The Case of

Terri Schiavo

MORE PRAISE FOR *THE CASE OF TERRI SCHIAVO*

"*The Case of Terri Schiavo* is an incredibly useful compilation of the multitude of materials generated by this case.

"The book is much more than an anthology of the public case materials, however. What makes the book particularly engaging is its inclusion of writings by philosophers (religious and lay), lawyers, and doctors, all of whom contribute their often varying perspectives on the situation represented by Ms. Schiavo's case. The case—and the issues with which it dealt—raised strong feelings all across the country, and this book shows why. I found particularly fascinating the materials setting forth the widely divergent views of issues surrounding death and dying that coexist within the Catholic Church. It is rare to find a compilation that is as multifaceted and complete as this one."

—Ellen Wertheimer
Professor of Law
Villanova University School of Law

"This work provides a balanced and interdisciplinary compendium of the medical, state, federal, and religious discussions regarding the tragic case of Terri Schiavo. The editors situate the case within the broader context of end-of-life treatment, and provide a timeline and bibliography that is an excellent resource for any student of bioethics. An excellent reference work, the text offers a resource to medical, legal, and ethical professionals."

—Patricia Talone, RSM, PhD
Vice President, Mission Services
Catholic Health Association
Saint Louis, Missouri

edited by
Arthur L. Caplan, James J. McCartney,
and Dominic A. Sisti

The Case of
Terri Schiavo

*Ethics
at the
End of Life*

foreword by Jay Wolfson, DrPH, JD
Terri Schiavo's Court-Appointed Guardian Ad Litem

Prometheus Books
59 John Glenn Drive
Amherst, New York 14228–2197

Published 2006 by Prometheus Books

Inquiries should be addressed to
Prometheus Books
59 John Glenn Drive
Amherst, New York 14228–2197
VOICE: 716–691–0133, ext. 207
FAX: 716–564–2711
WWW.PROMETHEUSBOOKS.COM

10 09 08 07 06   5 4 3 2 1

Library of Congress Cataloging-in-Publication Data

The case of Terri Schiavo : ethics at the end of life / Arthur L. Caplan, James J. McCartney, Dominic A. Sisti, co-editors.
        p. cm.
Includes bibliographical references.
ISBN 1–59102–398–X (pbk. : alk. paper)
1. Schiavo, Terri, 1963-2005. 2. Right to die—Moral and ethical aspects—United States—Case studies. 3. Terminal care—Moral and ethical aspects—United States—Case studies. 4. Medical ethics—United States—Case studies. 5. Coma—Patients—United States—Biography. I. Caplan, Arthur L. II. McCartney, James J. III. Sisti, Dominic A. [DNLM: 1. Schiavo, Terri, 1963-2005. 2. Life Support Care—ethics. 3. Persistent Vegetative State. 4. Enteral Nutrition. 5. Famous Persons. 6. Life Support Care—legislation & jurisprudence. WB 60 C337 2006]

R726.C357 2006
179.7—dc22

                                                                2005035135

Printed in the United States of America on acid-free paper

For Meg.

—Arthur L. Caplan

Dedicated to Kevin O'Rourke for his faithfulness and courage.

—James J. McCartney

For my parents and sister.

—Dominic A. Sisti

Contents

PART 3: FEDERAL CONTROVERSIES

PART 4: CATHOLIC CONTROVERSIES

Foreword
Jay Wolfson, DrPH, JD

Theresa Marie Schiavo may have had the most public death of any private person in history. Video snippets of her face and her partially clad, obviously disabled body were broadcast around the world on television and tabloids. Her name and her circumstance were front-page news for months. She captured the interest and attention of the Florida governor and catapulted its legislature into a special session. She was the singular cause for an extraordinary session of the U.S. Congress to be called during Easter week, and for the president of the United States of America to be transported by Air Force One from his Texas vacation to Washington, DC, to sign a law authored expressly for her. She activated all of the civil court systems at the state and federal levels, including the Supreme Court of the United States. She inspired Pope John Paul II to issue a confounding, nonencyclical statement admonishing against removal of artificial nutrition; and she stirred controversy within nearly all denominations about end of life decisions, medical technology, self-determination, and divine intent.

Ms. Schiavo's dying was an elixir of timely issues for a nation gripped by critical political and apparent philosophical divisions; a nation in the midst of a difficult and expensive war against a new form of enemy—terrorism; and a nation addicted to reality television and violent video games. The story of Theresa Schiavo is a political and social documentary of the United States that cannot be easily captured in any single document. Her story and so much of what it reflects became a very active and permanent part of my life, unexpectedly, in 2003.

In October of 2003, Ms. Schiavo's feeding tube was removed, for the second time. Within days, the Florida legislature called a special session and passed what became known as "Terri's Law," affording Governor Jeb Bush the authority to reinsert the tube pending an investigation and report by a specially appointed guardian ad litem. [A "guardian ad litem" is a legal term meaning a guardian who is appointed temporarily to protect the rights of persons who cannot protect themselves in a specific case.—*Eds.*] I was named to serve as Ms. Schiavo's special guardian ad litem and was given thirty days to issue a report to the governor and the courts providing a comprehensive legal and medical review of the history and facts in the case. I was also charged with assessing the feasibility of conducting additional tests on Ms. Schiavo.

To accomplish this, I read the more than thirty thousand pages of medical and legal documents in the massive and complex court files. I spent time with her parents, her husband, and the attorneys for both sides. I also spent about twenty of those days with Ms. Schiavo, in her hospice room. I held her hand, stroked her hair, played music for her, and sought to elicit responsive rather than reflexive reactions. I begged and cajoled her to provide me with some indication that she was not conforming to the clinical signs and symptoms of a persistent vegetative state—the condition in which she had been formally diagnosed for fourteen years.

I sought to learn what kind of person Theresa Schiavo was. She was my ward, and her best interests were my primary responsibility. It became clear that she was universally known about—but that only a handful of people knew her at all. Yet she was embraced by interest groups that advocated death with dignity or right to life as if she had been an active spokesperson for those points of view. "Terri" became a person familiar to millions of people because she had spent hours in their homes on television, on their radios, as the topic of sermons, and as a political force of unprecedented magnitude. She had been a shy, fun-loving woman, who took in sick animals, painted pretty pictures, and wanted to have a child. She had transformed herself from a 250-pound teenager into a svelte, attractive woman who won the heart of her first boyfriend, Michael Schiavo. They wed, moved to Florida, and had all of the usual and reasonable ups and downs of any relationship. She continued to lose weight aggressively, until six years after their marriage she was only 110 pounds.

On the fateful early morning of February 25, 1990, Ms. Schiavo collapsed in her apartment and suffered a cardiac arrest. She was anoxic, without oxygen to her brain, for ten to twelve minutes—nearly twice as long as is generally necessary to cause profound, irreversible brain damage. She was resuscitated, placed on a respirator, and a month later emerged from a coma to be under the undisputed guardianship care of her husband. Mr. Schiavo, along with Theresa's mother, Mary Schindler, served as a loving and personally attentive team of caregivers for more than three and a half years. Mr. Schiavo even brought his wife to California for an experimental implantation of electrodes in her brain—to no avail. The initial and continuing diagnosis of irreversible and extreme brain damage and the finding that she was in a persistent vegetative state, while not denied by her family, was challenged by the hope and love they had for her.

A long-shot malpractice lawsuit against a fertility physician claimed that had he been more careful, Ms. Schiavo's possible eating disorder might have been diagnosed and she would not have collapsed. A jury judgment in the case, three and a half years after Ms. Schiavo's collapse, awarded Mr. Schiavo $300,000 for loss of consortium and some $700,000 was placed in a court-managed trust for her maintenance. There was no hope of rehabilitation. It was a family tragedy. But that tragedy erupted into what may have been the most litigated end-of-life case in history.

Within months of the conclusion of the malpractice case, Michael Schiavo, for the first time in nearly four years, stood back and gained perspective on the woman he loved. He had consistently been told that she was persistently vegetative and that there was no hope of recovery or improvement. On two occasions, during family funerals of persons who had been on artificial life-support systems, Ms. Schiavo reportedly expressed that she would never want to be in that kind of circumstance. Mr. Schiavo began the intellectual, emotional, and legal process of fulfilling what he believed his wife's intentions were.

What had been a loving and caring family devolved into a nasty feud. The Schindlers, Ms. Schiavo's parents, challenged, for the first time, Michael Schiavo's guardianship rights, which included initiating removal of Ms. Schiavo's artificial nutrition/hydration tube—the only thing that was keeping her alive. What ensued were years of court battles between her parents and her husband, between the governor of Florida and the Florida courts, and remarkable public diatribes that often became laced with invective.

The laws of the various states differ about end-of-life decisions. In the very year that Ms. Schiavo collapsed, the U.S. Supreme Court decision in *Cruzan*, firmly placed legal purview for the standards regarding end-of-life decisions within state laws. Indeed, many scholars thought that such matters were finally resolved.

An almost mystical aura shrouded the last few weeks of Theresa's life. On the day her feeding tube was removed for the last time, the ailing Pope John Paul had his inserted. It was the prelude to Easter week, and the express personal, intentional, painful struggle of the pope to sanctify life was contrasted with Ms. Schiavo's very public dying. It was indeed Ms. Schiavo's dying, more so than her death, that has defined her. And as the public, the press, and the politicians responded to her dying, the limits of life emerged as the underlying issue. All the while, Theresa's parents were torn with grief and the perception of futility, while her husband was targeted with death threats and vilified, though sometimes praised for doing what he thought she would have wanted.

Ms. Schiavo became a natural and timely vehicle for the antiabortion and pro-life movements. As the pragmatic forces of politics became increasingly sensitive about at least one vacancy likely to occur on the U.S. Supreme Court, a perfect storm of political, religious, and media forces gathered around Ms. Schiavo, with *Roe v. Wade* firmly rooted as a driving force.

The court systems responded consistently, applying the carefully crafted state laws about end-of-life decisions and guardianship against the rules of evidence and civil procedure. Florida State Judge George Greer, a conservative Republican, stood firmly by the application of Florida law; and the federal courts, through U.S. District Court Judge James Whittemore, confirmed that the clear, convincing, and competent evidence had established the bases for both Ms. Schiavo's medical condition and her husband's decision to remove life-support technology. Both judges were supported by state and federal appellate and Supreme Court actions. The clinical evidence introduced throughout the pendency of the case, which was reviewed and supported in the guardian's special report, was further validated upon autopsy: indeed, her condition was determined to have been far worse than earlier stated. The autopsy report further debunked unsubstantiated allegations that Ms. Schiavo had been subject to abuse.

The "lessons learned" from the Schiavo experience will for years be subject to interpretation by legislators, scholars, medical practitioners, ethicists, and theologians. A key to understanding the complex panoply of political, philosophical, and clinical matters lies in the documentation that was created around the case. In this important book, Arthur Caplan, James McCartney, and Dominic Sisti have assembled vital documents that define, in the broadest sense, the vicissitudes of Ms. Schiavo's case. Their selection of court and legislative documents, commentary, speeches, and articles provides a distinctively objective basis for considering and framing the complex issues that drove the case and that will define its trajectory. This is a timely contribution to the necessary examination of the Schiavo matter, and the anthology provides an essential basis for understanding the scope of issues that both drove the case and that were driven by it.

In the long run, Theresa Marie Schiavo's story was a family tragedy for which no good solution was possible. But it was also a clarion call to the sensibilities of public policy in the United States. The coeditors provide the basis for individual and societal reflection that should help to frame discussions about end-of-life decisions and the allocation of increasingly scarce healthcare resources. That discussion will be a most valuable tribute to the shy, quiet woman who unconsciously stirred the world.

Part 1

Setting the Stage

INTRODUCTION

Terri Schiavo suffered a devastating heart attack in her Florida home on February 25, 1990. As a result, she was left severely brain damaged. Not long after this tragic event, another young woman, also severely brain damaged, thirty-two-year-old Nancy Cruzan, died in a Missouri nursing home on December 26, 1990.

Nancy Cruzan, who was in a permanent vegetative state as the result of an automobile accident years before, died because the feeding tube that was keeping her alive was removed at the request of her parents and sister. These two women and their families were, despite the fact that they never met, about to become inextricably linked forever in the minds of the American people, especially those in the healthcare professions and the legal system.

Nancy Cruzan was the center of a national controversy at the time she died. Her parents and sister had fought with the administration at her nursing home and authorities in the state of Missouri, including then governor and former Attorney General John Ashcroft, to have the right to have her feeding tube removed. The fight over the fate of Nancy Cruzan, as would later be true of Terri Schiavo, took a lengthy course through state and federal courts. Cruzan's parents insisted that Nancy would not want to be kept alive in a state of permanent unconsciousness. The state of Missouri insisted that there was not sufficient evidence to determine what Nancy Cruzan would have wanted and that the overriding interest of the state of Missouri in this case was in preserving life, especially for a vulnerable person such as Nancy Cruzan.

The *Cruzan* case went all the way to the United States Supreme Court. The Court recognized that every American has a constitutional right to refuse medical treatment based upon both liberty and privacy. They explicitly noted that this right to refuse treatment included decisions to stop life-sustaining treatment, including artificial nutrition and hydration.

The Court recognized the right of families to make decisions to forgo treatment for their incapacitated loved ones so long as that decision was based on an understanding of what the patient would have desired. The states could set their own standard for determining what evidence was necessary to permit healthcare providers to comply with a familial request to stop medical care.

The US Supreme Court returned the case to the Missouri courts with the admonition that if the parents could produce more evidence which supported their view of what Nancy would have wanted and met Missouri's standard for sufficient evidence, then the feeding tube could be withdrawn. The parents did find friends of Nancy's who supported their position. The information was deemed sufficient by the trial court in Missouri, which then sanctioned the removal of her feeding tube.

When Nancy Cruzan died there were many protestors at her nursing home who fervently disagreed with the decision to allow her to die. Some threatened to break into the nursing home in a last-ditch attempt to feed her. Others spoke angrily to a rapt media about the culture of death that had swept through an America whose courts would tolerate "starving" a disabled woman to death. While there was no homemade videotape of Nancy Cruzan prepared by the family, the circumstances of her death were as bitter and in many ways as tasteless in terms of media exploitation as those that surrounded the death of Terri Schiavo.

The Cruzan family was terribly battered by all the media attention and public protest their daughter's plight had garnered. Joe Cruzan, who had complained bitterly about all the outside interference in decisions about his daughter's medical care, took his own life in 1996.

Why is the story of Nancy Cruzan so important in understanding the events surrounding the death of Terri Schiavo? *Cruzan* was a vitally important precedent case in that nearly all of the issues that wound up dominating the national controversy over the fate of Terri Schiavo were addressed in the legal and ethical disputes that surrounded the death of Nancy Cruzan. In particular, when the president of the United States, the leadership of the House and Senate, the pope, and many other leaders of the right-to-life movement and some in the disability community were attempting to block the death of Terri Schiavo in federal courts, American courts had already established in *Cruzan* that there is a right to stop medical care that does not evaporate when a person becomes disabled or unable to communicate, that there is no meaningful distinction between ordinary and extraordinary care in terms of the authority that an individual has to end medical treatment, that families have decision-making authority for their loved ones, and that feeding tubes are a form of medical treatment.

So why then the fight over the fate of Terri Schiavo? In the *Schiavo* case the family, unlike that of Nancy Cruzan, was divided, husband against parents and siblings. Their dispute had gone on for many years and had grown only more bitter over time.

The Cruzans, unlike the Schiavos, were not especially religious. Terri Schiavo's parents were very religious Catholics who could not bring themselves to accept the termination of a feeding tube for their daughter and found firm support for their view in the Vatican and among some in the Florida legislature; the avowedly religious Catholic governor of Florida, Jeb Bush; and among a large number of pro-life members of the U.S. House and Senate.

Right-to-life groups were very eager to provide intellectual and financial support to the Schindler family in their battle against Michael Schiavo. The fight over the termination of artificial feeding for Robert Wendland, a severely brain-injured but not permanently comatose California man, had primed these groups to move quickly when they learned that the Schindler family did not agree with their son-in-law about removing Terri Schiavo's feeding tube. And a world of round-the-clock cable news outlets brought a level of intensity to the Schiavo story that could not have occurred fifteen years earlier when Nancy Cruzan died.

To many in the bioethics, theology, and legal communities, the bitter battle over the fate of Terri Schiavo was a complete surprise. From an ethical and legal point of view many of the key issues that were being keenly debated regarding Terri Schiavo had long been settled. Numerous professional associations and consensus statements in medical journals had articulated the view that, under certain circumstances, life support, including food and water, could be ended for those who were terminally ill, in a permanent vegetative state, or suffering irremediably but unable to communicate.

The *Schiavo* case seemed to fit those circumstances. The husband stated he knew his wife's preferences and many other people came forward to verify his claim. The courts and legislature in Florida have long allowed confirmed oral testimony to be the basis for withdrawing treatment, including food and water given by tube. And despite a furious campaign by Terri's parents to discredit him, reviews by Florida courts and various court-appointed guardians found no basis to challenge Michael Schiavo's standing as her primary decision maker or the medical diagnosis and prognosis that she was in a PVS state.

Despite this consensus, many Americans were not persuaded. It is clear that deep divisions existed within religious circles about the morality of stopping food and water for any patient and about the reliability of a diagnosis of permanent vegetative state. It is also clear that many Americans did not buy into the consensus that the courts, state and federal advisory commissions, medicine, and bioethics had forged with respect to ending life support.

Still, as the first set of readings makes clear, there was a consensus that had been forged through religious, philosophical, legal, legislative, and medical deliberation over a long period of time about how to respect the fundamental rights of privacy and liberty for every American. And despite the furious attack that opponents of that consensus brought to bear against it, the consensus held. Nearly every hospital, nursing home, and hospice in America follows policies that are the same as those articulated in the consensus that evolved around the case of Nancy Cruzan. The attempt to overturn the consensus did not succeed.

The Preservation of Life (excerpts)

Charles J. McFadden

. . . (A) *INTRAVENOUS FEEDING.* Routine medical practice today utilizes intravenous feeding in a countless variety of cases. Certainly the physician regards this procedure as an *ordinary* means of preserving life. It is obviously able to be carried out, under normal hospital conditions, without any notable inconvenience. For this reason we must regard recourse to intravenous feeding, in the case of typical hospitalized patients, as an *ordinary* and morally compulsory procedure.

The above conclusion applies, as stated, to routine hospital cases where the procedure is envisioned as a *temporary* means of carrying a patient through a critical period. Surely any effort to sustain life *permanently* in this fashion would constitute a grave hardship and not be morally compulsory.

The Associated Press carried a release on February 16, 1973, telling of the death of Janet Shouse of Butler, Pennsylvania. The girl had been critically injured in an auto accident on April 23, 1951; she fell into a coma immediately which lasted for *twenty-two years* until her death from pneumonia. In the words of her doctor: "It's hard to say whether she ever comprehended anything; the only part of her body she ever moved was her head; she had to be spoon-fed. She was one of those cases who break your heart, where life is sacred but death would be a blessing; and there wasn't anything anyone could do."

The moral problem in this case is accentuated by the fact that there was

From *The Dignity of Life: Moral Values in a Changing Society* (Huntington, IN: Our Sunday Visitor, 1976), pp. 152–56.

enough of a reflex present to cause the child to react to a spoon placed at her mouth, a normal mode of eating. This contrasts rather sharply with the artificial procedure of intravenously injecting nourishment into a person. I appreciate that someone may say that this sounds like "splitting hairs." What is the difference, in a hopeless case, between forcing nourishment into the girl's veins versus holding it to her mouth? I will say only that the above words of her own physician, Dr. James H. McClelland, superintendent of Polk State Hospital, reflect my own sentiments in the case.

The United Press carried the account, in October 1972, of the death of Miguel Martinez in Madrid. He was thirty-four years old, a Spanish soccer star, who had been critically injured in a game in 1964 and who had been in a coma for *eight years*. Death was attributed to a kidney infection resulting from eight years of intravenous feeding. Personally, I know no more about this case than is contained in the above brief press release. On the basis of the mere facts stated above, I would regard the continued recourse to intravenous feeding, after there was no longer hope of recovery, as an *extraordinary* and *noncompulsory* means of continuing the life of the person.

A truly difficult type of case is that in which intravenous feeding (and/or the use of oxygen) was begun when it was thought that the patient had some chance of recovery. We are referring to a patient *who is still conscious and rational* but whose condition has deteriorated to the point that he is in a terminal, hopeless condition. What is the morality of withdrawing the intravenous feeding and oxygen at this point? In response, I think we must distinguish between a *theoretical* versus a *practical* answer to the problem.

In theory, the means are, at this stage, *extraordinary* and *noncompulsory*. If the patient were to have been brought into the hospital in this hopeless condition, there would have been no obligation to initiate the measures. There is therefore no moral obligation to continue using them once it is evident that they can serve no useful purpose.

In practice, however, I do *not* think the artificial life supports should be withdrawn. I believe that the fact that intravenous feeding (and oxygen) have already been in use necessitates a different outlook on the problem. This conclusion is based on these points:

First, the danger of scandal would be very real. Members of a family that knew that their loved one was expected to live some days or weeks would witness the withdrawal of nourishment and oxygen, followed by death within a day. They would almost surely believe that the life of the patient had been taken in a "mercy killing" fashion in order to avoid further, useless suffering.

Second, doctors who made the decision to cease these life supports, possibly after consultation with a hospital chaplain, might not appreciate the fine moral distinction involved. Soon they might find themselves carrying over the practice to countless cases wherein they regarded as useless the preservation of certain lives. Needless to say, lesser members of the medical staff (such as the nurses in attendance) who are rarely informed on all of the reasons for a doctor's action would probably believe that they had witnessed a "mercy killing."

Third, it is fundamentally the patient himself—*if he be conscious and rational*—who has the right to decide whether or not he shall continue with a *useless* and *extraordinary* means which will prolong his suffering. It would be rash, indeed, to pose the question to him in his present condition, and it might be equally rash for others to make the decision for him. Who but God knows what goes on in the mind of such a person? Who but God knows what spiritual benefit such suffering may hold for the patient—on the basis of intentions made before the suffering became so intense, but at a time when the patient anticipated them as a proximate reality?

Finally, who is willing to assume the responsibility for acting as if the patient has spiritually prepared himself for death? If the doctors believe that the patient might survive a week or more with continued life supports, it may be that the patient himself believes that he may recover. If such be the case, even the fact that the patient has received the Last Sacraments is no guarantee that they have been rightly and fruitfully received.

The above case of a *conscious and rational patient* in a terminal condition differs, I believe, from that of *one who has lapsed into what the doctors agree is a terminal coma from which he will never recover.* If this latter person has, to the best of our knowledge, been spiritually prepared for death and if there is no reasonable expectation that consciousness will ever be regained, it would appear morally permissible, both in theory and in practice, to cease all artificial life supports. I think the doctor and/or hospital chaplain could and should explain to the family and the nurses the medical and moral basis for the action—and I am confident that they will not construe the act as one of "mercy killing."

At this writing (October 1975), one such case is gripping the attention of the nation. Twenty-one-year-old Karen Quinlan has been in a coma for more than five months in St. Clare's Hospital, Denville, New Jersey. Expert medical testimony, based on EEG readings, is that the brain has been hopelessly damaged. Although the parents of Karen Quinlan want the artificial life-support machines to be removed and their daughter allowed to die, state authorities are reluctant to issue an order which would culminate in the patient's death. (A similar case involved seventeen-year-old Randal Carmen, who had been in a coma for three weeks in Elyria Memorial Hospital, Ohio. His parents also wanted the life-support systems removed, but state officials did not dare acquiesce to their request. Before the youth's parents could take extensive legal action, the boy died. He had gone into a coma September 21 and died October 11, 1975.)

The reluctance of the state to issue the above authorization is based on two points. *First,* in most states death is still defined in terms of "cessation of heartbeat and respiration." When an EEG reading shows that there are still some brain waves, the person is alive and the state is fearful that a charge of homicide might be made against the one who "pulls the plug." The state also wonders if it, the state itself, would not be obliged to charge the person who "pulls the plug" with homicide. *Second,* the state is very fearful of setting a precedent which could culminate in untold abuses. Our hospitals are full of people who are on life-support machines. Frankly, there are many people who would like to see other people pass away. It could be a member of a rich family who would have a lot to gain financially by the death of a relative. It could be a city or state that finds its hospitals overcrowded with nonpaying patients from the ghetto. One could encounter some very thin lines of judgment if there existed a general authorization to remove life supports from those patients that someone decided "will not survive anyway" or "if they do survive, it will be in a severely handicapped condition." It could develop into a rather frightening situation if a legal precedent were created for the widespread and uncontrolled removal of life supports.

My recommendations are as follows:

1. If there has been a prolonged cessation of brain waves, the person is *dead.* The state should call upon the medical profession to assist it in determining the length of time that it would insist upon for "flat" brain waves to indicate the presence of *certain* death.
2. In the case of patients who are still alive, that is, patients who are in a coma but still show brain waves, the state should call upon the medical profession to assist it in setting up standards by means of which an EEG reading would indicate *grave and irreparable brain damage* in the patient.
3. In both types of cases—when the mechanical life supports are still in

use—I would require a written request from the spouse, parents, or legal guardians to be submitted to the ethical committee of the hospital involved asking that such supports be removed. I would require the ethical committee to check into the specific case and to verify in the first type of situation that there are no brain waves and that the person is therefore dead; and, in the second type of situation to verify that the comatose patient, according to EEG readings, has suffered grave and irreparable brain damage. I would then require the ethical committee to request from the proper court legal authorization to remove the artificial life supports.

The above procedures would, I believe, solve the dilemmas which presently exist.

The Percutaneous Endoscopic Gastrostomy Tube

Medical and Ethical Issues in Placement

Floyd Angus, MD, and Robert Burakoff, MD

Department of Gastroenterology
Washington Hospital Center, Washington, DC

OBJECTIVE: Offering and recommending PEG tube placement to patients has been a topic of considerable interest in the medical literature. The role of individual healthcare professionals in the decision-making process is poorly defined. PEG tubes are often placed inappropriately because of unrealistic and inaccurate expectations of what they can accomplish in patients unable to tolerate adequate oral intake. We have developed an algorithm for PEG placement for the geriatric, oncology, and neurology patients based on a critical review of current literature.

METHODS: An extensive review of the literature was performed focusing on PEG tube placement in oncology, neurology, and geriatric patients. This algorithm was developed to provide both the primary-care provider and the specialist with appropriate indications for PEG placement in these patient populations.

RESULTS: Appropriate indications for PEG placement are: 1) Esophageal obstruction (e.g., esophageal cancer), 2) Neurologic etiology of dysphagia without obstruction (e.g., status post–cerebrovascular accident, pseudobulbar palsy), 3) Prolonged refusal to swallow without evidence of concomitant terminal illness (e.g., protracted pseudodementia due to severe depression), 4) Supplemental nutrition for patients undergoing chemotherapy or radiation therapy.

CONCLUSIONS: If no physiologic benefit is expected with PEG placement (anorexia-cachexia syndrome), the healthcare team has no oblig-

From the *American Journal of Gastroenterology* 98 (2003): 272–77.

ation to offer or perform an intervention. This same principle would apply if intervention improves physiologic states but has no effect on quality of life (e.g., permanent vegetative state). Small-bore feeding tubes are cost effective and relatively safe for enteral feedings of up to 6–8 weeks. This is especially pertinent in the population with acute neurological deficits, in which prognostication on extent of impairment is best estimated by communication with neurologist. In the geriatric population there is no proved benefit in weight gain or markers of nutrition (albumin, prealbumin) in patients with malnutrition due to impaired oral intake.

INTRODUCTION

The decision on whether to offer and recommend percutaneous endoscopic gastrostomy (PEG) tube placement to patients has been a topic of considerable interest in the medical literature. In defining which patients should receive supplemental feeding through PEG tubes, issues such as perceived changes in quality of life and anticipated outcome can cause significant confusion and even animosity among patients and caregivers. Unfortunately, the role of healthcare professionals in the decision-making process is poorly defined. PEG tubes are often placed inappropriately because of unrealistic expectations of what they can accomplish in patients unable to tolerate *p.o.* intake. In a 1999 review, Gauderer (1), who was involved in the development of the PEG procedure, stated his concern that efforts be directed at the ethical aspects of placement. He also emphasized the need "to demonstrate that our interventions truly benefit the patient" (1). Data regarding the outcome of PEG placements from patients with a wide range of illnesses/major neurological deficits should be made available to the patients/caregivers. The purpose of this article is to provide an up-to-date review and evaluation of medical and ethical issues regarding the decision on starting supplemental enteral feeding through a PEG tube. This article should also spur communication between specialties and develop a framework that, although providing guidance on appropriate placement, is not overly rigid and allows for patients' and caregivers' desires of maximizing quality of life.

ETHICAL ISSUES

As with all medical care, the decision to place a PEG tube should be determined based on whether it will provide an actual benefit to the patient. Often, healthcare workers feel compelled to offer PEG tube placement because they believe that they are legally/ethically obligated to provide artificial nutrition and hydration (ANH). It is both ethically and legally accepted that ANH is a medical treatment. As with other medical treatments, determining whether ANH is appropriate for a particular patient is based on assessing the effectiveness of achieving the goals of treatment and weighing the risks and benefits. Approximately 80% of those who die today are in hospitals and healthcare facilities (2). According to the American Hospital Association, 70% of these deaths are preceded by a decision to stop or withhold some form of care (3). Using these figures, over half of all patients who die (or their family members) are involved with end-of-life decisions to withdraw or to withhold some form of medical treatment. However, despite these numbers, many patients and their families view ANH as basic healthcare that should never be denied to any patient. This myth continues to be held by healthcare providers who may feel obligated to offer some form of treatment to a patient who is otherwise dying.

As with all medical care, the decision to place a PEG tube should be determined on the basis of whether it will provide an actual benefit to the patient. Benefit to patient is determined ethically by two major factors—potential medical benefits and benefits as determined by the patient and/or the patient's appropriately designated surrogate decision maker. The ethical obligation to provide ANH is based upon medical need, medical appropriateness, and potential for benefit to the patient. As with any other medical treatment, determination of whether PEG placement and subsequent ANH are appropriate for a particular patient is paramount. The patient's and/or surrogate's wishes are also considered in light of the goals of treatment, the weighing of risks and benefits of this medical therapy in a specific patient, and in the context of the spiritual and cultural beliefs of the patient. In all cases, physicians are not obligated to offer or to continue ANH unless potential benefit is anticipated. ANH is considered ethically akin to any other life-sustaining treatment such as ventilator support, dialysis, antibiotics, etc. There are unique aspects of PEG tubes as a "medical treatment" that should be recognized as contributing to decisions on placement. These aspects include an emotional component that perceives withholding ANH as "starving" the patient, underlying biases of physicians as to which patients are appropriate for PEG placement, and barriers to discharge planning because of nursing home requirements.

The 1976 Quinlan case brought to the general public's attention the distinction between euthanasia and allowing a patient, who was being kept alive by artificial means, to die. Though the Supreme Court allowed individual states to set standards for decision making in patients considered to be incompetent, it was clearly noted that ANH was a medical treatment that could be withheld and withdrawn. A presidential commission on ethics found that ANH was not needed or justified in all cases (4, 5). In 1986, the American Medical Association published a statement that ANH is a "life-prolonging treatment." This policy statement has been supported by similar guidelines from groups including the American Academy of Neurology (6) and the American Nurses Association (7).

ISSUES FOR GERIATRIC POPULATION

The use of PEG tubes in the geriatric population residing in nursing homes is a controversial issue often complicated by lack of information and misinformation. The number of patients older than sixty-five years who have received PEG tubes have dramatically increased (15,000 in 1989, 75,000 in 1992, and 123,000 in 1995) (8). Many elderly individuals are provided with PEGs during the final months of life because of the unfortunate expectation that enteral nutrition will somehow provide comfort to the dying elderly patient. These patients often have severe dementia because of Alzheimer's disease or multiple infarcts. Approximately 60% of cases of dementia in the elderly is a result of Alzheimer's disease. The number of nursing home residents with Alzheimer's disease is between 382,000–553,500, with an estimated one-half in an advanced stage. The majority of patients fail to achieve any meaningful improvement in nutritional status, functional status, or subjective health status after PEG placement. Grant and Rudberg demonstrated a thirty-day mortality of 23.9% in this population group (8). Rabenek had similar findings of 23.5% (18.9% for patients 65, 24.7% for patients 65–74, and 27.5% for patients 75) for in-hospital mortality in a Veterans Affairs study (9).

Unfortunately, the therapeutic goal of placing a PEG tube is often to assuage surrogate decision makers. Surrogates and laypeople often list slowing of malnutrition and sequelae, providing comfort, improving survival, and preventing aspiration pneumonia as reasons for PEG placement. There is no proven long-term benefit in weight gain or markers of nutrition (albumin, prealbumin) when these patients are compared with age-matched controls. The median survival postplacement in this group was 7.5 months (9). Nair found that PEG tubes do not prevent aspiration physiologically and are not associated with improved wound healing (10). Ciocon and Silverstone (11) performed one of the initial prospective studies looking at indication, benefits, and complications of tube feeding in elderly patients. This study evaluated institutionalized geriatric patients between sixty-five and ninety-five years old and found that nutritional response was usually maintenance of body weight for up to six months, beyond which time there was a tendency toward weight loss (which was possibly attributed to the severe concomitant illnesses in many of the patients) (11). Callahan and Haag (12) performed a prospective cohort study of 150 patients older than sixty who received PEG. The outcome of this study confirmed previous studies with findings of thirty-day mortality (22%) and one-year mortality (50%). In those patients who survived greater than sixty days, at least 70% had no significant improvement in nutritional, functional, and subjective health status. Thus, although PEG feeding can probably be accomplished safely in the chronically and severely ill, there are important burdens associated with its use, with minimal evidence that it significantly improves nutritional or functional parameters (12).

By stopping offending medications (such as anticholinergics, neuroleptics, benzodiazepines, nonsteroidal anti-inflammatory drugs, etc.), mental status in demented patients without significant neurological deficits can sometimes be improved enough for them to tolerate sufficient intake. By improving individual hand feedings in demented patients with poor intake (through staff education, personal assist devices, dentures, more tasteful foods, etc.), patients can often obtain nutritional benefits that negate the need for PEG placement for supplemental nutrition.

ISSUES FOR PATIENTS WITH NEUROLOGICAL DEFICITS

The most common indication for PEG tube placement is neurological deficit causing impairment in ability to obtain sufficient oral nutritional intake. The largest population is patients who have incurred a cerebrovascular accident (but also include patients with amyotrophic lateral sclerosis, cerebral palsy, multiple sclerosis, etc.). Dysphagia is found in 29–45% of patients in the acute stage of stroke and approximately 20% at four-month follow-up (13). Risk factors for persistent dysphagia after stroke with increased risk of aspiration include persistent obtundation, brainstem stroke (especially with gurgly voice, impaired cough, and coughing while eating), bilateral cerebrovascular accident (especially with impaired cough, and coughing while eating), and aspiration documented by videofluoroscopic modified barium study. James et al. evaluated long-term outcome in patients with severe dysphagic strokes and found that, although 28% died during index hospitalization, only 4% had significant recovery of swallowing function to justify early PEG placement (14). When one or more of these risk factors are present more than five days postacute event, there is a high likelihood that severe dysphagia will be protracted. In these cases, PEG tubes are warranted and are appropriate to be placed less than five days postacute event because of the probable long-term requirement for supplemental nutrition.

The effect of PEG placement on long-term quality of life optimal timing of gastrostomy placement is yet to be resolved. Prognostication on the extent of impairment is best estimated by communication with the neurologist caring for the patient. In addition to dysphagia, other deficits such as agnosia, apraxia, and depression might impair patients' ability to feed themselves, and these should be addressed by the healthcare team (15).

ISSUES FOR PATIENTS WITH CANCER

Malnutrition is common among cancer patients and is frequently referred to as cancer cachexia. Although cancer patients can develop deficiencies in essential vitamins and minerals, the most common form of nutritional depletion is that of protein calorie malnutrition manifested as a loss of body cell mass. Although this is a true malnutrition syndrome, it differs from protein calorie malnutrition seen in starvation. PEG tubes often play a role in providing enteral nutrition in cancer patients undergoing surgical procedures or those expected to have significant side effects from chemotherapy/radiation therapy. These patients often require intensive chemotherapy/radiation therapy, which in combination with surgery can further compromise their already fragile nutritional status and further reduce treatment tolerance. Anticancer therapy may not only directly affect nutrition and reduce the urge to eat but may also affect the ability to chew, swallow, and absorb food. Cozzi and Gavazzi (16) evaluated the use of PEG tubes in a total of fifty oncology patients undergoing active treatment of their disease (forty-two feeding/eight decompression/one transgastric drainage of duodenal fistula) and found that PEG feedings could provide essential nutrition without significant discomfort in this patient population. More definitive guidelines for enteral support in patients with cancer have been advocated. Enteral nutrition through a PEG tube should be considered in selected patients with malnutrition undergoing antitumor therapy with either reasonable expectation of response, or in whom the natural history of the untreated tumor is of a protracted nature wherein survival is expected to be greater than six months (15). Senft and Fietkau (17) studied the influence of supportive nutrition through a PEG tube looking at quality-of-life issues. They studied 212 patients with head/neck tumor undergoing radiotherapy with impaired nutrition who either received PEG placement or were continued on oral feedings. This group found that the quality of life (based on the Padilla index) did not deteriorate, contrasting with the rapid decrease seen in patients continued on oral feeding. Enteral nutrition through PEG is seldom indicated in patients with advanced cancer associated with significant deterioration of performance status or in those patients with documented unresectable disease who have been unresponsive to chemotherapy and radiation therapy. PEG tube placement is not indicated in patients with evidence of terminal disease, with rapidly progressive tumor, severe malnutrition, and life expectancy of less than 1–2 months (anorexia-cachexia syndrome), though in cases of comfort care, this decision should be discussed with patient/physician.

Although these criteria would seem to also apply to patients with end-stage AIDS with severe malnutrition and similar poor life expectancy, there appears to be a difference in etiology of wasting syndrome. Data from a study performed by Macallan and Noble suggest that the wasting syndrome of AIDS is secondary to decreased energy intake, rather than increased energy expenditure (18). Ockenga and Suttman (19) performed a prospective study evaluating outcome and risks in patients with debilitation caused by AIDS (criteria included body mass index 19 kg/m2, persistent eating/swallowing disorder, untreatable weight loss 10% of body weight within six months or less, or Centers for Disease Control and Prevention classification of stage IV or more severe). The authors compared these patients with HIV-seronegative patients with PEGs and AIDS patients without PEGs with a similar degree of debilitation and found that PEG feedings were safe and significantly improved clinical parameters of nutrition (body weight, total body fat, and serum albumin concentration) within 4–6 weeks. This study, how-ever, does not answer the most critical question of whether successful treat-ment of wasting syndrome improves survival in these patients (19).

Though seldom discussed between patients and healthcare providers, economic considerations have dictated decisions on placement in the past. Sartori and Trevisani (20) prospectively evaluated the cost of long-term feeding via PEG in patients with head and neck cancer. Three main items were considered in a total of 34 patients in this study: 1) cost of PEG place-ment (i.e., gastrostomy kit, staff); 2) nutrition (i.e., enteral feeding products, flexible tube connectors); and 3) patient care (i.e., home care, nursing visits/month). Sartori and Trevisani (20) found that, although the mean daily cost (Italian Lire) of using a PEG was slightly higher (28,890 Lire *vs.* 27,340 Lire), the mean duration of use (180 days) and low sixty-day mortality (8%) justified placement in this patient population. Looking at subjective improved quality of life in this population, the PEG tube can be considered the procedure of choice in patients with anticipated long-term impairment in ability to obtain *p.o.* intake and reasonably long predicted survival.

PEG TUBES

Since their introduction in 1980, PEG tubes have become the preferred alter-native to operative gastrostomy tubes for those patients requiring long-term intubation. Large cumulative studies have shown a mean procedure mortality rate of 0.6% (21) and a major complication rate of 3–5% (including aspira-tion pneumonia and peritonitis), and a minor complication rate of 13% (including wound infection, tube dislodgment, and stromal leak) (14). Increased risk of death post-PEG placement has been associated with diabetes mellitus, increased age, and male gender. Hull and Rawlings (22) performed one of the initial studies looking at the outcome of long-term nutrition in patients with PEG placement and found an early (thirty-day) mortality/mor-bidity of 8% and 22%. Of the 90% of patients surviving thirty days, 51% had no further complications. It seems that the low mortality and morbidity of this procedure have led to complacency among many healthcare professionals in requesting this procedure. Clinical decisions on placement should be based on the prediction that the patient will survive more than 4 weeks and will obtain actual benefit from the procedure. To make this determination will require adequate communication between primary-care staff and the subspecialties (oncology, geriatrics, neurology, etc.). Gastroenterologists should not act merely as technicians but should evaluate the underlying disease process and the ramifications of PEG placement on ultimate outcome.

INDICATIONS FOR PEG PLACEMENT

Appropriate indications for PEG placement are esophageal obstruction (e.g., esophageal cancer), dysphagia without obstruction (e.g., status post–cerebrovascular accident and pseudobulbar palsy), refusal to swallow without evidence of concomitant terminal illness (e.g., protracted pseudodementia caused by severe depression), supplemental nutrition for patients undergoing chemo/radiation therapy with or without surgery with impaired nutrition, and chronic gastric decompression in patients with benign/malignant obstruction who do not wish or cannot have a nasogastric tube placed. If no physiological benefit is expected with PEG placement (anorexia-cachexia syndrome), the healthcare team has no obligation to offer or perform intervention (12). This same principle would apply if intervention improves physiological states but has no effect on quality of life (e.g., permanent vegetative state). Abuksis and Mor (23) assessed PEG outcome for inpatients and outpatients based on criteria of morbidity, mortality, and survival and found a thirty-day mortality in hospitalized patients with documented combination of mental disorder (i.e., dementia/delirium) and acute medical illness and malnutrition of 29%. Previously reported mortality rate has been 4–26%. This supports the conclusion that patients with acute illness are at an increased risk of significant adverse events, and PEG placement should be deferred until stabilization of the index illness. Light and Slezak (24) go even further in suggesting a 30–60-day trial period of nasogastric tube feeding in patients hospitalized with acute severe illness before considering PEG placement.

THE DECISION-MAKING PROCESS

A useful decision-making algorithm was developed by Rabenek and McCullough (25) on PEG placement. For patients with anorexia-cachexia syndromes (e.g., terminal cancer/end-stage AIDS), PEG should not be offered because the patient will not be able to adequately use the nutrition, and there is no improvement in quality of life. Enteral nutrition should be considered for cancer patients with malnutrition when the natural history of the underlying tumor can be expected to permit a period of normal performance or whose treatment-associated toxicity precludes adequate oral intake. For patients with permanent vegetative state, physicians can offer, but recommend against, PEG placement because the patient will not be able to experience any significant improvement in quality of life. For patients with dysphagia without complications, physicians should both offer and recommend PEG because the patient can benefit from placement. In patients with dysphagia with multiple medical complications, it is appropriate to discuss PEG *versus* no PEG with the patient/caregiver (25). The clinical tenet of Rabenek and McCullough's algorithm is that physicians are well informed regarding the clinical ramifications of PEG tube placement. We propose a modification to Rabenek and McCullough's algorithm that would include a recommendation for PEG placement in cancer patients with severe malnutrition who undergo radiation therapy/chemotherapy and/or surgery with possibility of response to treatment. Also, we would include patients with gastric obstruction who can benefit from a PEG tube for decompression.

PEG TUBES *VERSUS* SMALL-BORE FEEDING TUBES

In many patients with only temporary inability for *p.o.* intake, the decision for evaluation and placement of PEG is often made inappropriately when a small-bore nasogastric feeding tube can provide adequate nutrition support. Small-bore feeding tubes (external diameter ranging from 5 to 12 F) are cost-effective and relatively safe for enteral feedings of up to 6–8 weeks (26). In comparing clinical outcomes of PEG and nasoenteric placement for nutritional support, both were equivalent with respect to maintaining performance status and nutrition (26). The most significant major complication for both PEG and nasoenteric placement was aspiration pneumonia. Although patients with PEG initially had an increased rate of aspiration pneumonia, this difference was not sustained beyond the first fourteen days and did not have any significant impact on mortality (26). In looking at both major (aspiration pneumonia, misplacement, self-extubation) and minor complications (clogged tubing, kinking, difficult insertion), the literature indicates that there was similar morbidity at two-week postplacement. Survival in both groups is similar at all intervals of follow-up. In patients with anticipated need for supplemental enteral feeding of less than eight weeks, PEG tube feeding did not offer any substantial medical benefit in comparison with nasoenteric tube feeding. For the agitated patient with anticipated requirement of supplemental enteral feeding for more than two weeks, PEG tubes are generally better tolerated than nasogastric tube, though there is still a significant risk of extubation if appropriate safety measures are not in place (i.e., abdominal binder, soft restraints).

CONCLUSIONS

ANH is considered a medical treatment. As such, decisions for or against the treatment should be made in a shared decision model with the patient or surrogate, weighing the benefits and burdens of the specific treatment. When ANH cannot achieve the goals of care as defined by patients' values and what is considered appropriate medically, then ANH need not be provided. Physicians must recognize the emotional nature of the topic of ANH and frame these discussions in terms of achievable medical goals. The challenge of the decision-making process is to facilitate communication, respect the ethical principles of autonomy and beneficence, and tolerate a plurality of belief systems while safeguarding the vulnerable patient. Hopefully, by following the above tenets, the healthcare team will have a better understanding of the decision-making process to place a PEG tube and will facilitate greater communication among clinicians and patients/caregivers.

REFERENCES

1. Gauderer M. Twenty Years of Percutaneous Endoscopic Gastrostomy: Origin and Evolution of a Concept and Its Expanded Applications. *Gastrointes Endosc.* 1999;50:879–883.

2. McCarrick P. Withholding or Withdrawing Nutrition or Hydration. Washington, DC: National Reference Center for Bioethics Literature; 2000:1–17.

3. Taylor CA, Larson DE. Predictors of Outcome after Percutaneous Endoscopic Gastrostomy. *J May Clin Proc.* 1992;67:1042–1049.

4. Huang ZB, Ahronheim J. Nutrition and Hydration in Terminally Ill Patients. *Clin Geriatr Med.* 2000;16:313–325.

5. President's Commission for the Study of Ethical Problems in Biomedical and Behavioral Research. Deciding to Forego Life-sustaining Treatment. Washington, DC: U.S. Government Printing Office, 1983.

6. American Academy of Neurology. Position of the American Academy of Neurology on Certain Aspects of the Care and Management of the Persistent Vegetative State Patient. *Neurology.* 1989;39:125–126.

7. American Nurses Association. ANA Guidelines on Withdrawing or Withholding Food and Fluid. *Main Nurse.* 1988;74:3.

8. Grant MD, Rudberg MA. Gastrostomy Placement and Mortality among Hospitalized Medicare Beneficiaries. *JAMA.* 1998;279:1973–1976.

9. Rabeneck L. Longterm Outcomes of Patients Receiving PEG Tubes. *J Gen Intern Med.* 1996;11:287–293.

10. Nair S. Hypoalbumenemia Is a Poor Predictor of Survival after PEG in Elderly Patients with Dementia. *Am J Gastroenterol.* 2000;95:133–136.

11. Ciocon JO, Silverstone FA. Tube Feedings in Elderly Patients: Indications, Benefits, and Complications. *Arch Intern Med.* 1988;148:429–433.

12. Callahan CM, Haag KM. Outcomes of Percutaneous Endoscopic Gastrostomy among Older Adults in a Community Setting. *J Am Geriatr Soc.* 2000; 48:1048–1054.

13. Gillick MR. Rethinking the Role of Tube Feeding in Patients with Advanced Dementia. *N Engl J Med.* 2000;342:206–210.

14. James A, Kapur K. Long-term Outcome of Percutaneous Endoscopic Gastrostomy Feeding in Patients with Dysphagic Stroke. *Aging.* 1998;27:671–676.

15. Finestone H. Safe Feeding Methods in Stroke Patients. *Lancet.* 2000; 355:1662–1663.

16. Cozzi G, Gavazzi C. Percutaneous Gastrostomy in Oncologic Patients: Analysis of Results and Expansion of Indications. *Abdom Imag.* 2000;25:239–242.

17. Senft M, Fietkau R. The Influence of Supportive Nutritional Therapy via PEG on the Quality of Life of Cancer Patients. *Support Care Cancer.* 1993;1: 272–275.

18. Macallan DC, Noble C. Prospective Analysis of Patterns of Weight Change in Stage IV Human Immunodeficiency Virus Infection. *Am J Clin Nutr.* 1993;58: 417–424.

19. Ockenga J, Suttman U. Percutaneous Endoscopic Gastrostomy in AIDS and Control Patients: Risks and Outcome. *Am J Gastroenterol.* 1996;91:1817–1822.

20. Sartori S, Trevisani L. Cost Analysis of Long-term Feeding by Percutaneous Endoscopic Gastrostomy in Cancer Patients in Italian Health District. *Support Care Cancer.* 1996;4:21–26.

21. Miller RE, Castlemain BN. Percutaneous Endoscopic Gastrostomy. *Surg Endosc.* 1989;3:186–190.

22. Hull M, Rawlings J. Audit of Outcome of Long-term Enteral Nutrition by Percutaneous Endoscopic Gastrostomy. *Lancet.* 1993;341:869–872.

23. Abuksis G, Mor M. Percutaneous Endoscopic Gastrostomy: High Mortality Rates in Hospitalized Patients. *Am J Gastroenterol.* 2000;95:128–132.

24. Light VL, Slezak FA. Predictive Factors for Early Mortality after PEG. *Gastrointest Endosc*. 1995;42:330–335.

25. Rabenek L, McCullough L. Ethically Justified, Clinically Comprehensive Guidelines for Percutaneous Endoscopic Gastrostomy Tube Placement. *Lancet*. 1997;349:496–498.

26. Fay DE, Poplausky M. Long-term Enteral Feeding: A Retrospective Comparison of Delivery via PEG and Nasoenteric Tubes. *Am J Gastroenterol*. 1991;86: 1604–1609.

Deciding to Forego Life-Sustaining Treatment:
Ethical, Medical, and Legal Issues in Treatment Decisions

President's Commission for the Study of Ethical Problems in
Medicine and Biomedical and Behavioral Research

March 1983

Appendix G

Permanent Loss of Consciousness: Expert Opinion and Community Standards

Expert Opinion*

Fred Plum, MD

This is in follow-up of our telephone conversation of December 18 in which you asked my informed opinion about prognosis in patients with so-called permanent loss of consciousness or what might be called the vegetative state.

As you know, there are only a limited number of published data on this subject. Included in the figures are some from Jennett's study of head injury, some from our own studies of nontraumatic coma, a series published from Japan, and a few reasonably well verified anecdotal reports. The results of all this material can be stated in the following manner:

1. Prognosis in permanently unconscious patients varies somewhat according to the nature of the underlying disease. In patients with traumatic brain damage, especially younger patients, a small number, perhaps 5%, can recover from such states lasting as long as 4–6 weeks. If complete unconsciousness lasts for longer than that period, I know of no evidence of a subject who has improved beyond the level of severe disability, and very few of the latter exist.

From the President's Commission for the Study of Ethical Problems in Medicine and Biomedical and Behavioral Research, *Deciding to Forego Life-Sustaining Treatment: Ethical, Medical, and Legal Issues in Treatment Decisions* (Washington, DC, 1983).

*Letter from Dr. Fred Plum (Anne Parrish Titzell Professor of Neurology, Cornell University Medical College; Neurologist-in-Chief, The New York Hospital, New York, NY) to Dr. Joanne Lynn regarding reliability of prognosis for permanently unconscious patients (December 22, 1981).

2. In ischemic brain injury, good recovery after a period of complete unconsciousness longer than two weeks is very rare, and longer than one month probably does not occur in more than a fraction of 1%. Even those few in whom late evidence of cognitive awareness has reappeared had to be classified as having a severe disability both from the standpoint of physical and intellectual residua. I know of no example of such a patient who has returned to what can be considered independent intellectual or motor function. Wakefulness, of course, in the sense of having sleep and wake cycles, returns in almost all these subjects.

3. In conditions such as brain tumor, Alzheimer's disease, or other progressive dementias, loss of consciousness for a period lasting as long as one month dictates a hopeless prognosis. I suppose it is conceivable that such a patient could be overmedicated for a period of that duration, but I know of no example either by direct contact or anecdotal report of such a patient who has ever recovered any measure of cognition when all consciousness had been lost for a continuous period of thirty days or more. In my experience, a major problem in this area lies with poor medical diagnosis. Many patients who are severely disoriented, agitated, or locked-in are sometimes called unconscious by physicians. The statements above, of course, can only apply when the diagnosis is secure.

If I can expand on these comments in any way, I will be pleased to. In the meantime, I hope this has been useful. Please call me if there are any questions.

Sincerely,
(signed)
Fred Plum, MD

Joyce Cruzan, Nancy's parents and co-guardians, sought a court order directing the withdrawal of their daughter's artificial feeding and hydration equipment after it became apparent that she had virtually no chance of recovering her cognitive faculties. The Supreme Court of Missouri held that because there was no clear and convincing evidence of Nancy's desire to have life-sustaining treatment withdrawn under such circumstances, her parents lacked authority to effectuate such a request. We granted certiorari, 492 U.S. 917 (1989), and now affirm.

On the night of January 11, 1983, Nancy Cruzan lost control of her car as she traveled down Elm Road in Jasper County, Missouri. The vehicle overturned, and Cruzan was discovered lying face down in a ditch without detectable respiratory or cardiac function. Paramedics were able to restore her breathing and heartbeat at the accident site, and she was transported to a hospital in an unconscious state. An attending neurosurgeon diagnosed her as having sustained probable cerebral contusions compounded by significant anoxia (lack of oxygen). The Missouri trial court in this case found that permanent brain damage generally results after six minutes in an anoxic state; it was estimated that Cruzan was deprived of oxygen from twelve to fourteen minutes. She remained in a coma for approximately three weeks and then progressed to an unconscious state in which she was able to orally ingest some nutrition. In order to ease feeding and further the recovery, surgeons implanted a gastrostomy feeding and hydration tube in Cruzan with the consent of her then husband. Subsequent rehabilitative efforts proved unavailing. She now lies in a Missouri state hospital in what is commonly referred to as a persistent vegetative state: generally, a condition in which a person exhibits motor reflexes but evinces no indications of significant cognitive function.[1] The State of Missouri is bearing the cost of her care.

After it had become apparent that Nancy Cruzan had virtually no chance of regaining her mental faculties, her parents asked hospital employees to terminate the artificial nutrition and hydration procedures. All agree that such a removal would cause her death. The employees refused to honor the request without court approval. The parents then sought and received authorization from the state trial court for termination. The court found that a person in Nancy's condition had a fundamental right under the State and Federal Constitutions to refuse or direct the withdrawal of "death prolonging procedures." *App. to Pet. for Cert.* A99. The court also found that Nancy's "expressed thoughts at age twenty-five in somewhat serious conversation with a housemate friend that if sick or injured she would not wish to continue her life unless she could live at least halfway normally suggests that given her present condition she would not wish to continue on with her nutrition and hydration." Id., at A97–A98.

The Supreme Court of Missouri reversed by a divided vote. The court recognized a right to refuse treatment embodied in the common-law doctrine of informed consent, but expressed skepticism about the application of that doctrine in the circumstances of this case. *Cruzan v. Harmon*, 760 S.W.2d 408, 416–417 (1988) (en banc). The court also declined to read a broad right of privacy into the State Constitution which would "support the right of a person to refuse medical treatment in every circumstance," and expressed doubt as to whether such a right existed under the *United States Constitution.* Id., at 417–418. It then decided that the Missouri Living Will statute, *Mo Rev. Stat.* § 459.010 et seq. (1986), embodied a state policy strongly favoring the preservation of life. 760 S.W.2d at 419–420. The court found that Cruzan's statements to her roommate regarding her desire to live or die under certain conditions were "unreliable for the purpose of determining her intent," id., at 424, "and thus insufficient to support the co-guardians' claim to exercise substituted judgment on Nancy's behalf." Id., at 426. It rejected the argument that Cruzan's parents were entitled to order the termination of her medical treatment, concluding that "no person can assume that choice for an incompetent in the absence of the formalities required under Missouri's Living Will statutes or the clear and convincing, inherently reliable evidence absent here." Id., at 425. The court also expressed its view that "broad policy questions bearing on life and death are more properly addressed by representative assemblies" than judicial bodies. Id., at 426.

We granted certiorari to consider the question whether Cruzan has a right under the United States Constitution which would require the hospital to withdraw life-sustaining treatment from her under these circumstances.

At common law, even the touching of one person by another without consent and without legal justification was a battery. See W. Keeton, D. Dobbs, R. Keeton, & D. Owen, Prosser and Keeton on *Law of Torts* § 9, pp. 39–42 (5th ed. 1984). Before the turn of the century, this Court observed that "no right is held more sacred, or is more carefully guarded, by the common law, than the right of every individual to the possession and control of his own person, free from all restraint or interference of others, unless by clear and unquestionable authority of law." *Union Pacific R. Co. v. Botsford*, 141 U.S. 250, 251, 35 L. Ed. 734, 11 S. Ct. 1000 (1891). This notion of bodily integrity has been embodied in the requirement that informed consent is generally required for medical treatment. Justice Cardozo, while on the Court of Appeals of New York, aptly described this doctrine: "Every human being of adult years and sound mind has a right to determine what shall be done with his own body; and a surgeon who performs an operation without his patient's consent commits an assault, for which he is liable in damages." *Schloendorff v. Society of New York Hospital*, 211 N.Y. 125, 129–130, 105 N.E. 92, 93 (1914). The informed consent doctrine has become firmly entrenched in American tort law. See Keeton, Dobbs, Keeton, & Owen, *supra*, § 32, pp. 189–192; F. Rozovsky, *Consent to Treatment, A Practical Guide* 1–98 (2d ed. 1990).

The logical corollary of the doctrine of informed consent is that the patient generally possesses the right not to consent, that is, to refuse treatment. Until about fifteen years ago and the seminal decision in *In re Quinlan*, 70 N.J. 10, 355 A.2d 647, cert. denied sub nom. *Garger v. New Jersey*, 429 U.S. 922, 50 L. Ed. 2d 289, 97 S. Ct. 319 (1976), the number of right-to-refuse-treatment decisions was relatively few.[2] Most of the earlier cases involved patients who refused medical treatment forbidden by their religious beliefs, thus implicating First Amendment rights as well as common-law rights of self-determination.[3] More recently, however, with the advance of medical technology capable of sustaining life well past the point where natural forces would have brought certain death in earlier times, cases involving the right to refuse life-sustaining treatment have burgeoned. See 760 S.W.2d at 412, n. 4 (collecting fifty-four reported decisions from 1976 through 1988).

In the *Quinlan* case, young Karen Quinlan suffered severe brain damage as the result of anoxia and entered a persistent vegetative state. Karen's father sought judicial approval to disconnect his daughter's respirator. The New Jersey Supreme Court granted the relief, holding that Karen had a right of privacy grounded in the Federal Constitution to terminate treatment. *In re Quinlan*, 70 N.J. at 38–42, 355 A.2d at 662–664. Recognizing that this right was not absolute, however, the court balanced it against asserted state interests. Noting that the State's interest "weakens and the individual's right to privacy grows as the degree of bodily invasion increases and the prognosis dims," the court concluded that the state interests had to give way in that case. Id., at 41, 355 A.2d at 664. The court also concluded that the "only practical way" to prevent the loss of Karen's privacy right due to her incompetence was to allow her guardian and family to decide "whether she would exercise it in these circumstances." Ibid.

After *Quinlan*, however, most courts have based a right to refuse treatment either solely on the common-law right to informed consent or on both the common-law right and a constitutional privacy right. See L. Tribe, *American Constitutional Law* § 15-11, p. 1365 (2d ed. 1988). In *Superintendent of Belchertown State School v. Saikewicz*, 373 Mass. 728, 370 N.E.2d 417 (1977), the Supreme Judicial Court of Massachusetts relied on both the right of privacy and the right of informed consent to permit the withholding of chemotherapy from a profoundly retarded sixty-seven-year-old man suffering from leukemia. Id., at 737–738, 370 N.E.2d at 424. Reasoning that an incompetent person retains the same rights as a competent individual "because the value of human dignity extends to both," the court adopted a "substituted judgment" standard whereby courts were to determine what an incompetent individual's decision would have been under the circumstances. Id., at 745, 752–753, 757–758, 370 N.E.2d at 427, 431, 434. Distilling certain state interests from prior case law—the preservation of life, the protection of the interests of innocent third parties, the prevention of suicide, and the maintenance of the ethical integrity of the medical profession—the court recognized the first interest as paramount and noted it was greatest when an affliction was curable, "as opposed to the State interest where, as here, the issue is not whether, but when, for how long, and at what cost to the individual a life may be briefly extended." Id., at 742, 370 N.E.2d at 426.

In *In re Storar*, 52 N.Y.2d 363, 420 N.E.2d 64, 438 N.Y.S.2d 266, cert. denied, 454 U.S. 858, 70 L. Ed. 2d 153, 102 S. Ct. 309 (1981), the New York Court of Appeals declined to base a right to refuse treatment on a constitutional privacy right. Instead, it found such a right "adequately supported" by the informed consent doctrine. Id., at 376–377, 420 N.E.2d at 70. In *In re Eichner* (decided with *In re Storar*, supra), an eighty-three-year-old man who had suffered brain damage from anoxia entered a vegetative state and was thus incompetent to consent to the removal of his respirator. The court, however, found it unnecessary to reach the question whether his rights could be exercised by others since it found the evidence clear and convincing from statements made by the patient when competent that he "did not want to be maintained in a vegetative coma by use of a respirator." Id., at 380, 420 N.E.2d at 72. In the companion *Storar* case, a fifty-two-year-old man suffering from bladder cancer had been profoundly retarded during most of his life. Implicitly rejecting the approach taken in *Saikewicz*, supra, the court reasoned that due to such life-long incompetency, "it is unrealistic to attempt to determine whether he would want to continue potentially life prolonging treatment if he were competent." 52 N.Y.2d at 380, 420 N.E.2d at 72. As the evidence showed that the patient's required blood transfusions did not involve excessive pain and without them his mental and physical abilities would deteriorate, the court concluded that it should not "allow an incompetent patient to bleed to death because someone, even someone as close as a parent or sibling, feels that this is best for one with an incurable disease." Id., at 382, 420 N.E.2d at 73.

Many of the later cases build on the principles established in *Quinlan*, *Saikewicz*, and *Storar/Eichner*. For instance, in *In re Conroy*, 98 N.J. 321, 486 A.2d 1209 (1985), the same court that decided *Quinlan* considered whether a nasogastric feeding tube could be removed from an eighty-four-year-old incompetent nursing-home resident suffering irreversible mental and physical ailments. While recognizing that a federal right of privacy might apply in the case, the court, contrary to its approach in *Quinlan*, decided to base its decision on the common-law right to self-determination and informed consent. 98 N.J. at 348, 486 A.2d at 1223. "On balance, the right to self-determination ordinarily outweighs any countervailing state interests, and competent persons generally are permitted to refuse medical treatment, even at the risk of death. Most of the cases that have held otherwise, unless they involved the interest in protecting innocent third parties, have concerned the patient's competency to make a rational and considered choice." Id., at 353–354, 486 A.2d at 1225.

Reasoning that the right of self-determination should not be lost merely because an individual is unable to sense a violation of it, the court held that incompetent individuals retain a right to refuse treatment. It also held that such a right could be exercised by a surrogate decision maker using a "subjective" standard when there was clear evidence that the incompetent person would have exercised it. Where such evidence was lacking, the court held that an individual's right could still be invoked in certain circumstances under objective "best interest" standards. Id., at 361–368, 486 A.2d at 1229–1233. Thus, if some trustworthy evidence existed that the individual would have wanted to terminate treatment, but not enough to clearly establish a person's wishes for purposes of the subjective standard, and the burden of a prolonged life from the experience of pain and suffering markedly outweighed its satisfactions, treatment could be terminated under a "limited-objective" standard. Where no trustworthy evidence existed, and a person's suffering would make the administration of life-sustaining treatment inhumane, a "pure-objective" standard could be used to terminate treatment. If none of these conditions obtained, the court held it was best to err in favor of preserving life. Id., at 364–368, 486 A.2d at 1231–1233.

The court also rejected certain categorical distinctions that had been drawn in prior refusal-of-treatment cases as lacking substance for decision purposes: the distinction between actively hastening death by terminating treatment and passively allowing a person to die of a disease; between treating individuals as an initial matter versus withdrawing treatment afterwards; between ordinary versus extraordinary treatment; and between treatment by artificial feeding versus other forms of life-sustaining medical procedures. Id., at 369–374, 486 A.2d at 1233–1237. As to the last item, the court acknowledged the "emotional significance" of food, but noted that feeding by implanted tubes is a "medical procedure with inherent risks and possible side effects, instituted by skilled healthcare providers to compensate for impaired physical functioning" which analytically was equivalent to artificial breathing using a respirator. Id., at 373, 486 A.2d at 1236.[4]

In contrast to *Conroy*, the Court of Appeals of New York recently refused to accept less than the clearly expressed wishes of a patient before permitting the exercise of her right to refuse treatment by a surrogate decision maker. *In re Westchester County Medical Center on behalf of O'Connor*, 72 N.Y.2d 517, 531 N.E.2d 607, 534 N.Y.S.2d 886 (1988) (*O'Connor*). There, the court, over the objection of the patient's family members, granted an order to insert a feeding tube into a seventy-seven-year-old woman rendered incompetent as a result of several strokes. While continuing to recognize a common-law right to refuse treatment, the court rejected the substituted judgment approach for asserting it "because it is inconsistent with our fundamental commitment to the notion that no person or court should substitute its judgment as to what would be an acceptable quality of life for another. Consequently, we adhere to the view that, despite its pitfalls and inevitable uncertainties, the inquiry must always be narrowed to the patient's expressed intent, with every effort made to minimize the opportunity for error." Id., at 530, 531 N.E.2d at 613 (citation omitted). The court held that the record lacked the requisite clear and convincing evidence of the patient's expressed intent to withhold life-sustaining treatment. Id., at 531–534, 531 N.E.2d at 613–615.

Other courts have found state statutory law relevant to the resolution of these issues. *In Conservatorship of Drabick*, 200 Cal. App. 3d 185, 245 Cal. Rptr. 840, cert. denied, 488 U.S. 958 (1988), the California Court of Appeal authorized the removal of a nasogastric feeding tube from a forty-four-year-old man who was in a persistent vegetative state as a result of an auto accident. Noting that the right to refuse treatment was grounded in both the common law and a constitutional right of privacy, the court held that a state probate statute authorized the patient's conservator to order the withdrawal of life-sustaining treatment when such a decision was made in good faith based on medical advice and the conservatee's best interests. While acknowledging that "to claim that a patient's 'right to choose' survives incompetence is a legal fiction at best," the court reasoned that the respect society accords to persons as individuals is not lost upon incompetence and is best preserved by allowing others "to make a decision that reflects a patient's interests more closely than would a purely technological decision to do whatever is possible."[5] Id., at 208, 245 Cal. Rptr. at 854–855. See also *In re Conservatorship of Torres*, 357 N.W.2d 332 (Minn. 1984) (Minnesota court had constitutional and statutory authority to authorize a conservator to order the removal of an incompetent individual's respirator since in patient's best interests).

In *In re Estate of Longeway*, 133 Ill. 2d 33, 549 N.E.2d 292, 139 Ill. Dec. 780 (1989), the Supreme Court of Illinois considered whether a seventy-six-year-old woman rendered incompetent from a series of strokes had a right to the discontinuance of artificial nutrition and hydration. Noting that the boundaries of a federal right of privacy were uncertain, the court found a right to refuse treatment in the doctrine of informed consent. Id., at 43–45, 549 N.E.2d at 296–297. The court further held that the State Probate Act impliedly authorized a guardian to exercise a ward's right to refuse artificial sustenance in the event that the ward was terminally ill and irreversibly comatose. Id., at 45–47, 549 N.E.2d at 298. Declining to adopt a best interests standard for deciding when it would be appropriate to exercise a ward's right because it "lets another make a determination of a patient's quality of life," the court opted instead for a substituted judgment standard. Id., at 49, 549 N.E.2d at 299. Finding the "expressed intent" standard utilized in *O'Connor*, supra, too rigid, the court noted that other clear and convincing evidence of the patient's intent could be considered. 133 Ill. 2d at 50–51, 549 N.E.2d at 300. The court also adopted the "consensus opinion that treats artificial nutrition and hydration as medical treatment." Id., at 42, 549 N.E.2d at 296. Cf. *McConnell v. Beverly Enterprises-Connecticut, Inc.*, 209 Conn. 692, 705, 553 A.2d 596, 603 (1989) (right to withdraw artificial nutrition and hydration found in the Connecticut Removal of Life Support Systems Act, which "provides functional guidelines for the exercise of the common law and constitutional rights of self-determination"; attending physician authorized to remove treatment after finding that patient is in a terminal condition, obtaining consent of family, and considering expressed wishes of patient).[6]

As these cases demonstrate, the common-law doctrine of informed consent is viewed as generally encompassing the right of a competent individual to refuse medical treatment. Beyond that, these cases demonstrate both similarity and diversity in their approaches to decision of what all agree is a perplexing question with unusually strong moral and ethical overtones. State courts have available to them for decision a number of sources—state constitutions, statutes, and common law—which are not available to us. In this Court, the question is simply and starkly whether the United States Constitution prohibits Missouri from choosing the rule of decision which it did. This is the first case in which we have been squarely presented with the issue whether the United States Constitution grants what is in common parlance referred to as a "right to die." We follow the judicious counsel of our decision in *Twin City Bank v. Nebeker*, 167 U.S. 196, 202, 42 L. Ed. 134, 17 S. Ct. 766 (1897), where we said that in deciding "a question of such magnitude and importance . . . it is the better part of wisdom not to attempt, by any general statement, to cover every possible phase of the subject."

The Fourteenth Amendment provides that no State shall "deprive any person of life, liberty, or property, without due process of law." The principle that a competent person has a constitutionally protected liberty interest in refusing unwanted medical treatment may be inferred from our prior decisions. In *Jacobson v. Massachusetts*, 197 U.S. 11, 24–30, 49 L. Ed. 643, 25 S. Ct. 358 (1905), for instance, the Court balanced an individual's liberty interest in declining an unwanted smallpox vaccine against the State's interest in preventing disease. Decisions prior to the incorporation of the Fourth Amendment into the Fourteenth Amendment analyzed searches and seizures involving the body under the Due Process Clause and were thought to implicate substantial liberty interests. See, e.g., *Breithaupt v. Abram*, 352 U.S. 432, 439, 1 L. Ed. 2d 448, 77 S. Ct. 408 (1957) ("As against the right of an individual that his person be held inviolable . . . must be set the interests of society . . .").

Just this Term, in the course of holding that a State's procedures for administering antipsychotic medication to prisoners were sufficient to satisfy due process concerns, we recognized that prisoners possess "a significant liberty interest in avoiding the unwanted administration of antipsychotic drugs under the Due Process Clause of the Fourteenth Amendment." *Washington v. Harper*, 494 U.S. 210, 221–222, 108 L. Ed. 2d 178, 110 S. Ct. 1028 (1990); see also id., at 229 ("The forcible injection of medication into a nonconsenting person's body represents a substantial interference with that person's liberty"). Still other cases support the recognition of a general liberty interest in refusing medical treatment. *Vitek v. Jones,* 445 U.S. 480, 494, 63 L. Ed. 2d 552, 100 S. Ct. 1254 (1980) (transfer to mental hospital coupled with mandatory behavior modification treatment implicated liberty interests); *Parham v. J. R.*, 442 U.S. 584, 600, 61 L. Ed. 2d 101, 99 S. Ct. 2493 (1979) ("A child, in common with adults, has a substantial liberty interest in not being confined unnecessarily for medical treatment").

But determining that a person has a "liberty interest" under the Due Process Clause does not end the inquiry;[7] "whether respondent's constitutional rights have been violated must be determined by balancing his liberty interests against the relevant state interests." *Youngberg v. Romeo*, 457 U.S. 307, 321, 73 L. Ed. 2d 28, 102 S. Ct. 2452 (1982). See also *Mills v. Rogers,* 457 U.S. 291, 299, 73 L. Ed. 2d 16, 102 S. Ct. 2442 (1982).

NOTES

1. The State Supreme Court, adopting much of the trial court's findings, described Nancy Cruzan's medical condition as follows:

". . . (1) Her respiration and circulation are not artificially maintained and are within the normal limits of a thirty-year-old female; (2) she is oblivious to her environment except for reflexive responses to sound and perhaps painful stimuli; (3) she suffered anoxia of the brain resulting in a massive enlargement of the ventricles filling with cerebrospinal fluid in the area where the brain has degenerated and her cerebral cortical atrophy is irreversible, permanent, progressive, and ongoing; (4) her highest cognitive brain function is exhibited by her grimacing perhaps in recognition of ordinarily painful stimuli, indicating the experience of pain and apparent response to sound; (5) she is a spastic quadriplegic; (6) her four extremities are contracted with irreversible muscular and tendon damage to all extremities; (7) she has no cognitive or reflexive ability to swallow food or water to maintain her daily essential needs and . . . she will never recover her ability to swallow sufficient [sic] to satisfy her needs. In sum, Nancy is diagnosed as in a persistent vegetative state. She is not dead. She is not terminally ill. Medical experts testified that she could live another thirty years." *Cruzan v. Harmon*, 760 S.W.2d 408, 411 (Mo. 1989) (en banc) (quotations omitted; footnote omitted).

In observing that Cruzan was not dead, the court referred to the following Missouri statute:

"For all legal purposes, the occurrence of human death shall be determined in accordance with the usual and customary standards of medical practice, provided that death shall not be determined to have occurred unless the following minimal conditions have been met:

"(1) When respiration and circulation are not artificially maintained, there is an irreversible cessation of spontaneous respiration and circulation; or

"(2) When respiration and circulation are artificially maintained, and there is total and irreversible cessation of all brain function, including the brain stem and that such determination is made by a licensed physician." *Mo. Rev. Stat.* § 194.005 (1986).

Since Cruzan's respiration and circulation were not being artificially maintained, she obviously fit within the first proviso of the statute.

Dr. Fred Plum, the creator of the term "persistent vegetative state" and a renowned expert on the subject, has described the "vegetative state" in the following terms:

"'Vegetative state' describes a body which is functioning entirely in terms of its internal controls. It maintains temperature. It maintains heart beat and pulmonary ventilation. It maintains digestive activity. It maintains reflex activity of muscles and nerves for low level conditioned responses. But there is no behavioral evidence of either self-awareness or awareness of the surroundings in a learned manner.'" *In re Jobes*, 108 N.J. 394, 403, 529 A.2d 434, 438 (1987).

See also Brief for American Medical Association et al. as Amici Curiae 6 ("The persistent vegetative state can best be understood as one of the conditions in which patients have suffered a loss of consciousness").

2. See generally Karnezis, Patient's Right to Refuse Treatment Allegedly Necessary to Sustain Life, 93 *A. L. R.* 3d 67 (1979) (collecting cases); Cantor, A Patient's Decision to Decline Life-Saving Medical Treatment: Bodily Integrity Versus the Preservation of Life, 26 *Rutgers L. Rev.* 228, 229, and n. 5 (1973) (noting paucity of cases).

3. See Chapman, The Uniform Rights of the Terminally Ill Act: Too Little, Too Late? 42 *Ark. L. Rev.* 319, 324, n.15 (1989); see also F. Rozovsky, *Consent to Treatment: A Practical Guide*, Boston: Little, Brown; 1984:415–423.

4. In a later trilogy of cases, the New Jersey Supreme Court stressed that the analytic framework adopted in *Conroy* was limited to elderly, incompetent patients with shortened life expectancies, and established alternative approaches to deal with a different set of situations. See *In re Farrell*, 108 N.J. 335, 529 A.2d 404 (1987) (thirty-seven-year-old competent mother with terminal illness had right to removal of respirator based on common law and constitutional principles which overrode competing state interests); *In re Peter*, 108 N.J. 365, 529 A.2d 419 (1987) (sixty-five-year-old woman in persistent vegetative state had right to removal of nasogastric feeding tube—under *Conroy* subjective test, power of attorney and hearsay testimony constituted clear and convincing proof of patient's intent to have treatment

withdrawn); *In re Jobes*, 108 N.J. 394, 529 A.2d 434 (1987) (thirty-one-year-old woman in persistent vegetative state entitled to removal of jejunostomy feeding tube—even though hearsay testimony regarding patient's intent insufficient to meet clear and convincing standard of proof, under *Quinlan*, family or close friends entitled to make a substituted judgment for patient).

5. The *Drabick* court drew support for its analysis from earlier, influential decisions rendered by California Courts of Appeal. See *Bouvia v. Superior Court*, 179 Cal. App. 3d 1127, 225 Cal. Rptr. 297 (1986) (competent twenty-eight-year-old quadriplegic had right to removal of nasogastric feeding tube inserted against her will); *Bartling v. Superior Court*, 163 Cal. App. 3d 186, 209 Cal. Rptr. 220 (1984) (competent seventy-year-old, seriously ill man had right to the removal of respirator); *Barber v. Superior Court*, 147 Cal. App. 3d 1006, 195 Cal. Rptr. 484 (1983) (physicians could not be prosecuted for homicide on account of removing respirator and intravenous feeding tubes of patient in persistent vegetative state).

6. Besides the Missouri Supreme Court in *Cruzan* and the courts in *McConnell*, *Longeway*, *Drabick*, *Bouvia*, *Barber*, *O'Connor*, *Conroy*, *Jobes*, and *Peter*, appellate courts of at least four other States and one Federal District Court have specifically considered and discussed the issue of withholding or withdrawing artificial nutrition and hydration from incompetent individuals. See *Gray v. Romeo*, 697 F. Supp. 580 (RI 1988); *In re Gardner*, 534 A.2d 947 (Me. 1987); *In re Grant*, 109 Wash. 2d 545, 747 P.2d 445 (1987); *Brophy v. New England Sinai Hospital, Inc.*, 398 Mass. 417, 497 N.E.2d 626 (1986); *Corbett v. D'Alessandro*, 487 So. 2d 368 (Fla. App. 1986). All of these courts permitted or would permit the termination of such measures based on rights grounded in the common law, or in the State or Federal Constitution.

7. Although many state courts have held that a right to refuse treatment is encompassed by a generalized constitutional right of privacy, we have never so held. We believe this issue is more properly analyzed in terms of a Fourteenth Amendment liberty interest. See *Bowers v. Hardwick*, 478 U.S. 186, 194–195, 92 L. Ed. 2d 140, 106 S. Ct. 2841 (1986).

The *Wendland* Case

Withdrawing Life Support from Incompetent Patients Who Are Not Terminally Ill

Bernard Lo, MD, Laurie Dornbrand, MD, MPH, Leslie E. Wolf, JD, MPH, and Michelle Groman, AB

Almost all patients want their family members to make decisions about life-sustaining treatment for them if they become incompetent.[1] Asking family members to make such decisions is standard clinical practice and has strong ethical justification.[2] However, dilemmas arise when family members disagree about life-sustaining treatment.

In an important, unanimous decision, the California Supreme Court sharply restricted the authority of a patient's wife, who was also her husband's conservator, to limit life-sustaining interventions in the face of opposition from the patient's mother.[3] Unlike most incompetent patients for whom decisions must be made about life-sustaining interventions, this patient was conscious and was expected to survive for many years if the interventions were continued. If the ruling in this case were extended to other clinical situations, a patient could be subjected to burdensome interventions that offered little clinical benefit and that the patient might well not have wanted.

THE *WENDLAND* CASE

In 1993, forty-two-year-old Robert Wendland, while under the influence of alcohol, lost control of his truck, which rolled over at high speed; he was left comatose. When he regained consciousness fourteen months later, he had

From the *New England Journal of Medicine* 34, no. 19 (2002): 1489–93. Copyright © 2002 Massachusetts Medical Society. All rights reserved.

hemiparesis. He could not be fed by mouth and was unable to control his bowels and bladder, dress or bathe himself, or communicate consistently. At his best, he could draw simple shapes and follow two-step commands with prompting and cueing.

Wendland's feeding tube became dislodged several times. In 1995, his wife, Rose, refused to authorize its reinsertion because she believed he would not have wanted it replaced. The patient's daughter and brother, the hospital's ethics committee, and the county ombudsman for patients supported her decision. However, his mother, Florence, went to court to block the plan. Rose was named conservator, but the court ordered that tube feedings be continued pending a judicial ruling. A court-appointed counsel for Robert also supported the request to remove the tube.

In 1997, doctors asked Robert a series of yes-or-no questions. He was unable to answer correctly most of the time when asked whether he was sitting up or lying down. He answered yes or no when asked whether he had pain, whether he wanted more physical therapy, and whether he wanted to get into a chair. However, when asked, "Do you want to die?" he gave no answer.[4] His doctors expected him to survive for many years, despite recurrent infections, but they did not expect any neurologic improvement.

Robert's wife, brother, and daughter recalled statements he had made before his accident. Three months before the accident, his father-in-law had died after ventilatory support had been withdrawn at the family's request. Robert said at the time, "I would never want to live like that, and I wouldn't want my children to see me like that."[5] Five days before the accident, while Robert was recovering from a drinking bout, his brother predicted that he would have an accident while driving under the influence of alcohol and would end up in a vegetative state. Robert said, "Mike, whatever you do, don't let that happen. Don't let them do that to me."[6] His daughter, Katie, remembered him saying that "if he could not be a provider for his family, if he could not do all the things that he enjoyed doing, just enjoying the outdoors, just basic things, feeding himself, talking, communicating, . . . he would not want to live."[7]

After a series of lower-court rulings and appeals, the California Supreme Court accepted the case. In July 2001, after a two-week hospitalization for refractory pneumonia and while the court was still deliberating, Wendland died.[8]

THE CALIFORNIA SUPREME COURT RULING

In August 2001, the California Supreme Court ruled by a vote of 6 to 0 that Wendland's tube feedings could not have been discontinued.[9] The court acknowledged that in California conservators have the authority under appropriate circumstances to "withhold or withdraw artificial nutrition and hydration and all other forms of healthcare."[10] However, the court stipulated that in the case of a conscious patient, like Wendland, a conservator may withhold or withdraw life-sustaining treatment "for the purpose of causing [the patient's death]" only if there is clear and convincing evidence that the patient "wished to refuse life-sustaining treatment or that to withhold such treatment would have been in his best interest."[11] The court determined that Wendland's statements were not clear and convincing because they did not address his current condition, were not sufficiently specific, and were not necessarily intended to direct his medical care.

The court pointed out that a patient in Robert Wendland's situation might want life-sustaining treatment continued but be unable to express his or her wishes. The judges were also concerned that a conscious patient might suffer from dehydration or starvation. The court ruled that Rose Wendland had failed to provide sufficient evidence that her decision was in her husband's best interests. As conservator, she was required to show clear and convincing evidence that this was the case.

THE LEGAL CONTEXT OF THE RULING

The *Wendland* decision is one of a series of court rulings concerning life-sustaining interventions for incompetent persons who were not terminally ill. Perhaps the best-known case is the first—the 1976 *Quinlan* case. Karen Quinlan had been in a persistent vegetative state since 1975, after consuming drugs and alcohol. The New Jersey Supreme Court allowed her father to withdraw ventilatory support. Quinlan was expected to die when the ventilatory support was withdrawn. Even if it had been continued, she would not have been expected to live for more than a year. In fact, she survived for almost ten years. Although a detailed analysis of Karen's wishes was not conducted, the court was convinced she would have wanted life support discontinued. The court noted that the state's interest in preserving life "weakens . . . as the degree of bodily invasion increases and the prognosis dims."[12] Unlike Karen Quinlan, Robert Wendland was conscious. In subsequent cases, courts have given closer scrutiny to the evidence that the patient would not have wanted the treatment.

The ruling in the *Wendland* case is in accordance with other state rulings that require clear and convincing evidence of an incompetent patient's wishes—that is, written advance directives or specific oral directives.[13] Courts worry that patients' oral statements to family members may not be intended to guide future care or may be emotional reactions rather than carefully considered decisions.

The standard of clear and convincing evidence may be impractical. Patients usually cannot anticipate specific situations that may occur, and few patients provide written advance directives. However, it is unlikely that courts would use the less-demanding standard of a preponderance of the evidence to establish an incompetent patient's wishes. The standard of clear and convincing evidence is used in other civil cases to "protect particularly important individual interests" that are "more substantial than mere loss of money."[14] The California Supreme Court noted that a decision to withdraw life-sustaining interventions would have been irreversible and would have led to Wendland's death. The court regarded an erroneous decision to withdraw treatment as more perilous than an erroneous decision to continue treatment, which is reversible and maintains the status quo.[15] The U.S. Supreme Court has required that the standard of clear and convincing evidence be used in cases involving involuntary commitment to a mental hospital, termination of parental rights, or deportation.[16]

In 1990, the U.S. Supreme Court ruled on the case of Nancy Cruzan, a thirty-three-year-old woman who had been in a persistent vegetative state since an automobile accident in 1983. In a 5–4 ruling, the Court determined that the Constitution allows states to require clear and convincing evidence of an incompetent patient's wishes with regard to life-sustaining interventions.[17] Three dissenting justices declared that the standard of clear and convincing evidence would not improve the accuracy of a determination of the patient's wishes and would hinder the patient's ability to exercise the right to be free of unwanted life-sustaining treatment.[18] Cruzan died later in 1990, twelve days after a state court had allowed the feeding tube to be withdrawn on the basis of new evidence of her wishes.[19]

In Robert Wendland's case, the hospital's ethics committee, an ombudsman, and a court-appointed lawyer for the patient concurred with his wife's decision to withdraw the feeding tube. Other rulings suggest that such procedural safeguards help ensure impartial and thorough deliberations.[20] Nonetheless, the California Supreme Court did not allow Wendland's wife, who was also his conservator, to authorize the withdrawal of the feeding tube. The judges gave considerable weight to the clinical facts that Wendland could interact with others in limited ways and that a simple intervention with minor physical risks was expected to keep him in a stable condition for years. Thus, the ruling can be seen as protecting persons with severe but stable disabilities.

CONCERNS ABOUT THE RULING

Although the California Supreme Court declared that its ruling applied to patients who were "minimally conscious" and not terminally ill, its reasoning may not be limited to such patients. News reports about the decision reinforce a broad interpretation of the case.[21] The court's ruling might be interpreted as applying to other incompetent patients, such as those who are terminally ill or whose family members are in agreement about limiting life-sustaining interventions. We believe the situation in the *Wendland* case should be distinguished from other, more common situations involving life-sustaining interventions. The court's reasoning should not be applied too widely.

To Whom Does the Ruling Apply?

In noting that Wendland was not terminally ill, the court suggested that its restrictions on surrogate decision making might not apply to terminally ill patients. A competent patient's right to refuse unwanted treatment does not depend on his or her prognosis.[22] However, in numerous rulings, courts have refused to allow life-sustaining interventions to be limited for incompetent patients who are not terminally ill.[23] Although the courts often refer to "terminally ill" patients without explicitly defining terminal illness, physicians are most familiar with the criterion used by Medicare to determine eligibility for hospice care: an expected survival of six months or less.[24] Use of the term "terminally ill" is problematic for characterizing patients to whom the *Wendland* ruling should not apply. First, the criterion of terminal illness is too narrow in practice. Physicians substantially overestimate life expectancy for patients whom they characterize as terminally ill.[25] Second, there are conceptual problems with the criterion. Advanced cancer can be described as a terminal illness because it progresses relentlessly. However, it is difficult to apply this term to serious chronic illnesses, such as severe congestive heart failure, that are characterized by intermittent exacerbations, the timing and severity of which cannot be predicted.[26] Moreover, patients who have an acute illness that worsens despite appropriate therapy are not usually considered to be terminally ill.

For patients like Wendland, the California Supreme Court noted that if death occurred "despite the administration of life-sustaining treatment," it would be "unexpected."[27] However, for many seriously ill patients, death within a year would not be unexpected.[28] Clinically, the criterion that death would not be unexpected may be more useful than the criterion of terminal illness. Patients may also implicitly use this prognostic concept when making decisions about life-sustaining interventions.[29]

If a patient's death would not be unexpected, it is unreasonable to say, as in the *Wendland* case, that the "less perilous result" is to continue life-sustaining interventions.[30] As the prognosis worsens, the peril of imposing such interventions becomes greater, and it may be appropriate to avoid burdensome measures. Nor does it make sense to say that the proxy's decision to withhold treatment ends the patient's life under these circumstances; it is the disease that causes the patient's death.

How Were the Issues Framed?

The California Supreme Court's ruling characterized Rose Wendland's decision as intentionally ending the patient's life. The court sought to protect incompetent patients who would not be able to express a wish to remain alive. The court did not consider the opposite possibility. Incompetent patients might want to refuse life-sustaining treatment but be unable to state their refusal. Thus, they might be forced to continue an existence they considered undignified and inhumane.[31]

The court's framing of the issues might make sense because even though Robert Wendland was severely disabled, his condition was expected to remain stable with tube feedings. More typically, however, limiting life-sustaining interventions is considered when the condition of an incompetent patient worsens despite appropriate treatment or when the patient is unlikely to recover his or her base-line function. Hence, the choice is between certain death and a substantial likelihood of death despite interventions that may be invasive, pose medical risks, and be considered dehumanizing.

RESPONDING TO THE *WENDLAND* RULING

Physicians must often make decisions about life-sustaining interventions for incompetent patients who have not appointed a healthcare agent or expressed specific wishes about care. In California, physicians should consider how to respond—and how not to overrespond—to the *Wendland* decision. Physicians in other states can use the ruling as an impetus to improve decisions about life-sustaining interventions.

Discussing Surrogate Decision Making with Competent Patients

Only a minority of patients complete legal documents appointing surrogates to make medical decisions if they become incompetent.[32] Generally, these documents must be witnessed or notarized. In California and several other states, a competent patient can appoint a healthcare agent through an oral statement to a physician.[33] However, these appointments are limited. In California, an oral appointment of a surrogate decision maker is valid only for a particular hospitalization, episode of illness, or treatment.[34] Physicians should routinely ask patients with serious chronic illness and those who are elderly, "Who should make decisions for you if you are too sick to decide yourself?" The emphasis should be on the person who should make decisions rather than on what the patient would want. Physicians should confirm that the patient would allow the surrogate decision maker to limit life-sustaining interventions and to decide what the patient would want or what would be best for the patient. Helpful information about state laws on advance directives can be obtained from state medical societies and Partnership for Caring.[35]

Attempting to Make Joint Decisions with Families of Incompetent Patients

In clinical practice, physicians assume that an incompetent patient who is married would want his or her spouse to make decisions on the patient's behalf, in the absence of evidence to the contrary. The spouse, who generally has a relationship with the patient that is characterized by intimacy and mutual trust, is considered most likely to know what the patient would want and to make decisions in good faith. The assumption that the spouse should be the surrogate decision maker can be overturned—for example, if the couple has separated or if there has been domestic violence. Also, physicians should not follow a spouse's decision if it contradicts previously expressed wishes of the patient that are so specific and to the point that they would meet the legal standard of clear and convincing evidence. However, if the clinical situation differs substantially from the situation that the patient envisioned when stating his or her wishes, it might be appropriate for a surrogate to override the patient's prior statements.[36]

As a practical matter, it is wise to involve close relatives who are readily available in such decisions, even if there is a primary decision maker designated by the patient, by state law, or by the customary practice of turning to the next of kin.[37] Many families prefer to make decisions by consensus. Discussions among family members also give the physician an opportunity to identify and respond to disagreement with a plan of care.

Trying to Change the Law

Physicians should promote legal reforms that both safeguard incompetent patients and avoid imposing undue burdens on close family members who could appropriately make decisions about life-sustaining interventions. First, the scope of oral advance directives to physicians should be broadened. Statements patients make to physicians about life-sustaining interventions differ from statements to relatives or friends. When a patient says to a physician, "I wouldn't want to be kept alive like that," it is reasonable to assume that the patient wants to direct his or her own care.[38] Physicians should document such statements in the medical record. Courts are likely to consider these documented statements as clear and convincing evidence of the patient's wishes. In California, the law should be changed so that decisions made by orally appointed surrogates are not restricted to a specific hospitalization, episode of illness, or treatment.[39] States that do not currently authorize the oral appointment of healthcare proxies should consider doing so.

Second, spouses should be given more explicit authority to make decisions on behalf of incompetent patients. This could be done in several ways. State laws could make explicit the assumption that a married patient would want his or her spouse to serve as a healthcare proxy if the patient became incompetent, in the absence of evidence to the contrary. Hence, a spouse would have the same authority as a proxy specifically appointed by a patient. Alternatively, several states have enacted laws that specify a hierarchy of family members who have the authority to make decisions about life-sustaining interventions for an incompetent patient who did not appoint a proxy when he or she was competent.[40] The spouse is at the top of the hierarchy, with parents and adult children at a lower level. Such laws should also allow patients to disqualify potential surrogates in such hierarchies through oral statements to physicians.[41]

Doing What Is Appropriate despite a Possible Legal Risk

In the light of the *Wendland* ruling, physicians may be reluctant to limit life-sustaining interventions, even when it is appropriate to do so. For instance, family members may agree that an incompetent patient in the intensive care unit who has multi-organ failure and whose condition has not improved despite appropriate treatment would not want life-sustaining interventions continued. However, if the patient has not given clear and convincing advance directives, physicians may be unwilling to discontinue life support.

Some physicians may be tempted to respond to the ruling by appearing to comply with it—for instance, by suggesting to the family how the patient might have expressed his wishes for care in clear and convincing terms. Or they might distort the usual meanings of clinical terms—for example, calling a patient in Wendland's situation terminally ill because all human beings are mortal. Although these approaches might be motivated by compassion, they are deceptive and morally problematic. Deception erodes the integrity of physicians, undermines trust in the medical profession, and makes judges skeptical about decision making on the part of physicians and families.[42]

Some physicians may conclude that it is legally prudent to continue life-sustaining interventions, regardless of the patient's circumstances. If the burden imposed by these interventions outweighs their benefits, however, this approach violates the ethical obligations of the physician to act in the best interests of the patient.[43] Fear of legal liability should not drive physicians to provide interventions that contradict widely accepted standards of practice and sound clinical judgment. Consensus guidelines for limiting life-sustaining interventions have helped establish standards for practice.[44] Just as doctors accept a degree of medical uncertainty when they decide not to order every possible test or therapy, they should accept a degree of legal uncertainty in order to do what is ethically and clinically appropriate.[45]

NOTES

1. Singer PA, Martin DK, Lavery JV, Thiel EC, Kelner M, Mendelssohn DC. Reconceptualizing Advance Care Planning from the Patient's Perspective. *Arch Intern Med.* 1998;158:879–884.

Blendon RJ, Szalay US, Knox RA. Should Physicians Aid Their Patients in Dying? The Public Perspective. *JAMA.* 1992;267:2658–2662.

2. President's Commission for the Study of Ethical Problems in Medicine and Biomedical and Behavioral Research. Deciding to Forego Life-sustaining Treatment: A Report on the Ethical, Medical, and Legal Issues in Treatment Decisions. Washington, DC: Government Printing Office, 1983.

Meisel A. *The Right to Die.* 2d ed. New York: John Wiley; 1995.

Lo B. *Resolving Ethical Dilemmas: A Guide for Clinicians.* 2d ed. Philadelphia: Lippincott Williams & Wilkins; 2000.

3. *Wendland v. Wendland*, 26 Cal. 4th 519, 28 P.3d 151 (2001).

4. Ibid.

5. Ibid.

6. Ibid.

7. Ibid.

8. Dolan M. Injured Man in Life Support Case Dies. *Los Angeles Times.* July 18, 2001:B1.

9. *Wendland v. Wendland*, 26 Cal. 4th 519, 28 P.3d 151 (2001).

10. Ibid.

11. Ibid.

12. *In re Karen Quinlan*, 70 N.J. 10, 335 A.2d 647 (1976).

13. *In re Martin*, 450 Mich. 204; 538 N.W.2d 399 (1995).

In re Edna M.F., 563 N.W.2d 485 (Wis. 1997).

Cruzan v. Missouri Department of Health, 497 U.S. 261, 110 S. Ct. 2841 (1990).

In re O'Connor, 72 N.Y.2d 517, 531 N.E.2d 607, 534 N.Y.S.2d 886 (1988).

In re Conroy, 98 N.J. 321, 486 A.2d 1209 (1985).

14. *Addington v. Texas*, 441 U.S. 418; 99 S. Ct. 1804 (1979).

15. *Wendland v. Wendland*, 26 Cal. 4th 519, 28 P.3d 151 (2001).

16. *Addington v. Texas*, 441 U.S. 418; 99 S. Ct. 1804 (1979).

17. *Cruzan v. Missouri Department of Health*, 497 U.S. 261, 110 S. Ct. 2841 (1990).

18. *Cruzan v. Missouri Department of Health*, 497 U.S. 261, 301 (1990) (Brennan J, dissenting).

19. Steinbrook R. Comatose Woman Dies 12 Days after Life Support Is Halted. *Los Angeles Times.* December 27, 1990:A17.

20. *In re Karen Quinlan*, 70 N.J. 10, 335 A.2d 647 (1976); *In re Conroy*, 98 N.J.

321, 486 A.2d 1209 (1985); *In re Colyer*, 99 Wn.2d 114, 660 P.2d 738 (1983); *In re Hamlin*, 102 Wn.2d 810, 689 P.2d 1372 (1984); *In re Farrell*, 108 N.J. 335, 529 A.2d 404 (1987); *In re Torres*, 357 N.W.2d 332 (Minn. 1984).

21. Dolan M. Justices Deal Setback to Right-to-die Movement. *Los Angeles Times*. August 10, 2001:A1.

Chiang H. Right-to-die Case Loses in State Court. *San Francisco Chronicle*. August 10, 2001:A1.

McKee M. Conservators Can't Choose Death. In: *The Recorder*. San Francisco: American Lawyer Media; August 10, 2001:1.

22. Meisel A. *The Right to Die*.

23. *In re Martin*, 450 Mich. 204; 538 N.W.2d 399 (1995); *In re Edna M.F.*, 563 N.W.2d 485 (Wis. 1997); *In re O'Connor*, 72 N.Y.2d 517, 531 N.E.2d 607, 534 N.Y.S.2d 886 (1988); *In re Conroy*, 98 N.J. 321, 486 A.2d 1209 (1985); *Cruzan v. Harmon*, 760 S.W.2d 408 (Mo. 1988).

24. 42 U.S.C.S. § 1395x(dd) (2002).

25. Christakis NA, Lamont EB. Extent and Determinants of Error in Doctors' Prognoses in Terminally Ill Patients: Prospective Cohort Study. *BMJ*. 2000;320:469–472.

26. Lynn J. An 88-year-old Woman Facing the End of Life. *JAMA*. 1997;227: 1633–1640.

27. *Wendland v. Wendland*, 26 Cal. 4th 519, 28 P.3d 151 (2001).

28. The SUPPORT Principal Investigators. A Controlled Trial to Improve Care for Seriously Ill Hospitalized Patients: The Study to Understand Prognoses and Preferences for Outcomes and Risks of Treatments (SUPPORT). *JAMA*. 1995;274: 1591–1598. [Erratum, *JAMA*. 1996;275:1232.]

29. Weeks JC, Cook EF, O'Day SJ, et al. Relationship between Cancer Patients' Predictions of Prognosis and Their Treatment Preferences. *JAMA*. 1998;279:1709–1714. [Erratum, *JAMA*. 2000;283:203.]

30. *Wendland v. Wendland*, 26 Cal. 4th 519, 28 P.3d 151 (2001).

31. *Cruzan v. Missouri Department of Health*, 497 U.S. 261, 301 (1990) (Brennan J, dissenting).

32. Meier DE, Fuss BR, O'Rourke D, Baskin SA, Lewis M, Morrison RS. Marked Improvement in Recognition and Completion of Healthcare Proxies: A Randomized Controlled Trial of Counseling by Hospital Patient Representatives. *Arch Intern Med*. 1996;156:1227–1232.

Gordon NP, Shade SB. Advance Directives Are More Likely among Seniors Asked about End-of-life Care Preferences. *Arch Intern Med*. 1999;159:701–704.

Brown JB, Beck A, Boles M, Barrett P. Practical Methods to Increase Use of Advance Medical Directives. *J Gen Intern Med*. 1999;14:21–26.

33. Meisel A. *The Right to Die*; Cal. Prob. Code § 4670 (2001); Cal. Prob. Code § 4711 (2001).

34. Cal. Prob. Code § 4711 (2001).

35. Partnership for Caring home page. http://www.partnershipforcaring.org. Accessed April 19, 2002.

36. Sehgal A, Galbraith A, Chesney M, Schoenfeld P, Charles G, Lo B. How Strictly Do Dialysis Patients Want Their Advance Directives Followed? *JAMA.* 1992;267:59–63.

37. Alpers A, Lo B. Avoiding Family Feuds: Responding to Surrogates' Demands for Life-sustaining interventions. *J Law Med Ethics.* 1999;27:74–80.

38. Lo B. *Resolving Ethical Dilemmas: A Guide for Clinicians.*

39. Cal. Prob. Code § 4711 (2001).

40. Meisel A. *The Right to Die.*

Menikoff JA, Sachs GA, Siegler M. Beyond Advance Directives—Health Care Surrogate Laws. *N Engl J Med.* 1992;327:1165–1169.

Me. Rev. Stat. Ann. tit. 18-A, § 5-805 (West 2001).

755 Ill. Comp. Stat. 40/25 (West 2001).

N.M. Stat. Ann. § 24-7A-5 (Michie 2001).

41. Me. Rev. Stat. Ann. tit. 18-A, § 5-805 (West 2001); N.M. Stat. Ann. § 24-7A-5 (Michie 2001).

42. Lo B. *Resolving Ethical Dilemmas: A Guide for Clinicians.*

Beauchamp TL, Childress JF. *Principles of Biomedical Ethics.* 4th ed. New York: Oxford University Press; 1994.

43. Lo B. *Resolving Ethical Dilemmas: A Guide for Clinicians.*

Beauchamp TL, Childress JF. *Principles of Biomedical Ethics.*

Pellegrino ED, Thomasma DG. *For the Patient's Good: The Restoration of Beneficence in Health Care.* New York: Oxford University Press; 1988.

44. Halevy A, Brody B. A Multi-institutional Collaborative Policy on Medical Futility. *JAMA.* 1996;276:571–574.

45. Annas GJ. Asking the Courts to Set the Standard of Emergency Care—The Case of Baby K. *N Engl J Med.* 1994;330:1542–1545.

Diagnosing the Permanent Vegetative State
Ronald Cranford, MD

Modern medicine and newer life-saving treatments have not only resulted in the saving of an untold number of lives and preservation and restoration of health but, as an unfortunate and unavoidable by-product, they have created syndromes of severe brain damage rarely seen, if at all, prior to these advances in medical therapy. These syndromes include brain death, the minimally conscious state, locked-in syndrome, and, probably the most widely known example, the permanent vegetative state. In the middle of the last century, most physicians would have thought it strange to envision a neurological syndrome wherein the patient manifests sleep-wake cycles with periods of eyes open and yet possesses no consciousness whatsoever during those wakeful periods. This state—the permanent vegetative state—is a condition of wakeful unawareness, a form of permanent unconsciousness.

Originally described and named by Fred Plum and Brian Jennet in 1972, this neurological syndrome is now well known to most doctors who treat neurological disorders. Furthermore, many of the landmark right-to-die legal cases in the United States have involved patients in a permanent vegetative state, beginning with Karen Quinlan, the first major termination-of-treatment case in the United States to reach the state supreme court level (in New Jersey, 1975); Nancy Cruzan, the first right-to-die case to reach the United States Supreme Court (1990), and, more recently, the widely publicized case of Terri Schiavo, now pending before the Florida Supreme Court. Although

From the *American Medical Association Virtual Mentor*, http:///www.ama-assn.org/ama/pub/category/12720.html (accessed July 2005).

cases of the permanent vegetative state were undoubtedly rare prior to the 1960s, the Multi-Society Task Force on the Persistent Vegetative State estimated in 1994 that there were 10,000 to 25,000 adults and 4,000 to 10,000 children in persistent vegetative states in the United States.

The reason why these patients experience periods of wakeful unawareness is readily explainable by the underlying characteristic neuropathological changes present in most patients. Whatever the primary cause of the vegetative state, such as hypoxic-ischemic encephalopathy secondary to a cardiac or pulmonary arrest, or shearing injuries in brain trauma, there is extensive damage to the higher centers of the brain, with relative preservation of the brain stem structures. Hence, the cognitive functions of the cerebral cortex are absent, while the arousal system (the reticular activating system) in the brain stem is intact.

MAKING THE PVS DIAGNOSIS

Given this situation, the clinical diagnosis of PVS can be a difficult, and scary, diagnosis to make, unless a physician has adequate experience and expertise in evaluating neurological syndromes. To the families and loved ones, and to inexperienced healthcare professionals, PVS patients often look fairly "normal." Their eyes are open and moving about during the periods of wakefulness that alternate with periods of sleep; there may be spontaneous movements of the arms and legs, and at times these patients appear to smile, grimace, laugh, utter guttural sounds, groan and moan, and manifest other facial expressions and sounds that appear to reflect cognitive functions and emotions, especially in the eyes of the family.

But the cardinal features that distinguish the vegetative state from other syndromes of lesser brain damage, such as the minimally conscious state, are the absence of sustained visual pursuit (visual tracking) and visual fixation. The eyes do not follow objects or persons, nor do they fixate on these objects or persons. And, when patients do emerge from the vegetative state, almost invariably the first and most reliable sign of improvement is the ability to visually track objects or persons in a consistent, sustained, and reproducible fashion. The question is often asked, what exactly does "consistent, sustained, and reproducible fashion" mean in this context? None of the guidelines in the literature precisely defines these terms, but when the patients do develop sustained visual pursuit, it is usually readily apparent to anyone seeing the patient, families and healthcare professionals alike, and it is so consistent and reproducible that it is present almost 100% of the time during the periods of wakefulness.

PERSISTENT AND PERMANENT VEGETATIVE STATES

Extensive dialogue and debate has centered on when the vegetative state becomes permanent. Originally, and in common usage today, the term "persistent" was equated with "permanent." But the two terms should be distinguished, because some persistent vegetative state patients, especially those with traumatic head injuries, may gradually improve to higher levels of cognitive and motor functions in the first few months. It is now well established in the literature and among clinicians with over three decades of experience in this condition that, for both children and adults in vegetative states secondary to hypoxic-ischemic encephalopathy, the chance of any meaningful recovery beyond 3–6 months is negligible. In patients with traumatic brain injuries, the chances of meaningful recovery are practically nonexistent beyond one year. Reports of dramatic "miracle" recoveries surface in the lay press on a regular basis every few years, but these cases, when thoroughly investigated, have not substantially undermined the recovery period statistics given above. So the term "persistent" should be restricted to patients in a vegetative state of at least one-month duration, while "permanent" should be used when it can be determined with an extremely high degree of certainty that the condition is irreversible.

The diagnosis of the permanent vegetative state is primarily clinical, with repeated neurological examination necessary over a period of time to establish absence of cognitive functions and irreversibility. Laboratory studies may be useful and confirmatory in some cases. For example, EEGs will show severe background slowing. When monitored over a few years, CT scans and MRIs will show progressive cerebral cortical atrophy. While the degree of cerebral cortical atrophy does not necessarily correlate with the complete loss of cerebral cortical functions, it does, however, help to confirm that the underlying process, given the severity of destruction seen on these neuroimaging studies, is irreversible, thus establishing to a high degree of certainty that the condition is permanent. Clinical studies evaluating the usefulness of PET (positron emission tomography) have confirmed the absence of consciousness in these patients by conclusively demonstrating levels of oxygen and glucose metabolism in the cerebral cortex consistent with deep levels of coma, and other forms of deep unconsciousness.

SUGGESTED READING

Bernet JL. The Boundaries of the Persistent Vegetative State. *J Clin Ethics*. 1992; 3:176–180.

Cranford RE. The Persistent Vegetative State: The Medical Reality (Getting the Facts Straight). *Hastings Cent Rep*. 1988;18:27–32.

Giacino JT, Ashwal S, Childs N, et al. The Minimally Conscious State: Definition and Diagnostic Criteria. *Neurology*. 2002;58:349–353.

Jennett B, Plum F. Persistent Vegetative State after Brain Damage: A Syndrome in Search of a Name. *Lancet*. 1972;1:734–737.

Jennett B. *The Vegetative State: Medical Facts, Ethical and Legal Dilemmas*. New York: Cambridge University Press; 2002.

Levy DE, Sidtis JJ, Rottenberg DA, et al. Differences in Cerebral Blood Flow and Glucose Utilization in Vegetative versus Locked-in Patients. *Ann Neurol*. 1987; 22:673–682.

Multi-Society Task Force on the Persistent Vegetative State. Medical Aspects of the Persistent Vegetative State, Part I. *N Engl J Med*. 1994;330:1499–1508.

Multi-Society Task Force on the Persistent Vegetative State. Medical Aspects of the Persistent Vegetative State, Part II. *N Engl J Med*. 1994;330:1572–1579.

Position of the American Academy of Neurology on Certain Aspects of the Care and Management of the Persistent Vegetative State Patient: Adopted by the Executive Board, American Academy of Neurology, April 21, 1988, Cincinnati, Ohio. *Neurology*. 1989;39:125–126.

President's Commission for the Study of Ethical Problems in Medicine and Biomedical and Behavioral Research. *Deciding to Forgo Life-sustaining Treatment: A Report on the Ethical, Medical, and Legal Issues in Treatment Decisions*. Washington, DC: Government Printing Office. 1983:171–192.

Part 2

Florida Controversies

INTRODUCTION

The state of Florida has seen its share of political and legal controversy over the last five years. One only has to hear the phrase "hanging chad" to remember Florida's role in the presidential election of 2000, how the difficulty of determining how to recount ballots which would have decided the presidency was argued politically and then in the Florida courts, until at last the US Supreme Court in a 5–4 vote ended the legal proceedings and in effect declared George W. Bush the winner of the Florida election as well as making him the president-elect. While this scenario could have played out in any state with a significant number of electoral votes, it is quite surprising that the case of Mrs. Terri Schiavo should have happened in the state of Florida.

Since the mid-1980s, both Florida statutory and case law have supported the rights of patients and their surrogates or proxies to either accept or refuse medical interventions based on their religious or personal rights, on the prognosis of terminal illness, or on the diagnosis that the patient is in a persistent vegetative state. Florida law, beginning with the Florida Second District Court of Appeals case of *Corbett v. D'Alessandro* (upheld by the Supreme Court of Florida by its refusal to review the case), has held that artificially delivered nutrition and hydration is a medical treatment, not basic care, and may be withheld or withdrawn when it is medically appropriate and when it is the patient's wish. In *In re Guardianship of Browning* (1990) the Supreme Court of Florida explicitly incorporated many of the ideas and legal protec-

71

tions found in *Corbett*. Ideally patients should make healthcare decisions for themselves (after having consulted a physician or other healthcare professional), or at least should appoint a surrogate who can make decisions on their behalf if they do not have decision-making capacity, and Florida statutory law now supports both these possibilities as well as the possibility of using both the substituted judgment standard as well as the best interest standard when deciding to withdraw artificially delivered nutrition and hydration to those in a persistent vegetative state.

But Florida law goes further than this! Unlike many other states that leave healthcare decision making open-ended if the patient hasn't appointed a surrogate, Florida's Life Prolonging Procedure Act (FS 765) provides a lexical ordering of proxies who may act on the patient's behalf if the patient hasn't appointed a surrogate in writing. First on this list is a legal guardian if one has been appointed by a court—a judicially appointed guardian (this is done for wards of the state and is not the same as a "guardian ad litem," sometimes appointed by a court to assure that the best interests of a child or a patient who does not have healthcare decisional capacity is protected during a legal procedure). Next on the list (and in effect first, since most people don't have a legal guardian) is the spouse of the patient who should base healthcare decisions on what he or she believes the patient would have wanted (substituted judgment standard) or what is in the best interests of the patient (best interests standard) if the patient is terminally ill or in a persistent vegetative state. If someone contests the decision of the statutory proxy, it is up to the courts to determine if the proxy is the appropriate decision maker and is making a judgment based on either substituted judgment or the best interests of the patient and all legitimately concerned with the case.

Since Florida case and statutory law have tried to consider every possibility of patient self-determination in healthcare as indicated above, why was it possible for the *Schiavo* case, with all its complexity, to have taken place there? The reason is that the law assumes family solidarity in cases like this, even though by statute it is clear who the decision maker is. In the *Schiavo* case, since the family was claiming that they knew the patient's wishes better than her husband who was the legal proxy, this conflict had to be adjudicated in the courts. But it should be pointed out that since the law lists the husband as the (practically first) legal and legitimate proxy, the burden of proof was on the family to show that the husband was not the appropriate healthcare decision maker in the case, a burden that the courts ultimately decided they failed to meet.

This is the *Schiavo* case in a nutshell. But what we shall consider in part 2 is the involvement of all three branches of Florida government—legislative, executive, and judicial—in the ethical and legal controversies surrounding this case. We shall also present the views of Florida's bishops, since one of the Schiavo family's most frequent claims was that Terri Schiavo would not have chosen to refuse artificial nutrition and hydration because it was contrary to her religious belief as a Catholic. The Catholic Church's mixed teaching on this issue will be covered more thoroughly in part 4 exploring controversies within the Catholic Church in dealing with the issue of the withdrawal of artificially delivered nutrition and hydration.

The first selection in this part is an excerpt from FS 765, Florida's Life Prolonging Procedures Act. In this excerpt are presented some of the definitions included in the act and specifically the stipulated legal definition of the "persistent vegetative state"; also included is the section dealing with proxy decision making and the statutory lexical ordering of proxies; finally, a section (not really relevant for the *Schiavo* case as it unfolded) which shows that Florida law allows a judicially appointed guardian, even in the absence of the wishes of the patient, to discontinue treatment if he or she believes that this decision is in the best interests of the patient. If this is true for a court-appointed guardian, it should have applied even more to someone who was the legitimate and legal proxy.

The precedent-setting case of *Corbett v. D'Alessandro* was decided by the Second District Court of Appeals of Florida in 1986. As mentioned previously, the *Corbett* court decided, among other important things, that medically administered nutrition and hydration is a medical treatment which can be legitimately refused by a patient, surrogate, or proxy; and the court also cited with approval (in a footnote) the American Medical Association's Council on Ethical and Judicial Affairs statement that "Even if death is not imminent but a patient's coma is beyond doubt irreversible and there are adequate safeguards to confirm the accuracy of the diagnosis and with the concurrence of those who have responsibility for the diagnosis and with the concurrence of those who have responsibility for the care of the patient, it is not unethical to discontinue all means of life-prolonging medical treatment."

The Roman Catholic Bishops of Florida have made two statements related to the issue of medically administered nutrition and hydration in the Schiavo case. Both statements urge caution and a presumption in favor of providing nutrition and hydration, but the earlier statement (2003) is much more nuanced (and reflective of official Church teaching at that time) than the statement made in 2005. These statements are relevant because, as previously mentioned, the parents of Terri Schiavo claimed consistently that, as a practicing Roman Catholic, Terri would not have wanted her feeding tube removed.

It is interesting to compare and contrast the reports of two of the guardians ad litem assigned to the Schiavo case, one in 1998 and one in 2003. The former report evaluates the whole setting of the case and ultimately recommends to the court that the petition for the removal of the feeding tube be denied. However, this guardian ad litem bases his recommendations on the Florida Supreme Court decision in *In re Guardianship of Browning* and claims that Mr. Schiavo must have clear and convincing evidence of Terri Schiavo's wishes. This is in error, first because *Browning* does not deal with someone who was in a PVS, and secondly because the relevant statute (*supra.*) allows decisions to be made using a best interests standard as well as a substituted judgment standard in the case of patients in a PVS. The latter report is more circumspect and makes recommendations to Governor Jeb Bush based on contrasting hypotheticals, but ultimately supports the decision of the court that the feeding tube could be removed. Governor Bush's response to this report is more reflective of his own views (and those of the earlier guardian ad litem) than they are responses to the report. This part will conclude with a presentation of "Terri's Law," the hastily prepared piece of legislation which empowered Governor Bush to have the feeding tube reinserted after the court had ordered it removed, and with the Florida Supreme Court decision in *Bush v. Schiavo* which nicely summarizes the whole case and which held "Terri's Law" to be unconstitutional.

Florida Law (State Statute)

FL 765: HEALTHCARE ADVANCE DIRECTIVES

765.101 DEFINITIONS.—AS USED IN THIS CHAPTER

(1) "Advance directive" means a witnessed written document or oral statement in which instructions are given by a principal or in which the principal's desires are expressed concerning any aspect of the principal's healthcare, and includes, but is not limited to, the designation of a healthcare surrogate, a living will, or an anatomical gift made pursuant to part X of chapter 732.

(2) "Attending physician" means the primary physician who has responsibility for the treatment and care of the patient.

(3) "Close personal friend" means any person eighteen years of age or older who has exhibited special care and concern for the patient, and who presents an affidavit to the healthcare facility or to the attending or treating physician stating that he or she is a friend of the patient; is willing and able to become involved in the patient's healthcare; and has maintained such regular contact with the patient so as to be familiar with the patient's activities, health, and religious or moral beliefs.

(4) "End-stage condition" means an irreversible condition that is caused by injury, disease, or illness which has resulted in progressively severe and permanent deterioration, and which, to a reasonable degree of medical probability, treatment of the condition would be ineffective.

(5) "Healthcare decision" means:

(a) Informed consent, refusal of consent, or withdrawal of consent to any and all healthcare, including life-prolonging procedures.

(b) The decision to apply for private, public, government, or veterans' benefits to defray the cost of healthcare.

(c) The right of access to all records of the principal reasonably necessary for a healthcare surrogate to make decisions involving healthcare and to apply for benefits.

(d) The decision to make an anatomical gift pursuant to part X of chapter 732.

(6) "Healthcare facility" means a hospital, nursing home, hospice, home health agency, or health maintenance organization licensed in this state, or any facility subject to part I of chapter 394.

(7) "Healthcare provider" or "provider" means any person licensed, certified, or otherwise authorized by law to administer healthcare in the ordinary course of business or practice of a profession.

(8) "Incapacity" or "incompetent" means the patient is physically or mentally unable to communicate a willful and knowing healthcare decision. For the purposes of making an anatomical gift, the term also includes a patient who is deceased.

(9) "Informed consent" means consent voluntarily given by a person after a sufficient explanation and disclosure of the subject matter involved to enable that person to have a general understanding of the treatment or procedure and the medically acceptable alternatives, including the substantial risks and hazards inherent in the proposed treatment or procedures, and to make a knowing healthcare decision without coercion or undue influence.

(10) "Life-prolonging procedure" means any medical procedure, treatment, or intervention, including artificially provided sustenance and hydration, which sustains, restores, or supplants a spontaneous vital function. The term does not include the administration of medication or performance of medical procedure, when such medication or procedure is deemed necessary to provide comfort care or to alleviate pain.

(11) "Living will" or "declaration" means:

(a) A witnessed document in writing, voluntarily executed by the principal in accordance with s. 765.302; or

(b) A witnessed oral statement made by the principal expressing the principal's instructions concerning life-prolonging procedures.

(12) "Persistent vegetative state" means a permanent and irreversible condition of unconsciousness in which there is:

(a) The absence of voluntary action or cognitive behavior of any kind.

(b) An inability to communicate or interact purposefully with the environment.

(13) "Physician" means a person licensed pursuant to chapter 458 or chapter 459.

(14) "Principal" means a competent adult executing an advance directive and on whose behalf healthcare decisions are to be made.

(15) "Proxy" means a competent adult who has not been expressly designated to make healthcare decisions for a particular incapacitated individual, but who, nevertheless, is authorized pursuant to s. 765.401 to make healthcare decisions for such individual.

(16) "Surrogate" means any competent adult expressly designated by a principal to make healthcare decisions on behalf of the principal upon the principal's incapacity.

(17) "Terminal condition" means a condition caused by injury, disease, or illness from which there is no reasonable medical probability of recovery and which, without treatment, can be expected to cause death. . . .

765.401 THE PROXY

(1) If an incapacitated or developmentally disabled patient has not executed an advance directive, or designated a surrogate to execute an advance directive, or the designated or alternate surrogate is no longer available to make healthcare decisions, healthcare decisions may be made for the patient by any of the following individuals, in the following order of priority, if no individual in a prior class is reasonably available, willing, or competent to act:

(a) The judicially appointed guardian of the patient or the guardian advocate of the person having a developmental disability as defined in s. 393.063, who has been authorized to consent to medical treatment, if such guardian has previously been appointed; however, this paragraph shall not be construed to require such appointment before a treatment decision can be made under this subsection;

(b) The patient's spouse;

(c) An adult child of the patient, or if the patient has more than one adult child, a majority of the adult children who are reasonably available for consultation;

(d) A parent of the patient;

(e) The adult sibling of the patient or, if the patient has more than one sibling, a majority of the adult siblings who are reasonably available for consultation;

(f) An adult relative of the patient who has exhibited special care and concern for the patient and who has maintained regular contact with the patient and who is familiar with the patient's activities, health, and religious or moral beliefs; or

(g) A close friend of the patient.

(h) A clinical social worker licensed pursuant to chapter 491, or who is a graduate of a court-approved guardianship program. Such a proxy must be selected by the provider's bioethics committee and must not be employed by the provider. If the provider does not have a bioethics committee, then such a proxy may be chosen through an arrangement with the bioethics committee of another provider. The proxy will be notified that, upon request, the provider shall make available a second physician, not involved in the patient's care to assist the proxy in evaluating treatment. Decisions to withhold or withdraw life-prolonging procedures will be reviewed by the facility's bioethics committee. Documentation of efforts to locate proxies from prior classes must be recorded in the patient record.

(2) Any healthcare decision made under this part must be based on the proxy's informed consent and on the decision the proxy reasonably believes the patient would have made under the circumstances. If there is no indication of what the patient would have chosen, the proxy may consider the patient's best interest in deciding that proposed treatments are to be withheld or that treatments currently in effect are to be withdrawn.

(3) Before exercising the incapacitated patient's rights to select or decline healthcare, the proxy must comply with the provisions of §§ 765.205 and 765.305, except that a proxy's decision to withhold or withdraw life-prolonging procedures must be supported by clear and convincing evidence that the decision would have been the one the patient would have chosen had the patient been competent or, if there is no indication of what the patient would have chosen, that the decision is in the patient's best interest.

(4) Nothing in this section shall be construed to preempt the designation of persons who may consent to the medical care or treatment of minors established pursuant to s. 743.0645.

765.404 PERSISTENT VEGETATIVE STATE

For persons in a persistent vegetative state, as determined by the attending physician in accordance with currently accepted medical standards, who have no advance directive and for whom there is no evidence indicating what the person would have wanted under such conditions, and for whom, after a reasonably diligent inquiry, no family or friends are available or willing to serve as a proxy to make healthcare decisions for them, life-prolonging procedures may be withheld or withdrawn under the following conditions:

(1) The person has a judicially appointed guardian representing his or her best interest with authority to consent to medical treatment; and

(2) The guardian and the person's attending physician, in consultation with the medical ethics committee of the facility where the patient is located, conclude that the condition is permanent and that there is no reasonable medical probability for recovery and that withholding or withdrawing life-prolonging procedures is in the best interest of the patient. If there is no medical ethics committee at the facility, the facility must have an arrangement with the medical ethics committee of another facility or with a community-based ethics committee approved by the Florida Bioethics Network. The ethics committee shall review the case with the guardian, in consultation with the person's attending physician, to determine whether the condition is permanent and there is no reasonable medical probability for recovery. The individual committee members and the facility associated with an ethics committee shall not be held liable in any civil action related to the performance of any duties required in this subsection.

THOMAS E. CORBETT, Appellant, v. THE HONORABLE JOSEPH P. D'ALESSANDRO, Appellee

No. 85-1052

Court of Appeals of Florida, Second District

487 So. 2d 368; April 18, 1986

PRIOR HISTORY: Appeal from the Circuit Court for Lee County; James R. Thompson, Judge.

COUNSEL: Arnold L. Berman, John R. Day and Robert D. Miller of Shutts & Bowen, West Palm Beach, for Appellant.

Jim Smith, Attorney General, and Gerald B. Curington, Assistant Attorney General, Tallahassee, for Appellee.

Fanella Rouse, Staff Attorney, New York, on behalf of the Society For The Right To Die, Inc.

JUDGES: Campbell, Judge. Scheb, A.C.J., and Sanderlin, J., concur.

OPINION BY: CAMPBELL

OPINION: Appellant, Thomas E. Corbett, appeals a final declaratory judgment which refused appellant a judgment which would have permitted the discontinuance of furnishing nasogastric nutrition to Helen Corbett, appellant's terminally ill wife. Mrs. Corbett passed away naturally two days after the final hearing and prior to a decision by the trial judge. The trial judge rendered his decision in spite of Mrs. Corbett's death because he determined that the nature of the issues involved required a decision, relying upon *John F. Kennedy Memorial Hospital Inc. v. Bludworth*, 452 So.2d 921 (Fla. 1984). We, likewise, consider that a justiciable issue has been presented and will not decline to rule on the basis that the issue has been made moot by reason of the death of Mrs. Corbett. See also *John F. Kennedy Memorial*

From *Thomas E. Corbett, Appellant, v. The Honorable Joseph P. D'Alessandro, Appellee* Court of Appeals of Florida, Second District, 487 So. 2d 368; April 18, 1986.

Hospital Inc. v. Bludworth, 432 So.2d 611 (Fla. 4th DCA 1983), rev'd. on other grounds, 452 So.2d 921 (Fla. 1984).

The facts established in this case show that appellant and Mrs. Corbett were married on December 25, 1936. There were no children of the marriage. Mrs. Corbett had no living parents and no brothers or sisters. Mrs. Corbett, at the time appellant's petition for declaratory relief was filed on December 10, 1984, had been in a persistent vegetative state since March 13, 1982, and had received nutritional sustenance solely through a nasogastric tube since the Autumn of 1982. Mrs. Corbett's attending physician, a specialist in Internal Medicine, gave a written opinion on November 26, 1984, confirming that Mrs. Corbett was in a permanent vegetative state with no reasonable prospect of regaining cognitive brain function and was being sustained only through the use of nutrition supplied through a nasogastric tube. Two specialists in Neurology concurred, in writing, with the opinion of the attending physician.

At the time of the final hearing, Mrs. Corbett was approximately seventy-five years of age. Mrs. Corbett did not have a living will specifying her desires regarding treatment, nor had she designated, in writing, anyone to make treatment decisions for her.

Appellant and the healthcare professionals attending Mrs. Corbett were reluctant to discontinue the nasogastric sustenance without judicial intervention and approval for fear of civil and/or criminal liability. Appellant, therefore, sought declaratory relief as to the propriety of the discontinuance of the nasogastric tube. The trial court denied appellant's request for relief.

Appellant's argument focuses on three issues. The first issue urges that "the trial court erred in ruling that the discontinuance of the use of the nasogastric tube in this case is not protected by the Federal and State Constitutions, entitling appellant to the relief sought." We agree that the trial judge erred in holding that there was no Federal or State Constitutional right of privacy on which appellant could sustain the withholding of nasogastric forced sustenance to Mrs. Corbett.

The United States Supreme Court has long recognized that several of the fundamental constitutional guarantees have created a penumbral right to privacy that is no less important than the rights specifically articulated in the constitution. *Griswold v. Connecticut*, 381 U.S. 479, 85 S. Ct. 1678, 14 L. Ed. 2d 510 (1965). The Florida Constitution, article I, section 23, provides an express right of privacy to natural persons, and we have held that that right extends to incompetent persons who are unable to exercise the right in their own behalf. *In re Guardianship of Barry*, 445 So.2d 365 (Fla. 2d DCA 1984).

The trial court apparently recognized that this right of privacy exists regarding the removal of extraordinary life-prolonging procedures. It was unable to find, however, that the withholding of sustenance by the withdrawing of the nasogastric tube equated with the right to privacy exercised by the withholding of "extraordinary life-prolonging procedures." The trial court was troubled by the fact that chapter 765, *Florida Statutes (Supp. 1984)* (Right to Decline Life-Prolonging Procedures), specifically excludes the "provision of sustenance" from its definition of "life-prolonging procedure," which may be the subject of the right to decline. See § 765.03(3)(b). The trial court failed to give full cognizance to the fact that chapter 765 was enacted as a method for a "competent adult" to provide, in advance, a written declaration directing the withholding of life-prolonging procedures in the event of a terminal condition. § 765.04. In the alternative, section 765.07 provides a method whereby certain enumerated persons, together with the attending physician, may act on behalf of an incompetent patient who has not made a declaration in accordance with section 765.04 when the express or implied intent of the patient can be established. Therefore, chapter 765 appears to have been enacted to apply in certain specified situations and was not intended to encompass the entire spectrum of instances in which these privacy rights may be exercised.

As evidence of that intent, section 765.15 provides that chapter 765 is "cumulative to the existing law . . . and do[es] not impair any existing rights . . . a patient . . . may have . . . under the common law or statutes of the state." We must construe section 765.15 to protect all constitutional rights a patient might have or else the statute would be unconstitutional. We hold, therefore, that although chapter 765, in those cases to which it applies, excludes the right to decline sustenance providing life-prolonging measures, that chapter does not affect the otherwise existing constitutional rights of persons in a permanent vegetative state with no reasonable prospect of regaining cognitive brain function to forego the use of artificial life-sustaining measures.

Our supreme court in *Kennedy v. Bludworth*, 452 So.2d at 923, stated: "We agree with the district court that terminally ill incompetent persons being sustained only through use of extraordinary artificial means have the same right to refuse to be held on the threshold of death as terminally ill competent persons." While no Florida case has previously addressed the termination of artificial feeding devices to sustain life or prolong the moment of death, we see no reason to differentiate between the multitude of artificial devices that may be available to prolong the moment of death. The supreme court, in its above-quoted statement, did not attempt to limit the right to refuse treatment to any particular category of extraordinary artificial means.

Judge Hersey, in his opinion for the fourth district in *Kennedy v. Bludworth*, 432 So.2d at 619, in a statement not commented upon but apparently approved by our supreme court in *Kennedy v. Bludworth*, 452 So.2d 921, wrote: "Life-sustaining procedures are medical procedures which utilize mechanical or other artificial means to sustain, restore, or supplant a vital function, which serve only or primarily to prolong the moment of death, and where, in the judgment of the attending and consulting physicians, as reflected in the patient's medical records, death is imminent if such procedures are not utilized."

We are unable to distinguish on a legal, scientific, or a moral basis between those artificial measures that sustain life—whether by means of "forced" sustenance or "forced" continuance of vital functions—of the vegetative, comatose patient who would soon expire without the use of those artificial means. Perhaps, mainly for the satisfaction of our own consciences, we want to acknowledge that we began our deliberations in this matter, as did those who drafted our Declaration of Independence, with the solemnity and the gratefulness of the knowledge "that all men are . . . endowed by their Creator with . . . Life." It was not without considerable searching of our hearts, souls, and minds, as well as the jurisprudence of this great Land that we have reached our conclusions. We forcefully affirm that Life having been endowed by our Creator should not be lightly taken nor relinquished. We recognize, however, that we are also endowed with a certain amount of dignity and the right to the "Pursuit of Happiness." When, therefore, it may be determined by reason of the advanced scientific and medical technologies of this day that Life has, through causes beyond our control, reached the unconscious and vegetative state where all that remains is the forced function of the body's vital functions, including the artificial sustenance of the body itself, then we recognize the right to allow the natural consequence of the removal of those artificial life-sustaining measures.[1] Thus, we conclude that the right to have a nasogastric tube removed is a constitutionally protected right that exists under the circumstances of the instant case in conformity with the safeguards as discussed and established in *Kennedy v. Bludworth*, 452 So.2d 921 (Fla. 1984), *Satz v. Perlmutter*, 379 So.2d 359 (Fla. 1980), and *In re Guardianship of Barry*, 445 So.2d 365 (Fla. 2d DCA 1984).

Appellant's second issue on appeal asserts that "the trial court erred in ruling that the Life-Prolonging Procedure Act of Florida controls and prohibits the relief sought." We have already addressed this issue in our previous discussion. Section 765.15 specifically provides that the act is supplemental to existing rights and law. The right protected is a constitutional right which could not be limited by legislation even if section 765.15 did not exist.

Appellant's third point is rendered moot by reason of our holding in regard to the other two points.

We, therefore, reverse the holdings of the trial court below. On remand, the intervening death of Mrs. Corbett renders moot any further action by the trial court.

SCHEB, A.C.J., and SANDERLIN, J., Concur.

NOTE

1. Reaching a similar conclusion, the American Medical Association's Council on Ethical and Judicial Affairs adopted the following statement on March 15, 1986, entitled "Withholding or Withdrawing Life-Prolonging Medical Treatment":

The social commitment of the physician is to sustain life and relieve suffering. Where the performance of one duty conflicts with the other, the choice of the patient, or his family or legal representative if the patient is incompetent to act in his own behalf, should prevail. In the absence of the patient's choice or an authorized proxy, the physician must act in the best interest of the patient.

For humane reasons, with informed consent, a physician may do what is medically necessary to alleviate severe pain, or cease or omit treatment to permit a terminally ill patient whose death is imminent to die. However, he should not intentionally cause death. In deciding whether the administration of potentially life-prolonging medical treatment is in the best interest of the patient who is incompetent to act in his own behalf, the physician should determine what the possibility is for extending life under humane and comfortable conditions and what are the prior expressed wishes of the patient and attitudes of the family or those who have responsibility for the custody of the patient.

Even if death is not imminent but a patient's coma is beyond doubt irreversible and there are adequate safeguards to confirm the accuracy of the diagnosis and with the concurrence of those who have responsibility for the care of the patient, it is not unethical to discontinue all means of life-prolonging medical treatment.

Life-prolonging medical treatment includes medication and artificially or technologically supplied respiration, nutrition, or hydration. In treating a terminally ill or irreversibly comatose patient, the physician should determine whether the benefits of treatment outweigh its burdens. At all times, the dignity of the patient should be maintained.

IN THE CIRCUIT COURT OF PINELLAS COUNTY, FLORIDA

PROBATE DIVISION

IN RE: THE GUARDIANSHIP OF THERESA SCHIAVO, CASE NO. 90-2908GD-003

AN INCAPACITATED PERSON.

REPORT OF GUARDIAN AD LITEM

RICHARD L. PEARSE, JR., as guardian ad litem for THERESA SCHIAVO, an incapacitated person, submits the following report to this Court:

1. AUTHORITY OF GUARDIAN AD LITEM. The undersigned guardian ad litem was appointed by order of this Court dated June 11, 1998. The order appointing the undersigned directed that "the Guardian Ad Litem shall make such inquiry as is deemed necessary and shall file a written report and recommendations with the Court." The undersigned guardian ad litem filed an oath of guardian ad litem with the clerk of this Court on or about June 22, 1998.

2. THE WARD. The ward is THERESA MARIE SCHIAVO, a 32-year-old white female who has resided at Palm Gardens of Largo, a skilled nursing facility located at 10500 Starkey Road, Seminole, Florida, since March, 1994.

The ward is the daughter of ROBERT SCHINDLER and MARY SCHINDLER, to whom she was born on December 3, 1963. The ward is the wife of MICHAEL SCHIAVO, to whom she was married on November 10, 1984. The ward has no children. The ward was raised as a Roman Catholic and, according to the ward's parents, continued to practice her religion.

In 1990, the ward suffered cardiac arrest. Although she was resuscitated, the ward sustained profound hypoxic brain damage and has been comatose ever since. She receives food and water through a gastric feeding tube which was placed shortly after the arrest occurred. She is incontinent of bowel and bladder.

From Case no. 90-2908gd-003, *Report of Guardian* Ad Litem, December 29, 1998.

The ward has been neurologically evaluated several times since suffering the cardiac arrest. The most recent such evaluation by Dr. Jeffrey Karp dated September 11, 1998, indicates that the ward is "in a chronic vegetative state" and that the ward exhibits "an absence of voluntary activity or cognitive behavior, and [an] inability to communicate or interact purposefully with her environment." According to Dr. Karp, based on the duration of the ward's condition, "her chance of any improvement to a functional level is essentially zero."

Based on examination of the ward's medical records by the undersigned and a telephone interview with the ward's current primary-care physician, Dr. Vincent Gambone, it appears that Dr. Karp's opinion of the ward's condition and prognosis is substantially shared among those physicians who have recently been involved in her treatment.

Concerning her physical health, the ward is presently stable. She has no infections or skin breakdown. She has developed contractures of certain of her joints despite receiving regular physical therapy. Although, according to Dr. Gambone, the ward's susceptibility to infection and injury is heightened by her chronic vegetative state, there is a potential that she may live a normal life span.

According to the ward's mother, MARY SCHINDLER, the ward exhibits certain reactions to her presence which she ascribes to some kind of low-level cognitive function. The same reactions have been observed by nursing home staff members who indicated that they are random and not predictably in response to any specific stimulus.

The only consistent response related to the undersigned guardian ad litem is that the ward will respond to a deep pain stimulus by moaning and will open her eyes in response to noise. Otherwise, the ward appears totally nonresponsive.

The ward apparently never executed a living will or any writing expressing her intention concerning the withholding or withdrawal of artificial life prolonging procedures. No person interviewed by the undersigned indicated having any knowledge of any written advance directive of the ward.

3. THE WARD'S HUSBAND. The ward's husband is MICHAEL SCHIAVO, a 35-year-old white male. He and the ward have been married since November 10, 1984. They have no children.

Prior to the ward's cardiac arrest, according to Mr. SCHIAVO the two enjoyed a happy marriage and were looking forward to having a family. He worked as a restaurant manager and had held several different jobs after moving to Florida shortly after the marriage.

The ward's husband was appointed guardian of her person and has served in that capacity.

From the time of the ward's initial cardiac arrest through February, 1993, the ward's husband played a very active and aggressive role in pursuing treatment for her, all with the cooperation of the ward's parents, ROBERT and MARY SCHINDLER. He pursued aggressive medical and surgical treatment of the ward, including the surgical placement of experimental electrodes in an effort to stimulate the ward's damaged brain to restore itself. He visited the ward regularly and was actively and closely involved with every aspect of her care and rehabilitation. He was an aggressive advocate for the ward, and never hesitated to question the nursing home staff concerning matters he didn't understand or like. A previously appointed guardian ad litem for the ward referred to Mr. SCHIAVO as "a nursing home administrator's nightmare."

In addition, the ward's husband pursued negligence litigation arising from the ward's treatment following her cardiac arrest which eventually resulted in judgments for the ward netting the ward's estate in excess of $750,000 as well as a substantial personal award for his loss of the ward's consortium which were paid in early 1993.

In February, 1993, the ward's husband and her parents had a falling out. Mr. SCHIAVO claims the argument arose because he refused to share the settlement money with the SCHINDLERS. They, on the other hand, claim that Mr. SCHIAVO failed to honor commitments he had previously made to continue to seek aggressive treatments for the ward's condition. The SCHINDLERS retained counsel and sought Mr. SCHIAVO's removal as guardian, but were ultimately unsuccessful.

After February, 1993, Mr. SCHIAVO'S attitude concerning treatment for the ward apparently changed. Early in 1994, for example, he refused to consent to treat an infection from which the ward was then suffering and ordered that she not be resuscitated in the event of cardiac arrest. The nursing home where she resided at that time sought to intervene, which ultimately led the ward's husband to reverse his decision and authorize antibiotic treatment. It also resulted in a transfer of the ward to the nursing home where she now resides. Mr. SCHIAVO admitted to the undersigned that he essentially gave up hope that the ward would recover about four years after the accident.

Regarding the pending petition filed by Mr. SCHIAVO to withdraw the gastric feeding tube which sustains the ward, he claims that the ward told him after their marriage that she would not want to be kept alive artificially. He indicates that she related her feelings to an uncle of hers who was severely injured in an automobile accident and was comatose for a time. At one point, according to Mr. SCHIAVO, during a train trip from Pennsylvania to Florida in the mid-1980s, the ward told her husband that if she were ever in a situation of being artificially maintained that she wanted the life support removed. Mr. SCHIAVO indicated strongly to the undersigned that his petition to withdraw life support has nothing to do with the money held in the guardianship estate, which he would inherit upon the ward's death as her sole heir-at-law.

Mr. SCHIAVO has admitted at least two romantic involvements since the ward's accident. It is apparent that he has reached a point where he has no hope of the ward's recovery and wants to get on with his own life. He indicates that he wants the life support withdrawn because that is what the ward would want, and that she is his responsibility because he is her husband.

4. THE WARD'S PARENTS. The ward's parents are ROBERT and MARY SCHINDLER who reside in St. Petersburg, Florida.

Prior to the ward's accident, her parents indicated that they had a close relationship with her. The ward spent a great deal of time in her parents' home, especially when her husband was at work. Contrary to the ward's husband's assertions, the ward's parents believed that the ward's marriage to her husband was in difficulty during the months prior to the accident. Mrs. SCHINDLER has indicated in prior testimony that the ward told her that she was no longer in love with her husband and was considering ending their marriage. The ward's husband denies this, as indicated above.

From the time of the ward's accident, the ward's parents have been vitally interested in her welfare. Until February, 1993, the SCHINDLERS worked cooperatively with Mr. SCHIAVO: in fact, he lived with them in their home for a number of months following the ward's accident.

After the falling out between the ward's parents and her husband, Mr. and Mrs. SCHINDLER pursued removal litigation in an effort to have Mr. SCHIAVO removed as their daughter's guardian and to have themselves appointed guardians of her person. Their efforts in removing the ward's husband were unsuccessful and were ultimately dropped. They have also pursued litigation against him to gain access to medical and financial information concerning the ward which was withheld by the ward's husband, with only partial success. They express extreme frustration with the current situation in which they have virtually no input into the decision-making progress concerning their own daughter.

The ward's parents visit her regularly but at a time when they won't have to confront Mr. SCHIAVO. Mrs. SCHINDLER feels strongly that the ward does respond to her presence during these visits as evidenced by various reactions of the ward being talked to and touched. The reactions of the ward have been observed by nursing home staff members, but they believe that such reactions are coincidental. Nevertheless, Mr. and Mrs. SCHINDLER harbor a deeply held belief that the ward is aware of their presence at some level.

The ward's parents both acknowledged that the ward never discussed with them what her intentions would have been concerning the withholding or withdrawal of artificial life-prolonging procedures. They also have no knowledge that the ward spoke of these matters with anyone else.

The ward's parents' goal is to have their daughter restored to their care. They indicate that they understand Mr. SCHIAVO'S desire to get on with his own life and would have no objection to his seeking a divorce from their daughter. Their plan would be to care for her with the feeding tube in place until she died naturally, using the guardianship estate as a means of supporting her.

5. FINANCIAL STATUS. A review of the inventory and various annual financial returns reveals that the initial inventoried value of the guardianship estate was $776,254.69 and that the latest reported market value as of the close of the fiscal year ending 4/30/98 was $713,828.85. The estate is presently administered by SouthTrust Bank as guardian of the ward's property. The estate is invested in a diversified portfolio of stocks, bonds, mutual funds, and other securities. The undersigned guardian ad litem is aware of no evidence that the ward's estate has been mismanaged.

6. POTENTIAL CONFLICTS OF INTEREST. The pending application by the ward's husband for withdrawal of the ward's feeding tube which would ultimately result in the ward's death creates at least the appearance of, if not actual, conflicts of interest involving both the ward's husband and her parents.

All parties to this proceeding acknowledge that the ward has no will so that, upon her death, her entire estate will pass to her intestate heir(s). Thus, if the ward dies while married to Mr. SCHIAVO, he inherits the entire guardianship estate. On the other hand, if the marriage between the ward and her husband is dissolved the ward's parents become her intestate heirs and they (or the survivor of them) will inherit the ward's estate upon her death. Thus, Mr. SCHIAVO will realize a substantial and fairly immediate financial gain if his application for withdrawal of life support is granted. On the other hand, [*if*] Mr. SCHIAVO's petition for withdrawal of life support is denied, it may be anticipated that he would seek to dissolve his marriage to the ward, in which case the ward's parents become her sole heirs-at-law. Of course, given the potential that the ward may have a normal life expectancy, there is no way to quantify the projected financial gain to the ward's parents upon her eventual death because there is no reliable way of predicting how much of her estate will be left.

7. SUMMARY OF APPLICABLE LAW. The governing statute in this proceeding is Chapter 765, Florida Statutes, dealing with advance directives for health care. Specifically, *Fla. Stat.* 765.401 provides:

(1) If the patient has not executed an advance directive, or designated a surrogate to execute an advance directive, or the designated or alternate surrogate is no longer available to make healthcare decisions, healthcare decisions may be made for the patient by any of the following individuals, in the following order of priority, if no individual in a prior class is reasonably available, willing, or competent to act:

    (a) The judicially appointed guardian of the patient, who has been authorized to consent to medical treatment, if such guardian has previously been appointed; however, this paragraph shall not be construed to require such appointment before a treatment decision can be made under this subsection;

    (b) The patient's spouse;

    (c) An adult child of the patient, or if the patient has more than one adult child, a majority of the adult children who are reasonably available for consultation;

    (d) A parent of the patient;

    (e) The adult sibling of the patient or, if the patient has more than one sibling, a majority of the adult siblings who are reasonably available for consultation.

    (f) An adult relative of the patient who has exhibited special care and concern for the patient and who has maintained regular contact with the patient and who is familiar with the patient's activities, health, and religious or moral beliefs; or

    (g) A close friend of the patient.

(2) Any healthcare decision made under this part must be based on the proxy's informed consent and on the decision the proxy reasonably believes the patient would have made under the circumstances.

(3) Before exercising the incapacitated patient's rights to select or decline healthcare, the proxy must comply with the pertinent provisions applicable to surrogates under this chapter, except that a proxy's decision to withhold or withdraw life-prolonging procedures must be supported by

> clear and convincing evidence that the decision would have been the one the patient would have chosen had the patient been competent.
>
> (4)   Nothing in this section shall be construed to preempt the designation of persons who may consent to the medical care of treatment of minors established pursuant to s. 743.0645

The controlling case is *In re Guardianship of Browning*, 568 So. 2d 4 (Fla. 1990), wherein the Supreme Court of Florida held that a competent individual has the right [*to*] choose or refuse medical treatment, including artificial life-prolonging procedures; that such right extends to incapacitated persons and may, under appropriate circumstances, be exercised by an appointed surrogate or proxy; and that in the absence of a written direction by the principal the decision to withhold or withdraw life support must be supported by clear and convincing evidence to do so would have been the principal's decision if he or she could have made it.

Also instructive are *In Re Guardianship of Browning*, 543 So. 2d 258 (Fla. 2d DCA 1989); *Slomowitz v. Walker*, 429 So.2d 797, 800 (Fla. 4th DCA 1983); and *Migliore v. Migliore*, 717 So.2d 1077 (Fla. 4th DCA 1998), which deals with the "clear and convincing" standard applicable in this case.

8. GUARDIAN AD LITEM'S OPINION AND RECOMMENDATIONS. The principal issue presented in this case is whether the ward, if capable, would direct removal of her feeding tube given her present circumstances.

There is no written advance directive of the ward in this case. Based on *Browning*, there is no presumption that evidence of oral statements of the ward is clear and convincing; that burden remains with the Petitioner.

The only direct evidence probative of the issue of the ward's intent is the hearsay testimony of her husband, Mr. SCHIAVO, who seeks withdrawal of the ward's feeding tube which would inevitably result in her death. However, his credibility is necessarily affected by the obvious financial benefit to him of being the ward's sole heir-at-law in the event of her death while still married to him. Her death also permits him to go on with his own life.

In the opinion of the undersigned guardian ad litem, Mr. SCHIAVO's credibility is also adversely affected by his chronology of this case. For the first four years (approximately) following the ward's accident, he aggressively pursued every manner of treatment and rehabilitation conceivable, as well as lawsuits to compensate the ward for her injuries in connection with which he presumably argued she would require substantial funds for future care and treatment. At or around the time the litigation was finally concluded, he has a change of heart concerning further treatment which led, according to the ward's parents, to his falling out with them. From that point forward, the ward's husband has isolated the ward from her parents, has on at least one occasion refused to consent for the ward to be treated for an infection, and, ultimately, four years later, has filed the instant petition for the withdrawal of life support on the basis of evidence apparently known only to him which could have been asserted at any time during the ward's illness.

Since there is no corroborative evidence of the ward's intentions, and since the only witness claiming to have such evidence is the one person who will realize a direct and substantial financial benefit from the ward's death, the undersigned guardian ad litem is of the opinion that the evidence of the ward's intentions developed by the guardian ad litem's investigation does not meet the clear and convincing standard. Based on *Migliore v. Migliore*, 717 So.2d 1077 (Fla. 4th DCA 1998), the credibility of the witness is a factor to be considered in determining whether evidence is clear and convincing.

Given the inherent evidentiary problems already mentioned, together with the fact that the ward has been maintained on the life support measures sought to be withdrawn for the past 8 years, it is the recommendation of the guardian ad litem that the petition for removal be denied.

In fairness to the Petitioner, should this Court disagree with the foregoing analysis of the evidence and find it to clearly and convincingly reflect the actual wishes and intentions of the ward, the guardian ad litem believes that *Browning* controls and, in this case, the feeding tube should be removed.

The undersigned guardian ad litem further asserts and recommends that due process requires that the ward's interests continue to be represented in all further proceedings herein, whether by the undersigned guardian ad litem or another appointed guardian ad litem or other appropriate fiduciary.

Under penalties of perjury, I declare that I have read the foregoing and the facts and matters alleged therein are true and correct to the best of my knowledge and belief.

I HEREBY CERTIFY that a true copy of the foregoing was furnished by U.S. Mail, postage prepaid, to PAMELA A.M. CAMBELL, 535 Central Avenue, Suite 403, St. Petersburg, FL 33701-3701, DEBORAH A. BUSH-NELL, 204 Scotland Avenue, Dunedin, FL 34698, and GEORGE J. FELOS, 640 Douglas Avenue, Dunedin, FL 34698, on this 29th Day of December, 1998.

Florida Bishops Urge Safer Course for Terri Schiavo

By the Undersigned Catholic Bishops of Florida

We continue our fervent prayers for Terri Schiavo, for her family, and all involved in this most difficult and heart-wrenching situation. After a fourth consideration of her case, the 2nd District Court of Appeals has upheld the latest order of the trial court judge to withdraw her hydration and nutrition tube. An emergency appeal to the Florida Supreme Court was denied. Barring unforeseen legal intervention, the trial court will soon reschedule the removal of Mrs. Schiavo's feeding tube. It is most unfortunate that family members have not been able to agree on her care, forcing the Court's involvement.

Bishop Robert N. Lynch of the Diocese of St. Petersburg has spoken in detail to this case (*Concerning Terri Schiavo*). His statement followed careful consultation with his brother Bishops and we fully support it. Because of so much uncertainty and dispute, we reiterate his plea that her treatment be continued while all parties pursue a more clear understanding of her actual physical condition.

Bishop Lynch's statement clarifies the teaching of the Church that nourishment or hydration may be withheld or withdrawn where that treatment itself is causing harm to the patient or is useless because the patient's death is imminent. Church teaching is clear that there should be a presumption in favor of providing medically assisted nutrition and hydration to all patients as long as it is of sufficient benefit to outweigh the burdens involved to the patient.

The Church cannot make this decision, but her teaching guides those who

From Catholic Bishops of Florida, August 27, 2003. http://www.flacathconf.org/Publications/Bishops Statements/Bpst2000/TerriSchiavo.htm (accessed November 23, 2005).

must: the patient or those legally entitled to do so if the patient is unable. If Mrs. Schiavo's feeding tube were to be removed because the nutrition she receives is of no use to her, or because she is near death, or because it is unreasonably burdensome for her, her family, or caregivers, it could be seen as permissible. But if her feeding tube were to be removed to intentionally cause her death, or because her life is perceived to be useless, or because it is believed that the quality of her life is such that she would be better off, this would be wrong.

Without question, removal of Mrs. Schiavo's feeding tube will result in her death. We respect the need for finality of the court's decision, but we urge additional time to allow greater certainty as to her true condition. We respect, too, the limitations on new evidence being considered by the court, but in matters of life and death, exceptions should be made. If additional medical treatment can be shown to be helpful to her condition, we urge that all parties involved take the safer course and allow it to be used.

Just as we are concerned for Terri Schiavo, we are also concerned for others who are weak and vulnerable. There is an inherent danger in assuming that food and water can simply be withheld without clearly knowing a patient's wishes. There is reason to be circumspect and ever careful in these cases. We reject outright the euthanasia movement and its utilitarian standard that some lives are not worth living. Every life is precious and unrepeatable.

And finally, we remember there are times when one may refuse treatment that will result in a precarious and burdensome prolongation of life. Properly, this may be seen as an expression of our hope in the life to come. Let each of us communicate ahead of time with our families and loved ones, our wishes for treatment at the end of our lives. To do so will give great comfort to them in an emotionally stressful time.

We join our prayers with the family and loved ones of Terri Schiavo in this most difficult time.

Archbishop John C. Favalora
Archdiocese of Miami

Bishop John J. Nevins
Diocese of Venice

Bishop Norbert M. Dorsey, CP
Diocese of Orlando

Bishop John H. Ricard, SSJ
Diocese of Pensacola/Tallahassee

Bishop Victor Galeone
Diocese of St. Augustine

Bishop Robert N. Lynch
Diocese of St. Petersburg

Bishop-Designate Gerald M. Barbarito, JCL
Diocese of Palm Beach

Coadjutor Bishop Thomas G. Wenski
Diocese of Orlando

Continued Concerns for Terri Schiavo

By the Undersigned Catholic Bishops of Florida

Terri Schindler Schiavo has been the center of national media attention, and the focus of a debate that touches all three branches of government. Mrs. Schiavo is not "brain dead" or comatose. She has lived in a nursing home for years, presently a hospice facility, generally needing only nursing care and assistance in receiving nourishment. Some experts say she is in a "persistent vegetative state"; others say she is not. Her husband wants to remove her feeding tube, insisting she expressed clearly this would be her wish; her parents and siblings vigorously disagree, and have offered to care for her as long as she lives. Questions about her prognosis and wishes persist, raising doubt as to what she would truly want.

No longer able to speak on her own behalf, Mrs. Schiavo is a defenseless human being with inherent dignity, deserving of our respect, care, and concern. Her plight dramatizes one of the most critical questions we face: To be a truly human society, how should we care for those we may not be able to cure?

In our past statements concerning Terri Schiavo, as well as those by Bishop Robert N. Lynch of the Diocese of St. Petersburg, we have made it clear that there should be a presumption in favor of providing nutrition and hydration even by artificial means as long as it is of sufficient benefit to outweigh the burdens involved to the patient. We reiterate our plea that Mrs. Schiavo continues to receive all treatments and care that will be of benefit to her.

From Catholic Bishops of Florida, February 28, 2005. http://www.flacathconf.org/Health/Schaivo%20
Statement%202-28-05.htm (accessed November 23, 2005).

In a statement provided in March 2004, Pope John Paul II urges us to see every patient in a so-called vegetative state as a fellow human being, retaining his or her full dignity despite diminished abilities. Regarding nourishment for such patients, he said:

> I should like particularly to underline how the administration of water and food, even when provided by artificial means, always represents a natural means of preserving life, not a medical act. Its use, furthermore, should be considered, in principle, ordinary and proportionate, and as such morally obligatory, insofar as and until it is seen to have attained its proper finality, which in the present case consists in providing nourishment to the patient and alleviation of his suffering.

Simply put, we are called to provide basic means of sustenance such as food and water unless they are doing more harm than good to the patient, or are useless because the patient's death is imminent. As long as they effectively provide nourishment and help provide comfort, we should see them as part of what we owe to all who are helpless and in our care. In certain situations a patient may morally refuse medical treatment and such decisions may properly be seen as an expression of our hope of union with God in the life to come.

We pray that Terri Schindler Schiavo's family and friends, and all who hold power over her fate, will see that she continues to receive nourishment, comfort, and loving care.

Archbishop John C. Favalora
Archdiocese of Miami

Bishop John J. Nevins
Diocese of Venice

Bishop John H. Ricard, SSJ
Diocese of Pensacola/Tallahassee

Bishop Robert N. Lynch
Diocese of St. Petersburg

Bishop Victor Galeone
Diocese of St. Augustine

Bishop Gerald M. Barbarito, JCL
Diocese of Palm Beach

Bishop Thomas G. Wenski
Diocese of Orlando

Auxiliary Bishop Felipe J. Estévez
Archdiocese of Miami

A REPORT TO GOVERNOR JEB BUSH AND THE 6TH JUDICIAL CIRCUIT IN THE MATTER OF THERESA MARIE SCHIAVO

Jay Wolfson

Pursuant to the requirements of H.B. 35-E (Chapter 2003-418, Laws of Florida) and the Order of the Hon. David Demers, Chief Judge, Florida 6th Judicial Circuit regarding the appointment and duties of a Guardian Ad Litem in the matter of Theresa Marie Schiavo, Incapacitated.

Respectfully Submitted
Jay Wolfson, DrPH, JD, Guardian Ad Litem for Theresa Marie Schiavo

1 December 2003

INTRODUCTION

Sometimes good law is not enough, good medicine is not enough, and all too often, good intentions do not suffice. Sometimes, the answer is in the process, not the presumed outcome. We must be left with hope that the right thing will be done well.

We are, each of us, standing in Theresa Marie Schiavo's shoes. Each of us is profoundly affected by the decisions that have and will be made in this case. Advocates of privacy rights and death with dignity, and advocates of right to life and rights of the disabled provide the compelling definitional parameters of this matter.

From "*In Re: Theresa Marie Schiavo, Incapacitated*: Report to Gov. Jeb Bush and the 6th Florida Judicial Circuit," December 1, 2003.

On 31 October 2003, pursuant to the requirements of Florida H.B. 35-E (Chapter 2003-418, Laws of Florida) and the order of the Hon. David Demers, Chief Judge, Florida 6th Judicial Circuit, a Guardian Ad Litem was appointed for a period of thirty days with the following charge:

". . . make a report and recommendations to the Governor as to whether the Governor should lift the stay that he previously entered. The report will specifically address the feasibility and value of swallow tests for this ward and the feasibility and value of swallow therapy. Additionally, the report will include a thorough summary of everything that has taken place in the trial court and the appellate court concerning this case."

The legislature instructed the court to appoint a Guardian Ad Litem to report to the court and the Governor. Florida law regarding the duties and powers of the Guardian Ad Litem afford considerable scope and flexibility. The specific court-ordered charge is narrowly constructed, particularly with respect to the questions to be addressed.

The recommendations proffered herein are intended for both the Governor and the court, on behalf of Theresa Marie Schiavo. . . .

SUMMARY OF GUARDIAN AD LITEM RECOMMENDATIONS

Restatement of Questions and Recommendations

1. Should the Governor lift the stay that he previously entered relative to Theresa Schiavo's feeding tube?

a. Yes. The Governor should lift the stay, if valid, independent scientific medical evidence clearly indicates that Theresa has no reasonable medical hope of regaining any swallowing function and/or if there is no evidence of cognitive function and no hope of improvement.

b. No. The Governor should not lift the stay if valid, independent scientific medical evidence clearly indicates that Theresa has a reasonable medical hope of regaining any swallowing function and/or if there is evidence of cognitive function with or without hope of improvement.

2. Is there feasibility and value in swallowing tests and swallowing therapy given the totality of circumstances?

a. Yes. There is feasibility and value in swallowing tests and swallowing therapy being administered if the parties agree in advance as to how the results of these tests will be used with respect to the decision about Theresa's future. If the parties do not agree in advance as to how the tests will be used, then the court must be prepared to once again make a final judgment on the matter. Given the history of the case, this would not, in and of itself, assure a resolution, and is not, therefore, deemed either feasible or of value to Theresa Schiavo without prior agreement.

The GAL concludes from the medical records and consultations with medical experts that the scope and weight of the medical information within the file concerning Theresa Schiavo consists of competent, well-documented information that she is in a persistent vegetative state with no likelihood of improvement, and that the neurological and speech pathology evidence in the file support the contention that she cannot take oral nutrition or hydration and cannot consciously interact with her environment. The GAL concludes that the trier of fact and the evidence that served as the basis for the decisions regarding Theresa Schiavo were firmly grounded within Florida statutory and case law, which clearly and unequivocally provide for the removal of artificial nutrition in cases of persistent vegetative states, where there is no advance directive, through substituted/proxy judgment of the guardian and/or the court as guardian, and with the use of evidence regarding the medical condition and the intent of the parties that was deemed, by the trier of fact to be clear and convincing.

The GAL concludes the Guardian Ad Litem appointment be extended until a resolution is concluded in the matter of Theresa Maria Schiavo.

The rules were adhered to and they are the laws of this state. Again, Justice Rehnquist in *Cruzan*: "But the Constitution does not require general rules to work faultlessly; no general rule can." *Cruzan v. Director, MDH*, 497, U.S. 261 (1990)

We remain in Theresa Schiavo's shoes.

In Re: Theresa Marie Schiavo, Incapacitated
Report to Gov. Jeb Bush and the 6th Florida Judicial Circuit 1 December 2003
Jay Wolfson, as Guardian Ad Litem to Theresa Marie Schiavo

STATEMENT BY:
GOVERNOR JEB BUSH
GUARDIAN AD LITEM'S REPORT

TALLAHASSEE—I appreciate Dr. Wolfson's time and effort in this endeavor. I also respect the tremendous challenge of preparing an accurate, independent, and thorough review of nearly ten years of information in only thirty days. That Dr. Wolfson recognizes the continued need for an independent third party Guardian Ad Litem is encouraging, as is his recommendation that Mrs. Schiavo undergo swallowing tests and therapy. Based on this third-party analysis, I am hopeful that Mr. Schiavo and his attorney will no longer prevent this vital testing from taking place. This would be a first step in the fresh, clean-hands start that Dr. Wolfson recommended at the end of his report.

Taken as a whole, however, I am concerned that too many open questions still remain. Chief among them is the issue of Mrs. Schiavo's wishes, and whether or not there is clear and convincing evidence as to what those wishes were. The current court proceedings have not addressed this issue, or her current guardian's conflicts of interest, nor have I been given the opportunity to develop evidence, or test the accuracy of Mr. Schiavo's assertions on this matter.

I am also concerned we do not know the expertise of the individuals who provided the "answers" to the questions that are addressed in the report. I am sure that Dr. Wolfson, who indicated his reliance on "good science-based medicine," understands the importance of knowing which good scientists and good doctors he relied on to reach certain conclusions.

As I have said from the beginning, the state must protect every Floridian's right to life, and in so doing, err on the side of life. As Governor, I will continue to do just that. Nothing in Dr. Wolfson's report leads me to believe the stay should be lifted at this time, or that Mrs. Schiavo should be deprived of her right to live.

From "Guardian Ad Litem's Report: Statement by Governor Jeb Bush," December 2, 2003.

THE LAW PASSED BY THE FLORIDA LEGISLATURE

(in Relation to the Schiavo Case)

SECTION 1.

(1) The Governor shall have the authority to issue a one-time stay to prevent the withholding of nutrition and hydration from a patient if, as of October 15, 2003:

(a) That patient has no written advance directive;

(b) The court has found that patient to be in a persistent vegetative state;

(c) That patient has had nutrition and hydration withheld; and

(d) A member of that patient's family has challenged the withholding of nutrition and hydration.

(2) The Governor's authority to issue the stay expires fifteen days after the effective date of this act, and the expiration of that authority does not impact the validity or the effect of any stay issued pursuant to this act. The Governor may lift the stay authorized under this act at any time. A person may not be held civilly liable and is not subject to regulatory or disciplinary sanctions for taking any action to comply with a stay issued by the Governor pursuant to this act.

(3) Upon the issuance of a stay, the chief judge of the circuit court shall appoint a guardian ad litem for the patient to make recommendations to the Governor and the court.

SECTION 2. THIS ACT SHALL TAKE EFFECT UPON BECOMING A LAW.

From Bill No. HB 35-E. The Law Passed by the Florida Legislature (In Relation to the Schiavo Case); "Terri's Law."

102

JEB BUSH, Governor of Florida, et al., Appellants, v. MICHAEL SCHIAVO, Guardian of Theresa Schiavo, Appellee.

No. SC04-925

SUPREME COURT OF FLORIDA

885 So. 2d 321;

September 23, 2004, Decided

DISPOSITION: Trial court affirmed.

JUDGES: PARIENTE, C.J. WELLS, ANSTEAD, LEWIS, QUINCE, CANTERO, and BELL, JJ., concur.

OPINION BY: PARIENTE

OPINION: CORRECTED OPINION

PARIENTE, C.J.

The narrow issue in this case requires this Court to decide the constitutionality of a law passed by the Legislature that directly affected Theresa Schiavo, who has been in a persistent vegetative state since 1990.[1] This Court, after careful consideration of the arguments of the parties and Amici, the constitutional issues raised, the precise wording of the challenged law, and the underlying procedural history of this case, concludes that the law violates the fundamental constitutional tenet of separation of powers and is therefore unconstitutional both on its face and as applied to Theresa Schiavo. Accordingly, we affirm the trial court's order declaring the law unconstitutional.

From *Jeb Bush, Governor of Florida, et al., Appellants, v. Michael Schiavo, Guardian of Theresa Schiavo, Appellee.* No. SC04-925. Supreme Court of Florida 885 So. 2d 321; Decided September 23, 2004.

FACTS AND PROCEDURAL HISTORY

The resolution of the discrete separation of powers issue presented in this case does not turn on the facts of the underlying guardianship proceedings that resulted in the removal of Theresa's nutrition and hydration tube. The underlying litigation, which has pitted Theresa's husband, Michael Schiavo, against Theresa's parents, turned on whether the procedures sustaining Theresa's life should be discontinued. However, the procedural history is important because it provides the backdrop to the Legislature's enactment of the challenged law. We also detail the facts and procedural history in light of the Governor's assertion that chapter 2003-418, Laws of Florida (hereinafter sometimes referred to as "the Act"), was passed in order to protect the due process rights of Theresa and other individuals in her position.

As set forth in the Second District's first opinion in this case, which upheld the guardianship court's final order, Theresa Marie Schindler was born on December 3, 1963, and lived with or near her parents in Pennsylvania until she married Michael Schiavo on November 10, 1984. Michael and Theresa moved to Florida in 1986. They were happily married and both were employed. They had no children.

On February 25, 1990, their lives changed. Theresa, age 27, suffered a cardiac arrest as a result of a potassium imbalance. Michael called 911, and Theresa was rushed to the hospital. She never regained consciousness.

Since 1990, Theresa has lived in nursing homes with constant care. She is fed and hydrated by tubes. The staff changes her diapers regularly. She has had numerous health problems, but none have been life threatening.

For the first three years after this tragedy, Michael and Theresa's parents, Robert and Mary Schindler, enjoyed an amicable relationship. However, that relationship ended in 1993 and the parties literally stopped speaking to each other. In May of 1998, eight years after Theresa lost consciousness, Michael petitioned the guardianship court to authorize the termination of life-prolonging procedures. See id. By filing this petition, which the Schindlers opposed, Michael placed the difficult decision in the hands of the court.

After a trial, at which both Michael and the Schindlers presented evidence, the guardianship court issued an extensive written order authorizing the discontinuance of artificial life support. The trial court found by clear and convincing evidence that Theresa Schiavo was in a persistent vegetative state and that Theresa would elect to cease life-prolonging procedures if she were competent to make her own decision. This order was affirmed on direct appeal, see *Schiavo I*, 780 So. 2d at 177, and we denied review. See *In re Guardianship of Schiavo*, 789 So. 2d 348 (Fla. 2001).

The severity of Theresa's medical condition was explained by the Second District as follows:

The evidence is overwhelming that Theresa is in a permanent or persistent vegetative state. It is important to understand that a persistent vegetative state is not simply a coma. She is not asleep. She has cycles of apparent wakefulness and apparent sleep without any cognition or awareness. As she breathes, she often makes moaning sounds. Theresa has severe contractures of her hands, elbows, knees, and feet.

Over the span of this last decade, Theresa's brain has deteriorated because of the lack of oxygen it suffered at the time of the heart attack. By mid-1996, the CAT scans of her brain showed a severely abnormal structure. At this point, much of her cerebral cortex is simply gone and has been replaced by cerebral spinal fluid. Medicine cannot cure this condition. Unless an act of God, a true miracle, were to re-create her brain, Theresa will always remain in an unconscious, reflexive state, totally dependent upon others to feed her and care for her most private needs. She could remain in this state for many years.

Schiavo I, 780 So. 2d at 177. In affirming the trial court's order, the Second District concluded by stating:

In the final analysis, the difficult question that faced the trial court was whether Theresa Marie Schindler Schiavo, not after a few weeks in a coma, but after ten years in a persistent vegetative state that has robbed her of most of her cerebrum and all but the most instinctive of neurological functions, with no hope of a medical cure but with sufficient money and strength of body to live indefinitely, would choose to continue the constant nursing care and the supporting tubes in hopes that a miracle would somehow re-create her missing brain tissue, or whether she would wish to permit a natural death process to take its course and for her family members and loved ones to be free to continue their lives. After due consideration, we conclude that the trial judge had clear and convincing evidence to answer this question as he did. *Schiavo I*, 780 So. 2d at 180.

Although the guardianship court's final order authorizing the termination of life-prolonging procedures was affirmed on direct appeal, the litigation continued because the Schindlers began an attack on the final order. The Schindlers filed a motion for relief from judgment under Florida Rule of Civil Procedure 1.540(b)(2) and (3) in the guardianship court, alleging newly discovered evidence and intrinsic fraud. The Schindlers also filed a separate complaint in the civil division of the circuit court, challenging the final judgment of the guardianship court. See *In re Guardianship of Schiavo*, 792 So. 2d 551, 555–56 (Fla. 2d DCA 2001) (*Schiavo II*).

The trial court determined that the post-judgment motion was untimely and the Schindlers appealed. The Second District agreed that the guardianship court had appropriately denied the rule 1.540(b)(2) and (3) motion as untimely. See *Schiavo II*, 792 So. 2d at 558. The Second District also reversed an injunction entered in the case pending before the civil division of the circuit court. See id. at 562. However, the Second District determined that the Schindlers, as "interested parties," had standing to file either a motion for relief from judgment under Florida Rule of Civil Procedure 1.540(b)(5) or an independent action in the guardianship court to challenge the judgment on the ground that it is "no longer equitable for the trial court to enforce its earlier order." *Schiavo II*, 792 So. 2d at 560. Nonetheless, the Second District pointedly cautioned that any proceeding to challenge a final order on this basis is extraordinary and should not be filed merely to delay an order with which an interested party disagrees or to retry an adversary proceeding. The interested party must establish that new circumstances make it no longer equitable to enforce the earlier order. In this case, if the Schindlers believe a valid basis for relief from the order exists, they must plead and prove newly discovered evidence of such a substantial nature that it proves either (1) that Mrs. Schiavo would not have made the decision to withdraw life-prolonging procedures fourteen months earlier when the final order was entered, or (2) that Mrs. Schiavo would make a different decision at this time based on developments subsequent to the earlier court order. Id. at 554.

On remand, the Schindlers filed a timely motion for relief from judgment pursuant to rule 1.540(b)(5). See *In re Guardianship of Schiavo*, 800 So. 2d 640, 642 (Fla. 2d DCA 2001) (*Schiavo III*). The trial court summarily denied the motion but the Second District reversed and remanded to the guardianship court for the purpose of conducting a limited evidentiary hearing:

Of the four issues resolved in the original trial . . . , we conclude that the motion establishes a colorable entitlement only as to the fourth issue. As to that issue—whether there was clear and convincing evidence to support the determination that Mrs. Schiavo would choose to withdraw the life-prolonging procedures—the motion for relief from judgment alleges evidence of a new treatment that could dramatically improve Mrs. Schiavo's condition and allow her to have cognitive function to the level of speech. In our last opinion we stated that the Schindlers had "presented no medical evidence suggesting that any new treatment could restore to Mrs. Schiavo a level of function within the cerebral cortex that would allow her to understand her perceptions of sight and sound or to communicate or respond cognitively to those perceptions." *Schiavo II*, 792 So. 2d at 560. Although we have expressed some lay skepticism about the new affidavits, the Schindlers now have presented some evidence, in the form of the affidavit of Dr. [Fred] Webber, of such a potential new treatment. Id. at 645.

The Second District permitted the Schindlers to present evidence to establish by a preponderance of the evidence that the judgment was no longer equitable and specifically held:

To meet this burden, they must establish that new treatment offers suffi-cient promise of increased cognitive function in Mrs. Schiavo's cerebral cortex—significantly improving the quality of Mrs. Schiavo's life—so that she herself would elect to undergo this treatment and would reverse the prior decision to withdraw life-prolonging procedures.

Id. The Second District required an additional set of medical examinations of Theresa and instructed that one of the physicians must be a new, indepen-dent physician selected either by the agreement of the parties or, if they could not agree, by the appointment of the guardianship court. See id. at 646.

After conducting a hearing for the purpose set forth in the Second Dis-trict's decision, the guardianship court denied the Schindlers' motion for relief from judgment. See *In re Guardianship of Schiavo*, 851 So. 2d 182, 183 (Fla. 2d DCA 2003) (*Schiavo IV*). In reviewing the trial court's order, the Second District explained that it was "not reviewing a final judgment in this appellate proceeding. The final judgment was entered several years ago and has already been affirmed by this court." Id. at 185–86. However, the Second District carefully examined the record:

Despite our decision that the appropriate standard of review is abuse of discretion, this court has closely examined all of the evidence in this record. We have repeatedly examined the videotapes, not merely watching short seg-ments but carefully observing the tapes in their entirety. We have examined the brain scans with the eyes of educated laypersons and considered the explanations provided by the doctors in the transcripts. We have concluded that, if we were called upon to review the guardianship court's decision de novo, we would still affirm it. Id. at 186. Finally, the Second District con-cluded its fourth opinion in the Schiavo case with the following observation:

The judges on this panel are called upon to make a collective, objective decision concerning a question of law. Each of us, however, has our own family, our own loved ones, our own children. From our review of the video-tapes of Mrs. Schiavo, despite the irrefutable evidence that her cerebral cortex has sustained the most severe of irreparable injuries, we understand why a parent who had raised and nurtured a child from conception would hold out hope that some level of cognitive function remained. If Mrs. Schiavo were our own daughter, we could not but hold to such a faith.

But in the end, this case is not about the aspirations that loving parents have for their children. It is about Theresa Schiavo's right to make her own decision, independent of her parents and independent of her husband. . . . It may be unfortunate that when families cannot agree, the best forum we can offer for this private, personal decision is a public courtroom and the best decision-maker we can provide is a judge with no prior knowledge of the ward, but the law currently provides no better solution that adequately protects the interests of promoting the value of life. We have previously affirmed the guardianship court's decision in this regard, and we now affirm the denial of a motion for relief from that judgment. Id. at 186–87. We denied review, see *In re Guardianship of Schiavo*, 855 So. 2d 621 (Fla. 2003), and Theresa's nutrition and hydration tube was removed on October 15, 2003.

On October 21, 2003, the Legislature enacted chapter 2003-418, the Governor signed the Act into law, and the Governor issued executive order No. 03-201 to stay the continued withholding of nutrition and hydration from Theresa. The nutrition and hydration tube was reinserted pursuant to the Governor's executive order.

On the same day, Michael Schiavo brought the action for declaratory judgment in the circuit court. Relying on undisputed facts and legal argument, the circuit court entered a final summary judgment on May 6, 2004, in favor of Michael Schiavo, finding the Act unconstitutional both on its face and as applied to Theresa. Specifically, the circuit court found that chapter 2003-418 was unconstitutional on its face as an unlawful delegation of legislative authority and as a violation of the right to privacy, and unconstitutional as applied because it allowed the Governor to encroach upon the judicial power and to retroactively abolish Theresa's vested right to privacy.[2]

ANALYSIS

We begin our discussion by emphasizing that our task in this case is to review the constitutionality of chapter 2003-418, not to reexamine the guardianship court's orders directing the removal of Theresa's nutrition and hydration tube, or to review the Second District's numerous decisions in the guardianship case. Although we recognize that the parties continue to dispute the findings made in the prior proceedings, these proceedings are relevant to our decision only to the extent that they occurred and resulted in a final judgment directing the withdrawal of life-prolonging procedures.[3]

The language of chapter 2003-418 is clear. It states in full:

Section 1. (1) The Governor shall have the authority to issue a one-time stay to prevent the withholding of nutrition and hydration from a patient if, as of October 15, 2003:

(a) That patient has no written advance directive;

(b) The court has found that patient to be in a persistent vegetative state;

(c) That patient has had nutrition and hydration withheld; and

(d) A member of that patient's family has challenged the withholding of nutrition and hydration.

(2) The Governor's authority to issue the stay expires 15 days after the effective date of this act, and the expiration of the authority does not impact the validity or the effect of any stay issued pursuant to this act. The Governor may lift the stay authorized under this act at any time. A person may not be held civilly liable and is not subject to regulatory or disciplinary sanctions for taking any action to comply with a stay issued by the Governor pursuant to this act.

(3) Upon issuance of a stay, the chief judge of the circuit court shall appoint a guardian ad litem for the patient to make recommendations to the Governor and the court.

Section 2. This act shall take effect upon becoming a law.

Ch. 2003-418, *Laws of Fla.* Thus, chapter 2003-418 allowed the Governor to issue a stay to prevent the withholding of nutrition and hydration from a patient under the circumstances provided for in subsections (1)(a)–(d). Under the fifteen-day sunset provision, the Governor's authority to issue the stay expired on November 5, 2003. See id. The Governor's authority to lift the stay continues indefinitely.

SEPARATION OF POWERS

The cornerstone of American democracy known as separation of powers recognizes three separate branches of government—the executive, the legislative, and the judicial—each with its own powers and responsibilities. In Florida, the constitutional doctrine has been expressly codified in article II, section 3 of the Florida Constitution, which not only divides state government into three branches but also expressly prohibits one branch from exercising the powers of the other two branches:

Branches of Government.—The powers of the state government shall be divided into legislative, executive and judicial branches. No person belonging to one branch shall exercise any powers appertaining to either of the other branches unless expressly provided herein.

"This Court . . . has traditionally applied a strict separation of powers doctrine," *State v. Cotton*, 769 So. 2d 345, 353 (Fla. 2000), and has explained that this doctrine "encompasses two fundamental prohibitions. The first is that no branch may encroach upon the powers of another. The second is that no branch may delegate to another branch its constitutionally assigned power." *Chiles v. Children A, B, C, D, E, & F,* 589 So. 2d 260, 264 (Fla. 1991).

The circuit court found that chapter 2003-418 violates both of these prohibitions, and we address each separately below. Our standard of review is de novo. See *Major League Baseball v. Morsani,* 790 So. 2d 1071, 1074 (Fla. 2001) (stating that a trial court's ruling on a motion for summary judgment posing a pure question of law is subject to de novo review).

Encroachment on the Judicial Branch

We begin by addressing the argument that, as applied to Theresa Schiavo, the Act encroaches on the power and authority of the judicial branch. More than 140 years ago this Court explained the foundation of Florida's express separation of powers provision:

The framers of the Constitution of Florida, doubtless, had in mind the omnipotent power often exercised by the British Parliament, the exercise of judicial power by the Legislature in those States where there are no written Constitutions restraining them, when they wisely prohibited the exercise of such powers in our State.

That Convention was composed of men of the best legal minds in the country—men of experience and skilled in the law—who had witnessed the breaking down by unrestrained legislation all the security of property derived from contract, the divesting of vested rights by doing away the force of the law as decided, the overturning of solemn decisions of the Courts of the last resort, by, under the pretence of remedial acts, enacting for one or the other party litigants such provisions as would dictate to the judiciary their decision, and leaving everything which should be expounded by the judiciary to the variable and ever-changing mind of the popular branch of the Government. *Trustees Internal Improvement Fund v. Bailey*, 10 Fla. 238, 250 (1863). Similarly, the framers of the United States Constitution recognized the need to establish a judiciary independent of the legislative branch. Indeed, the desire to prevent Congress from using its power to interfere with the judgments of the courts was one of the primary motivations for the separation of powers established at this nation's founding:

This sense of a sharp necessity to separate the legislative from the judicial power, prompted by the crescendo of legislative interference with private judgments of the courts, triumphed among the Framers of the new Federal Constitution. The Convention made the critical decision to establish a judicial department independent of the Legislative Branch. . . . Before and during the debates on ratification, Madison, Jefferson, and Hamilton each wrote of the factional disorders and disarray that the system of legislative equity had produced in the years before the framing; and each thought that the separation of the legislative from the judicial power in the new Constitution would cure them. Madison's *Federalist* No. 48, the famous description of the process by which "the legislative department is every where extending the sphere of its activity, and drawing all power into its impetuous vortex," referred to the report of the Pennsylvania Council of Censors to show that in that State "cases belonging to the judiciary department [had been] frequently drawn within legislative cognizance and determination." Madison relied as well on Jefferson's Notes on the State of Virginia, which mentioned, as one example of the dangerous concentration of governmental powers into the hands of the legislature, that "the Legislature . . . in many instances decided rights which should have been left to judiciary controversy." *Plaut v. Spendthrift Farm, Inc.*, 514 U.S. 211, 221–22, 131 L. Ed. 2d 328, 115 S. Ct. 1447 (1995).

Under the express separation of powers provision in our state constitution, "the judiciary is a coequal branch of the Florida government vested with the sole authority to exercise the judicial power," and "the legislature cannot, short of constitutional amendment, reallocate the balance of power expressly delineated in the constitution among the three coequal branches." *Children A, B, C, D, E, & F*, 589 So. 2d at 268–69; see also *Office of State Attorney v. Parrotino*, 628 So. 2d 1097, 1099 (Fla. 1993) ("The legislature cannot take actions that would undermine the independence of Florida's judicial . . . offices.").

As the United States Supreme Court has explained, the power of the judiciary is "not merely to rule on cases, but to decide them, subject to review only by superior courts" and "having achieved finality . . . a judicial decision becomes the last word of the judicial department with regard to a particular case or controversy." *Plaut*, 514 U.S. at 218–19, 227. Moreover, "purely judicial acts . . . are not subject to review as to their accuracy by the Governor." *In re Advisory Opinion to the Governor*, 213 So. 2d 716, 720 (Fla. 1968); see also *Children A, B, C, D, E, & F*, 589 So. 2d at 269 ("The judicial branch cannot be subject in any manner to oversight by the executive branch.").

In *Advisory Opinion*, the Governor asked the Court whether he had the "constitutional authority to review the judicial accuracy and propriety of [a judge] and to suspend him from office if it does not appear . . . that the Judge has exercised proper judicial discretion and wisdom." 213 So. 2d at 718. The Court agreed that the Governor had the authority to suspend a judge on the grounds of incompetency "if the physical or mental incompetency is established and determined within the Judicial Branch by a court of competent jurisdiction." Id. at 720. However, the Court held that the Governor did not have the power to "review the judicial discretion and wisdom of a . . . Judge while he is engaged in the judicial process." Id. The Court explained that article V of the Florida Constitution provides for appellate review for the benefit of litigants aggrieved by the decisions of the lower court, and that "appeal is the exclusive remedy." Id.

In this case, the undisputed facts show that the guardianship court authorized Michael to proceed with the discontinuance of Theresa's life support after the issue was fully litigated in a proceeding in which the Schindlers were afforded the opportunity to present evidence on all issues. This order as well as the order denying the Schindlers' motion for relief from judgment were affirmed on direct appeal. See *Schiavo I*, 780 So. 2d at 177; *Schiavo IV*, 851 So. 2d at 183. The Schindlers sought review in this Court, which was denied. Thereafter, the tube was removed. Subsequently, pursuant to the Governor's executive order, the nutrition and hydration tube was reinserted. Thus, the Act, as applied in this case, resulted in an executive order that effectively reversed a properly rendered final judgment and thereby constituted an unconstitutional encroachment on the power that has been reserved for the independent judiciary. Cf. Bailey, 10 Fla. at 249–50 (noting that had the statute under review "directed a rehearing, the hearing of the case would necessarily carry with it the right to set aside the judgment of the Court, and there would be unquestionably an exercise of judicial power").

The Governor and Amici assert that the Act does not reverse a final court order because an order to discontinue life-prolonging procedures may be challenged at any time prior to the death of the ward. In advancing this argument, the Governor and Amici rely on the Second District's conclusion that as long as the ward is alive, an order discontinuing life-prolonging procedures "is subject to recall and is executory in nature." *Schiavo II*, 792 So. 2d at 559. However, the Second District did not hold that the guardianship court's order was not a final judgment but, rather, that the Schindlers, as interested parties, could file a motion for relief from judgment under *Florida Rule of Civil Procedure* 1.540(b)(5) if they sufficiently alleged that it is no longer equitable that the judgment have prospective application. See id. at 561. Rule 1.540(b) expressly states that a motion filed pursuant to its terms "does not affect the finality of a judgment." Further, the fact that a final judgment may be subject to recall under a rule of procedure, if certain circumstances can be proved, does not negate its finality. Unless and until the judgment is vacated by judicial order, it is "the last word of the judicial department with regard to a particular case or controversy." *Plaut*, 514 U.S. at 227.

Under procedures enacted by the Legislature, effective both before the passage of the Act and after its fifteen-day effective period expired, circuit courts are charged with adjudicating issues regarding incompetent individuals. The trial courts of this State are called upon to make many of the most difficult decisions facing society. In proceedings under chapter 765, *Florida Statutes* (2003), these decisions literally affect the lives or deaths of patients. The trial courts also handle other weighty decisions affecting the welfare of children such as termination of parental rights and child custody. See § 61.13(2)(b)(1), *Fla. Stat.* (2003) ("The court shall determine all matters relating to custody of each minor child of the parties in accordance with the best interests of the child and in accordance with the Uniform Child Custody Jurisdiction and Enforcement Act."); § 39.801(2), *Fla. Stat.* (2003) ("The circuit court shall have exclusive original jurisdiction of a proceeding involving termination of parental rights."). When the prescribed procedures are followed according to our rules of court and the governing statutes, a final judgment is issued, and all post-judgment procedures are followed, it is without question an invasion of the authority of the judicial branch for the Legislature to pass a law that allows the executive branch to interfere with the final judicial determination in a case. That is precisely what occurred here and for that reason the Act is unconstitutional as applied to Theresa Schiavo.

Delegation of Legislative Authority

In addition to concluding that the Act is unconstitutional as applied in this case because it encroaches on the power of the judicial branch, we further conclude that the Act is unconstitutional on its face because it delegates legislative power to the Governor. The Legislature is permitted to transfer subordinate functions "to permit administration of legislative policy by an agency with the expertise and flexibility to deal with complex and fluid conditions." *Microtel, Inc. v. Fla. Public Serv. Comm'n*, 464 So. 2d 1189, 1191 (Fla. 1985). However, under article II, section 3 of the constitution the Legislature "may not delegate the power to enact a law or the right to exercise unrestricted discretion in applying the law." *Sims v. State*, 754 So. 2d 657, 668 (Fla. 2000). This prohibition, known as the nondelegation doctrine, requires that "fundamental and primary policy decisions . . . be made by members of the legislature who are elected to perform those tasks, and [that the] administration of legislative programs must be pursuant to some minimal standards and guidelines ascertainable by reference to the enactment establishing the program." *Askew v. Cross Key Waterways*, 372 So. 2d 913, 925 (Fla. 1978); see also *Avatar Dev. Corp. v. State*, 723 So. 2d 199, 202 (Fla. 1998) (citing Askew with approval). In other words, statutes granting power to the executive branch "must clearly announce adequate standards to guide . . . in the execution of the powers delegated. The statute must so clearly define the power delegated that the [executive] is precluded from acting through whim, showing favoritism, or exercising unbridled discretion." *Lewis v. Bank of Pasco County*, 346 So. 2d 53, 55–56 (Fla. 1976). The requirement that the Legislature provide sufficient guidelines also ensures the availability of meaningful judicial review:

In the final analysis it is the courts, upon a challenge to the exercise or nonexercise of administrative action, which must determine whether the administrative agency has performed consistently with the mandate of the legislature. When legislation is so lacking in guidelines that neither the agency nor the courts can determine whether the agency is carrying out the intent of the legislature in its conduct, then, in fact, the agency becomes the lawgiver rather than the administrator of the law. *Askew*, 372 So. 2d at 918–19.

We have recognized that the "specificity of the guidelines [set forth in the legislation] will depend on the complexity of the subject and the 'degree of difficulty involved in articulating finite standards.'" *Brown v. Apalachee Regional Planning Council*, 560 So. 2d 782, 784 (Fla. 1990) (quoting *Askew*,

372 So. 2d at 918). However, we have also made clear that "even where a general approach would be more practical than a detailed scheme of legislation, enactments may not be drafted in terms so general and unrestrictive that administrators are left without standards for the guidance of their official acts." *State Dep't of Citrus v. Griffin*, 239 So. 2d 577, 581 (Fla. 1970).

In both *Askew* and *Lewis*, this Court held that the respective statutes under review violated the nondelegation doctrine because they failed to provide the executive branch with adequate guidelines and criteria. In *Askew*, the Court invalidated a statute that directed the executive branch to designate certain areas of the state as areas of critical state concern but did not contain sufficient standards to allow "a reviewing court to ascertain whether the priorities recognized by the Administration Commission comport with the intent of the legislature." 372 So. 2d at 919. The statute in question enunciated the following criteria for the Division of State Planning to use in identifying a particular area as one of critical state concern:

(a) An area containing, or having a significant impact upon, environmental, historical, natural, or archaeological resources of regional or statewide importance.

(b) An area significantly affected by, or having a significant effect upon, an existing or proposed major public facility or other area of major public investment.

(c) A proposed area of major development potential, which may include a proposed site of a new community, designated in a state land development plan. Id. at 914–15 (quoting section 380.05[2], *Florida Statutes* [1975]). The Court concluded that the criteria for designation of an area of critical concern set forth in subsections (a) and (b) were defective because they gave the executive agency "the fundamental legislative task of determining which geographic areas and resources [were] in greatest need of protection." Id. at 919. With regard to subsection (a), this Court agreed with the district court that the deficiency resulted from the Legislature's failure to "establish or provide for establishing priorities or other means for identifying and choosing among the resources the Act is intended to preserve." Id. (quoting *Cross Key Waterways v. Askew*, 351 So. 2d 1062, 1069 [Fla. 1st DCA 1977]). Subsection (b) suffered a similar defect by expanding "the choice to include areas which in unstated ways affect or are affected by any 'major public facility' which is defined in Section 380.031(10), or any 'major public investment,' which is not." Id.

Lewis involved a statute that gave the state comptroller the unrestricted power to release banking records to the public that were otherwise considered confidential under the Public Records Act. See 346 So. 2d at 55. The statute at issue provided in pertinent part:

Division records.

All bank or trust company applications, investigation reports, examination reports, and related information, including any duly authorized copies in possession of any banking organization, foreign banking corporation, or any other person or agency, shall be confidential communications, other than such documents as are required by law to be published, and shall not be made public, unless with the consent of the department, pursuant to a court order, or in response to legislative subpoena as provided by law.

Lewis, 346 So. 2d at 54 (quoting section 658.10, *Florida Statutes* [1975]) (alteration in original). This Court held that the law was "couched in vague and uncertain terms or is so broad in scope that . . . it must be held unconstitutional as attempting to grant to the . . . [comptroller] the power to say what the law shall be." 346 So. 2d at 56 (quoting *Sarasota County v. Barg*, 302 So. 2d 737, 742 [Fla. 1974]) (alterations in original).

In this case, the circuit court found that chapter 2003-418 contains no guidelines or standards that "would serve to limit the Governor from exercising completely unrestricted discretion in applying the law to" those who fall within its terms. The circuit court explained:

The terms of the Act affirmatively confirm the discretionary power conferred upon the Governor. He is given the "authority to issue a one-time stay to prevent the withholding of nutrition and hydration from a patient" under certain circumstances, but he is not required to do so. Likewise, the Act provides that the Governor "may lift the stay authorized under this act at any time. The Governor may revoke the stay upon a finding that a change in the condition of the patient warrants revocation. "In both instances there is nothing to provide the Governor with any direction or guidelines for the exercise of this delegated authority. The Act does not suggest what constitutes "a change in condition of the patient" that could "warrant revocation." Even when such an undefined "change" occurs, the Governor is not compelled to act. The Act confers upon the Governor the unfettered discretion to determine what the terms of the Act mean and when, or if, he may act under it.

We agree with this analysis. In enacting chapter 2003-418, the Legislature failed to provide any standards by which the Governor should determine whether, in any given case, a stay should be issued and how long a stay should remain in effect. Further, the Legislature has failed to provide any criteria for lifting the stay. This absolute, unfettered discretion to decide whether to issue and then when to lift a stay makes the Governor's decision virtually unreviewable.

The Governor asserts that by enacting chapter 2003-418 the Legislature determined that he should be permitted to act as proxy for an incompetent patient in very narrow circumstances and, therefore, that his discretion is limited by the provisions of chapter 765. However, the Act does not refer to the provisions of chapter 765. Specifically, the Act does not amend section 765.401(1), *Florida Statutes* (2003), which sets forth an order of priority for determining who should act as proxy for an incapacitated patient who has no advance directive. Nor does the Act require that the Governor's decision be made in conformity with the requirement of section 765.401 that the proxy's decision be based on "the decision the proxy reasonably believes that patient would have made under the circumstances" or, if there is no indication of what the patient would have chosen, in the patient's best interests. § 765.401(2)–(3), *Fla. Stat.* (2003). Finally, the Act does not provide for review of the Governor's decision as proxy as required by section 765.105, *Florida Statutes* (2003). In short, there is no indication in the language of chapter 2003-418 that the Legislature intended the Governor's discretion to be limited in any way. Even if we were to read chapter 2003-418 in *pari materia* with chapter 765, as the Governor suggests, there is nothing in chapter 765 to guide the Governor's discretion in issuing a stay because chapter 765 does not contemplate that a proxy will have the type of open-ended power delegated to the Governor under the Act.

We also reject the Governor's argument that this legislation provides an additional layer of due process protection to those who are unable to communicate their wishes regarding end-of-life decisions. Parts I, II, III, and IV of chapter 765, enacted by the Legislature in 1992 and amended several times,[4] provide detailed protections for those who are adjudicated incompetent, including that the proxy's decision be based on what the patient would have chosen under the circumstances or is in the patient's best interest, and be supported by competent, substantial evidence. See § 765.401(2)–(3). Chapter 765 also provides for judicial review if "the patient's family, the healthcare facility, or the attending physician, or any other interested person who may reasonably be expected to be directly affected by the surrogate or proxy's decision . . . believes [that] the surrogate or proxy's decision is not in accord with the patient's known desires or the provisions of this chapter." § 765.105(1), *Fla. Stat.* (2003).

In contrast to the protections set forth in chapter 765, chapter 2003-418's standardless, open-ended delegation of authority by the Legislature to the Governor provides no guarantee that the incompetent patient's right to withdraw life-prolonging procedures will in fact be honored. See *In re Guardianship of Browning*, 568 So. 2d 4, 12 (Fla. 1990) (reaffirming that an incompetent person has the same right to refuse medical treatment as a competent person). As noted above, the Act does not even require that the Governor consider the patient's wishes in deciding whether to issue a stay, and instead allows a unilateral decision by the Governor to stay the withholding of life-prolonging procedures without affording any procedural process to the patient.

Finally, we reject the Governor's argument that the Legislature's grant of authority to issue the stay under chapter 2003-418 is a valid exercise of the state's parens patriae power. Although unquestionably the Legislature may enact laws to protect those citizens who are incapable of protecting their own interests, see, e.g., *In re Byrne*, 402 So. 2d 383 (Fla. 1981), such laws must comply with the constitution. Chapter 2003-418 fails to do so.

Moreover, the argument that the Act broadly protects those who cannot protect themselves is belied by the case-specific criteria under which the Governor can exercise his discretion. The Act applies only if a court has found the individual to be in a persistent vegetative state and food and hydration have been ordered withdrawn. It does not authorize the Governor to intervene if a person in a persistent vegetative state is dependent upon another form of life support. Nor does the Act apply to a person who is not in a persistent vegetative state but a court finds, contrary to the wishes of another family member, that life support should be withdrawn. In theory, the Act could have applied during its fifteen-day window to more than one person, but it is undeniable that in fact the criteria fit only Theresa Schiavo.

In sum, although chapter 2003-418 applies to a limited class of people, it provides no criteria to guide the Governor's decision about whether to act. In addition, once the Governor has issued a stay as provided for in the Act, there are no criteria for the Governor to evaluate in deciding whether to lift the stay. Thus, chapter 2003-418 allows the Governor to act "through whim, show favoritism, or exercise unbridled discretion," *Lewis*, 346 So. 2d at 56, and is therefore an unconstitutional delegation of legislative authority.

CONCLUSION

We recognize that the tragic circumstances underlying this case make it difficult to put emotions aside and focus solely on the legal issue presented. We are not insensitive to the struggle that all members of Theresa's family have endured since she fell unconscious in 1990. However, we are a nation of laws and we must govern our decisions by the rule of law and not by our own emotions. Our hearts can fully comprehend the grief so fully demonstrated by Theresa's family members on this record. But our hearts are not the law. What is in the Constitution always must prevail over emotion. Our oaths as judges require that this principle is our polestar, and it alone.

As the Second District noted in one of the multiple appeals in this case, we "are called upon to make a collective, objective decision concerning a question of law. Each of us, however, has our own family, our own loved ones, our own children. . . . But in the end, this case is not about the aspirations that loving parents have for their children." *Schiavo IV*, 851 So. 2d at 186. Rather, as our decision today makes clear, this case is about maintaining the integrity of a constitutional system of government with three independent and coequal branches, none of which can either encroach upon the powers of another branch or improperly delegate its own responsibilities.

The continuing vitality of our system of separation of powers precludes the other two branches from nullifying the judicial branch's final orders. If the Legislature with the assent of the Governor can do what was attempted here, the judicial branch would be subordinated to the final directive of the other branches. Also subordinated would be the rights of individuals, including the well-established privacy right to self-determination. See *Browning*, 568 So. 2d at 11–13. No court judgment could ever be considered truly final and no constitutional right truly secure, because the precedent of this case would hold to the contrary. Vested rights could be stripped away based on popular clamor. The essential core of what the Founding Fathers sought to change from their experience with English rule would be lost, especially their belief that our courts exist precisely to preserve the rights of individuals, even when doing so is contrary to popular will.

The trial court's decision regarding Theresa Schiavo was made in accordance with the procedures and protections set forth by the judicial branch and in accordance with the statutes passed by the Legislature in effect at that time. That decision is final and the Legislature's attempt to alter that final adjudication is unconstitutional as applied to Theresa Schiavo. Further, even if there had been no final judgment in this case, the Legislature provided the Governor constitutionally inadequate standards for the application of the legislative authority delegated in chapter 2003-418. Because chapter 2003-418 runs afoul of article II, section 3 of the Florida Constitution in both respects, we affirm the circuit court's final summary judgment.

It is so ordered.

WELLS, ANSTEAD, LEWIS, QUINCE, CANTERO, and BELL, JJ., concur.

IN THIS CASE DUE TO ITS EXPEDITED NATURE ANY REHEARING MOTION SHALL BE FILED NO LATER THAN 10 DAYS FROM THE DATE OF THIS OPINION AND ANY RESPONSE FILED 5 DAYS THEREAFTER. NO REPLY SHALL BE ALLOWED AND NO MOTIONS FOR EXTENSION OF TIME ENTERTAINED.

NOTES

1. The trial court, in an extensive written order, declared that the law was unconstitutional as a violation of separation of powers, as a violation of the right of privacy, and as unconstitutional retroactive legislation. The Second District Court of Appeal certified this case as one of great public importance and requiring immediate resolution by this Court. We have jurisdiction. See art. V, § 3(b)(5), Fla. Const.

2. Because we find the separation of powers issue to be dispositive in this case, we do not reach the other constitutional issues addressed by the circuit court.

3. The parties stipulated that the circuit court was authorized to take judicial notice of three orders of the guardianship court. The circuit court relied only on the existence of these orders in finding chapter 2003-418 unconstitutional as applied.

4. Prior to this Court's decision in *In re Guardianship of Browning*, 568 So. 2d 4 (Fla. 1990), statutory law provided a procedure by which a competent adult could provide a declaration instructing his or her physician to withhold or withdraw life-prolonging procedures, or designating another to make the treatment decision. See §§ 765.01–765.17, *Fla. Stat.* (1991). This law had been in effect since 1984.

In 1992, the Legislature repealed sections 765.01–765.17, see ch. 92-199, § 10 at 1852, *Laws of Fla.*, and enacted Parts I, II, III, and IV of chapter 765. See id. §§ 2–5. The Legislature provided that in the absence of an advance directive, a proxy may make healthcare decisions for an incapacitated patient. See ch. 92-199, § 5 at 1850 *Laws of Fla.*; § 765.401 *Fla. Stat.* (2003). "Healthcare decisions" include "informed consent, refusal of consent, or withdrawal of consent to any and all healthcare, including life-prolonging procedures." Ch. 92-199, § 2 at 1840, *Laws of Fla.*; § 765.101(5)(a) *Fla. Stat.* (2003). When the statute was enacted in 1992, the Legislature defined life-prolonging procedures as:

any medical procedure, treatment, or intervention which:

(a) Utilizes mechanical or other artificial means to sustain, restore, or supplant a spontaneous vital function; and

(b) When applied to a patient in a terminal condition, serves only to prolong the process of dying.

Ch. 92-199, § 2 at 1840–41. However, in 1999, the Legislature rewrote the definitions section and defined life-prolonging procedures as:

any medical procedure, treatment, or intervention, including artificially provided sustenance and hydration, which sustains, restores, or supplants a spontaneous vital function. The term does not include the administration of medication or performance of medical procedure, when such medication or procedure is deemed necessary to provide comfort care or to alleviate pain. Ch. 99-331, § 16 at 3464, *Laws of Fla.*; § 765.101(10), *Fla. Stat.* (2003).

In order to determine who is to act as a patient's proxy, the Legislature set forth a detailed order of priority. See ch. 92-199, § 5 at 1851. This order of priority has been amended only once since 1992 to allow a clinical social worker to act as the patient's proxy if none of the other potential proxies are available. See ch. 2003-57, § 5, *Laws of Fla.* The Legislature also provided that a "proxy's decision to withhold or withdraw life-prolonging procedures must by supported by clear and convincing evidence that the decision would have been the one the patient would have chosen had [the patient] been competent." Ch. 92-199, § 5 at 1851, *Laws of Fla.*; see also § 765.401(3), Fla. Stat. (2003).

Finally, the Legislature provided for judicial review of a proxy's decision if "the patient's family, the healthcare facility, or the attending physician, or any other interested person who may reasonably be expected to be directly affected by the surrogate or proxy's decision . . . believes (1) The surrogate or proxy's decision is not in accord with the patient's known desires or the provisions of this chapter." Ch. 92-199, § 2 at 1842, *Laws of Fla*; § 765.105, *Fla. Stat.* (2003).

Part 3

Federal Controversies

INTRODUCTION

In March 2005, the furor surrounding the case of Theresa Marie Schiavo climaxed as each branch of the federal government became involved. Although earlier attempts by the Schindlers to take their case to federal court had failed, a new method to force federal intervention was devised.

On March 8, 2005, U.S. representative David Weldon, MD (R-FL) introduced the Incapacitated Persons' Legal Protection Act (H.R. 1151) that proposed utilizing the habeas corpus remedy. By extending habeas corpus protections to Schiavo, the federal government could then intervene and, it was argued, restore to her the liberty of which she had been deprived by the state of Florida. In this way, the bill likened Schiavo to a death-row inmate requesting a stay of execution and made it possible for a federal court to review the case and possibly trump the state court's decisions. Pennsylvania Republican senator Rick Santorum bemoaned what he claimed was a clear injustice: convicted murderer Scott Peterson who had just been sentenced to death was ensured "due process and fair consideration," while Terri Schiavo was meeting the same fate "for not filing a living will."

H.R. 1151 morphed into H.R. 1332, a bill sponsored by Senator James Sensenbrenner and designed to authorize federal courts to review de novo specific cases wherein the state court decision to allow withholding or withdrawal of life support is contested by a "next friend." H.R. 1132 passed from the House to the Senate.

123

Meanwhile, the Schindlers continued to litigate in the Florida courts, requesting a stay on the withdrawal of Schiavo's feeding tube. Pinellas-Pasco circuit judge George W. Greer time and again refused to grant a stay and set March 18 as the day Schiavo's tube was to be removed. Florida congressman David Weldon described Greer's steadfastness as "troubling and inhumane."

On Thursday, March 17, Republican Majority Leader Bill Frist, a transplant surgeon, publicly challenged Schiavo's diagnosis from the Senate floor. After viewing about one hour of family videotape, Frist questioned the findings of neurological assessments and confidently stated Schiavo "certainly seems to respond to visual stimuli." Frist further claimed the video "depicts something very different than persistent vegetative state." Frist's controversial medical opinions are presented in this part. (Autopsy findings presented in part 5 confirmed Schiavo was in fact blind and unaware.)

The next day, in an attempt to circumvent Judge Greer's decisions, the House Government Reform Committee issued subpoenas to Michael and Terri Schiavo ordering them to appear at a congressional hearing and the Senate Health Committee formally invited the Schiavos to testify. Since it would be a federal crime to interfere with a person's ability to meet a congressional summons, the doctors and healthcare workers charged with removing Schiavo's tubes could be criminally prosecuted along with Michael Schiavo if he failed to go Washington with Terri. Nonetheless, Greer maintained that these legislative maneuvers had no impact on his injunction, and ordered that Schiavo's tube was to be removed "forthwith."

Early in the afternoon of March 18, doctors disconnected Terri Schiavo's percutaneous endoscopic gastrostomy (PEG) tube. Legislative activity in Washington became frenetic. Because of differences between lawmakers in the House and Senate, H.R. 1332 and related Senate bills did not pass the full Congress. Instead, on Saturday, March 19, a "private" Senate bill was introduced—S.686 For the Relief of the Parents of Theresa Marie Schiavo. The bill, reprinted in this part, granted the Federal District Court the jurisdiction to hear the Schindlers' case. Importantly, in order to obtain unanimous consent to consider the bill in the Senate, the final version of the bill purposefully omitted language that would have mandated a stay of state court proceedings pending federal consideration of the case. This was a crucial omission.

Congress returned from Easter recess and worked from Saturday through the night of Palm Sunday. Sunday night Air Force One winged President Bush back to Washington from his Easter vacation in Crawford, Texas.

Bill S.686 passed both chambers of Congress early Monday morning. The president signed S.686 into law shortly after 1:00 AM on Monday, March 21.

With the Relief Act in hand, Monday morning found the Schindler legal team in Middle District Federal Court of Florida in Tampa. They presented arguments in an attempt to have Schiavo's tube reinserted. Finding the Schindlers' claim would unlikely be successful because the Relief Act did not address the traditional requirements for temporary injunctive relief, Federal District Judge James Whittemore refused to grant a restraining order and to reinitiate Schiavo's medical nutrition and hydration. In his opinion, an extract of which is presented in this part, Whittemore also expressed his ambivalence about the constitutionality of the Relief Act.

The Schindlers appealed Whittemore's decision to U.S. Court of Appeals for the Eleventh Circuit in Atlanta. The appeals court refused to hear their appeals. The U.S. Supreme Court refused the Schindlers' case on March 24. The Schindlers returned to Judge Whittemore with new claims. He again denied the Schindlers' motions. Another round of refused appeals on March 25 ended the federal judicial action.

All the while, action at the state level continued. William Cheshire, a neurologist and fellow at the Center for Bioethics and Human Dignity, reevaluated Schiavo at the behest of Governor Bush. Cheshire claimed in an affidavit, presented here, that Schiavo was not in a persistent vegetative state. Rather, Cheshire claimed, Schiavo was minimally conscious and that he "could not withhold life-sustaining nutrition and hydration from this beautiful lady whose face brightens in the presence of others." On March 23, Judge Greer rejected the findings of the Cheshire affidavit included in a petition from Florida Department of Children and Families (DCF). Governor Jeb Bush had continued to press the DCF to take Schiavo into state custody based on allegations Michael had abused her. Judge Greer dismissed claims of abuse and issued a restraining order against the DCF, prohibiting state intervention.

During those days a groupthink seemed to envelop the U.S. Congress as lawmakers took on the Schiavo case almost obsessively. Senators like Rick Santorum (R-PA) were the most vocal, accusing the courts of "thumbing their nose at congressional intent" and fating "Terri to death by dehydration and starvation—a sentence that would not be placed on the worst criminal." In a joint statement included here, Speaker of the House J. Dennis Hastert and Senate Majority Leader Bill Frist expressed congressional solidarity, "We will be working through the weekend to resolve the differences and reach an effective solution that can clear our chambers and be signed by the president." It was during this time a memo was circulated among Republican lawmakers suggesting the Schiavo controversy be exploited as "a great political issue." After falling into the hands of Democrat Tom Harkin, it was discovered that the memo originated from the office of Senator Mel Martinez (R-FL), the cosponsor of a stalled habeas corpus bill in the Senate and an early version of the Relief Bill.

Relatively few in Congress stood up against the political momentum of federal intervention. Statements of those who did are included here. Congressman Robert Wexler (D-FL) accused the Republican administration and congressional majority of using "Ms. Schiavo as their political pawn to kowtow to their conservative base." Wexler also claimed hypocrisy among Republican lawmakers who just weeks prior cut billions from the Medicaid rolls. Representative Debbie Wasserman Schultz (D-FL) pointedly questioned the consistency of President Bush's support of federal intervention in the Schiavo case in light of policies he helped formulate as governor of Texas. Congressman Elijah Cummings, a supporter of the Schiavo legislation, nonetheless expressed deep reservations about the "pro-life" ethic said to be driving federal intervention. In his essay, Cummings claims the "culture of life" movement has ignored a blatant disparity of health coverage among Americans, an injustice that has led to the loss of almost a million black Americans who "died before their time."

The ethical problems of federal intervention, especially by Congress's pro-life constituency, are described in Arthur Caplan's op-ed included in part 3. Jon Eisenberg, author of an *amicus brief* signed by bioethicists, expresses through personal narrative the ethical and judicial mechanisms in place to facilitate medical decisions for incapacitated patients when disagreement among family members occurs. He is equally critical of the interventionist approach by executives and lawmakers at the state and federal levels.

During late March, protestors, journalists, and camera crews camped out in front of The Hospice of the Florida Suncoast where Schiavo lay dying. The media fixated on the case as the public waited with bated breathe to learn whether Schiavo would live or die in the days to come. Despite the vocal presence of dozens of protestors, all polls indicated the majority of Americans were troubled by the federal intervention in the case and supported the removal of Schiavo's feeding tube. In one poll conducted by the Gallup Organization, 80% of respondents were opposed to the legislative actions taken by Congress to intervene in the Schiavo case and a majority of

Americans agreed with the Supreme Court's decision to refuse the case. In several polls conducted by Fox News, ABC, and Gallup, a clear majority of Americans said that they would remove the feeding tube if they were Schiavo's guardian or the guardian of a loved one who was in a persistent vegetative state.

Bloggers on the left wrote of an impending theocratic revolution, the invasion of hospital rooms by politicians, and the use of Schiavo to distract the nation from the increasingly unpopular war in Iraq and to reverse the president's steadily declining approval ratings. (By May 2005, CNN reported Bush's job approval rating sank to 46%.) Bloggers on the right decried the state of American morality, likening Schiavo's imminent death as the first mile along the road toward an American Final Solution. Amid all of the media frenzy, clinical confusion, haphazard prognosticating, and political grandstanding, the central issue of the case became completely obfuscated: would Terri Schiavo have wanted to live in this condition?

Terri Schiavo died on March 31, close to two weeks after the removal of her feeding tube. A statement issued by The Hospice of the Florida Suncoast encapsulated the depth of the questions that had emerged during those weeks in March, "Our profound spiritual reflection has led us to grapple with some of life's most difficult issues and reflect on our own values and beliefs about life and death, about marriage and family, about our democracy itself."

CONGRESSIONAL STATEMENTS AND ACTIONS RELATED TO THE SCHIAVO CASE

U.S. REPRESENTATIVE DAVE WELDON

WELDON INTRODUCES THE "INCAPACITATED PERSONS LEGAL PROTECTION ACT"

H.R. 1151 Would Clarify Lifesaving "Habeas Corpus" Due Process Rights for Incapacitated Persons Unable to Speak for Themselves

Washington, Mar. 8—

On Tuesday, March 8, U.S. Representative Dave Weldon, MD (FL-15), introduced H.R. 1151, the "Incapacitated Person's Legal Protection Act." This bill would explicitly clarify fundamental due process rights for those who are incapacitated, are under court-ordered removal of nutrition and hydration, and have no written advanced medical directive in effect.

"Terri Schiavo, and men and women like her, deserve the same due process rights that death row inmates are granted. When a court is making a life-or-death decision for a disabled person who has been charged with no crime, shouldn't they be afforded independent counsel to speak on their behalf?" Weldon said.

Terri is in the center of a dispute between her husband—who insists on her death, and her parents—who say Terri wants to live. The court has never considered independent council representing Terri—despite conflicting

From news release, March 8, 2005.

reports as to her condition—and the court's decision could cost Terri her life. This bill would act as a safeguard for people like Terri by giving them a voice of their own.

"Our Constitution guarantees that no life will be taken without due process of law and guarantees equal protection under the law. We need to make sure that these protections are clearly available to the disabled and incapacitated," said Weldon.

Due process protections, like habeas corpus appeals, are legal procedures that allow courts to review whether someone is being unlawfully deprived of the fundamental protection of liberty. In a life-or-death situation, such as inmates on death row, this procedure is used to avoid the death of an innocent person by conducting fact-finding procedures. Current law does not explicitly apply this same right to disabled or incapacitated individuals who are subject to court-ordered removal of food and water.

U.S. REPRESENTATIVE DAVE WELDON

WELDON STATEMENT ON JUDGE GEORGE W. GREER RULINGS

Washington, DC, Mar. 11—

U.S. Representative Dave Weldon, MD, released the following statement regarding Judge George W. Greer's recent rulings on Terri Schindler Schiavo's case:

"Of the many rulings that Judge Greer has invoked on Terri Schindler Schiavo, the most troubling and inhuman was his recent decision to deny food or water to touch her lips should the death order come into effect. When our judicial branch refuses to defend the weakest among us, it has lost its constitutional bearings and deserves to be criticized and given society's highest disapproval," said U.S. Representative Dave Weldon.

On Tuesday, Weldon introduced H.R. 1151, the "Incapacitated Person's Legal Protection Act." This bill would explicitly clarify fundamental due process rights for those who are incapacitated, are under court-ordered removal of nutrition and hydration, and have no written advanced medical directive in effect.

From news release, March 11, 2005.

U.S. SENATOR RICK SANTORUM

Santorum Fights to Save Life of Terri Schiavo

March 17, 2005—

FOR IMMEDIATE RELEASE March 17, 2005

Washington, DC—U.S. Senator Rick Santorum (R-PA), Chairman of the Senate Republican Conference, today offered comments following Senate passage of a bill that enables the parents of Terri Schiavo to appeal to federal court for review of state court proceedings to ensure that due process has been upheld and that Terri's rights were protected by the state court with regards to her feeding and hydration tube:

"We work in Washington to pass legislation that impacts the lives of all Americans. Today, a vote by the U.S. Senate could mean the difference between life and death for one Florida woman fighting for her life.

"Terri Schiavo, a daughter, a sister, and most importantly an innocent person who is being penalized by a court system that grants convicted murderers fair treatment under the law, but not a woman who has committed no crime and whose life hangs in the balance.

"The actions on the part of the Florida court are unconscionable. Yesterday in California, Scott Peterson, a convicted murderer, was sentenced to death, yet his constitutional rights were upheld to ensure that he received due process and fair consideration in court. The Florida court has been trying to ultimately end the life of Terri Schiavo, who committed no crime, but is being penalized for not filing a living will.

"I applaud my Senate colleagues for heeding my calls for immediate action on this, most especially the legislation's sponsor, Senator Mel Martinez from Florida. It is absolutely critical for the House of Representatives to pass this legislation in a timely fashion. We cannot allow Terri, an innocent woman, to die a slow, painful death due to starvation and dehydration when her feeding tube is removed tomorrow at 1:00 PM."

From news release, March 17, 2005.

SENATE MAJORITY LEADER BILL FRIST

STATEMENT ON TERRI SCHIAVO BILL

Floor Statement

March 17th, 2005—Mr. President, in closing tonight, I want to take a few final moments to speak on an issue that I opened with earlier this morning, and it has to do with the Terri Schiavo case in Florida. I'd like to close this evening speaking more as a physician than as a United States Senator and really speak to my involvement as a physician and—and as a Senator and as leader in the United States Senate in what has been a fascinating course of events for us over the last forty-eight hours. A saga which has not ended but one which we took major steps toward tonight by seeing that this woman is not starved to death tomorrow beginning at 1:00 PM.

When I first heard about the situation facing Terri Schiavo, I immediately wanted to know more about the case from a medical standpoint. I asked myself, just looking at the newspaper reports, is Terri clearly in this diagnosis called persistent vegetative state?

I was interested in it in part because it is a very difficult diagnosis to make and I've been in a situation such as this many, many times before as a transplant surgeon. When we do heart transplants and lung transplants, the transplanted organs come from someone who is brain-dead and death is clearly defined with a series of standardized clinical exams over a period of time. Brain death is a difficult diagnosis to make and short of brain death, there are stages of incapacitation that go from coma to this persistent vegetative state to a minimally conscious state, and they're a tough diagnosis to make.

You can make brain death with certainty, but short of that, it's a difficult diagnosis and one that takes a series of evaluations over a period of time because of fluctuating consciousness. And so I was a little bit surprised to hear that a decision had been made to starve to death a woman based on a clinical exam that took place over a very short period of time by a neurologist who was called in to make the diagnosis. It's almost unheard of. And so that raised the first question in my mind.

I asked myself: does Terri clearly have no hope of being rehabilitated or improved in—in any way? And if you are in a true persistent vegetative state,

From *Congressional Record* S3090-S3092, March 17, 2005.

that may be the case. But again, it's [a] very tough diagnosis to make, and only by putting forth that rehabilitative therapy and following over time do you know if somebody's going to improve. And at least from the reporting that was being done, that has not been the case.

I asked myself, because we have living wills now and we have written directives which are very commonplace now. But ten years ago they weren't that common. And to be honest with you, a lot of twenty- and thirty-year-olds don't think about their own mortality. So I asked does she have a written directive or did she at the time?

And the answer was no. And did she have a clear-cut oral directive, and the answer was no. With that my curiosity piqued, so I asked to see all of the court affidavits and I received those court affidavits and had the opportunity to read through those over the last forty-eight hours. And my curiosity was piqued even further because of what seemed to be unusual about the case. And so I called one of the neurologists who did evaluate her and evaluated her more extensively than what at least was alleged other neurologists had, and he told me very directly that she is not in a persistent vegetative state. And I said, well, give me a spectrum from this neurologist who examined her, and to be fair, he examined her about two years ago, and to the best of my knowledge, no neurologist has been able to examine her—I'm not positive about that but that's what I've been told—but at that time that clearly she was not in a persistent vegetative state. And of one hundred patients this neurologist would take care of, she wasn't at the extreme end of her disability.

She might have been the seventieth but not the eightieth, ninetieth, or one-hundredth in terms of degree of disability. And so then I became really curious that a neurologist who had spent time with her, said she is not in a persistent vegetative state, yet she is going to be starved tomorrow because of what another neurologist had said.

I talked to her family and had the opportunity to meet her [brother], and her [brother] told me that she is responsive. She has a severe disability, a lot of people with cerebral palsy and disabilities have severe disabilities. Her brother said that she responds to her parents and to him. And that is not somebody in persistent vegetative state. I then met with the chairman of the Judiciary Committee two days ago in Florida to discuss the case, and he told me that they had exhausted all options in the state of Florida to reverse what was going to be inevitable tomorrow, Friday, the eighteenth of March. He said the courts have been exhausted and that all of the court decisions and the court cases had not been based on the facts because the facts were very limited and were the conclusions of one judge, and two neurologists and that was it.

There was something like thirty-four affidavits from other doctors who said that she could be improved with rehabilitation. So then it came to, what do you do?

Here is—here is the United States Senate, which normally does not and should not get involved in all of these private-action cases. It's not our primary responsibility here in the United States Senate, but with an exhaustion of state legislature, exhaustion of the court system in a state, yet all of this is based on what one—one judge had decided on what at least initially to me looks like wrong data, incomplete data, but somebody is being condemned to death, somebody who's alive—there's no question she's alive—is being condemned to death. It takes an action to pull out a feeding tube. It takes an action to stop feeding. The inaction of feeding becomes an action.

And, thus, as I started talking about it this morning, the question was what do we do? Bills have been put forth broadly on the floor and Senator Martinez had very effective legislation but it had to do with habeas corpus, a very large issue that we haven't had hearings on and debated. So what we've decided to do is to fashion a bill that was very narrow, aimed specifically at this case that would say she's not going to be starved to death tomorrow but let's go and collect more information, have neurologists come in and obtain a body of facts before such a decision would be made. That's what we've done, as Senator Martinez said and Senator Santorum said. We're not there yet. We've got three different tracks going on. It'll be going on over the course of tonight. In my office right now letters are being written and being sent out and we'll not give up.

We've passed the bill here tonight. The House has a bill and I'm confident if we continue working—we're going to stay in session until we complete action. Let me just comment a little bit about the Terri Schiavo case because what I said is how we got involved and what I'm about to say is a little bit more information than what we've been able to talk about on the floor today because of the focus on the budget committee.

Terri Schiavo is right now in a Florida hospice. She is breathing on her own. She's not on a ventilator. She is not a terminal case. She is, as I said, disabled. When her feeding tube is removed, she does not receive food, she starves to death. Her parents, Bob and Mary Schindler, have been fighting for over ten years to prevent her death. Imagine if you and your spouse, and you had a daughter, and you said, don't let her die. We will take care of her.

We will financially take care of her. How in the world can you have some-body come in and remove a feeding tube?

And that's what they've been saying for ten years. They love her. They say that she responds to her. They would welcome the chance, welcome the chance, to be her guardian. As I understand it, Terri's husband will not divorce Terri and will not allow her parents to take care of her. Terri's husband, who I've not met, does have a girlfriend that he lives with and they have children of their own. The single Florida judge ruled that Terri is in this persistent veg-etative state and this is the same judge that has denied new testing, new exam-inations of Terri by independent and qualified medical professionals.

They've not been allowed. As I mentioned, the attorney for Terri's par-ents [has] submitted thirty-three affidavits from doctors and other medical professionals, all of whom say that Terri should be reevaluated. At least four-teen of these affidavits are from board-certified neurologists. Some of these doctors very specifically say they believe on the data that they had seen that Terri could benefit from therapy. There have been many comments that her legal guardian—that's Terri's husband—has not—it is either he has not been aggressive to rehabilitation, to other reports that say that he has thwarted rehabilitation since 1992. I can only report what I have read there because I haven't met him.

Persistent vegetative state, which is what the court has ruled—I question it. I question it based on a review of the video footage which I spent an hour or so looking at last night in my office here in the Capitol. And that footage, to me, depicts something very different than persistent vegetative state. One of the classic textbooks that we use in medicine today is called *Harrison's Principles of Internal Medicine*. In the sixteenth edition, which was pub-lished just this year, 2005, on page 1625, it reads, "the vegetative state sig-nifies an awake but unresponsive state. These patients have emerged from coma after a period of days or weeks to an unresponsive state in which the eyelids are open, giving the appearance of wakefulness." I'll stop quoting from the classic internal medicine textbook, but one last sentence, "in the closely related, minimally conscious state, the patient may make intermit-tent, rudimentary vocal and motor responses."

I would simply ask, maybe she is not in this vegetative state and she's in this minimally conscious state. In which case the diagnosis upon which this whole case has been based would be incorrect. Fifteen neurologists have signed affidavits that Terri should have additional testing by unbiased, inde-pendent neurologists. I'm told that Terri never had an MRI or a PET scan of her head. And that disturbs me only because it suggests that she hasn't been fully evaluated by today's standards. You don't have to have an MRI scan or a PET scan to the diagnosis of a vegetative state. But if you are going to put somebody to death I would think you would want a complete neurological exam in reaching that conclusion.

In 1996 a British medical journal study conducted at England's Royal Hospital for Neurodisability concluded that there was a 43% error rate in the diagnosis of PVS. It takes a lot of time, as I mentioned earlier, to make this diagnosis with a very high error rate. If you're going to be causing somebody to die with purposeful action, you're not going to want to make a mistake in terms of the diagnosis. I mentioned that Terri's brother told me that Terri laughs, smiles, and tries to speak. Doesn't sound like a woman in persistent vegetative state.

So our Congress has acted tonight and the House of Representatives acted last night. The approaches are a bit different and I hope that we can resolve those differences. It is clear to me that Congress has a responsibility since other aspects of government at the state level have failed to address this issue. There just seems to be insufficient information to conclude that Terri Schiavo is persistent vegetative state, securing the facts I believe is the first and proper step at this juncture. Whoever does spend time making the diagnosis with Terri does need to spend enough time to make an appropriate diagnosis.

Prudence and caution and respect for the dignity of life must be the principles in this case.

Let me close with an e-mail that I received, a friend of mine sent me this e-mail once they saw that we as a body were involved in this case.

And the e-mail reads: "I know you are dealing with so many major issues but I believe this one threatens to send us down another shameful path we may never recover from. I don't think I ever had an occasion to tell you that I have a severely brain damaged adult daughter that I cared for in my home for twenty years. Sasha's functioning level is far below Terri's but she's been such a blessing in my life. Senator Frist, as you fight this battle today, hold fast. If ever the weak needed a champion, it is now. On behalf of my sweet Sasha." I close tonight with those words—powerful words.

SENATE MAJORITY LEADER BILL FRIST

March 18th, 2005—WASHINGTON, DC—U.S. Senate Majority Leader Bill Frist, MD (R-TN), today made the following statement:

"The Senate and the House remain dedicated to saving Terri Schiavo's life. While discussions over possible legislative remedies continue, the Senate and the House are taking action to keep her alive in the interim."

HELP Committee Chairman Mike Enzi has requested the presence of Mr. and Mrs. Schiavo at an official committee hearing. He has sent a letter to the Schiavos to appear at a hearing on Monday, March 28, 2005 regarding "Health Care Provided to Nonambulatory Persons." The purpose of the hearing is to review healthcare policies and practices relevant to the care of nonambulatory persons such as Mrs. Schiavo.

Federal criminal law protects witnesses called before official congressional committee proceedings from anyone who may obstruct or impede a witness's attendance or testimony. More specifically, the law protects a witness from anyone who—by threats, force, or by any threatening letter or communication—influences, obstructs, or impedes an inquiry or investigation by Congress. Anyone who violates this law is subject to criminal fines and imprisonment.

JOINT STATEMENT OF SENATE MAJORITY LEADER BILL FRIST AND SPEAKER OF THE HOUSE J. DENNIS HASTERT ON TERRI SCHIAVO

Congress to Work Through Weekend to Save Mrs. Schiavo's Life

March 18th, 2005—WASHINGTON, DC—Speaker of the House J. Dennis Hastert and Senate Majority Leader Bill Frist released the following statement today:

"We're very disappointed by the Florida court's decision to allow Terri Schiavo's feeding tube to be removed. The House and Senate leadership are committed to reaching agreement on legislation that provides an opportunity to save Mrs. Schiavo's life. Now that the House and Senate have each passed

---

Both from news releases, March 18, 2005.

different legislative remedies, the House and Senate Committees are working urgently together. We will be working through the weekend to resolve the differences and reach an effective solution that can clear our chambers and be signed by the President."

REP. DEBBIE WASSERMAN SCHULTZ

Congresswoman from Florida's Twentieth Congressional District

Excerpt of Rep. Debbie Wasserman Schultz's Terri Schiavo Floor Statement

March 20, 2005—

I notice today that President Bush has returned from Crawford hoping to sign this legislation if it is passed by Congress. I think it is important to note that President Bush when he was governor of Texas in 1999 signed a Texas law that is on the books today that was just used a few days ago to allow a hospital to withdraw, over the parents' objections, the life support of a six-month-old boy, over the parents' objections.

President Bush signed a law called the Texas Advanced Directives Act, when he was governor of Texas. This law, that has been used several times and as recently as a few days ago, liberalized the situations under which a person in Texas can avoid artificial life support. Under it, life support can be withheld or withdrawn if you have an irreversible condition in Texas from which you are expected to eventually pass away.

Indeed, this law, signed by then governor Bush, allows doctors to remove a patient from life support if the hospital's ethics committee agrees, even over the objections of a family member, only allowing the family ten days to find another facility that might accept the patient, barring any state judicial intervention.

It appears that President Bush felt, as governor, that there was a point at which, when doctors felt there was no further hope for the patient, that it is appropriate for an end-of-life decision to be made, even over the objections of family members. That was a law that President Bush did not just allow to become law without his signature, he came back from a campaign trip to sign it.

From *Congressional Record* H1700-H1728, March 20, 2005.

There is an obvious conflict here between the president's feelings on this matter now as compared to when he was governor of Texas, so I thought that was an important conflict that should be raised here this evening in our discussion.

Let me just close my remarks by reiterating there is no room for the federal government in this most personal of private angst-ridden family matters, in which a family has to make the most personal of decisions when dealing with the course of care of a loved one. We should not politicize this very personal family matter.

HOUSE MAJORITY LEADER TOM DELAY

DeLay: Palm Sunday Compromise Will Give Terri a Chance

Urges Objectors to Let House Vote Before It's Too Late

Washington, Mar. 20, 2005—

WASHINGTON—House Majority Leader Tom DeLay (R-Texas) today spoke at a press availability on the latest efforts to save the life of Terri Schiavo. The following are excerpts from his remarks:

"Last night, as you know, House and Senate negotiators reached a bipartisan, bicameral compromise proposal to provide Terri Schiavo a clear and appropriate avenue to have her case heard in federal court. The bill we're working on has majority support in the House and the Senate, and it is going to pass. The only question is when. The few, objecting House Democrats have so far cost Mrs. Schiavo two meals already today, and we're working now to resolve this in time for her to get some food and water tonight.

"Mrs. Schiavo's condition, I believe, has been at times misrepresented by the media, but far more often has simply gone unreported all together. Terri Schiavo is not on a respirator; she can breathe on her own. Terri Schiavo is not brain-dead; she talks and she laughs, and she expresses happiness and discomfort. Terri Schiavo is not on life-support.

"She's not being 'kept alive'; she is alive. It won't take a miracle to help Terri Schiavo; it will only take the medical care and therapy that all patients deserve. Mrs. Schiavo is not being denied heroic measures; she's being denied basic, basic, basic medical and personal care.

From news release, March 20, 2005.

"The legal issues, I grant everyone, are complicated, but the moral ones are not. What will it hurt to have a federal judge take a fresh look at all this evidence and apply it against fifteen years' worth of advances in medical technology? We have a bill—the Palm Sunday compromise—that will give her that chance. It is bipartisan and bicameral and has overwhelming support in both houses. It will eventually pass. We just hope the objectors let us vote on it before it's too late."

U.S. REPRESENTATIVE DAVE WELDON

WELDON STATEMENT ON PASSAGE OF SCHIAVO BILL

Bill Signed into Law by President Bush Late Last Night

Washington, DC, Mar. 21—

U.S. Representative Dave Weldon, MD, released the following statement in response to the passage of S. 626 for the relief of the parents of Terri Schiavo:

"By passing this bipartisan bill tonight, Congress has sent a clear message that Terri Schiavo deserves the same due process rights to a federal court review that death row inmates receive. I am pleased that the Congress has been able to act swiftly on behalf of this important matter," Weldon said.

SENATE MAJORITY LEADER FRIST
LETTER TO GOVERNOR JEB BUSH

March 22nd, 2005—

The Honorable Jeb Bush
Governor
400 S. Monroe Street
The Capitol
Tallahassee, Florida 32399-0001

Weldon: from news release, March 21, 2005.
Frist: from news release, March 22, 2005.

Dear Governor Bush:

Thank you for your courageous stand on behalf of Terri Schiavo. You have been doing important work to preserve and protect her rights.

As you know, in the last week, the House and Senate have each passed two bills to give Terri Schiavo another chance in the judicial process. These bills affirm the commitment of Congress to preserve the sanctity of life. Our efforts culminated with the passage of S. 686, (P.L. 109-3), which affords Terri's parents the opportunity to protect their daughter's rights in the federal courts.

Given the uncertain judicial outcome of this case, currently pending before the 11th Circuit Court of Appeals, it is all the more important that the Florida legislature act expeditiously on Terri's behalf. The new law has opened the federal courthouse doors for Terri, but federal action should not be her only remaining option. The extraordinary nature of this case requires that every avenue be pursued to protect her life.

Thanks again for your outspoken and courageous efforts on behalf of Terri Schiavo's right to life.

Sincerely,

William H. Frist, MD
Majority Leader
United States Senate

CONGRESSMAN ROBERT WEXLER

March 23, 2005

Wexler: Delay's Political Use of Schiavo Case Deplorable

Republican Hypocrisy Exposed as They Cut Billions From Medicaid While Claiming to Fight for Medicaid's Highest-Profile Patient—Terri Schiavo (Washington, DC)—

From news release, March 23, 2005.

Congressman Robert Wexler (D-FL) believes that the "politically motivated" actions of House Majority Leader Tom Delay (R-TX) and Republicans in Congress regarding the case of Terri Schiavo are deplorable. Last
Friday, Mr. Delay speaking to the Family Research Council, a Christian conservative group, stated the following regarding the case of Terri Schiavo—
"One thing that God has brought to us is Terri Schiavo, to help elevate the
visibility of what is going on in America," he said. "This is exactly the issue
that is going on in America, of attacks against the conservative movement,
against me and against many others." Delay's divisive comments come at
time when the Majority Leader and some Republicans in Congress have
brazenly thumbed their nose at Florida's courts by intervening in the Schiavo
case. And now, despite their failed last-minute attempt to produce their
desired result, Mr. Delay, Senate Majority Leader Frist and the Republican
leadership are rumored to be considering further congressional intervention
to undermine their own so-called remedy. This threatened action blatantly
contradicts Republican claims on Sunday that all they wanted to do was
allow Ms. Schiavo's parents access to federal courts. "Mr. Delay's comments
and actions in the Schiavo case underscore an unfortunate willingness on his
part to use this difficult situation for political cover exactly at a time when
he is being publicly scrutinized. What happened to Ms. Schiavo is a tragedy,
and her husband and family have endured unimaginably painful years in
coming to terms with her condition. They have had to face decisions all of
us pray we will never have to make for ourselves or our loved ones. I find it
shameful that Mr. Delay and Republicans have used Ms. Schiavo as their
political pawn to kowtow to their conservative base. In the process, they
have decided that the rule of law is only worth respecting if they agree with
the results. These manipulative actions are anything but compassionate and
set an absolutely frightening precedent. "I am equally outraged that while
Mr. Delay and Republican leaders intervene in the Schiavo case, they simul-
taneously have slashed Medicaid funding in their budget by $20 billion over
the next five years. While Republicans have fought vociferously to protect
the well-being of one individual, they are unconscionably cutting Medicaid
funding by billions leaving the most vulnerable in our society—women,
children, the elderly, and the disabled to fend for themselves. "The oppor-
tunistic actions of Mr. Delay and Republicans in Congress speak volumes to
their political motivations in the Schiavo case. I urge Mr. Delay and Republican leaders to explain to all Medicaid recipients why they support leaving
America's most vulnerable without adequate health coverage and why they

bers and to painful stimuli and what this may indicate about her level of consciousness.

It is further unclear what Terri's intent was prior to her cardiac arrest— would she want to live or die if in her current state? Michael Schiavo argues that despite the absence of any written expression of her wishes, Terri told him that she would never want to be kept alive "artificially." However, Terri's parents, Bob and Mary Schindler, have fought to prevent the removal of her feeding tube and argue that Terri never expressed an opinion relating to a situation similar to her current situation.

Because we do not know if Terri is in fact living "artificially" and what her intent was, Congress should always, as President Bush has said, "err on the side of life." And so, we stepped forward to make sure that Terri's civil rights were upheld. Our U.S. Constitution guarantees all Americans the right to due process. Just last week in California, Scott Peterson, a convicted murderer, was sentenced to death, yet his constitutional rights were upheld to ensure that he received due process and fair consideration in court. There should be no question that Terri Schiavo should have the same due process and fair treatment in accordance with the law.

Furthermore, when it is obvious that certain judges and courts have distorted several facts surrounding a case under the balance of powers, it is Congress's duty to challenge their decisions. It was necessary for Congress to enact legislation to ensure that Terri's constitutional right to equal protection is fully exercised and for a court to review her case, including all of the outstanding evidence.

Congress worked hard to do all they could to provide relief to Terri and to delay the extraction of the feeding tube. In unprecedented acts by Congress and President Bush, a private relief bill was signed into law enabling the parents of Terri Schiavo to appeal to federal court for review of state court proceedings to ensure that due process was upheld, and that Terri's rights were protected by the state court. This legislation remains consistent with the will of the people of Florida who have been repeatedly frustrated by the state courts.

It was our hope that while the U.S. Supreme Court exercised this discretion, the tube would have been replaced, allowing nourishment to be restored to Terri while the review of her case continued. However, the Supreme Court denied taking up the case, thumbing their nose at congressional intent, and Terri's life was further jeopardized. I am disheartened by the state and federal courts' refusal to review Terri Schiavo's case. Their actions are unconscionable. They have sentenced Terri to death by dehydration and starvation—a sentence that would not be placed on the worst criminal.

I commend the efforts of President Bush, Congress, and Governor Jeb Bush to help ensure protection of Terri's rights, and to attempt to save her life. Congress was right in passing legislation to let Terri live and not die a slow painful death.

FRIST STATEMENT ON PASSING OF TERRI SCHIAVO

March 31st, 2005—WASHINGTON, DC—U.S. Senate Majority Leader Bill Frist made the following statement regarding Terri Schiavo's passing:

"Today I join with all those mourning Terri Schiavo's passing. I am deeply saddened by her loss. I pray for her mother and father, her family, and all those involved in this regrettable loss of life. May God bless her memory."

CONGRESSMAN ELIJAH E. CUMMINGS

We All Deserve the Full Measure of Our Lives

This month, Americans have struggled with two very difficult, but related, questions about what it means to foster a "culture of life."

The first of these questions, the Terri Schiavo controversy, has flooded the public arena so completely that all three branches of our federal government have been involved. Nevertheless, most Americans now understand that the end-of-life questions raised by the Schiavo family's tragedy are within each person's right (and power) to answer, without inviting the government to intervene.

The other "culture of life" question that was raised again this month—the unequal mortality of people of color in this society—has been largely ignored, both by the media and by the Congress of the United States.

Yet, a complete answer to this challenge to life will require far more effective action by the federal government—a development that can occur only in the context of a renewed national commitment to universal civil rights.

Frist: from news release, March 31, 2005.
Cummings: from the *Baltimore AFRO-American*, April 2, 2005, http://www.house.gov/cummings/articles/art05_09.htm (accessed November 21, 2005).

It is understandable that the American people would respond with compassion to the televised pictures of a woman lying helpless and vulnerable in her Florida hospice bed. Our basic humanity would have been subject to serious and legitimate questions had we not put ourselves in the place of Terri Schiavo and her family.

We have all asked ourselves what we would do if we were in their place. Yet, the basic principle of our system of government is that the Congress should act for all Americans—not respond to an individual case.

When the Schiavo controversy was brought before the Congress, we had little to guide our decision but conscience applied to the facts at hand. I gave heavy weight to the doubts about Mrs. Schiavo's condition that had been raised by the Senate's Majority Leader, Dr. Bill Frist.

Although I understood why some of my colleagues voted the other way, under these circumstances, I could not vote to deny Terri Schiavo's parents one last chance in federal court to argue her constitutional claim.

I left the Capitol that evening feeling in my heart that I did the right thing. Yet, as a lawyer for more than twenty-eight years, I also understand that the most immediate lesson for us to draw from this American tragedy is the importance of making these end-of-life decisions for ourselves—and in writing.

We each have the capability to spare those closest to us the agony experienced by Terri Schiavo's family. Legally sufficient documents for accomplishing this goal—written in plain language—are available from national organizations like the American Association of Retired Persons and—here in Maryland—from the Office of our Attorney General [http://www.oag.state.md.us/].

A far more difficult challenge for this nation, as people who strive to be humane, is the growing (and well-founded) indictment of this nation's system of healthcare.

This month, a high-caliber research team that included Dr. David Satcher, former Surgeon General of the United States, released its evaluation of this country's mortality figures for the 1990s. During the last decade, the Satcher team concluded, more than 886,000 Americans of color died before their time.

Stated in the language of national healthcare policy, more than 886,000 African American deaths could have been prevented had these Americans received the same healthcare that was provided to White Americans by this society.

To place this staggering number of deaths in perspective, consider this. The avoidable mortality of African Americans during the last fourteen years at least equals the number of deaths in the Darfur region of Sudan.

Following the lead of the Congressional Black Caucus, the Congress of the United States has called the carnage in that troubled African country "genocide." What, then, should the Congress call the same number of African American lives ended before their time?

This question must be at the center of any national debate about a renewed "culture of life."

In this context, all Americans should be deeply troubled by the President's misguided and inadequate budget for healthcare. How could cutting federal funds for Medicaid possibly affirm a culture of life? Don't the poor and disabled of our society share Terri Schiavo's right to live out their lives?

At the same time, I remain cautiously hopeful that we may be able to make some bipartisan progress in this Congress toward reducing racial disparities in healthcare. Mr. Dean Rosen, the top health policy aide to Senate Majority Leader Bill Frist, recently acknowledged that Dr. Frist understands that minority health disparities are "alarming and troubling . . . challenges that need to be addressed."

For all the controversy that has followed the Terri Schiavo debate, one principle—shared by advocates on all sides of this controversy—offers an insight that may further bipartisan solutions to the broader healthcare issues that we face.

Every human life has value.

Perhaps the President and Congress will now agree that all Americans deserve the full measure of our lives.

The Honorable Elijah E. Cummings represents the 7th Congressional District of Maryland in the United States House of Representatives.

BARNEY FRANK

April 10, 2005

Congress Should Revisit Issues of Schiavo Case

The fact that Congress adopted a bad law in the Terri Schiavo case—unwise, unprincipled, and unconstitutional—does not mean Congress must never

From the *Boston Globe*, April 10, 2005, Boston.com, http://www.boston.com/news/globe/editorial_opinion/oped/articles/2005/04/10/congress_should_revisit_issues_of_schiavo_case (accessed November 21, 2005).

again return to the subject. It is too early to adopt any legislation, but it is appropriate for Congress to begin discussing what public policy ought to be with regard to the anguishing issues in this case. The legislation adopted on March 27 offers a useful negative reference point for such an effort. Our approach in the future should in every important respect be exactly the opposite of what we have done so far this year. First, the distinction between the judicial and legislative functions must be maintained. On March 27, Congress did not legislate. We constituted ourselves as an ad hoc super court, cancelled the lengthy, careful judicial deliberations of the entire court system of Florida, and sent the case to a federal District Court with very specific instructions about how to proceed in deciding it. Members of Congress brought to that decision our ideologies, our concern for reelection, our interests in advancing our parties' political positions, and our need to maintain good relationships with our political leaderships and colleagues—elements that should have had no place in this decision. Future legislative efforts must remember that if we do not wish decisions to be made on a political basis, we should not ask 536 politicians to make them. Second, the division of responsibility between the state and federal governments, while not as absolute in importance to our liberty as that between the judging and legislative functions, is still important. Some have claimed as precedent for the Schiavo bill federal efforts to protect African American citizens against the mistreatment that had been the practice in many Southern states. But that was a significant exception to the general principle that regulating personal life is best left to the states. And the civil rights actions came only after a national conclusion that there had been a massive failure of the states' responsibility in this regard. No such conclusion could possibly be reached today about the role of the states here. Third, if we take any action it must be a balanced one, recognizing both the right of individuals not to have their lives ended prematurely and, equally important, the right not to have life in a severely diminished form prolonged far beyond what might be desired. Both the bills specifically dealing with Terri Schiavo and the broader one, which passed the House and was defeated in the Senate, were entirely one-sided. They mandated federal preemption of decisions resulting in the end of life but said nothing about situations in which state authorities might block individual decisions to allow death to occur in accordance with the wishes of the affected individual. In the current climate, it is this latter right that may well be in the greater jeopardy. That is certainly the message of a recent survey of state actions in the wake of the Schiavo case which reported that a

AN ACT

For the relief of the parents of Theresa Marie Schiavo.

Be it enacted by the Senate and House of Representatives of the United States of America in Congress assembled,

SECTION 1. RELIEF OF THE PARENTS OF THERESA MARIE SCHIAVO

The United States District Court for the Middle District of Florida shall have jurisdiction to hear, determine, and render judgment on a suit or claim by or on behalf of Theresa Marie Schiavo for the alleged violation of any right of Theresa Marie Schiavo under the Constitution or laws of the United States relating to the withholding or withdrawal of food, fluids, or medical treatment necessary to sustain her life.

SEC. 2. PROCEDURE

Any parent of Theresa Marie Schiavo shall have standing to bring a suit under this Act. The suit may be brought against any other person who was a party to State court proceedings relating to the withholding or withdrawal of food, fluids, or medical treatment necessary to sustain the life of Theresa Marie Schiavo, or who may act pursuant to a State court order authorizing or directing the withholding or withdrawal of food, fluids, or medical treatment necessary to sustain her life. In such a suit, the District Court shall determine *de novo* any claim of a violation of any right of Theresa Marie Schiavo within the scope of this Act, notwithstanding any prior State court

From Library of Congress THOMAS.

149

determination and regardless of whether such a claim has previously been raised, considered, or decided in State court proceedings. The District Court shall entertain and determine the suit without any delay or abstention in favor of State court proceedings, and regardless of whether remedies available in the State courts have been exhausted.

SEC. 3. RELIEF

After a determination of the merits of a suit brought under this Act, the District Court shall issue such declaratory and injunctive relief as may be necessary to protect the rights of Theresa Marie Schiavo under the Constitution and laws of the United States relating to the withholding or withdrawal of food, fluids, or medical treatment necessary to sustain her life.

SEC. 4. TIME FOR FILING

Notwithstanding any other time limitation, any suit or claim under this Act shall be timely if filed within thirty days after the date of enactment of this Act.

SEC. 5. NO CHANGE OF SUBSTANTIVE RIGHTS

Nothing in this Act shall be construed to create substantive rights not otherwise secured by the Constitution and laws of the United States or of the several States.

SEC. 6. NO EFFECT ON ASSISTING SUICIDE

Nothing in this Act shall be construed to confer additional jurisdiction on any court to consider any claim related—

(1) to assisting suicide, or
(2) a State law regarding assisting suicide.

SEC. 7. NO PRECEDENT FOR FUTURE LEGISLATION

Nothing in this Act shall constitute a precedent with respect to future legislation, including the provision of private relief bills.

SEC. 8. NO AFFECT ON THE PATIENT SELF-DETERMINATION ACT OF 1990

Nothing in this Act shall affect the rights of any person under the Patient Self-Determination Act of 1990.

SEC. 9. SENSE OF THE CONGRESS

It is the Sense of Congress that the 109th Congress should consider policies regarding the status and legal rights of incapacitated individuals who are incapable of making decisions concerning the provision, withholding, or withdrawal of foods, fluid, or medical care.

President George W. Bush's Statement on S. 686, Allowing Federal Courts to Hear Claim of Terri Schiavo

Today, I signed into law a bill that will allow federal courts to hear a claim by or on behalf of Terri Schiavo for violation of her rights relating to the withholding or withdrawal of food, fluids, or medical treatment necessary to sustain her life. In cases like this one, where there are serious questions and substantial doubts, our society, our laws, and our courts should have a presumption in favor of life. This presumption is especially critical for those like Terri Schiavo who live at the mercy of others. I appreciate the bipartisan action by the Members of Congress to pass this bill. I will continue to stand on the side of those defending life for all Americans, including those with disabilities.

From news release, March 21, 2005.

UNITED STATES DISTRICT COURT MIDDLE DISTRICT OF FLORIDA TAMPA DIVISION

THERESA MARIE SCHINDLER SCHIAVO
Incapacitated ex rel., ROBERT SCHINDLER
and MARY SCHINDLER, her Parents and
Next Friends,
    Plaintiffs,

    Case No. 8:05-CV-530-T-27TBM

v.

MICHAEL SCHIAVO, JUDGE GEORGE W.
GREER and THE HOSPICE OF THE FLORIDA
SUNCOAST, INC.
    Defendants.

ORDER

BEFORE THE COURT is Plaintiffs' Motion for Temporary Restraining Order (Dkt. 2). In their motion, Plaintiffs seek an order directing Defendants Schiavo and Hospice to transport Theresa Schiavo to Morton Plant Hospital for any necessary medical treatment to sustain her life and to reestablish her nutrition and hydration. This action and Plaintiffs' motion were filed in response to an order of Pinellas County Probate Judge George W. Greer directing Defendant Schiavo, Theresa Schiavo's husband and plenary guardian, to discontinue her nutrition and hydration.

The court conducted a hearing on Plaintiffs' motion after notice to Defendants. Upon consideration, Plaintiffs' Motion for Temporary Restraining Order is denied.

From Judge James D. Whittemore, United States District Court, Middle District of Florida, Tampa Division, *Theresa Marie Schindler Schiavo Incapacitated ex rel., Robert Schindler and Mary Schindler, Her Parents and Next Friends, v. Michael Schiavo, Judge George W. Greer and The Hospice of the Florida Suncoast, Inc.* Case No. 8:05-CV-530-T-27TBM. Decided March 22, 2005.

Plaintiffs, the parents of Theresa Marie Schindler Schiavo, brought this action pursuant to a Congressional Act signed into law by the President during the early morning hours of March 21,2005.[1] The Act, entitled "An Act for the relief of the parents of Theresa Marie Schiavo," provides that the:

> United States District Court for the Middle District of Florida shall have jurisdiction to hear, determine, and render judgment on a suit or claim by or on behalf of Theresa Marie Schiavo for the alleged violation of any right of Theresa Marie Schiavo under the Constitution or laws of the United States relating to the withholding or withdrawal of food, fluids, or medical treatment necessary to sustain life.

Jurisdiction and Standing

The federal district courts are courts of limited jurisdiction, "empowered to hear only those cases , . . . which have been entrusted to them by a jurisdictional grant authorized by Congress." *University of S. Ala. v. American Tobacco Co.,* 168 F.3d 405, 409 (11th Cir. 1999) (quoting *Taylor v. Appleton,* 30 F.3d 1365, 1367 [11th Cir. 1994]). The plain language of the Act establishes jurisdiction in this court to determine *de novo* "any claim of a violation of any right of Theresa Schiavo within the scope of this Act." The Act expressly confers standing to Plaintiffs as her parents to bring any such claims. There can be no substantial question, therefore, that Plaintiffs may bring an action against a party to the state court proceedings in this court for claimed constitutional deprivations or violations of federal law occasioned on their daughter relating to the withholding or withdrawal of food, fluids, or medical treatment necessary to sustain her life. Whether the Plaintiffs may bring claims in federal court is not the issue confronting the court today, however. The issue confronting the court is whether temporary injunctive relief is warranted.

Applicable Standards

While there may be substantial issues concerning the constitutionality of the Act, for purposes of considering temporary injunctive relief, the Act is presumed to be constitutional. *Benning v. Georgia,* 391 F.3d 1299, 1303 (11th Cir. 2004). The purpose of a temporary restraining order, like a preliminary injunction, is to protect against irreparable injury and preserve the status quo until the district court renders a meaningful decision on the merits. *Canal*

Auth. of State of Florida v. Callaway, 489 F.2d 567, 572 (5th Cir. 1974). A district court may grant a preliminary injunction only if the moving party shows that:

(1) it has a substantial likelihood of success on the merits;
(2) irreparable injury will be suffered unless the injunction issues;
(3) the threatened injury to the movant outweighs whatever damage the proposed injunction may cause the opposing party; and
(4) if issued, the injunction would not be adverse to the public interest.

Klay v. United Healthgroup, Inc., 376 F.3d 1092, 1097 (11th Cir. 2004); *Suntrust Bank v. Houghton Mifflin Co.*, 268 F.3d 1257, 1265 (11th Cir. 2001). A preliminary injunction is "an extraordinary and drastic remedy" and is "not to be granted unless the movant 'clearly established the burden of persuasion' as to the four prerequisites." *United States v. Jefferson County*, 720 F.2d 1511, 1519 (11th Cir. 1983) (*quoting Canal Auth. of State of Florida*, 489 F.2d at 573).[2] It is apparent that Theresa Schiavo will die unless temporary injunctive relief is granted. This circumstance satisfies the requirement of irreparable injury. Moreover, that threatened injury outweighs any harm the proposed injunction would cause. To the extent Defendants urge that Theresa Schiavo would be harmed by the invasive procedure reinserting the feeding tube, this court finds that death outweighs any such harm. Finally, the court is satisfied that an injunction would not be adverse to the public interest. Notwithstanding these findings, it is essential that Plaintiffs establish a substantial likelihood of success on the merits, which the court finds they have not done. . . .

A. COUNT I—VIOLATION OF FOURTEENTH AMENDMENT DUE PROCESS RIGHT TO A FAIR AND IMPARTIAL TRIAL

. . . Plaintiffs' argument effectively ignores the role of the presiding judge as judicial fact finder and decision maker under the Florida statutory scheme. By fulfilling his statutory judicial responsibilities, the judge was not transformed into an advocate merely because his rulings are unfavorable to a litigant. Plaintiffs' contention that the statutory scheme followed by Judge Greer deprived Theresa Schiavo of an impartial trial is accordingly without merit. Defendant is correct that no federal constitutional right is implicated when a judge merely grants relief to a litigant in accordance with the law he is sworn to uphold and follow. This Court concludes that Plaintiffs cannot establish a substantial likelihood of success on the merits of Count I.

B. COUNT II—VIOLATION OF FOURTEENTH AMENDMENT PROCEDURAL DUE PROCESS RIGHTS

... Balancing the three factors [Editors' note: referring to the *Mathews* balancing test—*Mathews v. Eldridge*, 424 U.S. 319 (1976)—discussed previously by the judge], this court concludes that Theresa Schiavo's life and liberty interests were adequately protected by the extensive process provided in the state courts. Defendant Michael Schiavo and Plaintiffs, assisted by counsel, thoroughly advocated their competing perspectives on Theresa Schiavo's wishes. Another lawyer appointed by the court could not have offered more protection of Theresa Schiavo's interests. Accordingly, Plaintiffs have not established a substantial likelihood of success on the merits on Count II.

... This court appreciates the gravity of the consequences of denying injunctive relief. Even under these difficult and time strained circumstances, however, and notwithstanding Congress' expressed interest in the welfare of Theresa Schiavo, this court is constrained to apply the law to the issues before it. As Plaintiffs have not established a substantial likelihood of success on the merits, Plaintiffs' Motion for Temporary Restraining Order (Dkt, 2) must be **DENIED**.

DONE AND ORDERED in chambers this 22nd day of March, 2005.

(signed) James D. Whittemore
United States District Judge

NOTES

1. Pub. L. No. 109-3 (March 21, 2005).
2. The Act does not address the traditional requirements for temporary injunctive relief. Accordingly, these standards control whether temporary injunctive relief is warranted, notwithstanding Congress' intent that the federal courts examine *de novo* the merits of Theresa Schiavo's claimed constitutional deprivations.

IN THE UNITED STATES COURT OF APPEALS FOR THE ELEVENTH CIRCUIT

No. 05-11628
D.C. Docket No. 05-00530-CY-T-2

THERESA MARIE SCHINDLER SCHIAVO,
incapacitated ex rel, Robert Schindler and
Mary Schindler, her parents and next friends,
Plaintiff-Appellant,

versus

MICHAEL SCHIAVO,
as guardian of the person of
Theresa Marie Schindler Schiavo, incapacitated,
JUDGE GEORGE W. GREER,
THE HOSPICE OF THE FLORIDA SUNCOAST, INC.,
Defendants-Appellees.

Appeal from the United States District Court

for the Middle District of Florida

ON PETITION FOR EXPEDITED REHEARING EN BANC

(Opinion March 25, 2005)

Before EDMONDSON, Chief Judge, TJOFLAT, ANDERSON, BIRCH, DUBINA, BLACK, CARNES, BARKETT, HULL, MARCUS, WILSON, and PRYOR, * Circuit Judges.

From J. L. Edmondson, *Theresa Marie Schindler Schiavo, incapacitated ex rel, Robert Schindler and Mary Schindler, her parents and next friends, Plaintiff-Appellant, versus Michael Schiavo, as guardian of the person of Theresa Marie Schindler Schiavo, incapacitated, Judge George W. Greer, The Hospice of The Florida Suncoast, Inc., Defendants-Appellees.* Appeal from the United States District Court for the Middle District of Florida on Petition for Expedited Rehearing En Banc. Decided March 25, 2005.

*Judge William H. Pryor Jr. did not participate in the consideration of the Petition because he is recovering from surgery.

157

ORDER:

The Court having been polled at the request of one of the members of the Court and a majority of the Circuit Judges who are in regular active service not having voted in favor of it (Rule 35, Federal Rules of Appellate Procedure; Eleventh Circuit Rule 35-5), the Emergency Petition for Rehearing En Banc is **DENIED**.

/s J. L. EDMONDSON
CHIEF JUDGE

The Time Has Come to Let Terri Schiavo Die

Politicians, Courts Must Allow Husband to Make Final Decision

Arthur L. Caplan

We have now reached the endgame in the case of Terri Schiavo. Her husband, Michael, remains unwavering in his view that she would not want to live in the state she is in. Despite the fact that he has been made the target of an incredible organized campaign of vilification, slander, and just plain nastiness, he remains unmoved. Even a pathetic effort to bribe him into changing his mind with the offer of $1 million did not budge him. He says he loves his wife and will do whatever it takes to end an existence that he believes she would not want to endure. He thinks that she would want her feeding tube stopped and that she would wish to die rather than remain bed-bound in a nursing home in a permanent vegetative state for the rest of her days.

The Schindler parents and their other children remain equally convinced that Michael is wrong. They say that Terri would want to live, that she is not as brain-damaged as Michael contends, and that there is still hope for her recovery despite the fact that she has failed to show any real improvement in sixteen years. They argue that there are still more treatments to be tried and that as a Catholic Terri would want to honor recent papal teachings that feeding tubes should not be removed from those in permanent vegetative states.

From MSNBC.com, March 18, 2005, http://www.msnbc.msn.com/id/7231440 (accessed November 21, 2005). Copyright © 2005 Arthur L. Caplan. Reprinted by permission.

159

WHO'S RIGHT AND WHO'S WRONG?

Congress, or at least the pro-life constituency in the House and Senate, is doing its best to halt Schiavo's death. Last-minute bills invoking habeas corpus, a legal doctrine that has historically only been used for those held in federal custody, along with incredibly zany and inappropriate subpoenas to doctors and nurses requiring that Terri Schiavo be brought to Washington, show a level of grandstanding that is normally reserved for issues such as the use of steroids by major-league baseball players. So now that this miserable case is moving toward a resolution, what can be said about who is right and who is wrong? And what is the likely legacy of the battle over the fate of Terri Schiavo? Ever since the New Jersey Supreme Court allowed a respirator to be removed from Karen Ann Quinlan and the U.S. Supreme Court declared that feeding tubes are medical treatments just like respirators, heart-lung machines, dialysis, and antibiotics, it has been crystal clear in U.S. law and medical ethics that those who cannot speak can have their feeding tubes stopped. The authority to make that decision has fallen to those closest to the person who cannot make their own views known. First come husbands or wives, then adult children, then parents and other relatives. That is why Michael Schiavo, despite all the hatred that is now directed against him, has the right to decide his wife's fate. The decision about Terri's life does not belong to the U.S. Congress, President Bush, Representative Tom Delay of Texas, Florida Governor Jeb Bush, the Florida legislature, clerics in Rome, self-proclaimed disability activists, Operation Rescue founder Randall Terry, conservative commentators, bioethicists, or Terri's parents. The decision is Michael's and Michael's alone.

SANCTITY OF MARRIAGE

Remember the recent debate about gay marriage and the sanctity of the bond between husband and wife? Nearly all of those now trying to push their views forward about what should be done with Terri Schiavo told us that marriage is a sacred trust between a man and a woman. Well, if that is what marriage means then it is very clear who should be making the medical decisions for Terri—her husband. But, isn't it true that tough questions have been raised about whether he has her best interests at heart? They have. But, these charges against Michael Schiavo have been heard in court again and again and again. And no court has found them persuasive. Has there really been careful review of this case? Is Terri really unable to think or feel or sense? Will she never recover? The flurry of activity in Washington and Tallahassee might make you think there has not. But that is not so.

There have been at least eleven applications to the Florida Court of Appeal in this case resulting in four published decisions; four applications to the Florida Supreme Court with one published decision (*Bush v. Schiavo*); three lawsuits in federal district court; three applications to the U.S. Supreme Court, and nearly untold motions in the trial court. This has got to be the most extensively litigated "right-to-die" case in U.S. history. No one looking at what has gone on in the courts in this case could possibly deny that all parties have had ample opportunity for objective and independent review by earnest and prudent judges of the facts and trial court orders.

THE TIME HAS COME

So, it is clear that the time has come to let Terri die. Not because everyone who is brain damaged should be allowed to die. Not because her quality of life is too poor for anyone to think it meaningful to go on. Not even because she costs a lot of money to continue to care for. Simply because her husband who loves her and has stuck by her for more than fifteen years says she would not want to live the way she is living. If Terri is allowed to starve to death what next? Undoubtedly there will be efforts to pass laws to prohibit feeding tubes from being taken away from others like Terri in the future. And there may even be efforts made to push right-to-die cases out of state courts and into federal courts. These are bad ideas. We have had a consensus in this country that you have a right to refuse any and all medical care that you might not want.

Christian Scientists do not have to accept medical care nor do Jehovah's Witnesses need to accept blood transfusions or fundamentalist Protestants who would rather pray than get chemotherapy. Those who are disabled and cannot communicate have the exact same rights. Their closest family members have the power to speak for them. The state courts of this country have the power to review termination of treatment cases and have done so with compassion, skill, and wisdom for many years. Those who would change a system that has worked—and worked well for the millions of Americans who face the most difficult of medical decisions—should think very hard about whether Senator Bill Frist, Congressman De Lay, Senator Hillary Clinton, Governor Bush and President Bush, Senator John Kerry, or the governor of your state needs to be consulted before you and your doctor can decide that it is time to stop life-prolonging medical care.

tent vegetative state (PVS), I would like to disclose that I came into this case with the belief that it can be ethically permissible to discontinue artificially provided nutrition and hydration for persons in a permanent vegetative state. Having now reviewed the relevant facts, having met and observed Ms. Schiavo in person, and having reflected deeply on the moral and ethical issues, I would like to explain why I have changed my mind in regard to this particular case.

In my daily conversation with colleagues, I have been interested to hear what others have thought about the issues surrounding this case. I have heard from neurologists, other physicians, nurses, other paramedical professionals, attorneys, ethicists, clergy, geriatricians, teachers, the elderly, and the young. I have heard from people of many faiths, Roman Catholic, Protestant, Jewish, and people without a particular faith commitment. Generally, I have found that many people who have thought seriously about this case say that they have been unable to reach a judgment. They acknowledge valid principles on both sides of the arguments, and they recognize the difficulty of ascertaining from the media accurate and complete facts needed to reach a trustworthy conclusion. All agree that this is an extraordinarily difficult case and that the family members on both sides must be suffering greatly.

There is, at the heart of this case, uncertainty regarding the neurological diagnosis on which treatment decisions have rested. The courts have ruled, on the basis of credible expert testimony, that Terri is permanently in a persistent vegetative state (PVS), which is a specific neurologic diagnosis meaning wakefulness without awareness. Patients in a PVS lack integrated function of the cerebral cortex while retaining involuntary brain stem reflexes that regulate heart rate, digestive, circulatory, sleep, and other involuntary bodily functions. Their behaviors are automatic, nonpurposeful, uninhibited reflexes no longer under voluntary control by higher brain centers.

On the other hand, there have been repeated claims that Terri at times seems more responsive, even intentional and interactive. Such observations, if true, would be inconsistent with a diagnosis of PVS, the diagnosis upon which medical and legal decisions have been based. The question thus arises, whether Terri might be in what neurologists call a "minimally conscious state." This question is important, for in making decisions that affect the life and welfare of Terri, one would like to know whether she is aware of her environment, aware of others, aware of her own bodily discomfort, or has thoughts that we would regard as human even if she cannot communicate them to us. As my charge is to investigate the possibility of abuse or neglects, it matters whether Terri would be able to recognize and feel the consequences of abuse or neglect. Some actions might even be unintentionally neglectful if performed by persons unaware of Terri's level of awareness.

There are many behaviors typical for patients in PVS that someone without neurological training could easily mistake as voluntary. The nonneurologist seldom has experience in observing how the brain stem and basal ganglia behave when deprived of input from the cerebral cortex where consciousness is believed to reside. It is quite common for dedicated and caring family members, hoping desperately for a sign from their loved one, to misinterpret these reflexes as evidence of communication. Such behaviors can include involuntary arousal, eye opening, random eye movements (nystagmus and horizontal scanning), brief eye contact, reflexive withdrawal from a noxious stimulant, movement of the lips or mouth or turning of the head in response to oral stimulation (suck and rooting reflexes which also occur in newborn infants), spontaneous grimacing or smiling or displays of emotion (affective release, usually a momentary gesture), and certain other nonsustained behaviors usually not seen in healthy adults. Some of the video clips of Terri Schiavo that have been presented in the media display such involuntary behaviors. It is the responsibility of neurologists in cases like this to educate family members so that they will not develop a false hope of recovery.

Where is the neurologist in this case at this time? It is my understanding that nearly three years have passed since Terri has had the benefit of neurological consultation. How, then, are we to be certain about her current neurologic status? There remain, in fact, huge uncertainties in regard to Terri's true neurologic status. Although exploring such questions may be uncomfortable, I believe that medicine has an obligation to ascertain the neurological facts to the highest possible degree of certainty.

Some studies have indicated, upon follow-up over time, a high rate of false initial diagnosis of PVS.[1] Furthermore, the diagnosis of minimally conscious state had not yet become standard parlance in the field of neurology at the time of Terri's initial diagnosis. The minimally conscious state has emerged as a distinct diagnosis entity only within the last few years.[2]

Although Terri has undergone structural imaging studies of her brain (such as the CT scan which I have reviewed), she has not, to my knowledge, undergone functional imaging studies, such as positron emission tomography (PET) or functional magnetic resonance imaging (fMRI). The structural studies have shown substantial loss of cerebral cortex which was deprived of blood supply for more than forty minutes in 1990, but there does remain some cerebral cortex.

New facts have come to light in the last few years that should be weighed in the neurologic assessment of Terri Schiavo. Significant strides have been made in the scientific understanding of PVS and minimally conscious states since Terri last underwent neurological evaluation. As usually happens in science, the newest evidence is prompting the medical community to think about this field in new ways. With new evidence comes fresh appreciation for what is actually happening in the brains of persons with profound cognitive impairment. And there is a great deal more to be learned.

Of particular interest was the fMRI study published just year by Schiff and colleagues of two patients at Cornell University. When these patients, who had been diagnosed as being in a minimally conscious state, listened to narratives read by a family person, large areas of cerebral cortex normally involved in language recognition and processing lit up. The presence of metabolic activity in those brain cells was far more than expected given their inability to follow simple instructions reliably or otherwise demonstrate at the bedside evidence of comprehension or communication.[3] From this study one may conclude that there is still a great deal we do not know about what previously unsuspected cerebral cortex functions may yet be occurring in the minds of persons who have sustained profound brain damage and are no longer able to communicate outwardly what their thoughts may be.

Based on my review of extensive medical records documenting Terri's care over the years, on my personal observations of Terri, and on my observations of Terri's responses in the many hours of videotapes taken in 2002, she demonstrates a number of behaviors that I believe cast reasonable doubt on the prior diagnosis of PVS. These include:

1. Her behavior is frequently context-specific. For example, her facial expression brightens and she smiles in response to the voice of familiar persons such as her parents or her nurse. Her agitation subsides and her facial demeanor softens when quiet music is played. When jubilant piano music is played, her face brightens, she lifts her eyebrows, smiles, and even laughs. Her lateral gaze toward the tape player is sustained for many minutes. Several times I witnessed Terri briefly, albeit inconsistently, laugh in response to a humorous comment someone in the room had made. I did not see her laugh in the absence of someone else's laughter.

2. Although she does not seem to track or follow visual object consistently or for long periods of time, she does fixate her gaze on colorful objects or human faces for some fifteen seconds at a time and occasionally follows with her eyes at least briefly as these objects move from side to side. When I

first walked into her room, she immediately turned her head toward me and looked directly at my face. There was a look of curiosity or expectation in her expression, and she maintained eye contact for about half a minute. Later, when she again looked at me, she brought her lips together as if to pronounce the letter "O," and although for a moment it appeared that she might be making an intentional effort to speak, her face then fell blank, and no words came out.

3. Although I did not hear Terri utter distinct words, she demonstrates emotional expressivity by her use of single syllable vocalizations such as "ah," making cooing sounds, or by expressing guttural sounds of annoyance or moaning appropriate to the context of the situation. The context-specific range and variability of her vocalizations suggest at least a reasonable probability of the processing of emotional thought within her brain. There have been reports of Terri rarely using actual words specific to her situational context. The July 25, 2003, affidavit of speech pathologist Sara Green Mole, MS, on page 6, reads, "The records of Mediplex reflect the fact that she has said 'stop' in apparent response to a medical procedure being done to her." The Adult Protective Services team has been unable to retrieve those original medical records in this instance.

4. Although Terri has not consistently followed commands, there appear to be some notable exceptions. In the taped examination by Dr. Hammesfahr from 2002, when asked to close her eyes she began to blink repeatedly. Although it was unclear whether she squeezed her grip when asked, she did appear to raise her right leg four times in succession each time she was asked to do so. Rehabilitation notes from 1991 indicate that she tracked inconsistently, and although did not develop a yes/no communication system, did follow some commands inconsistently and demonstrated good eye contact to family members.

5. There is a remarkable moment in the videotape of the September 3, 2002, examination by Dr. Hammesfahr that seemed to go unnoticed at the time. At 2:44 PM, Dr. Hammesfahr had just turned Terri onto her right side to examine her back with a painful sharp stimulus (a sharp piece of wood), to which Terri had responded with signs of discomfort. Well after he ceased applying the stimulus and had returned Terri to a comfortable position, he says to her parents, "So we're going to have to roll her over . . ." Immediately Terri cries. She vocalizes a crying sound, "Ugh, ha, ha, ha," presses her eyebrows together, and sadly grimaces. It is important to note that, at that moment, no one is touching Terri or causing actual pain. Rather, she appears to comprehend the meaning of Dr. Hammesfahr's comment and signals her *anticipation*

of pain. This response suggests some degree of language processing and inter-pretation at the level of the cerebral cortex. It also suggests that she may be aware of pain beyond what could be explained by simple reflex withdrawal.

6. According to the definition of PVS published by the American Academy of Neurology, "persistent vegetative state patients do not have the capacity to experience pain or suffering. Pain and suffering are attributes of consciousness requiring cerebral cortical functioning, and patients who are permanently and completely unconscious cannot experience these symptoms."[4] And yet, in my review of Terri's medical records, pain issues keep surfacing. The nurses at Woodside Hospice told us that she often has pain with menstrual cramps. Men-strual flow is associated with agitation, repeated or sustained moaning, facial grimacing, limb posturing, and facial flushing, all of which subside once she is given ibuprofen. Some of the records document moaning, crying, and other painful behavior in the setting of urinary tract infections.

The neurologic literature has traditionally distinguished between, on one hand, the pattered reflex responses resulting from mere activation of spinal and brain stem pain circuits in PVS and, on the other hand, conscious aware-ness of pain which requires participation by the cerebral cortex, including interpretation, felt emotional awareness, and volitional avoidance behavior that would not be expected to occur in PVS. Recent studies suggest, how-ever, that such a distinction may not be the clear bright line previously imag-ined. Laureys and colleagues demonstrated, for example, neuronal pro-cessing activity in the primary somatosensory area of the cerebral cortex in response to noxious stimuli in patients with PVS.[5]

Regardless of what objective measures may be available, the conscious experience of pain remains a phenomenon directly discernable only through introspective awareness, which means that one cannot directly know with certainty the pain another person experiences. If, as the authors of the con-sensus statement on PVS wrote in 1994, there are some cases in which "the absence of a response cannot be taken as proof of the absence of conscious-ness"[6] then should not the clear presence of pain be given serious consider-ation as possibly indicating conscious awareness in Terri Schiavo? The fact that Terri's responses to pain have been context-specific, sustained, and, in the taped example I cited, in response to a spoken sentence, all suggest the possibility that she may be at some level consciously aware of pain.

Terri has received analgesic medication as treatment for her pain behavior. This seems to be appropriate medical treatment if one cannot know with cer-tainty whether her behavior indicates conscious awareness of pain. If a patient behaves as if in pain, then the clinically prudent and compassionate response, when in doubt, is to treat pain. If a patient behaves at times as though there may be some remnant of conscious awareness, then the clinically prudent and compassionate response, when in doubt, is to treat that patient with respect and care. If Terri is consciously aware of pain, and therefore is capable of suffering, then her diagnosis of PVS may be tragically mistaken.

7. To enter the room of Terri Schiavo is nothing like entering the room of a patient who is comatose or brain-dead or in some neurological sense no longer there. Although Terri did not demonstrate during our ninety-minute visit compelling evidence of verbalization, conscious awareness, or volitional behavior, yet the visitor has the distinct sense of the presence of a living human being who seems at some level to be aware of some things around her.

As I looked at Terri, and she gazed directly back at me, I asked myself whether, if I were her attending physician, I could in good conscience withdraw her feeding and hydration. No, I could not. I could not withdraw life support if I were asked. I could not withhold life-sustaining nutrition and hydration from this beautiful lady whose face brightens in the presence of others.

The neurological signs are in many ways ambiguous. There is no guarantee that more sophisticated testing would definitely resolve that ambiguity to everyone's satisfaction. There would be value, I think, in obtaining a functional fMRI scan if that is possible.

This situation differs fundamentally from end-of-life scenarios where it is appropriate to withdraw life-sustaining medical interventions that no longer benefit or are burdensome to patient in the terminal stages of illness. Terri's feeding tube is not a burden to her. It is not painful, it is not infected, is not eroding her stomach lining or causing any medical complications. But for the decision to withdraw her feeding tube, Terri cannot be considered medically terminal. But for the withdrawal of food and water, she would not die.

In summary, Terri Schiavo demonstrates behaviors in a variety of cognitive domains that call into question the previous neurologic diagnosis of persistent vegetative state. Specifically, she has demonstrated behaviors that are context-specific, sustained, and indicative of cerebral cortical processing that, upon careful neurologic consideration, would not be expected in a persistent vegetative state.

Based on this evidence, I believe that, within a reasonable degree of medical certainty, there is a greater likelihood that Terri is in a minimally conscious state than a persistent vegetative state. This distinction makes an enormous difference in making ethical decisions on Terri's behalf. If Terri is sufficiently aware of her surroundings that she can feel pleasure and suffer, if she is capable of understanding to some degree how she is being treated, then in my judgment it would be wrong to bring about her death by withdrawing food and water.

At the time of this writing, Terri Schiavo, as the result of decisions based on what I have argued to be a faulty diagnosis of persistent vegetative state, has been without food or water for five days. She is thus at risk of death or serious injury unless the provision of food and water can be restored. Terri Schiavo lacks the capacity to consent to emergency protective services and must trust others to act on her behalf. If she were to be transferred to another facility, it would be medically necessary first to initiate hydration and ensure that her serum electrolytes are within normal values.

How medicine and society choose to think about Terri Schiavo will influence what kind of people we will be as we evaluate and respond to the needs of the most vulnerable people among us. When serious doubts exist as to whether a cognitively impaired person is or is not consciously aware, even if these doubts cannot be conclusively resolved, it is better to err on the side of protecting the vulnerable life.

Respectfully submitted,
William Polk Cheshire Jr., MD, MA, FAAN
Sworn to (or affirmed) and subscribed before me this 23 day of March, 2005
by William Polk Cheshire Jr., MD

NOTES

1. Andrews K, Murphy L, Munday R, et Al. Misdiagnosis of the Vegetative State: Retrospective Study in a Rehabilitation Unit. *British Medical Journal.* 1996;313:13–16.

Childs NL, Mercer WN, Childs HW. Accuracy of Diagnosis of Persistent Vegetative State. *Neurology.* 1993;43: 1465–1467.

2. Giancino JT, Ashwal S, Childs N, Cranford R, Jenner B, Katz DJ, Kelley JP, Rosenberg JH, Whyte J, Zafonte RD, Zasler ND. The Minimally Conscious State: Definition and Diagnosis Criteria. *Neurology.* 2002;38:349–353.

Laureys S, Owen AM, Schiff ND, Brain Function in Coma, Vegetative State and Relaxed Disorders. *Lancet Neurology.* 2004;3:537–546.

3. Schiff ND, Rodriguez-Moreno D, Kamal A, Kino KHS, Giancino JT, Flam F, Hirsch J. fMRI Reveals Large-scale Network Activation in Minimally Conscious Patients. *Neurology.* 2004;64:514–523.

4. http://www.aan.com/about/ethics/109556.pdf.

5. Laureys S, Faymonville MB, Peigneux P, Damas P, Lambermont B, Del Flore G, Degueldre C, Aerts J, Luxen A, Franck G, Larry M, Moonen G, Maques F. Cortical Processing of Noxious Somatosensory Stimuli in the Persistent Vegetative State. *Neuroimage*. 2002;17:732–741.

6. Multi-Society Task Force on PVS. Medical Aspects of the Persistent Vegetative State—A Second of Two Parts. *New England Journal of Medicine*. 1994;330:157–159.

ORDER IN PENDING CASE 04A825 SCHIAVO, EX REL. SCHINDLER V. SCHIAVO, MICHAEL, ET AL.

(ORDER LIST: 544 U.S.)
THURSDAY, MARCH 24, 2005

The application for stay of enforcement of judgment pending the filing and disposition of a petition for writ of certiorari presented to Justice Kennedy and by him referred to the Court is denied.

From U.S. Supreme Court, Order in Pending Case 04A825 *Schiavo, ex rel. Schindler v. Schiavo, Michael, et al.*, Thursday, March 24, 2005.

Attorney Shares Experience, Pain, in Michael Schiavo's Defense

Jon B. Eisenberg

I joined Michael Schiavo's legal team last month, after having represented a group of bioethicists who had previously supported him in a "friend of the court" brief, because I understand his painful task more than most. End-of-life surrogate decision making is not easy. I know from personal experience.

Eight years ago, my beloved cousin Ros suffered a devastating stroke that left her with what the doctors called "global aphasia." As one of them put it, "Nothing is getting through to her, and nothing can come out." I spent days at her bedside trying to communicate. I held her hand and asked her to squeeze it. Nothing. I told her to blink if she could hear me. Nothing. I kissed her cheek. Nothing.

Yet she was not in a coma. Her eyes were often open, and sometimes they tracked me as I crossed the room. Once I handed her my favorite photograph of her, standing in a grove of trees in Yosemite Valley, whimsically raising her arms upwards toward the sky. She took it, seemed to look at it uncomprehendingly, and then dropped it and went blank again.

Was she in a persistent vegetative state? None of the doctors ever said.

Was she in a minimally conscious state? That diagnosis did not yet even exist. Could she improve? This the doctors could tell me: no. There was nothing they could do.

Except for one thing: They could keep her alive with a feeding tube inserted through her nose into her stomach. The problem, however, was that she kept pulling the tube out. She did it three times, and each time the doctors reinserted it.

From the *San Francisco Daily Journal*, April 5, 2005. Reprinted by permission of the author.

Ros had previously made a will and named me her executor. She had given me legal power of attorney over her financial affairs should she become unable to handle them, and she had executed an advance written directive for healthcare decisions, making me her surrogate decision-maker. I had power over her life and death.

When Ros gave me the advance directive, I didn't think much about it. But I knew what she wanted.

Ros had told my wife and me for years, over many dinner conversations, especially in the wake of the Karen Ann Quinlan and Nancy Cruzan right-to-die cases, that she would never want to be kept alive artificially if she became unable to communicate. Her comments never got any more specific than that. She never said the words "persistent vegetative state," a phrase most Americans never heard until a few weeks ago. But I knew what she meant. I knew her values, I knew the life she had lived, and I knew the life she did not want to live. And I, as her closest relative at that point, knew these things better than anyone else.

So, when the time came to exercise the awesome power Ros had given me, I knew what I had to do. I had to tell the doctors not to reinsert the feeding tube for a fourth time. We had to let her go.

This was not a simple thing to accomplish. The hospital first insisted on convening a meeting of its ethics committee, where I was called on to make the case for ending Ros's life. I had her advance written directive, but it was a simple form, saying nothing about her specific wishes. I had to tell the committee members what Ros had previously said to me. My wife and two friends of Ros told similar stories. Then, after some debate, the doctors, bioethicists, and clergy at the meeting agreed that the feeding tube should not be reinserted, convinced that would have been Ros's wish.

The doctors told me it would take a week or two for Ros to die, of what they call "terminal dehydration." I feared she would suffer. They assured me that she was not cognitive enough to suffer. They told me of medical studies showing that terminal dehydration under such circumstances is not painful and that any possible discomfort can be effectively treated by moistening the patient's mouth and skin, and by administering morphine if necessary.

I was skeptical. I resolved to watch Ros closely to make sure, as best I could, that she wasn't suffering as she slowly died. But I never saw any signs of suffering.

She died on the ninth day. It was a quiet death. Not pretty, but quiet.

I would even say peaceful.

But did that really matter? What I knew for sure was that Ros would have wanted to die this way. I knew this in my heart, as her closest relative. Even if painful, she would have preferred such a death over an artificially sustained life that she would have abhorred.

So I know what Michael Schiavo has gone through. He did what I had to do, but under far more painful circumstances, under intense public scrutiny, suffering accusations of murder and abuse and enduring the meddling of politicians who knew nothing of his and his wife's lives and values.

Was Terri Schiavo in a "persistent vegetative state" or a "minimally conscious state"? Most doctors said the former, a few said the latter.

Would she have wanted her life sustained? Some of her family and friends said no; others said yes. But the person closest to her—her husband—said no.

When families disagree amongst themselves about end-of-life decisions, someone has to resolve the dispute. Our American legal system calls on judges, not politicians, to do so. The judge in this case decided that Terri Schiavo was in a persistent vegetative state and would not have wanted her life to be artificially sustained under such circumstances.

Dozens of appellate judges, all the way up to the United States Supreme Court, upheld that decision.

This is the legal system we live by, and die by. Judges, not politicians, resolve these agonizing disputes. Congress and Florida governor Jeb Bush stepped way over the constitutional line in trying to do so.

In the end, we have all suffered: Michael Schiavo, the Schindler family, the millions of Americans who were riveted to the drama of the past few weeks, and the American legal system itself.

But surely none have suffered more than Michael Schiavo in simply carrying out his wife's wishes, vastly more than I suffered in making the decision, on behalf of Ros, to end her life as I knew she would have wished. That is why I joined Michael Schiavo's legal team during the last weeks of Terri Schiavo's life.

Part 4

Catholic Controversies

INTRODUCTION

Terri Schiavo's parents are practicing Catholics and they claim that Terri herself actively professed her Catholic faith. Governor Jeb Bush is also Catholic. Both the Schiavos and Governor Bush argued that because Terri was Catholic, she couldn't and wouldn't have wanted her feeding tube removed. The intent of part 4 is to show that this picture of Catholic teaching is not as clear as the governor or Terri's parents would have it; in fact, many traditional Catholic moral theologians and some bishops have argued that providing artificially delivered nutrition and hydration to persons in a persistent vegetative state (PVS) is often disproportionate because it prevents a lethal pathology (the inability to swallow) from achieving its end (natural death), and therefore is ethically optional. But to be fair to Terri's parents and the governor, this section also presents the view of those Catholic moralists who have argued that discontinuing the artificial delivery of feeding and fluids to those in a PVS is the moral equivalent of euthanasia by omission because the motive behind such discontinuation is intentionally to cause the death of the person who is in the PVS.

We start with a very influential article written some years ago by William E. May et al. which very forcefully argues that it is wrong to discontinue artificially delivered feeding and fluids in situations comparable to the Schiavo case. May and his coauthors are rightly concerned about the "devaluation" of persons which often occurs in contemporary society, and how this devalua-

177

tion can easily lead to a casual acceptance of euthanasia. They are troubled by the traditional burden/benefit analysis in refusing healthcare interventions and point out that "medical" burdens can easily, and wrongly in their opinion, be translated into the "burden" of continued living for which euthanasia is the answer. They cite the Christian obligation of "feeding the hungry" to show that persons who are severely debilitated but not dying must be fed, by tubes if necessary. They do allow some possibility of cessation "*if it is really useless or excessively burdensome* to provide someone with nutrition and hydration," but they see this as the exception, not as the rule. They consider many elements that the Catholic tradition has accepted as constituting burdensomeness, such as expense or psychological aversion or even pain, but they dismiss these as generally incommensurable with the value of prolonging biological life. They conclude that it is almost always morally obligatory to provide artificially delivered nutrition and hydration to those who are debilitated (including those in a PVS) but not imminently dying.

The next two articles are from two Bishops' Conferences (a semi-official grouping of bishops in each state), one from Texas and one from Pennsylvania. The Texas bishops agree with the general theological analysis of May et al., but when they apply the teaching to those in a PVS they state the following: "Patients, competently diagnosed to be in a persistent vegetative state or in an irreversible coma, remain human persons. Nonetheless, those individuals are stricken with a lethal pathology which, without artificial nutrition and hydration, will lead to death." Because they believe this to be the case, the Texas bishops hold that it is ethically acceptable in the Catholic tradition to let the fatal pathology, the inability to swallow, run its course; thus they accept that withdrawing artificially delivered food and fluids may be an ethically acceptable allowing to die, not an ethically objectionable intention to kill. The Pennsylvania Bishops Conference statement is a carefully crafted document intended to give Catholics guidance in preparing advance directives. However, when it comes to the issue of providing artificially delivered nutrition and hydration to those who are debilitated mentally and cannot swallow, the bishops follow the lead of May et al. and conclude that "in almost every instance there is an obligation to continue supplying nutrition and hydration to the unconscious patient."

The next two articles by Catholic moral theologians attempt to clarify the debate. O'Rourke's article focuses on three positions relative to the cessation of artificially delivered nutrition and hydration and discusses each approach carefully. He clearly favors the third position, which is that "continuing life support for people with a PVS diagnosis does not offer 'hope of benefit' for the patient" because "healthcare seeks to enable people to strive for the purpose of life, not merely to function at the biological level," and "ultimately, the purpose in life is friendship with God," which those in a persistent vegetative state cannot experience this side of the grave. It should be pointed out that O'Rourke is one of two coauthors (with Benedict Ashley) of *Health Care Ethics: A Theological Analysis*, which has gone through several revisions and editions, and which is one of the most widely used textbooks on bioethics in American Catholic seminaries today. McCartney's piece summarizes traditional Catholic teaching regarding reverence for life and end-of-life ethics, and then applies this teaching to those who are in a persistent vegetative state. His approach is clearly that of the third position described by O'Rourke.

The next three articles focus on the address given by the late Pope John Paul II to the participants in the International Congress on "Life-Sustaining Treatments and Vegetative State: Scientific Advances and Ethical Dilemmas." Here the pope embraces the position of May et al. and argues that the provision of nutrition and hydration is ethically mandatory if it is prolonging life and providing comfort. The address is followed by two articles of Catholic moralists who question the relation of this address to official church teaching regarding the end of life. They also question some of the medical and other healthcare claims made in the address.

The final article is highly polemical and applies the arguments of May et al. specifically to the Schiavo case. It is representative of the vigorous and vocal extreme pro-(biological)life positions taken by many conservative Catholics over the last year. But it is still questionable as to whether this is the official position of the church on this issue. We invite readers to make up their own minds after having considered both sides of the debate.

Feeding and Hydrating the Permanently Unconscious and Other Vulnerable Persons

William E. May, Robert Barry, OP, Msgr. Orville Griese, Germain Grisez, Brian Johnstone, CSsR, Thomas J. Marzen, JD, Bishop James T. McHugh, SJD, Gilbert Meilaender, PhD, Mark Siegler, MD, and Msgr. William Smith

Recent court cases (such as those involving Claire Conroy, Paul Brophy, and Nancy Ellen Jobes) have called attention to the moral and legal questions concerning the provision by tube of food and fluids to the permanently unconscious (e.g., those diagnosed as being in a "persistent vegetative state") and other seriously debilitated but nondying persons. Is it ever morally right to withhold or withdraw such nutrition and hydration? If so, on what grounds? And what should be the role of law?

Before answering these questions, we think it necessary to state several crucially important presuppositions and principles relevant to the subject and also to reject a rationale offered by some ethicists—and apparently accepted by most courts—for withholding or withdrawing food and fluids provided by tubes from the permanently unconscious and other seriously debilitated but nondying persons.

PRESUPPOSITIONS AND PRINCIPLES

1. Human bodily life is a great good. Such life is personal, not subpersonal. It is a good *of* the person, not merely *for* the person. Such life is inherently good, not merely instrumental to other goods.

The original article appeared in William E. May et al., *Feeding and Hydrating the Permanently Unconscious and Other Vulnerable Persons*, 3 ISSUES IN LAW AND MEDICINE 203 (1987). Reprinted with permission. Copyright © 1987 by the National Legal Center for the Medically Dependent & Disabled, Inc.

2. It is never morally right to deliberately kill innocent human beings—that is, to adopt by choice and carry out a proposal to end their lives. (We here set aside questions about killing those who are not "innocent," i.e., those convicted of capital crimes, engaged in unjust military actions, or otherwise unjustly attacking others.)

3. It is possible to kill innocent persons by acts of omission as well as by acts of commission. Whenever the failure to provide adequate food and fluids carries out a proposal, adopted by choice, to end life, the omission of nutrition and hydration is an act of killing by omission.

4. The deliberate killing of the innocent, even if motivated by an anguished or merciful wish to terminate painful and burdened life—deliberate killing that will henceforth be called "euthanasia"— is not morally justified by that motive.

5. Like other killing of the innocent, euthanasia can be carried out by acts of omission ("passive euthanasia") as well as by acts of commission ("active euthanasia"). The distinction makes no moral difference.

6. Euthanasia can be voluntary (of a person who gives informed consent to being killed), nonvoluntary (of a person incapable of giving informed consent), or involuntary (of a person capable of giving informed consent who does not give it).

7. Morally, for a person who consents to be killed, voluntary euthanasia is a method of suicide. Nonvoluntary and involuntary euthanasia violate not only the dignity of innocent human life but also the right of the person who is killed not to be killed. The law of homicide should continue to apply to all forms and methods of euthanasia; none should be legalized. The law of homicide, in particular, must protect innocent human beings from being killed for reasons of mercy.

8. While competent persons have the moral and legal right to refuse any useless or excessively burdensome treatment, they must exercise great care in reaching the judgment that a treatment is useless or excessively burdensome. This is necessary both in order to avoid any intention to end life on the grounds that it is devoid of intrinsic worth and in order to fulfill properly the responsibility to respect human life.

9. Likewise, those who have the moral duty to make decisions for non-competent persons (such as infants or the permanently unconscious) have a moral right to refuse any useless or excessively burdensome treatment for them. This right must, however, be exercised with great care in order to avoid the temptation, unfortunately not uncommon in our society, to devalue

the lives of the noncompetent or to regard such persons chiefly in terms of the utilitarian values they may represent. Too often, unfortunately, the judgment that a treatment is useless or excessively burdensome does not reflect serious consideration of the objectively discernible features of the treatment, but is an expression of attitudes toward the life being treated. Moreover, a sound public policy to protect the rights and interests of noncompetent persons and to promote the common good may require regulation by law of the scope of treatment decisions made by families and other proxies *(cf.* the federal "Child Abuse Amendments of 1984").

10. Human life can be burdened in many ways. But no matter how burdened it may be, human life remains inherently a good of the person. Thus, remaining alive is never rightly regarded as a burden, and deliberately killing innocent human life is never rightly regarded as rendering a benefit.

CONTEMPORARY THREATS TO THE DIGNITY OF INNOCENT HUMAN LIFE

Some today morally approve and seek the legalization of euthanasia, both active and passive, voluntary and nonvoluntary. (At present, public advocacy of involuntary euthanasia is rare.)

One argument for euthanasia is based on the claim that competent persons have a right to be killed mercifully—a "right to die" when they think that they would be better off dead than alive. Another argument for euthanasia is based on the claim that competent persons can refuse all treatment and may choose to do so precisely in order to end their own lives. Assuming or claiming that it is justifiable to refuse treatment on this basis, some proponents of euthanasia argue that ending life with another's help through "active" euthanasia often would be quicker and easier than choosing death through "passive" euthanasia.

Some proponents of euthanasia employ dehumanizing language to support their proposal that noncompetent persons should be killed when their lives are judged by others to be valueless or excessively burdensome. Those to be killed often are defined as nonpersons or are called "vegetables." Some in poor but stable and nonterminal conditions are reclassified as "terminal." Others are defined as "brain-dead," even though some spontaneous functioning of the brain persists and the strict clinical criteria for declaring brain death are not verified.

Certain people claim to oppose euthanasia and do not advocate killing by acts of commission, but nevertheless support the view that treatment may rightly be withheld or withdrawn from noncompetent, nonterminal persons simply because their lives are thought by others to be valueless or excessively burdensome. Adopting this rationale, and accepting the assumption that life itself can be useless or an excessive burden, some American ethicists, physicians, and courts have judged that food and fluids may rightly be withheld or withdrawn from persons who are not terminally ill because they are permanently unconscious or otherwise seriously debilitated.

However, withholding or withdrawing food and fluids *on this rationale* is morally wrong because it is euthanasia by omission. The withholding or withdrawing of food and fluids carries out the proposal, adopted by choice, to end someone's life because that life itself is judged by others to be valueless or excessively burdensome. Moreover, the withholding or withdrawing of food and fluids *on this rationale* should be judged to violate fundamental principles of American law and equity, since it explicitly sanctions status-based discrimination—i.e., discrimination based on the debilitated physical or mental condition of the person. Such discrimination becomes a new basis for deliberate killing by omission—killing that is not justified by the plain language of applicable statutory or constitutional law.

It is cause for very great alarm that some influential physicians, ethicists, and courts have adopted this rationale for withholding or withdrawing food and fluids—and other means of preserving life from some persons. For in adopting this rationale, they approve and legally sanction euthanasia by omission—deliberate killing—in these cases. In order to prevent the sanctioning, even if unintended, of killing the innocent, everyone with relevant competence—especially ethicists, religious teachers, lawyers, jurists, physicians, and other healthcare personnel—must repudiate the withholding or withdrawal of food and fluids on this rationale.

If it becomes entrenched practice to kill by omission certain sorts of persons whose condition is very poor and whose lives are judged by others no longer to be worth living, then this method of killing surely will be extended to many other persons. Most of the cases that have attracted attention thus far have involved the very severely brain damaged—those who are permanently unconscious, severely damaged by strokes, in advanced stages of dementia due to Alzheimer's or another disease, and so on. But the various sorts of damage, defect, debility, and handicap that burden human lives occur in myriad degrees, so that there are always more and less severe cases differing from one another only by degree. Unfortunately, it is not difficult to imagine a future America in which human life may itself be judged excessively burdensome for all persons who cannot care for themselves and have no one willing and able to care for them. Since dying of thirst and starvation can often be slow, very painful, and disfiguring, the demand will inevitably follow that death be hastened by lethal overdose or injection. Thus, ironically, the purportedly "dignified death" of those who die from dehydration and malnutrition would occasion demands for deliberate killing by commission because of the indignity involved in such a death.

THE USE OF TUBES TO PROVIDE FOOD AND HYDRATION FOR THE PERMANENTLY UNCONSCIOUS AND OTHER SERIOUSLY ILL PERSONS

Providing food and fluids to noncompetent individuals such as infants and the unconscious is, except under extraordinary circumstances, a grave duty. The Second Vatican Council invoked a longstanding tradition of the Church Fathers when it urged individuals and governments: "Feed the man dying of hunger, because if you do not feed him you have killed him" *(Gaudium et spes,* n. 69). Deliberately to deny food and water to such innocent human beings in order to bring about their deaths is homicide, for it is the adoption by choice of a proposal to kill them by starvation and dehydration. Such killing can never be morally right and ought never to be legalized. It follows that it is never right and ought never to be legally permitted to withhold food and fluids from the permanently unconscious or from others who are seriously debilitated (e.g., with strokes, Alzheimer's disease, Lou Gehrig's disease, organic brain syndrome, or AIDS dementia) as a means of securing their deaths.

However, when specific objective conditions are met, the withholding and withdrawing of various forms of treatment, including the provision of food and fluids by artificial means, do not necessarily carry out a proposal to end life. One may rightly choose to withhold or withdraw a means of preserving life if the means employed is judged either useless or excessively burdensome. It is most necessary to note that the judgment made here is *not* that the person's *life* is useless or excessively burdensome; rather, the judgment made is that the *means used to preserve life* is useless or excessively burdensome.

Traditionally, a treatment has been judged useless or relatively useless if the benefits it provides to a person are nil (useless in a strict sense) or are insignificant in comparison to the burdens it imposes (useless in a wider sense). Traditionally, a treatment has been judged excessively burdensome when whatever benefits it offers are not worth pursuing for one or more of several reasons: it is too painful, too damaging to the patient's bodily self and functioning, too psychologically repugnant to the patient, too restrictive of the patient's liberty and preferred activities, too suppressive of the patient's mental life, or too expensive.

An exhaustive examination of each of these factors is beyond the scope of this statement. We stress, however, that moral certainty of excessive burdensomeness is required to justify foregoing nutrition or hydration. It is necessary, especially in the formulation of law and public policy, to identify with precision the circumstances in which nutrition and hydration may be legitimately foregone.

In judging whether treatment of a noncompetent person is excessively burdensome, one must be fair. Great care should be taken not to employ a double standard, by which consciously or unconsciously one attributes greater weight to burdens imposed by the treatment and less to benefits provided by it because the patient is cognitively impaired or physically debilitated. The logic of such a standard would lead to rationalizing the discriminatory withholding or withdrawing of care from anyone whose condition fails to meet some arbitrary norm for adequate quality of life.

Yet the damaged or debilitated condition of the patient has been the key factor taken into consideration in virtually all the recent court cases that have focused attention on the moral and legal questions concerning the provision by tube of food and fluids to permanently unconscious or other severely debilitated but nondying individuals. Decisions have been made to withdraw food and fluids not because continuing to provide them would be in itself excessively burdensome, but because sustaining life was judged to be no benefit to a person in such poor condition. These decisions have been unjust and, as noted above, they set a dangerous precedent for more extensive passive or even active euthanasia.

Nonetheless, *if it is really useless or excessively burdensome* to provide someone with nutrition and hydration, then these means may rightly be withheld or withdrawn, *provided* that this omission does not carry out a proposal to end the person's life, but rather is chosen to avoid the useless effort or the excessive burden of continuing to provide the food and fluids.

Plainly, when a person is imminently dying, a time often comes when it is really useless or excessively burdensome to continue hydration and nutrition, whether by tube or otherwise. But the question that concerns us is not about patients who are judged to be imminently dying, but rather about persons who are not.

In our judgment, feeding such patients and providing them with fluids by means of tubes is *not* useless in the strict sense because it does bring to these patients a great benefit, namely, the preservation of their lives and the prevention of their death through malnutrition and dehydration. We grant that provision of food and fluids by tubes or other means to such persons could become useless or futile if (a) the person in question is imminently dying, so that any effort to sustain life is futile, or (b) the person is no longer able to assimilate the nourishment or fluids thus provided. But unless these conditions are verified, it is unjust to claim that the provision of food and fluids is useless.

We recognize that provision of food and fluids by IVs and nasogastric tubes can have side effects (e.g., irritation of the nasal passages, sore throats, collapsing of veins, etc.) that might become serious enough in particular cases to render their use excessively burdensome. But the experience of many physicians and nurses suggests that these side effects are often transitory and capable of being ameliorated. Moreover, use of gastric tubes does not ordinarily cause the patient grave discomfort. There may be gas pains, diarrhea, or nose and throat irritation, but ordinarily such discomforts are of passing nature and can be ameliorated. We thus judge that providing food and fluids to the permanently unconscious and other categories of seriously debilitated but nondying persons (e.g., those with strokes or Alzheimer's disease) does not ordinarily impose excessive burdens by reason of pain or damage to bodily self and functioning. Psychological repugnance, restrictions on physical liberty and preferred activities, or harm to the person's mental life are not relevant considerations in the cases with which we are concerned.

The question remains whether providing food and water in this way to these patients is excessively burdensome because of its cost. At the outset we make two critical points. First, the cost of providing food and fluids by enteral tubes is not, in itself, excessive. Such feeding is generally no more costly than other forms of ordinary nursing care (such as cleaning or spoon-feeding a patient) or ordinary maintenance care (such as the maintenance of room temperature through heating or air conditioning). Second, one must also take into account the benefits that such care may provide both to the patient and to the caregivers.

It must be acknowledged that the care of persons in very poor but nonterminal condition, sometimes over a long time, can be quite costly when taken as a whole. For instance, the care of anyone who cannot eat and drink in a normal way requires not only tubal nutrition and hydration, but also a room, which must be supplied appropriately with heat and utilities, and regular nursing care to keep the patient clean, prevent bed sores, and so on. But these forms of care and maintenance are provided to many other classes of persons (e.g., those with severe mental illnesses or retardation, with other long-term disabilities, etc.). The "burdens" involved in each of these instances are similar to those involved in caring for nondying persons who cannot feed themselves.

Some of these patients (e.g., those suffering from strokes) might be cared for at home rather than in an institution; the regular provision of food and fluids by tube is usually not too difficult or complicated to be done by people without professional training if they are properly instructed and supervised. This is not to say that care of such patients, when feasible, is not costly in time and energy. Like care for a baby, it must be carried on constantly; and it may be more difficult in some cases because of the larger size of an adult body.

But such care is not without its benefits. Since it is necessary to sustain life, such care benefits the nondying patient by serving this fundamental personal good—human life itself—which, as we have explained, remains good in itself no matter how burdened it may become due to the patient's poor condition.

Moreover, caring for others expresses recognition of their personhood and responds appropriately to it. For example, care for a baby is the form parental love naturally takes; care for a helpless adult family member, neighbor, or stranger—expresses compassion and humane appreciation of his or her dignity. It also offers the possibility to the caregiver of nurturing such noble qualities as mercy and compassion.

It is possible to imagine situations in which a society might reasonably consider it too burdensome to continue to care for its helpless members. For example, in some very harsh environments, natural disasters, and war situations, the more able can be forced to make hard choices between caring for themselves (and their children) and providing life-sustaining care for those who are gravely disabled and helpless. However, our society is by no means in such straitened circumstances—in the aftermath of nuclear destruction we may face such a situation, but we are surely not facing one now.

Some Americans might prefer to abandon to death those who require long-term care at public or private expense. But comparing the costs of care with its benefits, only one who sets aside the Golden Rule will consider excessively burdensome the provision by our society of life-sustaining care to all its members who require it and can benefit from it. As the Catholic Church stated in its 1981 *Document for the International Year of Disabled Persons*: "The respect, the dedication, the time and means required for the care of handicapped persons, even of those whose mental faculties are gravely affected, is the price that a society should generously pay in order to remain truly human." To withhold or withdraw from those in poor condition the elemental care they need to survive would be to decide that our society no longer values its members insofar as they are persons with dignity—that is, with inherent value independent of what they can do and contribute but only insofar as they are useful, or so long as their lives have sufficient "quality."

We thus conclude that, in the ordinary circumstances of life in our society today, it is not morally right, nor ought it to be legally permissible, to withhold or withdraw nutrition and hydration provided by artificial means to the permanently unconscious or other categories of seriously debilitated but nonterminal persons. Rather, food and fluids are universally needed for the preservation of life, and can generally be provided without the burdens and expense of more aggressive means of supporting life. Therefore, both morality and law should recognize a strong presumption in favor of their use.

Furthermore, judgments that these means of supporting life have become optional in an individual case should be scrutinized with the utmost care, to ensure that such judgments are not guided by a discriminatory attitude regarding the value of the lives of persons with disabilities or by an intention of deliberately hastening the death of such persons.

AN INTERIM PASTORAL STATEMENT ON ARTIFICIAL NUTRITION AND HYDRATION

Bishops of Texas and the Texas Conference of Catholic Health Facilities

PREFACE

Human life is God's precious gift to each person. We possess and treasure it as a sacred trust. All persons, therefore, have a moral responsibility, in accord with their own capacities, roles, and personal vocation, to make those decisions and take those necessary steps to preserve and promote their own life and health and that of others. We firmly reiterate the Church's continued condemnation of euthanasia as defined in the Vatican's 1980 *Declaration on Euthanasia*.[1]

This responsibility for conserving life and health falls especially upon those persons and institutions directly involved in the healing ministry. Catholic Health Facilities have a special duty to reflect Roman Catholic teaching while carrying out the compassionate healing ministry of Jesus Christ.

In particular, this commitment to relevant Church teaching is exemplified in the treatment of all patients, including those who require life-sustaining procedures. Specifically, the highly controversial issue of the provision of artificial nutrition and hydration is of particular concern today because of the current anti-life ambiance in the United States.

The Texas Conference of Catholic Health Facilities, to insure consonance with the teachings of the Catholic Church in all of its activities, consulted the Bishops of Texas on the subject of foregoing and withdrawing of

From Chancery Office, Diocese of Dallas, Most Reverend Charles V. Grahmann, DD, Bishop of Dallas, May 7, 1990.

artificial nutrition and hydration. This consultation contributed to this statement which addresses the moral aspects of this issue.

MORAL VALUES TO BE PROMOTED AND PROTECTED

Human Personhood

Each human person is of incalculable worth because all humans are made in the image of God, redeemed by Christ, and are called to share the life of the Triune God.

A Holistic Integration

This value includes the spiritual, mental, emotional, and physical health in the unity of the person and communion of persons. The life and health of the total person and communion of persons are important in order for each person to hear and respond effectively under the influence of grace to God's call.

The Inherent Sacredness and Dignity of the Human Person

The life of each person has an inherent dignity which is to be respected by all other humans. So, each person, regardless of age or condition, has exactly the same basic right to life which deserves equal protection by society and its laws.

BASIC MORAL PRINCIPLES

Although life always is a good, there are conditions which, if present, lessen or remove one's obligation to sustain life.

While every reasonable effort should be made to maintain life and restore health, Pope Pius XII noted that there comes a time when these efforts may become excessively burdensome for the patient or others (see Address to International Congress of Anesthesiologists, November 24, 1957).[2]

If the reasonable foreseen benefits to the patient in the use of
any means outweigh the burdens to the patient or others,
then those means are morally obligatory.

Examples of benefits include cure, pain reduction, restoration of consciousness, restoration of function, and maintenance of life with reasonable hope
of recovery. Even without any hope of recovery it is an expression of love
and respect for the person to keep the patient clean, warm, and comfortable.
There is no moral distinction to be made between the foregoing and withdrawing of life-sustaining procedures.

If the means used to prolong life are disproportionately burdensome
compared with the benefits to the patient,
then those means need not be used, they are morally optional.

This principle, taught in the Vatican *Declaration on Euthanasia* (1980), was
built on the teaching of Pope Pius XII and the Church's moral tradition.[3]
Burdens are those undesirable aspects and consequences of the use of the
means themselves which fall upon the patient or others—family, care
provider, or community. Examples of disproportionate burdens include
excessive suffering for the patient; excessive expense for the family or the
community; investment in medical technology and personnel disproportionate to the expected results; inequitable resource allocation.[4]

The National Conference of Catholic Bishops' Committee for Pro-Life
Activities came to the same conclusion regarding the situation when the
burden is disproportionate to the benefits in their statement on the proposed
Uniform Rights of the Terminally Ill Act. The statement (July 2, 1986)
allowed that "laws dealing with medical treatments may have to take account
of exceptional circumstances, where even means for providing nourishment
may become too ineffective or burdensome to be obligatory" (*Origins,* July
24, 1986, p. 224).

The *Declaration on Euthanasia* as well as the teaching of Pius XII
explicitly state that such foregoing or withdrawing are not suicide;[5] rather,
they should be considered as the acceptance of the human condition and
simply letting nature takes its course. The omission of life-sustaining means
(whether it be a mechanical respirator, a cardiac pacemaker, a renal dialysis
machine, or artificial nutrition and hydration) can be acceptable under conditions which render those means morally nonobligatory. In those appro-

priate cases the decision maker is *not* guilty of murder, suicide, or assisted suicide since there is no moral obligation under these circumstances to impede the normal consequences of the underlying pathology. The physical cause of death is ultimately the pathology which required the use of those means in the first place. The proximate physical means are either the absence of the substance necessary for life (oxygen, water, nutrients) or the presence of toxic substances resulting from metabolic activities of the body.

APPLICATION TO PVS

Patients, competently diagnosed to be in a persistent vegetative state or in an irreversible coma, remain human persons. Nonetheless, those individuals are stricken with a lethal pathology which, without artificial nutrition and hydration, will lead to death.

The moral issue, then, is what conditions make it morally obligatory to intervene with artificial nutrition and hydration to prevent death which would otherwise occur as a consequence of the underlying pathology? While each case has to be judged on its own merits, the final decision should be based upon the application of the principles previously described regarding the burden/benefit analysis relative to the use of life-sustaining procedures. Decisions about treatment for unconscious or incompetent patients are to be made by an appropriate proxy (e.g., spouse, parent, adult children) in light of what the patient would have decided. This judgment should be based on the expressed wishes of the patient. The final decision, however, for patients with a fatal pathology but who are conscious and competent and in the judgment of physicians have no reasonable hope of recovery from it is to be made by the patients themselves and by no one else.

Patients, even those persons who are in a permanent vegetative state or irreversibly unconscious, should never be abandoned. They should be cared for lovingly—kept clean, warm, and treated with dignity. The morally appropriate foregoing or withdrawing of artificial nutrition and hydration from a permanently unconscious person is not abandoning that person. Rather, it is accepting the fact that the person has come to the end of his or her pilgrimage and should not be impeded from taking the final step. The foregoing or withdrawing of artificial nutrition and hydration should only occur after there has been sufficient deliberation based upon the best medical and personal information available.

CONCLUSION

The principles are applicable to any life-threatening situation where a person—regardless of age or condition—requires some intervention, especially artificially administered nutrition and hydration, in order to impede the threat to life. In a medical context, the decision needs to be made in each particular case as to whether the normal consequences of a disease or injury should be impeded by human intervention.

All care and treatment should be directed toward the total well-being of the person in need. Because of the high value of temporal health and life, the presumption is made that the necessary steps will be taken to restore health or, at least, avert death. However, the temporal concerns must always be subordinated to the patient's spiritual needs and obligations.

Catholic health facilities should be particularly sensitive to the pastoral needs of both patients and caregivers (family, friends, staff) especially in the context of death and dying.

In the event of doubt about meaning or application of Church teaching, the diocesan bishop or his delegate shall be consulted.

NOTES

1. "By euthanasia is understood an action or an omission which of itself or by intention causes death, in order that all suffering may in this way be eliminated. Euthanasia's terms of reference, therefore, are to be found in the intention of the will and in the methods used" (*Declaration on Euthanasia*, no. II).

2. "But normally one is held to use only ordinary means—according to circumstances of persons, places, times, and culture—that is to say, means that don't involve any grave burden for oneself or another. A more strict obligation would be too burdensome for most men and would render the attainment of the higher, more important good too difficult. Life, health, all temporal activities are in fact subordinated to spiritual ends. On the other hand, one is not forbidden to take more than the strictly necessary steps to preserve life and health, as long as he does not fail in some more serious duty" (Pope Pius XI: "Prolongation of Life," November 24, 1957, English translation, *The Pope Speaks*, vol. 4 [1958], pp. 393–398).

3. "In the past, moralists replied that one is never obliged to use 'extraordinary' means. This reply, which as a principle still holds good, is perhaps less clear today, by reasons of the imprecision of the term and the rapid progress made in the treatment of sickness. Thus some people prefer to speak of 'proportionate' and 'disproportionate' means" (*Declaration on Euthanasia*, no. IV, see also number 4, below).

4. "If there are no other sufficient remedies, it is permitted, with the patient's consent, to have recourse to the means provided by the most advanced medical techniques. Even if these means are still at the experimental stage and are not without a certain risk. By accepting them, the patient can even show generosity in the service of humanity.

"It is also permitted, with the patient's consent, to interrupt these means, where the results fall short of expectations. But for such a decision to be made, account will have to be taken of the reasonable wishes of the patient's family, as also of the advice of the doctors who are specially competent in the matter. The latter may in particular judge that the investment in instruments and personnel is disproportionate to the results foreseen; they may also judge that the techniques applied impose on the patient strain or suffering out of proportion with the benefits which he or she may gain from such techniques" (ibid.).

5. "It is also permissible to make do with the normal means that medicine can offer. Therefore one cannot impose on anyone the obligation to have recourse to a technique which is already in use but which carries a risk or is burdensome. Such a refusal is not the equivalent of suicide; on the contrary, it should be considered as an acceptance of the human condition, or a wish to avoid the application of a medical procedure disproportionate to the results that can be expected, or a desire not to impose excessive expense on the family or the community" (ibid.).

Nutrition and Hydration

Moral Considerations

A Statement of the
Catholic Bishops of Pennsylvania

FOREWORD

It is well known that there has been a great deal of discussion at every level in our Church and in society at large concerning "advance medical directives." These issues are already having a profound effect on the way in which we live. They influence not only our loved ones who are dying, but the very manner in which we view human life in general. Since all of us are mortal, these are issues which will also have an immense impact on each of us personally. Because of this, the Catholic Bishops of Pennsylvania have collaborated in the composition of the following statement which is an effort on our part to fulfill our responsibilities as bishops to give guidance to all the Catholic faithful of this state who are entrusted to our care. It is also our hope that these observations and the principles on which they are based will be of help to all who recognize the importance of deliberating at length on the moral aspects of the difficult question of providing food and fluids to patients. Our statement is intended to express, as well as we are currently able, the teaching of the Catholic Church as it affects these admittedly difficult cases. As we here profess our faith that all human life is sacred since it comes from God, we pray that all who read our statement will join us in our resolve truly to care for those in need among us.

From PA Catholic Conference, http://www.pacatholic.org/bishops'%20statements/qascr.htm (accessed November 23, 2005). Original version December 12, 1991; revised edition, 1999.

Anthony Cardinal Bevilacqua Archbishop of Philadelphia
The Feast of Our Lady of Guadalupe, December 12, 1991

INTRODUCTION

Recent court decisions and the enactment of federal and state laws governing advance medical directives (living will or durable power of attorney) have given many the impression that anything the courts or the civil laws allow is morally acceptable. The issue of the withholding or withdrawal of nutrition and hydration in particular has become controverted. We, as Catholic Bishops and fellow Pennsylvanians, hope that what follows will be of help to many of those who are confused about the present situation, but we especially seek to offer guidance to the Catholic faithful entrusted to our pastoral care. . . .

The purpose of our statement is multiple. [1] We wish to offer guidance to Catholics involved in decision making, especially pastors of souls, those in the healthcare profession and its beneficiaries. [2] We wish to offer our teaching as a way of engaging in a dialogue of public policy as it affects all those involved with legislative and judicial decisions. [3] We wish to present the developed tradition of a medical ethic which for centuries has guided doctors and patients alike to achieve the highest standards of healthcare and moral good. As Bishops we speak as official teachers and spokesmen for the Church, but we speak also as citizens concerned with the welfare of all in our society. . . .

STATE OF THE QUESTION

Modern medicine continues to deal with age-old questions, even though current knowledge and technologies offer treatments and procedures that would once have been impossible. One such area is the supplying of nutrition and hydration to patients who are incapable of feeding themselves and are unable to take nourishment orally even with assistance. It is now possible to sustain the lives of such patients with a variety of techniques, and so arises the question of the moral obligation to do so. This question of moral obligation touches not only the patient, who has primary responsibility for the reasonable care of health and life, but also those who have responsibility for the patient who is no longer able to exercise self-determination. . . .

STATES OF UNCONSCIOUSNESS

All states of unconsciousness are often referred to (even by medical personnel) as "coma." This is, in fact, not a correct designation. Coma is but one type of impaired consciousness. There are also others which we should consider because all of them present situations in which problems may arise in terms of the supplying of nutrition and hydration.

A true coma is a state of "unarousable unresponsiveness" with no response to external stimuli. The person is not dead, but is in a state of sleep. This condition is never permanent. It may last as long as six months, but it will resolve itself into some other state. The person may emerge into consciousness again or sink into another state, such as that which is referred to as the persistent vegetative state. It may take some time, even months, to diagnose the exact condition.

The persistent vegetative state (PVS) is deeper than a coma. The coma is a state of sleep; PVS is a form of deep unconsciousness. The cerebrum, the upper part of the brain, gives evidence of impaired or failed operation—and it is this portion of the brain, in its cortex or outer layer, which is responsible for those activities that we recognize as specifically human. Another portion of the brain, the brain stem, is, however, still functioning in the PVS patient. It is this portion of the brain which controls involuntary functions such as breathing, blinking, involuntary contractions, and cycles of waking and sleep. Thus PVS patients may open their eyes and sometimes follow movement with them or respond to loud and sudden noises (although these responses will be neither long sustained nor apparently purposeful). There will be cyclical stages of sleeping and waking, but such activity is a function of the brain stem and is not an indicator of purposeful human activity.

PVS is sometimes referred to as "cerebral death." This is an unfortunate terminology, since it seems to imply that there is "brain death" as described earlier. This is not true. There is a failure of function at one level in the brain, but not all, and the person in PVS is definitely not dead. Even medical personnel sometimes refer to such a patient as "brain-dead." This is simply not the case.

There is also a state which is referred to as psychiatric pseudocoma. This is a state of unconsciousness caused by shock or trauma which lead the victim to close off from the outside world. This may be so severe as to give the appearance of death, but it is not even truly a state of unconsciousness. It is simply total lack of response.

Finally, there is another condition which is referred to as the locked-in state. This condition is caused by an interruption in the descending motor pathways of the nervous system. In this condition, paralysis, not cognitive failure, leads to a lack of ability to communicate. The patient is fully conscious, but simply has no way in which to indicate conscious response. (In some cases, however, depending on where the motor pathways are interrupted, communication may be possible by such means as coded eye blinking.) It takes careful diagnosis not to mistake this patient for the PVS patient. PET scans can distinguish between the locked-in state and the persistent vegetative state. The EEG, however, cannot do so, since the patient in the locked-in state may show an abnormal response, while the PVS patient may produce readings that are near normal. Patients who have recovered from this condition reveal that they were indeed conscious and well aware of what was going on around them—and had a strong desire to continue to live.

In none of these classes of unconscious patients are we dealing with the dead. All of them are alive and some of them may well be expected to recover. The one case in which recovery becomes most unlikely is that of the PVS patient, and it is this patient who is likely to become the object of decision making in regard to continued treatment or care, or supplying of nourishment.

ORDINARY AND EXTRAORDINARY MEANS OF CARE

"The Catholic moral tradition holds that one is morally obliged to use the ordinary means of sustaining life, but is not obliged to make use of extraordinary means." Ordinary means are those which are available and do not require effort, suffering, or expense beyond that which most people would consider appropriate in a serious situation. This would include most of the developed procedures and techniques commonly practiced in medicine and surgery. However, moralists recognize that there are also subjective elements which influence our ability to make moral judgments. Subjective considerations of pain, expense, and personal abhorrence may act as obstacles to the fulfillment of this obligation. Furthermore, not all techniques have to be used in every instance. What would usually be ordinary means may, in certain cases, offer little hope of success and may prove more burdensome than beneficial to the user. In such situations one would not be morally obliged to use such means.

The distinction between ordinary means (which we are morally obliged to use) and extraordinary means (which we may choose to use, but are not obliged to) is not based solely on the commonness and availability of the means themselves, although this is taken into account. It is also based on the results that one can expect and on certain serious subjective considerations and attitudes as well. It takes into account the proportion between benefit and burden.

PRINCIPLES OF DECISION MAKING

Decisions on the use of appropriate means for the preservation of life and health can sometimes be complex. One way in which to approach them is to ask questions which can illuminate the process and direct the questioner to the best sources for the answers. Those sources involve moral teaching, medical information, and the concrete condition and means of the patient and the patient's family. What is being suggested here applies as a help to the decision-making process for all patients, including both the conscious and the unconscious. Obviously, however, the process for the unconscious patient will involve the use of some sort of "substituted judgment."

Is the procedure beneficial to the patient in terms of preservation of life or restoration of health? Is it serving a lifesaving purpose? Is it adding a serious burden? Is death already imminent, so that the proposed treatment may add briefly to the life span in such a way as simply to prolong the dying process without actually preserving life? Questions such as these must be directed to experts in the field of medicine, although in difficult cases even the experts may presently be unable to give final answers to all questions.

Is the procedure a grave burden to the patient, and has that burden become unbearable or intolerable? No one can actually answer that question except the patient or, perhaps, the patient's family. At the same time, suffering is a part of every life and has a spiritual and salutary significance. Judgments in this area must be tempered by the presence of the varying degrees of depression that any suffering patient or family may be experiencing. They may need help in overcoming the temptation simply to give up. At this point the pastoral counselor may be of considerable assistance. We must still recognize, however, the subjective aspect of "unbearableness" and must respect moral judgments made in good conscience. If the patient is not competent, then who is to make this sort of judgment? What motives will enter into that decision? Here again the pastoral counselor can be of considerable help and so, too, is the intimate knowledge that family members might be expected to have of the patient.

We must also realize that moralists and medical personnel may not always be using exactly the same definitions of ordinary and extraordinary means. Medical personnel often use the terms to refer to the means of treatment in themselves, considering them ordinary unless they are experimental or rarely used. The moralist must also take into account those other elements mentioned earlier, that is, the burdens and benefits the particular treatment may have for the patient or for others. Thus the moral terminology is usually more related to the condition of the patient, while the medical terminology is more related to the technique itself. The moral judgment is based on the benefit of the technique for the patient as compared to the accompanying burden, and not simply on the availability of the technique. Clarity on this point can help to remove one source of confusion.

Decision makers should also be aware that the decision to terminate a treatment is usually not morally different from the decision not to initiate that treatment in the first place. The same moral norms apply in each instance, but there are circumstantial differences. When treatment is initiated, the prognosis may not yet be clear. No one is able to predict the future course of events. The more definitive the prognosis, the more easily the moral norms can be applied in a concrete manner. However, it may take considerable time to determine that a patient has entered into a persistent vegetative state. The duration of unconsciousness itself is an important determinant in both diagnosis and prognosis. Maximum treatment is required in the earliest stages, while full or partial recovery still remains a greater possibility. Even the location or extent of brain or brain stem damage may not be an accurate indicator in every instance. Time and treatment are both required. In general, the younger the patient, the more likely is recovery. After three months the chance of recovery always lessens. Recovery after six months of the vegetative state is probably less than 1 in 100, and after twelve months almost never.

It is most often when the treatments have run their course and the patient is clearly not going to recover that the decisions must be made. Prognosis and the condition of the patient may be clearer than they were at first. Even then, there is still a serious obstacle to easy decision making. No matter how clear the case may be by the time a decision is made, the decision to withdraw a treatment or some form of care already in progress is psychologically more difficult, since it is always hard for the survivors not to feel that its withdrawal was the cause of death.

PROVISION OF NUTRITION AND HYDRATION

Feeding Methods

There are various ways to supply nourishment to the unconscious. The general categories would include at least these three: oral feeding, enteral feeding, and parenteral feeding.

Oral feeding simply means that food (which may be pureed) or drink can be placed in the mouth and the patient will then swallow it. For some patients, even in the persistent vegetative state, this may be enough, provided that the swallowing reflex is sufficiently unimpaired. At times, however, the medical staff will prefer not to use this method, even in cases where it could be used, since it can be quite time consuming for a staff that may already have a large number of patients to care for.

Enteral (within the bowel) feeding means that the nourishment is placed directly into the upper end of the small intestine. This can be accomplished by means of a nasogastric (through the nose and into the stomach) or naso-duodenal (through the nose and into the upper end of the small bowel) tube, or it can also be done through a gastrostomy (an opening directly into the stomach) or jejunostomy (an opening into the upper part of the small bowel). This method does not usually result in complications and, even if some complications do arise, they are usually not of a serious nature, but the method does presuppose that the gastrointestinal tract is intact and functioning.

Parenteral (outside the bowel) feeding refers to the supplying of nourishment intravenously. This may be done when the gastrointestinal tract is not intact or does not function. It may be accomplished for a short time by means of tubes inserted into the peripheral veins (e.g., in the arms or legs), but this can easily lead to thrombosis (clotting). Therefore, if it is to be used for longer periods, it is done by inserting a tube into the central venous system. There is need for daily monitoring of nutrients, waste products, and blood chemistry until the patient becomes stable, after which monitoring can be less frequent. This method of nutrition also carries with it greater risks of complications. Metabolic complications may arise, resulting in bone disease, liver dysfunction, or other problems. There may also be nonmetabolic complications, such as thrombosis or the introduction of infecting organisms. However, the relative simplicity of this method is evidenced by the fact that in some situations it has been used as a form of home care allowing some types of conscious patients to resume many of their normal activities.

Decisions in Relation to Nutrition and Hydration

There are instances in which it is relatively easy to apply moral principles to the decision to withhold or withdraw nutrition. In the case of a terminal cancer patient whose death is imminent, for instance, the decision to begin intravenous feeding or feeding by nasogastric tube or gastrostomy, may also mean that the patient is going to endure greater suffering for a somewhat longer period of time—without hope of recovery or even appreciable lengthening of life. Weighing the balance of benefits versus burdens makes it relatively easy to decide that this could fall into the category of extraordinary means and that such feeding procedures need not be initiated or may be discontinued.

We are faced with a different set of questions when we begin to examine the case of the long-term patient who must be fed by some of the means described above (i.e., those more complicated than assisted oral feeding). The question of patients in the persistent vegetative state is particularly important. There is no question here of "brain death, " even though that term is so frequently misused in the media (who cannot always be expected to know better) and by medical practitioners (who certainly ought to know better). The PVS patient is alive, but unconscious and, therefore, unable to take nourishment without assistance. It is clearly not a question of deciding to stop treatment because the patient has died.

Questions relative to the supplying of nutrition and hydration are often qualified by the term "artificial." The discussion thus tends to center on whether artificial nutrition and hydration are to be continued or not in certain cases. It is not, however, the question of whether a type of care is artificial or natural that makes the difference in terms of its continuance or discontinuance. The fact is that every mode of taking in food and drink is, to some extent, artificial. This is the case whether we speak of the patient receiving parenteral feeding or the honored guest at a banquet for royalty— a banquet which observes every nicety of the most sophisticated table manners and requires a certain expertise in the recognition of all appropriate cutlery. Both situations provide nourishment and both also use some artificial means to supply it. The real question, when it comes to decision making for the unconscious patient, depends in the final analysis on something other than a distinction between artificial and natural means. If the supplying of nutrition and hydration is of benefit to the patient and causes no undue burden of pain or suffering or excessive expenditure of resources, then it is our duty to take and to provide that nutrition and hydration. If the burdens have far surpassed the benefits, then our obligation has ceased.

A distinction is also often made between treatment and care. In the case of the patient in the persistent vegetative state, some would hold that we are obliged to continue to supply the proper care, but are not obliged to continue treatment. The reason for this statement is that treatment in this instance is no longer useful in resolving the unconscious state of the patient. For many, then, it becomes a question of whether feeding constitutes treatment or care. If the former, then it may be discontinued. If the latter, it must continue. Statements by the Pontifical Council on Health Affairs and the Pontifical Academy of Sciences both hold to this distinction and say that treatment may be discontinued, but they then go on to explain that they view the supplying of nutrition and hydration as care—which must, therefore, be continued (pre-supposing, of course, the distinctions already made in reference to the question of excessive burdens).

There is, however, another way to look at this. In the case of the immi-nently terminal patient one would suppose that treatment is intended to reverse the course of the disease or, at least, to better the condition of the patient. If it no longer does that, then its discontinuance is no more than a clear recognition of its futility. Even feeding methods other than oral thus become futile and can be stopped so as to attend more to the comfort of the one who is dying. In cer-tain clearly defined cases, then, even certain types of care might become extra-ordinary if they were futile or excessively burdensome.

However, the patient in the persistent vegetative state is not imminently terminal (provided that there is no other pathology present). The feeding—regardless of whether it be considered as treatment or as care—is serving a life-sustaining purpose. Therefore, it remains an ordinary means of sus-taining life and should be continued. In other words, the mere distinction between treatment and care does not of itself resolve the moral problem. Rather, its resolution still remains within the scope of the usual norms of ordinary and extraordinary means. Whether it is viewed as treatment or care, it would be morally wrong to discontinue nutrition and hydration when they are within the realm of ordinary means.

What obligations, then, do exist? The moral obligation to preserve life and health falls immediately on the one whose health it is. Is one morally obliged to submit to procedures to supply nutrition and hydration? Or are they in the category of extraordinary care, and therefore not obligatory? Of course, in the case of the PVS patient, these decisions will be made by others, since the patient is incapable of making them. Obviously, the primary focus should be on the patient. With this in mind, then, we can begin to find our moral response by answering the questions proposed earlier, when we discussed the process of decision making.

Questions Related to the Medical Condition of the Patient

Is the procedure (supplying of nutrition and hydration) beneficial to the patient in terms of preservation of life or restoration of health? Supplying nourishment sustains life; it does not of itself restore health to a former state. However, it is clearly beneficial in terms of preservation of life, since death would be inevitable without it and life will continue with it.

Is it serving a lifesaving purpose? There is no doubt about the fact that it is, since the patient could not survive without it and is unable to supply it for himself.

Is it adding a serious burden? In almost every case the answer is negative. The means of supplying food in themselves are all relatively simple and—barring complications—generally without pain.

While there should be a presumption in favor of medically assisted nutrition and hydration, the judgment can legitimately be made that, in a particular case, they can be extraordinary.

Is death already imminent, so that the proposed procedures (supplying of nourishment, in this case) may add briefly to the life span in such a way as simply to prolong the dying process without actually preserving life? The pathological condition which has caused the persistent vegetative state or which is concurrent with it may threaten imminent death. Or it may be such as simply to make it impossible for the patient to care for himself. In this latter case the condition would not in itself be immediately life-threatening, but the lack of nourishment would be. Supplying nourishment would not be an instance of simply prolonging the dying process without actually preserving life. Life would be preserved at length and not merely temporarily prolonged while waiting for an imminently terminal condition to complete its course.

Questions Related to the Internal Disposition of the Patient

Is the procedure a grave burden to the patient, and has that burden become unbearable or intolerable? In terms of the gravity of any burden, it is always the one who bears the burden who is in the best position to answer this sort of question. In the present case, however, we are dealing precisely with a patient who is incapable of giving any answer. So far as can be determined by observation, the unconscious patient is not experiencing the anguish that would be borne by a conscious person in these or similar circumstances. The parts of the brain responsible for the specifically human qualities of anticipation and anguish that so affect human pain are precisely those parts which are not now functioning. As to the intensity of any physical pain due to the increased atrophy of muscle, the discomfort of immobility, the feelings arising from various medical procedures, etc., there would seem to be no way at the present time to render final and definitive judgment, although the external signs in the unconscious patient do not indicate excessive discomfort which cannot be relieved by those who have charge of the patient's care.

The question as to whether the patient in the persistent vegetative state feels pain is not an easy one to address, since the patient is the very one who is incapable of answering any question about the situation. Some of the problem, of course, is based on the way in which we view pain. There is a distinction between pain as a physical sensation and pain as the affective response associated with human suffering. The response of the vegetative patient to noxious stimuli would indicate that there is a physical response to pain or discomfort. However, physical evidence also indicates that the affective level of human suffering is not present. Experience with such patients shows no behavioral indication of such suffering. Postmortem examinations usually reveal a degree of damage to the cerebral hemispheres sufficient to preclude the experience of suffering. PET scanning also shows a metabolic rate in the cortex so reduced as to be incompatible with consciousness.

We can say, therefore, that all appearances would generally seem to indicate that there is no excessive pain involved in the feeding process. The feeding procedures themselves, except where there may be some serious complications, may involve some discomfort, but nothing excessive (this can be determined from the reactions of conscious patients who for one reason or another have undergone such procedures). Feeding methods do not generally carry with them the sometimes serious discomfort which would be found in the patient on a respirator.

As to the discomfort of being in this condition for years, unable to communicate and unable to help oneself, it is not possible to make a final and decisive comment. If, indeed, the patient is unconscious then there is no awareness of these inabilities and, consequently, none of the anguish that would attend them. However, we should note that some of what is being said is conjecture, since we have no way of knowing what is going on in the mind of the unconscious person. If we could indeed establish that there is pain, and that there is, in fact, considerable pain, then our answers might be quite different. That question, however, remains to be answered, although present consensus argues against the existence of such pain, mental or physical.

Questions Related to Family and Caregivers

What motives will enter into "substituted judgments" given by others on behalf of the patient? There is no doubt that a family undergoes considerable pain as it watches a loved one who remains for months or years in the persistent vegetative state. It is not at all unusual that members of that family find themselves, at times, wondering if death would not be a better alternative for the one who is afflicted. This feeling can and does arise out of love, compassion, and concern for the sick person. It is also, almost always, influenced as well by the internal struggle experienced by those who are well. They experience the pain of loss as the person they love is now removed from conscious communication with them. They experience their own exhaustion if they are very directly involved in the care for the patient. All of these are emotions that one would expect to find in such a situation. The family members, however, must be careful not to allow their own fears or frustrations to become the basis for the moral decision making that now falls to them. They must exercise for the one who is ill the same stewardship of life that is the obligation of each of us in our own regard. The desire to escape from our own burdens cannot become the source of a decision which would end the life of someone else.

There are, of course, other far less worthy motives which can inspire people to decide to terminate nutrition for the unconscious patient. Anger, spite, greed, culpable lack of concern, and a host of other motivations can also be part of our human decisions. For this reason it is also desirable that the benefit of the doubt be given to the continued sustenance of the life of the unconscious person.

We must, however, take into real account situations in which the family has reached the moral limits of its abilities or its resources. In such a situation, they have done all that they can do and they are not morally obliged to do more. They would then have reached the limits of ordinary means. However, in the society in which we live this does not present a fully convincing argument. Resources are available from other sources and these can often be tapped before a family reaches dire financial straits. Such assistance has been and continues to be available.

EUTHANASIA OR ALLOWING TO DIE

It would be unwise to complete our consideration of these questions without addressing the question of euthanasia. The word once referred to the effort to help make one's dying process easier. It has come finally to refer to some sort of intervention which actually brings about death.

Etymologically speaking, in ancient times euthanasia meant an easy death without severe suffering. Today one no longer thinks of this original meaning of the word, but rather of some intervention of medicine whereby the sufferings of sickness or of the final agony are reduced, sometimes also with the danger of suppressing life prematurely. Ultimately, the word euthanasia is used in a more particular sense to mean "mercy killing," for the purpose of putting an end to extreme suffering, or saving abnormal babies, the mentally ill, or the incurably sick from the prolongation, perhaps for many years, of a miserable life, which could impose too heavy a burden on their families or on society.

It is necessary to state clearly in what sense the word is used in the present document.

By euthanasia is understood an action or an omission which of itself or by intention causes death, in order that all suffering may in this way be eliminated. Euthanasia's terms of reference, therefore, are to be found in the intention of the will and in the methods used.

Alleviation of suffering through the purposeful destruction of the life of the sufferer is clearly contrary to true Christian respect for life and Christian love of neighbor. Yet, in our own time, this solution is proposed more and more frequently and even by doctors, whose very profession should be geared to the preservation of life. It has been said that in the Netherlands as many as one sixth of all deaths are attributable to euthanasia.

The movement toward murder as a solution to problems has already begun in the societal attitude toward the killing of the unborn. It is rapidly entering into the realm of the "hopelessly" ill. It can just as easily be extended to include the seriously handicapped, either physically or mentally. In none of these cases is it a question of the good of the patient, but more a question of the exercise of a questionable autonomy founded in equally questionable "rights" of the individual. Decisions such as this are all too easily based on the desires or fears or even inconvenience of others and the patient's wishes may not even enter into the question. That is certainly the case with abortion, and can just as easily become the case with the incurably ill. In both cases the decision is based on an attitude that there is such a thing as a human life not worthy to be lived. Those who are defective in some way are destroyed rather than cared for. It is an attitude which easily dehumanizes not only the victim but the perpetrator as well.

In 1986 the Council of Ethical and Judicial Affairs of the American Medical Association stated that "it is not unethical to discontinue all means of life-prolonging medical treatment" for patients in irreversible comas. This statement has the weight of whatever prestige that council holds, even though it was not the decision of a referendum of the members and does not tell us anything about how many of the members would support it. Nor should one be misled into thinking that the statement is based on the fact that such patients are suffering some sort of severe pain caused by the care that is being given them. This has already been discussed above, with the conclusion that there is usually no excessive pain due to such feeding. In fact, that same council in 1990 said:

"One aspect of the debate about stopping treatment in PVS focuses on a concern that the afflicted person would experience suffering after treatment is stopped (e.g., will experience dyspnea after removal of a respirator or face discomfort associated with starvation and dehydration after removal of a feeding tube.) The most obvious contradiction to this projection is that, by definition, in PVS both the person's capacity to perceive a wide range of stimuli and the neocortical or higher brain functions that are needed to generate a self-perceived affective response to any such stimuli are destroyed. Pain cannot be experienced by brains that no longer retain the neural apparatus for suffering."

But if the pain of the inability to breathe or the pain of starvation and dehydration cannot be felt, then there is no reason at all to support the contention that the removal of nutrition and hydration is being done out of concern for the sufferings of the patient. It must, therefore, be based upon something else; and what is that something else if not the decision that the life of this particular patient is not worth living? Sad to say, the intent is not to relieve suffering but, rather, to cause the patient to die. Nor can it be argued that it is merely the intention to "allow" the patient to die, rather than to "cause his death." The patient in the persistent vegetative state is not thereby in a terminal condition, since nutrition and hydration and ordinary care will allow him to live for years. It is only if that care is taken away—and barring any other new disease or debilitation—that the patient will die. It is the removal of the nutrition and hydration that brings about the death. This is euthanasia by omission rather than by positive lethal action, but it is just as really euthanasia in its intent.

There is a vast difference between allowing a terminal patient to die and doing something to hasten the death. We find no moral problem in those situations in which treatments are withdrawn because they have become an excessive burden rather than a benefit to the terminal patient. We find no moral problem in the withdrawing even of nutrition and hydration from the patient if the supplying of them is futile or excessively burdensome. It is morally wrong, however, to take these extreme cases and make them the norm for all cases of persistent vegetative state patients, when treatment or care will allow that patient to continue to live and will do so without a burden of excessive pain or suffering. In such cases their removal is tantamount to passive euthanasia (killing by omission).

Much of the contemporary discussion seems to have lost sight entirely of the difference between allowing to die when no treatment or care can any longer save the patient and murder by omission. Recalling the moral truth that one is not obliged to employ means that are either futile or too burdensome, but must never intentionally act against innocent human life, we see a clear moral distinction between intending and allowing. The latter is permissible in some circumstances—those involving extraordinary means—the former is always immoral and therefore forbidden.

CONCLUSION

As a general conclusion, in almost every instance there is an obligation to continue supplying nutrition and hydration to the unconscious patient. There are situations in which this is not the case, but those are the exceptions and should not be made into the rule. We can and do offer our sympathy and support to those who must make such hard decisions in those difficult cases. We cannot and do not offer our support to those who are willing to remove from patients the means of sustaining nourishment on the ground that their lives are not worthy of our continued care and concern.

Respect for personal autonomy is a basic principle of medical ethics. This principle reinforces the duty of hospital personnel to secure the consent of patients or their surrogates before initiating or discontinuing treatment. It does not reduce them to mere functionaries who can do no more than carry out the orders of the patient or the patient's surrogate. The purpose of medicine is no more the mere satisfaction of patients' or surrogates' desires than the purpose of teaching is to give students only what they explicitly desire to learn. As a student of medicine the physician has a knowledge of health and the effects of disease. As a professional the physician is dedicated to keeping patients healthy or, at least, to relieving their suffering. When there are alternative treatments or courses of action, the physician will lay out the advantages and disadvantages of the various choices, and show respect for the autonomy of patients not by merely acceding to their wishes but by telling them the truth and enabling them to make the right decisions. Neither the patient nor the surrogates of the patient have the moral right to withhold or withdraw treatment that is ordinary. Neither does the physician have the right to do so simply because the patient or the surrogates ask or demand this. In this perspective the physician responds to patient desires only if those desires accord with the proper professional and moral judgment as to what will promote the health, preserve the life, or prevent the suffering of the patient. The physician's duty has not been properly done if there has been no effort to persuade the patient to follow the proper course of action. If the patient decides to refuse excessively burdensome or futile treatment, the physician may properly comply with that request. If the patient decides to refuse ordinary treatment, there may, in some instances, be little that the physician can do to prevent this, but there remains at least the duty to attempt to persuade the patient otherwise or, failing that, for the physician to remove himself from the case so as not to be guilty of complicity in suicide.

It is important to recall that historically the practitioners and researchers in medical science have steadfastly and, in some cases, heroically striven to offer the very best of care to their patients. If some solution to a medical problem were not available, they gave their time, energies, and sometimes even their lives and fortunes to find it, to invent it, to discover some way to preserve their patients' lives and alleviate their suffering. It is our hope that medical science will remain faithful to this wonderful heritage which has been of inestimable advantage to humanity. Using the talents that God has given them, those who have dedicated their lives to providing healthcare to their fellow human beings need to know that their work is respected and valued by all of us. The fact that there remains so much to do, even though so much has already been achieved, should not discourage them nor deter them from the search for further solutions to problems that we still face. New procedures may have to be found to resolve difficulties of suffering and discomfort. Cost effective and affordable treatments and care need to be developed so that the burden of caring for the ill will not impoverish families nor add unreasonably to their burdens. Diagnostic methods should be studied so that we can begin to ascertain with better certainty the pain that may actually be suffered by the unconscious. The tradition of health science shows that physicians and nurses have not avoided solving problems which human sickness and disease have presented in the past. We are confident that that same tradition will inspire present and future healthcare providers to do the same.

We ask also that those in the judicial and legislative fields bring their expertise to bear on these cases and that they will do so with full attention not only to the law alone but to the basic norms of morality and full respect for human life which ought to supply the proper basis for good law. Because of new circumstances generated by medical and scientific advances, there has been serious interest in advance medical directives such as the living will and durable power of attorney. It is quite reasonable to want to leave instructions regarding one's own healthcare in the event of incapacitation. It is not necessary to submit to procedures which are truly extraordinary or futile. But we caution all those involved in legislation and judgment that laws must have their true foundation in those same principles which guide our moral decisions. Recent court opinions have come very close to agreeing that simply because the patient wishes, nutrition and hydration can be discontinued, even when there is not a question of something that is overly burdensome or simply futile to the patient. The law and legal decisions should never be such as to encourage the removal of the essential means of life and thus yield to a clear intent to bring about death and not merely to the willingness to yield to the fact of human life that all must die and that the day will come for each of us when this is inevitable. The laws must be just and must be based on unequivocal principles which identify the taking of innocent human life and make it illegal, with full recognition that it is already immoral. We should be most cautious and develop these principles very carefully since many of the arguments we have heard in favor of the removal of nutrition and hydration from one group of patients, those in the PVS for example, could easily be applied in the cases of other groups, such as the retarded, the elderly, the incurably crippled, and any other whose diseases modern medicine has not yet been able to cure. Naturally, it would be irresponsible to stand by idly and let such a tragedy occur.

Care of PVS Patients

Catholic Opinion in the United States
Kevin O'Rourke, OP, and Patrick Norris, OP

Members of the Catholic community in the United States often disagree concerning the proper care of a person in a state of permanent unconsciousness. For example, a few years ago, Hugh Finn, suffering from brain damage incurred in an automobile accident, was the person about whom the dispute centered. Even though they foresaw that his death would occur following removal of life support, his wife Michelle and one of Hugh's sisters wanted to have artificial hydration and nutrition (AHN) removed because "it was not helping him." Though Hugh had stated before his accident that he would not desire life support if he were permanently unconscious, other members of his family desired to have AHN continued. Said Hugh's father, "It's murder as far as I am concerned."[1] Even though they were diametrically opposed, members of the Catholic community, claiming "to speak for the Church," supported both sides of the family.

Why is there still such disagreement in regard to this issue within the Catholic community? Usually, the official position of the Church is clear, and though some people may disagree with the official position, there is no doubt that they are dissenting from the official teaching and have no right "to speak for the Church." While general principles for removing life support have been stated in magisterial teaching,[2] there is no authoritative magisterial teaching in regard to specific treatment of people in a state of permanent unconsciousness,[3] so different theological opinions have been formulated.

Reprinted from *Linacre Quarterly*, official journal of the Catholic Medical Association 68 (3): 201–17, 2001.

This article will present the various opinions held by members of the Catholic Church in the United States in regard to removing AHN from people in a permanent state of unconsciousness (persistent vegetative state, PVS). The first opinion views AHN as ordinary care and morally obligatory. The second viewpoint contends that AHN is a medical treatment that should be offered unless it is physiologically futile or excessively burdensome. The third opinion states that AHN may be discontinued in the case of the patient in PVS primarily because it offers no benefit to the patient and secondarily because it may at times impose a grave burden. This article will seek to evaluate these opinions, and opt for one of them as being more in accord with the anthropology identified with Catholic tradition. . . .

THE FIRST OPINION

Basically there are three opinions held by people in the Catholic community in regard to the use of AHN for patients in PVS.[4] The first opinion looks upon the removal of AHN from a PVS patient as a serious violation of the right to life, and often implies that removal of AHN from a PVS patient is an act of euthanasia.[5] This opinion seems to be based upon the fact that death will follow removal of AHN and that for some, any act from which death follows is an act of euthanasia. Proponents of this opinion maintain that only when a patient is in a "terminal condition" and in "imminent danger of death" may life support be removed.[6] As long as AHN continues to do the job for which it was designed, to keep the person alive, it should not be removed. . . .

Occasionally, the argument is offered by proponents of this first position that a feeding tube and nutrition are very inexpensive and comparatively easy for the medical professionals to install so they could never be considered an extraordinary means to prolong life.[7] In other words, this opinion tends to judge whether the means to prolong life are ordinary or extraordinary (morally imperative or morally free) in the abstract, without reference to the condition of the patient. As Kevin Wildes pointed out in a thorough study of the means to prolong life, this attitude is not in accord with Catholic tradition.[8] It dehumanizes the person because it neglects the needs of the person by concentrating on the medical therapy alone. This first opinion was popular when the Nancy Beth Cruzan case was in the news in the late 1980s. Then its popularity seemed to wane, perhaps as a result of several court decisions which allowed removal of AHN from PVS patients and the opinions expressed by several professional societies.[9] But it seems to be gaining adherents once again as avid pro-life proponents seek to oppose any and all withdrawal of life support and persuade people to fill out their advance directives to insure that AHN will always be used, no matter what the circumstances.[10] While this opinion is often invoked by people maintaining that they are fighting the movement toward euthanasia in the United States, others allege that such an absolutist position disposes for euthanasia because this opinion would allow withdrawal of life support only if death were imminent, no matter what the quality of function or the suffering of the individual patient. . . .

Ultimately, the underlying conviction of people who hold this first opinion seems to be that AHN for PVS patients is not a medical device or medical treatment, but merely comfort or normal care which would be morally obligatory when physiologically effective.[11] The aforementioned opinions of medical societies, as well as the medical expertise needed to install AHN, and the fact that AHN does nothing to increase the comfort of the patient contradicts this conviction.[12]

THE SECOND OPINION

The second opinion extant in the Catholic community does not prohibit the removal of AHN from patients in PVS. However, as we shall see, in its interpretation of "hope of benefit" and "excessive burden," it does limit the criteria which may be used for removal. This opinion was expressed most authoritatively in 1992 by the U.S. Bishops Pro-Life Committee (PLC) and is held by some theologians and philosophers,[13] but was never adopted by the Administrative Board of the National Conference of Catholic Bishops (NCCB) nor by the NCCB as a whole. It is of considerable importance within the Catholic community in the United States as a pastoral statement, even though the PLC does not promulgate doctrinal statements. While the document of the PLC "repeats solid principles," it also contains "contingent and conjectural elements," which mitigate its doctrinal authority.[14] As the PLC itself declared, the document states "the first word" which may be revised before the "last word" is spoken. Briefly, this opinion may be expressed in the words of the committee:

. . . it is our considered judgment that while legitimate Catholic debate continues, decisions concerning these patients (PVS) should be guided by a presumption in favor of medically assisted nutrition and hydration. A decision to discontinue such measures should be made in light of a careful assessment of the burdens and benefits of nutrition and hydration for the individual patient and his or her family and community. Such measures must not be withdrawn in order to cause death, but they may be withdrawn if they offer no reasonable hope of sustaining life or pose excessive risks or burdens.[15]

There is no dispute in the United States Catholic community in regard to teaching and theology concerning the intention of removing life support. It must not be to kill the patient, but rather to stop doing something disproportionate (no hope of benefit) or to benefit the patient by removing a burdensome therapy (remove an excessive burden). In traditional Catholic theology, evidence that people act ethically when removing life support is drawn either from "no hope of benefit" or from "excessive burden." "No hope of benefit" simply means that the goods for which one seeks medical therapy are not forthcoming from the therapy; "excessive burden" means that any benefits forthcoming from use of a therapy are outweighed significantly by the burdens. Burdens may be spiritual, psychic, and economic as well as physiological. These criteria are stated in the *Ethical and Religious Directives for Catholic Health Care Services* (ERD),[16] a document prepared by the United States Bishops to maintain ethical standards in the provision of healthcare in Catholic healthcare facilities. If the medical therapy offers hope of benefit and does not impose an excessive burden, it is called an ordinary or proportionate means of preserving life. If it either offers no hope of benefit or imposes an excessive burden, it is called an extraordinary or disproportionate means to prolong life.[17] . . .

THE THIRD OPINION

The third opinion is held by many Catholic theologians and ethicists who work in clinical settings and by many medical societies who have studied the issue.[18] In addition, this opinion has been followed by some bishops who have been called upon to offer opinions in regard to well-publicized cases in their dioceses.[19] The opinion follows the traditional admonition that the death of the patient must not be the proximate intention of the persons either requesting the removal of life support or removing it from the patient. But it also maintains that once a firm prognosis of permanent unconsciousness has been made, AHN may be removed. This third opinion uses both of the criteria for removing life support, originated by Catholic theologians at Salamanca, Spain, in the sixteenth century: namely, hope of benefit to the patient or excessive burden to the patient, his or her family, and to the community which is involved in caring for the patient.[20]

The essential difference between the second and third opinions is that those who hold the third opinion maintain that continuing life support for people with a PVS diagnosis does not offer "hope of benefit" for the patient. Proponents of both the second and third opinion agree that the proximate intention of the people removing life support must not be to end the life of the patient. But the proponents of the third opinion maintain that the continued existence of the patient who is permanently unconscious offers objective evidence that life support may be removed because it is disproportionate or unnecessary.[21] Proponents of this position support their opinion by referring to the purpose of healthcare and the purpose of life. Healthcare seeks to enable people to strive for the purpose of life, not merely to function at the biological level.[22] Ultimately, the purpose in life is friendship with God.[23] Recall in another era we would answer the Catechism question, "Why did God make you?" with the response, "To know Him, love Him, and be happy with Him in this life and the next." To know, love, and be happy requires cognitive-affective function. If a person does not have the potential for cognitive-affective function, it does not mean that God does not love him or her or that the person is no longer a friend of God. But it does mean that the person cannot pursue the friendship of God, the purpose of life, through his or her free actions. Therefore, the moral imperative to help the person toward health and existence is no longer present if there is no potential for cognitive-affective function and treatment offers no palliative benefit. The truth of this explanation is confirmed by the care given to anencephalic infants in Catholic hospitals. Their lives could be prolonged, maybe even for a few years, but no care outside of comfort care is given because they do not have the capacity for cognitive-affective function. This manner of treatment has been approved by a recent statement of the Doctrine Committee of the National Conference of Catholic Bishops (NCCB) in the United States.[24] . . .

NOTES

1. Brooke Masters, "Family's Life and Death Battle Plays Out in Court," *Washington Post*, September 9, 1998, p. A1.
2. Congregation for the Doctrine of the Faith (CDF), "Vatican Declaration on Euthanasia," *Origins* 10 (1980): 154–57.

3. T. Kopfensteiner, "Developing Directive 58," *Health Progress* (May–June 2000): 20–27.

4. In stating only three opinions, we are excluding the position that would claim legitimacy for the intentional killing of patients through the deliberate omission of AHN. This opinion has never been compatible with Catholic teaching (see John Paul II, *Evangelium Vitae*, no. 65). For the full text, see *Origins* 24 (1995): 689–727.

5. Edward Richard, "Bioethical Magisterium on Normal Treatment and Ordinary Care: Medically Assisted Feeding and Hydration," unpublished paper, copyright 1999, distributed by Archbishop of Saint Louis to diocesan clergy, pp.1, 5.

6. Germain Grisez, *Living a Christian Life,* vol. 2 of *The Way of the Lord Jesus* (Quincy, IL: Franciscan Press, 1993), 284–86, 524–32. Cf. Robert Barry, "Feeding the Comatose and the Common Good in the Catholic Tradition," *The Thomist* 53 (1989): 1–30.

7. Cf., "Court Rules Against Christine Busalacchi," *National Right to Life News* (February 6, 1993).

8. Kevin Wildes, "Ordinary and Extraordinary Means and the Quality of Life," *Theological Studies* 57 (1996): 500–13.

9. Alan Meisel, "The Legal Consensus About Foregoing Life Sustaining Treatments: Its Status and Its Prospects," *Kennedy Institute of Ethics Journal* 2 (1992): 309–45. Court cases: *Brophy v. New England Sinai Hospital, Inc.*, 398 Mass 417, 497 N.E. 2nd 626 (1986); *Cruzan v. Director, Missouri Dept. of Health*, 497 U.S. 261, 110 S. Ct. 2841 (1990); John Paris, "Hugh Finn's 'Right to Die,'" *America* 179 (October 31, 1998): 13–15. Professional Societies: American Academy of Neurology (see note 3); Committee on Ethics, American Nurses Association, *Guidelines on Withdrawing or Withholding Food and Fluid* (Kansas City, MO, 1987); and American Medical Association Council on Ethical and Judicial Affairs, "Decisions Near the End of Life," *Journal of the American Medical Association* 267 (1992): 2229–33.

10. Amy Goldstein, "Pro-Life Activists Take on Death," *Washington Post,* November 10, 1998, p. A1.

11. William Saunders, "Euthanasia and Extraordinary Care, Parts I and II," *Arlington Catholic Herald* (October 15 and 22, 1998). See also George Graham, "Artificial Nutrition and Hydration: It Is Time to Take a Stand," *Homiletic and Pastoral Review* 99 (May 1999): 11.

12. Gastone Celestia, "Persistent Vegetative State: Clinical and Ethical Issues," *Theoretical Medicine* 18 (1997): 221–36; Jacquelyn Slomka, "What Do Apple Pie and Motherhood Have to Do with Feeding Tubes and Caring for the Patient?" *Archives of Internal Medicine* 155 (1995): 1258–63; and Thomas Finucane, Colleen Christmas, and Kathy Travis, "Tube Feeding in Patients with Advance Dementia," *Journal of the American Medical Association* 282 (1999): 1365–70.

13. U.S. Bishops Pro-Life Committee, "Nutrition and Hydration: Moral and Pastoral Reflections," *Origins* 21 (1992): 705–12; Joseph Boyle, "A Case for Sometimes Tube-Feeding Patients in Persistent Vegetative State," in *Euthanasia Examined,* ed. John Keown (Cambridge: Cambridge University Press, 1995), pp. 189–99; William May, "Tube Feeding and the 'Vegetative State' (Part I)," *Ethics and Medics* 23 (December 1998): 1–2 and "Tube Feeding and the 'Vegetative State' (Part II)," *Ethics and Medics* 24 (January 1999): 3–4.

14. CDF, "Instructions on the Ecclesial Vocation of the Theologian," n. 17. For full text, see *Origins* 20 (1990): 117–26.

15. U.S. Bishops Pro-Life Committee, "Nutrition and Hydration: Moral and Pastoral Reflections," *Origins* 21 (1992): 710.

16. National Conference of Catholic Bishops (NCCB), *Ethical and Religious Directives for Catholic Health Services* (ERD), fifth printing (Washington, DC: United States Catholic Conference, 1995), pp. 21–22 and Directive nos. 55–58.

17. Ibid., Directive nos. 56 and 57.

18. Paris, "Hugh Finn's 'Right to Die'"; Richard McCormick, "'Moral Considerations' Ill Considered," *America* 166 (March 14, 1992): 210–14; Dennis Brodeur, "The Ethics of Cruzan," *Health Progress* 71 (October 1990): 42–47; and Kevin O'Rourke, "Should Nutrition and Hydration be Provided to Permanently Unconscious and Other Mentally Disabled Persons?" *Issues in Law and Medicine* 5 (1989): 181–96. Cf. note 20 for medical societies that approve this practice.

19. U.S. Bishops Pro-Life Committee, "Nutrition and Hydration: Moral and Pastoral Reflections," *Origins* 21 (1992): 707–708.

20. Daniel Cronin, "Moral Law in Regard to the Ordinary and Extraordinary Means of Conserving Life," in *Conserving Human Life*, ed. Russell Smith (Braintree, MA: Pope John XXIII Center, 1989), pp. 33ff.

21. Archdiocese of Chicago, "Chicago Commission Speaks Out on Nutrition and Hydration," *Health Progress* 68 (December 1987): 35–36, 68.

22. Edmund Pellegrino and David Thomasma, *For the Patient's Good: The Restoration of Beneficence in Health Care* (New York: Oxford University Press, 1988), p. 80.

23. *Catechism of the Catholic Church* (English translation), 2nd ed. Liberia Editrice Vaticana, 1997, n. 1.

24. NCCB Doctrine Committee, "Moral Principles Concerning Infants with Anencephaly," 26 *Origins* (1996): 276; and Kevin O'Rourke, "Ethical Opinions in Regard to the Question of Early Delivery of Anencephalic Infants," *Linacre Quarterly* 63 (August 1996): 55–59.

Reverence for Human Life

James J. McCartney

In the book of Deuteronomy, Moses tells the Israelites "Choose life!" This motif has been a central vision of both Judaism and Christianity for millennia, and the values that spring from this vision have been consistently articulated and enriched over the centuries by adherents of both of these monotheistic faiths. In John's Gospel, Jesus of Nazareth is seen as the source of all life (as the Word of God made flesh) and especially the spiritual life of humans ("I have come that they might have life . . ."). Reverence for human life in all of its dimensions, biological, psychosocial, ethical, and spiritual, is one of the hallmarks of Christian life and practice, and the dignity and sanctity of human life, especially the lives of the poor, marginalized, disabled, or oppressed, is one of the constant holdings of Christian ethics. . . .

CHRISTIAN ETHICAL TEACHING REGARDING THE END OF BIOLOGICAL LIFE

In the Catholic tradition, compassionate care of the dying does include the provision of adequate palliative care and support, presence, touch, and spiritual comfort, and the right to refuse burdensome or useless treatments. It does not include assisted suicide and euthanasia. It should not come as a surprise that death and dying are of major theological interest for the Christian

From *Visions and Values: Ethical Viewpoints in the Catholic Tradition*, edited by Judith A. Dwyer (Washington, DC: Georgetown University Press, 1999), pp. 71, 82, 86–95.

220

tradition. Christians believe that it is precisely through the redemptive death and resurrection of Jesus of Nazareth that God's saving self-disclosure in human history has taken place. Christians participate in this Divine redemptive activity through Baptism wherein the believer promises to *die* to sin and live in Christ. Indeed part of the symbolism of Baptism by immersion is the figurative entering into the tomb (dying to the power of sin) and emerging from the tomb clothed in the radiant innocence of Jesus' resurrection and glorification.

Emphasis upon sacramental activity is a hallmark of Roman Catholic piety and spirituality. Catholics believe that God's saving power is mediated through earthly signs and symbols which touch us at special graced moments of our lives. And at least four of the sacraments—baptism, reconciliation, Eucharist, and anointing—are seen as appropriate in the situation of death and dying since this particular time is best spent preparing to enter into the fullness of God's kingdom.

Thus the notion of Christian death has always meant for Catholics a time of refocusing one's energies away from earthly survival and biological life towards spiritual realities and life with God in Christ whose Spirit we share. Death with dignity in the Catholic tradition means the ability to prepare oneself spiritually for the life to come since Catholics believe that when the body dies "life is changed, not ended" as the *Preface for the Dead* said at Masses for the dead proclaims so well. Yet at the same time the Catholic ethical tradition has emphasized that we should take reasonable means to preserve our biological life and health since we are stewards, not masters, of our own bodies. Oftentimes Catholics are confronted with whether they should try to focus their energies on staying alive, possibly at great burden or expense to themselves or others, or preparing for Christian death. . . .

Legitimate Refusal of Medical Treatment

The Catholic tradition puts high value on the promotion and preservation of life and health. It believes that biological life is a gift from God, and that we are stewards and conservators of this gift and must take those means generally available to preserve our lives and enhance our well-being. However, biological life is not considered an absolute value by the Catholic tradition and is in fact a relative good, because its purpose is to support and enable the possibility of spiritual life. Nevertheless, biological life is a most basic value and, in fact, is the source of all other human values and goods.

Catholic teaching sees the responsibility to care for one's life and health as a positive command, part of the affirmative natural law. Unlike some negative commands which, in principle, can bind absolutely (e.g., the command against directly taking the life of the innocent), affirmative commands may always, in principle, admit of exceptions. Thus the command to worship on Sunday by attending Mass does not bind absolutely, but allows for exception when sickness or other serious obstacles stand in the way. The responsibility to care for life and health, being an affirmative command, also does not bind absolutely. In fact, the Church, acknowledging human limitation and finitude, stresses that not everything possible need be done to preserve life and health because this would be a moral impossibility in some situations.

The Catholic Church has always honored the profession of medicine, seeing physicians as possessing certain skills and knowledge to enhance biological health, cure disease, and treat illness. Nonetheless, the Church has always seen the promotion of life and health as a personal responsibility, and has allowed people great discretion with regard to the means they consider necessary in the accomplishment of these laudable goals. Therefore, physicians must always get the informed consent of the patient in order to treat, and it is ultimately up to the patient, not the physician, to determine what treatment options will best meet the obligations of stewardship the patient has before God. This decision about treatment options, however, is not totally subjective and discretionary. Catholic teaching has suggested several standards in order to help people decide whether a given medical intervention is mandatory or not.

Ordinary versus Extraordinary

Unless another standard contravenes, Catholic teaching maintains that those medical interventions which would be customary, or usual, given the lifestyle of the person in relation with his or her society, should be considered ethically mandatory. Those interventions which would not be customary, or would be unusual within a given culture, would be considered extraordinary and medically optional. Perhaps better wording for this standard would be "usual versus unusual" since oftentimes "ordinary" has been interpreted as "standard medical treatment" and "extraordinary" as "experimental" treatment, clearly a misunderstanding of the Church's emphasis with regard to these terms.

An excellent example of the use of this criterion is provided by Gary

Atkinson[1] when he discusses the sixteenth-century moralist Francisco De Vitoria. Vitoria believes that if a person uses foods which people commonly use and in the quantity which customarily suffices for the conservation of strength, then the person is acting morally even if by acting in this way one's life is notably shortened. In addition, an individual would not be required to use the best, most delicate, most expensive foods, even if they were the most healthful. Vitoria says that if the doctor were to advise the person to eat chickens and partridges, the individual could still choose to eat eggs and other common items instead, even though the person knew for certain that life could be extended another twenty years by eating such foods. Abbots of monasteries often followed this advice when monks became ill since they were worried that if monks grew accustomed to more nutritious foods during time of sickness, perhaps when they got well they would not be able to return to their more simple manner of life.

In deciding whether a given medical intervention is ordinary or extraordinary, we should consider whether its use, *for this particular person*, would be perceived as usual/customary or not. Medical interventions which would generally be considered ordinary and usual would include medicines taken by mouth, injections, minor surgery, and most commonly used diagnostic interventions. Also included would be temporary intravenous feeding and medications as well as temporary modifications of diet and lifestyle. These all could become extraordinary and unusual if the person could honestly say that for some weighty reason, they were not the customary means to health as far as they were concerned, or because this was not the customary way of treatment within their culture or society. Obviously the criterion of ordinary versus extraordinary, even if very helpful at times, is a very ambiguous one.

Burden versus Benefit

Another standard often proposed and discussed within the Catholic tradition for determining whether or not a medical intervention is morally obligatory is the standard of burdensomeness. Often this criterion is coupled and contrasted with the notion of benefit and it is held that a medical intervention is truly burdensome when the difficulties of treatment outweigh any possible benefits to be gained. However, many times it is very difficult to assign moral weight to the interventions suggested and the results anticipated. This can cause the person to become genuinely confused as to whether an anticipated course of action will be more beneficial than burdensome, or vice versa. Using a benefit/burden calculus to determine burdensomeness greatly constricts and limits the notion of burden as it was traditionally understood by Catholic scholars and the Church.

Examples of burdensome interventions (as construed by the patient) have been provided by Catholic moralists through the years. These include moving to a more healthful climate (in the case, for example, of respiratory distress) if, by moving, one would have to uproot oneself from job, family, and other relationships; amputation surgery when it is believed that the disfigurement, pain, or crippling effect of the amputation will be too difficult to bear either physically or psychologically; chemotherapy for cancer when it is anticipated that the side effects of the drugs will be gravely debilitating; and major surgery when there is great expense involved or when the risk is very high. Notice that some of these examples clearly relate to how the person assesses his or her quality of life after the intervention. Therefore, to hold that decisions involving burdensomeness must only focus on the burdensomeness of intervention and not on the (anticipated) burdensomeness of life after the intervention is a clear misinterpretation of the doctrine of burdensomeness as it has been historically construed. We may, and indeed should, make quality of life judgments about ourselves when deciding which contemporary medical or surgical interventions we wish to accept or refuse. What we ought not to do is decide that another person's life is not worth living, because this directly contradicts the reverence for life that Christians should have. We may, however, make treatment refusals on behalf of another when that person has told us that he or she does not want continued treatment under certain specific circumstances because he or she would consider the situation too difficult and burdensome in these circumstances. We are also sometimes legally and ethically empowered to make decisions about another when that other hasn't told us what he or she would have wanted in that situation. In these cases decision making is very difficult because what must be considered is the best interests of all involved in the decision, including the patient and the caregivers alike. A colleague of mine and I have tried to deal with this issue by developing a decision-making grid that might be helpful in decisions dealing with newborns, children, or anyone who has not expressed his or her wishes with regard to treatment options in the situation of terminal illness or catastrophic injury.[2]

Generally the assessment of whether or not a given treatment option is a grave burden should be made by the patient or at least by his or her designated healthcare proxy. However, where an appointment of a proxy has not been made and where we do not know the wishes of the patient, the Catholic tradition suggests we consider the burden that the proposed intervention places on the family itself before deciding whether we should continue. Pope Pius XII expresses this clearly with regard to resuscitation: "Consequently, if it appears that the attempt at resuscitation constitutes such a burden for the family that one cannot in all conscience impose it upon them, they can lawfully insist that the doctor should discontinue these attempts, and the doctor can lawfully comply. . . . The rights and duties of the family depend in general upon the presumed will of the unconscious patient if he or she is of age and 'sui juris'. Where the proper and independent duty of the family is concerned, they are usually bound only to the use of ordinary means."[3] And although Pius in this allocution does relate ordinary means to the notion of burden, I believe that in this passage his notion of "ordinary" can best be construed as saying that the family must provide for the unconscious person what is customary and usual care, and not feel bound to medical interventions that are needlessly prolonging the process of dying, or are not restoring the person to health. In secular terms this is often referred to as the "best interest" principle.

Burdensome treatment options are those which the patient believes are jeopardizing his or her higher goals, or those which are not offset by comparable benefits, or those which cause great anxiety to the patient, either because of the intervention itself (anticipated pain, suffering, depression, financial ruin) or because of the poor quality of life rendered by the intervention (isolation or separation from significant others, disfigurement, economic burden to others).

Perhaps the person who has best articulated the Catholic tradition's understanding of burdensomeness is Pope Pius XII. In an address previously mentioned, the pope stressed that "normally one is held to use only . . . means that do not involve any grave burden for oneself or another. A more strict obligation would be too heavy for most people to bear and would render the attainment of the higher, more important good too difficult. Life, health, and all temporal activities are in fact subordinated to spiritual ends."[4] In this passage the pope seems to be focusing upon burdensomeness in and of itself without consideration of any countervailing benefit. I would thus argue that if a person perceives any medical intervention as too burdensome either because of the pain or suffering involved, or because the intervention will be disfiguring or crippling, or because it will cause the family too much grief and hardship, or even because it will cause the person or the family financial difficulties (although society has the responsibility to provide a level of healthcare that should make this type of burden less significant ethically), then this person is free to reject the intervention. I wish to emphasize that the determination of a grave burden should be made by the patient or at least by those who know and respect the values and beliefs of the patient. In addition, burdens are not only determined by considering physical interventions but also by assessing the psychological, economic, or spiritual harms as perceived by the patient or patient surrogate.

A good example of this kind of assessment of burdensomeness is provided by Jehovah's Witnesses, who, for religious reasons, believe that the acceptance of blood transfusions causes expulsion from their religious community and possibly condemnation by God. Jehovah's Witnesses construe the spiritual burden of expulsion and possible condemnation as weighty enough to refuse blood and blood products in almost all situations. And although Catholics do not share this interpretation of biblical revelation, Catholic healthcare facilities must, on the ground of religious freedom, respect the Witnesses' refusal of transfusions as an ethically optional choice because for them accepting transfusion constitutes a grave burden.

It is clear that the Catholic tradition, when considering burden as a reason for refusing a treatment option, does so in a broad and inclusive manner, and not in a narrow and strict way as some contemporary commentators of this tradition would have us believe.

Useful versus Useless

This distinction made by Catholic authors is of rather recent vintage and was developed most extensively by Gerald Kelly in the United States.[5] Simply stated, this distinction holds that even medical interventions considered as usual and not generally burdensome are not morally obligatory when they are medically useless, that is, when they do not offer a reasonable hope of benefit. In fact, Kelly would want to designate these interventions as ethically *extraordinary* precisely because of their uselessness. However, I mentioned before that this approach strips away the conceptual fullness of the original understanding of *ordinary*, which, as we have discussed, really meant usual or customary when it was first used in ethical discourse. Thus I would prefer to understand uselessness not as a criterion in itself, but as an instantiation of the burden/benefit distinction discussed in the previous section. There I mentioned that I accepted the burden/benefit calculus even though I also hold that it is very important psychologically to consider the burden (present or anticipated) in and of itself. In the case of a useless medical intervention, we are confronted with a situation in which there is some burden without any reasonable hope of benefit (as Kelly himself describes his notion of useless). Thus there is always a net effect of burdensomeness since there is in these situations no reasonable anticipated benefit to offset the burden however slight. I would, then, hold that useless medical interventions are ethically objectionable because they provide a burden (possibly minimal) which is not offset by a reasonable hope of benefit.

One significant problem that arises within the context of discussing useless interventions is exactly what constitutes them. For example, is the provision of artificial sustenance and hydration to a person in a persistent vegetative state (PVS) *useless* since it is not providing the benefit of restoration of health, or *useful* since it is keeping the individual alive (sometimes for long periods of time). It seems that Kelly introduced the distinction precisely because he was concerned about the use of intravenous feeding for people who were not going to recover. Thus, he would hold some restoration of health as necessary in order to consider a medical intervention useful. I will discuss my own approach to the sustenance issue in a later section where I will try to show that the artificial provision of sustenance for individuals in a PVS is ethically optional for several reasons, all of which relate to the criteria I have discussed here.

Proportionate versus Disproportionate

Treatment options can be ordinary or extraordinary, burdensome or beneficial, useless or useful, or some combination of any or all of these criteria. To determine whether a proposed treatment option is ethically mandatory in a given case, one would have to take all the relevant criteria into consideration. When one decides that a treatment option is morally obligatory, it is generally described as proportionate since there is a favorable proportion among all the values involved indicating that the proposed intervention ought to be chosen and accepted. When this weighing of values helps the person decide that a treatment is ethically optional since it involves an unusual, burdensome, or useless intervention, the treatment option is said to be disproportionate since the disvalues outweigh the values in this particular case. Thus the terms proportionate or disproportionate are really used as an ethical shorthand to indicate when a proposed intervention is ethically mandatory in a given case or not. It is important to stress that this weighing of values must be done for each individual case, and that oftentimes ongoing evaluation must be continued while the treatment option is being carried out. Some treatment options which initially seem promising and do not appear to have much burden attached to them are transformed into very burdensome and/or ineffective procedures as the disease progresses. The Catholic tradition has always allowed for the possibility that a treatment option construed as proportionate at the beginning of the intervention may become disproportionate because of a change of circumstances. Just because a treatment option has been accepted as ethically mandatory and initiated doesn't mean that it must be continued. As the circumstances of the case change, the ethical evaluation of medical interventions also may change and these may be discontinued once they are experienced as disproportionate and ethically optional.

Artificial Delivery of Nutrition and Hydration

It is my conviction that the artificial provision of nutrition and hydration by feeding tube (either through the nose or directly into the stomach) or by intravenous infusion is a medical treatment (and not basic care). I am supported in this conviction by the Supreme Courts of several states and of the United States, and also by the American Medical Association and other healthcare organizations. I believe that a person could decide, on the basis of the criteria I have presented above, that the artificial delivery of nutrition and hydration is morally disproportionate, therefore ethically optional and able to be refused. When persons make this evaluation and decide that they wish to refuse artificial nutrition and hydration if they should be terminally ill or in a PVS, and especially when they indicate this in writing in some sort of advance directive for healthcare, their wishes and values should be respected and followed. Pope Pius XII states this explicitly in the allocution cited above: "The rights and duties of the doctor are correlative to those of the patient. The doctor, in fact, has no separate or independent right where the patient is concerned. In general, the doctor can take action only if the patient explicitly or implicitly, directly or indirectly, gives permission."

How do the standards we have discussed earlier apply in the situation of the acceptance or refusal of the artificial delivery of nutrition or hydration? First of all, people are not generally fed through a feeding tube or an intravenous line. And while these interventions have short-term benefits for some patients, and it has become customary or usual to use them in these circumstances, it is not customary or usual (ordinary as I understand the term) to receive sustenance and hydration in this way for a long period of time. Certainly this is true in less well developed countries that have trouble providing enough food for their citizens to eat by mouth, but I believe that even here (in the United States) one could construe this procedure as not customary and usual and thus refuse it on the grounds that it is an extraordinary means of delivering nutrition and hydration and therefore able to be forgone.

I also hold that the artificial provision of nutrition and hydration could be seen as a grave burden. In the first place, this treatment is often accompanied by diarrhea and other discomforts and irritations which of themselves could be gravely burdensome, especially when the person is conscious. But, additionally, persons might rightly decide that continuing this treatment (especially if they were in a PVS) might place heavy psychological or economic burdens on other family members which the patient would not want them to bear. And although a comparison of benefits and burdens is difficult here because some will point to the benefit of continuing biological life as resolving the issue of continuing the provision once and for all, while others might point out that the prolongation of biological life without restoration of conscious awareness is not really a benefit but actually a burden, nevertheless, the other burdens of providing sustenance which I have considered are ample justification for considering it ethically optional no matter how beneficial one considers it to be.

A consideration of usefulness, unless the patient is terminally ill with little time to live, encounters the same sort of conceptual difficulty as a consideration of benefit and is not helpful in this discussion. What I mean is that those who see continued biological life as a great good will assess this intervention as very useful, while those who see continued biological life without the restoration of consciousness as a grave burden will consider the provision of sustenance and hydration as useless. Usefulness comes into play in this discussion when, for those patients who are in a borderline PVS and who may perceive pain, provision of sustenance and hydration is considered as a palliative treatment. If the evidence in a particular case is that it is useful in this regard, then it should be provided, unless the patient has specifically indicated refusal even with the knowledge that it might have a palliative application in his or her specific case.

With regard to assessing the provision of sustenance and hydration for incompetent patients who have not made their wishes known, I recommend caution and prudence as well as statutory safeguards to prevent against abuse. But I also recognize that there are situations in which families have the right to make decisions that will allow loved ones to die, either because they have a sense that this is what the person would have wanted in this situation even though the person has never told them so explicitly, or even because the total care and treatment of a family member is causing the family grave psychological, economic, or spiritual hardship. I repeat the words of Pius XII in this regard: "Where the proper and independent duty of the family is concerned, they are bound only to the use of ordinary means." With regard to nutrition and hydration, a useful rule of thumb is provided in the *Ethical and Religious Directives for Catholic Health Care Services* in Directive 58, which states: "There should be a presumption in favor of providing nutrition and hydration to all patients, including patients who require medically assisted nutrition and hydration, as long as this is of sufficient benefit to outweigh the burdens involved to the patient."

NOTES

1. G. M. Atkinson, "Theological History of Catholic Teaching on Prolonging Life," in *Moral Responsibility in Prolonging Life Decisions* (St. Louis: Pope John Center, 1981), pp. 95–115.

2. J. M. Trau and J. J. McCartney, "In the Best Interest of the Patient; Its Meaning and Application Today," *Health Progress* (April 1993): 50–56.

3. Pope Pius XII, "Allocution 'Le Dr. Bruno Haid,'" *Acta Apostolicae Sedis*, November 24, 1957, pp. 1031–32.

4. Ibid.

5. G. Kelly, "The Duty to Preserve Life," *Theological Studies* 12 (1951): 550–56.

To the Participants in the International Congress on "Life-Sustaining Treatments and Vegetative State: Scientific Advances and Ethical Dilemmas"

Pope John Paul II

Saturday, March 20, 2004

Distinguished Ladies and Gentlemen,

1. I cordially greet all of you who took part in the International Congress: "Life-Sustaining Treatments and Vegetative State: Scientific Advances and Ethical Dilemmas." I wish to extend a special greeting to Bishop Elio Sgreccia, Vice-President of the Pontifical Academy for Life, and to Prof. Gian Luigi Gigli, President of the International Federation of Catholic Medical Associations and selfless champion of the fundamental value of life, who has kindly expressed your shared feelings. This important Congress, organized jointly by the Pontifical Academy for Life and the International Federation of Catholic Medical Associations, is dealing with a very significant issue: *the clinical condition called the "vegetative state."* The complex scientific, ethical, social, and pastoral implications of such a condition require in-depth reflections and a fruitful interdisciplinary dialogue, as evidenced by the intense and carefully structured program of your work sessions.

2. With deep esteem and sincere hope, the Church encourages the efforts of men and women of science who, sometimes at great sacrifice, daily dedicate their task of study and research to the improvement of the diagnostic, therapeutic, prognostic, and rehabilitative possibilities confronting those

From March 20, 2004, http://www.vatican.va/holy_father/john_paul_ii/speeches/2004/march/documents/hf_jp-ii_spe_20040320_congress-fiamc_en.html (accessed November 23, 2005).

patients who rely completely on those who care for and assist them. The person in a vegetative state, in fact, shows no evident sign of self-awareness or of awareness of the environment, and seems unable to interact with others or to react to specific stimuli. Scientists and researchers realize that one must, first of all, arrive at a correct diagnosis, which usually requires prolonged and careful observation in specialized centers, given also the high number of diagnostic errors reported in the literature. Moreover, not a few of these persons, with appropriate treatment and with specific rehabilitation programs, have been able to emerge from a vegetative state. On the contrary, many others unfortunately remain prisoners of their condition even for long stretches of time and without needing technological support. In particular, the term *permanent vegetative state* has been coined to indicate the condition of those patients whose "vegetative state" continues for over a year. Actually, there is no different diagnosis that corresponds to such a definition, but only a conventional prognostic judgment, relative to the fact that the recovery of patients, statistically speaking, is ever more difficult as the condition of vegetative state is prolonged in time. However, we must neither forget nor underestimate that there are well-documented cases of at least partial recovery even after many years; we can thus state that medical science, up until now, is still unable to predict with certainty who among patients in this condition will recover and who will not.

3. Faced with patients in similar clinical conditions, there are some who cast doubt on the persistence of the "human quality" itself, almost as if the adjective "vegetative" (whose use is now solidly established), which symbolically describes a clinical state, could or should be instead applied to the sick as such, actually demeaning their value and personal dignity. In this sense, it must be noted that this term, even when confined to the clinical context, is certainly not the most felicitous when applied to human beings. In opposition to such trends of thought, I feel the duty to reaffirm strongly that the intrinsic value and personal dignity of every human being do not change, no matter what the concrete circumstances of his or her life. *A man, even if seriously ill or disabled in the exercise of his highest functions, is and always will be a man*, and he will never become a "vegetable" or an "animal." Even our brothers and sisters who find themselves in the clinical condition of a "vegetative state" retain their human dignity in all its fullness. The loving gaze of God the Father continues to fall upon them, acknowledging them as his sons and daughters, especially in need of help.

4. Medical doctors and healthcare personnel, society, and the Church

have moral duties toward these persons from which they cannot exempt themselves without lessening the demands both of professional ethics and human and Christian solidarity. The sick person in a vegetative state, awaiting recovery or a natural end, still has the right to basic healthcare (nutrition, hydration, cleanliness, warmth, etc.) and to the prevention of complications related to his confinement to bed. He also has the right to appropriate rehabilitative care and to be monitored for clinical signs of eventual recovery. I should like particularly to underline how the administration of water and food, even when provided by artificial means, always represents a *natural means* of preserving life, not a *medical act.* Its use, furthermore, should be considered, in principle, *ordinary* and *proportionate,* and as such morally obligatory, insofar as and until it is seen to have attained its proper finality, which in the present case consists in providing nourishment to the patient and alleviation of his suffering. The obligation to provide the "normal care due to the sick in such cases" (Congregation for the Doctrine of the Faith, *Iura et Bona,* p. iv) includes, in fact, the use of nutrition and hydration (cf. Pontifical Council "Cor Unum," *Dans le Cadre,* 2, 4, 4; Pontifical Council for Pastoral Assistance to Health Care Workers, *Charter of Health Care Workers,* n. 120). The evaluation of probabilities, founded on waning hopes for recovery when the vegetative state is prolonged beyond a year, cannot ethically justify the cessation or interruption of *minimal care* for the patient, including nutrition and hydration. Death by starvation or dehydration is, in fact, the only possible outcome as a result of their withdrawal. In this sense it ends up becoming, if done knowingly and willingly, true and proper euthanasia by omission. In this regard, I recall what I wrote in the Encyclical *Evangelium Vitae,* making it clear that "by *euthanasia in the true and proper sense* must be understood an action or omission which by its very nature and intention brings about death, with the purpose of eliminating all pain"; such an act is always "a *serious violation of the law of God,* since it is the deliberate and morally unacceptable killing of a human person" (n. 65). Besides, the moral principle is well known, according to which even the simple doubt of being in the presence of a living person already imposes the obligation of full respect and of abstaining from any act that aims at anticipating the person's death.

5. Considerations about the "quality of life," often actually dictated by psychological, social, and economic pressures, cannot take precedence over general principles. First of all, no evaluation of costs can outweigh the value of the fundamental good which we are trying to protect, that of human life.

Moreover, to admit that decisions regarding man's life can be based on the external acknowledgment of its quality is the same as acknowledging that increasing and decreasing levels of quality of life, and therefore of human dignity, can be attributed from an external perspective to any subject, thus introducing into social relations a discriminatory and eugenic principle. Moreover, it is not possible to rule out *a priori* that the withdrawal of nutrition and hydration, as reported by authoritative studies, is the source of considerable suffering for the sick person, even if we can see only the reactions at the level of the autonomic nervous system or of gestures. Modern clinical neurophysiology and neuro-imaging techniques, in fact, seem to point to the lasting quality in these patients of elementary forms of communication and analysis of stimuli.

6. However, it is not enough to reaffirm the general principle according to which the value of a man's life cannot be made subordinate to any judgment of its quality expressed by other men; it is necessary to promote the *taking of positive actions* as a stand against pressures to withdraw hydration and nutrition as a way to put an end to the lives of these patients. It is necessary, above all, *to support those families* who have had one of their loved ones struck down by this terrible clinical condition. They cannot be left alone with their heavy human, psychological, and financial burden. Although the care for these patients is not, in general, particularly costly, society must allot sufficient resources for the care of this sort of frailty, by way of bringing about appropriate, concrete initiatives such as, for example, the creation of a network of awakening centers with specialized treatment and rehabilitation programs; financial support and home assistance for families when patients are moved back home at the end of intensive rehabilitation programs; the establishment of facilities which can accommodate those cases in which there is no family able to deal with the problem or to provide "breaks" for those families who are at risk of psychological and moral burnout. Proper care for these patients and their families should, moreover, include the presence and the witness of a medical doctor and an entire team, who are asked to help the family understand that they are there as allies who are in this struggle with them. The participation of volunteers represents a basic support to enable the family to break out of its isolation and to help it to realize that it is a precious and not a forsaken part of the social fabric. In these situations, then, spiritual counseling and pastoral aid are particularly important as help for recovering the deepest meaning of an apparently desperate condition.

7. Distinguished Ladies and Gentlemen, in conclusion I exhort you, as

men and women of science responsible for the dignity of the medical profession, to guard jealously the principle according to which the true task of
medicine is "to cure if possible, always to care." As a pledge and support of
this, your authentic humanitarian mission to give comfort and support to
your suffering brothers and sisters, I remind you of the words of Jesus:
"Amen, I say to you, whatever you did for one of these least brothers of
mine, you did for me" (Matt. 25:40). In this light, I invoke upon you the
assistance of him, whom a meaningful saying of the Church Fathers
describes as *Christus medicus*, and in entrusting your work to the protection
of Mary, Consoler of the sick and Comforter of the dying, I lovingly bestow
on all of you a special Apostolic Blessing.

Implications of the
Papal Allocution on Feeding Tubes

Thomas A. Shannon and James J. Walter

The recent papal allocution to the International Congress on "Life-Sustaining Treatment and Vegetative State: Scientific Advances and Ethical Dilemmas" has been the occasion for much discussion concerning the use of artificial feeding tubes for nutrition and hydration. Briefly, the pope stated in the March address that such tubes were "not a medical act" and that their use "always represents a natural means of preserving life" and is part of "normal care." Therefore, their use is to be morally evaluated as ordinary and obligatory. "If done knowingly and willingly," the removal of such feeding tubes is "euthanasia by omission." The person's medical condition is not relevant in making a determination about the use of feeding tubes because the food and water delivered through such tubes is ordinary care and provides a benefit—"nourishment to the patient and alleviation of his suffering."[1]

What is interesting about this papal allocution is that it seems to represent a significant departure from the Roman Catholic bioethical tradition with respect to both the method and the basis upon which such decisions are made. The method announced by Pope John Paul II seems to be deontological. The use of feeding tubes to deliver artificial nutrition and hydration is declared "ordinary," and such an intervention apparently ought not be forgone or withdrawn. Historically, the method for making a determination about the use of a medical intervention was to consider the proportional benefits and its harms to the individual, family, and community. The method is a teleological balancing of the impact of the intervention. This has been the central teaching of the tradition from the mid-1600s through Pope Plus XII and the 1987 *Declaration on Euthanasia* by the Congregation for the Doctrine of the Faith.[2] The examples of disproportionately harmful impacts in the Roman Catholic tradition range from the use of expensive medications, food beyond the budget of the individual, and interventions that are painful in both the short and long term, to the refusal of a physical examination if that will cause excessive embarrassment to the individual. Included in such a listing and specifically noted in the *Declaration on Euthanasia* is the financial impact on both the patient and family. Interventions that will provide a significant financial hardship need not be utilized.

The question of the use of artificial feeding tubes has been much debated in Roman Catholic bioethics, especially when used for patients in persistent vegetative state.[3] One early statement was from the revered Jesuit moral theologian Gerald Kelly:

> I see no reason why even the most delicate professional standard should call for their [oxygen and intravenous nutrition and hydration for a patient in a terminal coma] use. In fact, it seems to me that, apart from very special circumstances, the artificial means not only need not but also should not be used, once the coma is reasonably diagnosed as terminal. Their use creates expense and nervous strain without conferring any real benefit.[4]

There were further arguments made on both sides of the issue by theologians, bishops, and bishop conferences. Over time a consensus seemed to develop that the forgoing or withdrawal of artificial feeding tubes could be judged morally optional in some circumstances.

The reason the papal statement is so startling to many is that it came out of the blue. It seems to depart from the tradition of Roman Catholic bioethics on how to analyze such questions and substitutes a deontological principle for the traditional weighing of benefits to burdens. Thus it raises a number of very practical questions for patients, theologians, medical personnel, and Catholic hospital administrators.

One question concerns the authority of the statement. Traditionally, allocutions are given to a variety of groups that meet in Rome, but they have not always been seen as the locus for announcing a major policy shift. Instead, they have been used by popes for discussing particular issues, as Plus XII was wont to do. He used allocutions to discuss organ transplantation[5] and the use of analgesics to relieve pain at the end of life.[6] Many of these allocutions were understood to be made in relation to the state of the question in moral theology, and it was well understood that the statements were subject to interpretation by moral theologians. So a first question is, What is the authority of this text?

A second question is whether the text should be read broadly or narrowly. That is, should the text be understood to apply to all instances in which a feeding tube is involved, or should it be restricted to the specific case of the patient in a persistent vegetative state? Profound personal and institutional implications follow from one's reading of the application of the text.

A third question concerns how the allocution will be implemented. That is, what will the U.S. bishops do with it? Will they consider it a directive that must be implemented in all Catholic healthcare institutions, will they need to study what it means in terms of its implications for Catholic healthcare, or will they leave its meaning up to individual healthcare institutions? The Catholic right-to-life movement may also influence the debate. Clearly, this movement holds that questions related to the beginning of life are to be resolved deontologically, with little or no attention given to circumstances. It may also now hold that end-of-life questions are to be resolved in a similar way. The political and religious power of the right-to-life movement was clearly manifest in the Terri Schiavo case in Florida. Such questions are of direct concern to Roman Catholics, but their resolution will have implications beyond Catholicism. Additionally, it must be noted that Pope John Paul II has appointed almost every single bishop in the United States, and it is clear that primary criteria for such appointments are fidelity to Church teaching and loyalty to the pope.

Another set of questions will have an impact on people and institutions. For the past several decades in the United States, people have been encouraged to make some sort of advance directive. The purpose of the directive, of course, is to help the individual clarify his or her wishes with respect to healthcare in the event that he or she becomes incompetent. Such directives help ensure that the person's wishes are carried out, can be the means by which a proxy decision maker is designated, and can reassure the family that the patient's wishes are being honored. In addition, advance directives might also ease the family's responsibilities at a time of great stress. If there is an advance directive, the family will know that they are doing what the patient wanted and this may be a great comfort.

Should Catholics no longer be encouraged to make advance directives? Or should they simply be directed to include no statement about the use of artificial feeding tubes? But suppose that the individual has already directed that he or she does not want a feeding tube, or that it should be removed when it no longer proves beneficial. Will family members be torn between the wishes of the patient and what they understand to be the teaching of the Catholic Church? By following what the family thinks is Church teaching, they will violate the wishes of the patient, and they may in fact cause harm to the patient. Yet if they do not follow what they think is Church teaching, they might think they are sinning or at least failing to be good Catholics. Practically speaking, the bedside of a dying patient is not the place to have a crisis of faith or morals.

What is a Catholic hospital, nursing home, or palliative care facility to do? If the bishop of the diocese in which a facility is located mandates a literal implementation of this directive, then presumably the facility would be under an obligation to develop policies that prohibit the forgoing or removal of feeding tubes regardless of the instructions of the patient, advance directive, and family. As a matter of practical fact, most Catholics probably will not know what, if any, instructions the local bishop has given, and they certainly will not know what policies the local Catholic hospital has. They will find out what the policies are when they confront the reality of the policies at a time of critical decision making—the absolutely worst time for such a discovery.

Several difficult situations might present themselves here. One can envision patients or families insisting on either forgoing or removing a feeding tube, and one can then see hospitals refusing such a request. The medical staff is then caught in the middle, and in the United States, one will consequently have a lawsuit with major implications for the church-state relationship, one that will make the mandating of the provision of contraceptives in the California Supreme Court ruling in March 2004 against Catholic Charities of Sacramento pale in comparison. One solution that has been proposed is for the patient to be transferred to another hospital if one's insurance plan would facilitate such a transfer or another hospital would accept the patient under these circumstances.

Another solution would be for patients who might want feeding tubes withdrawn or foregone not be admitted to such a facility to begin with. Upon admission to a hospital, patients are informed about advance directives and given the opportunity to fill one out. This practice could be complemented with a statement that, because the health facility they are entering is owned by the Catholic Church, any instructions concerning the forgoing or removal of feeding tubes will be disregarded. The patient could then determine whether to be admitted.

But the problems with this solution are almost infinite: this facility is where the physician sent the patient; this is the facility that performs this particular procedure; this is the hospital covered by the insurance plan; and so on. And what of people admitted to the facility through the emergency room?

There may be any number of administrators and physicians, nurses, or other healthcare providers who will conscientiously object to a strict interpretation and unilateral application of the new teaching. This will present a problem for the hospital at least with respect to the sort of privileges that it grants to physicians. What should the facility do with administrators and staff, the ethics committee, the various chaplains, and other people involved in the daily working of the facility who might conscientiously disagree with the allocution?

What if the patient in the facility is not a Catholic and demands either the forgoing or removal of a feeding tube? Will there be exemptions for non-Catholics? On what basis would these be granted, since the papal allocution states that such a practice would be euthanasia by omission? One would assume that a Catholic facility instructed by a bishop to implement the pope's allocution strictly would do so across the board, lest it participate in euthanasia by omission.

The fact that this allocution is understood by many Catholic moral theologians to sit uneasily with the dominant method and basis for determining when a treatment is ordinary or extraordinary pales in comparison with the myriad of personal and institutional issues that the allocution raises. Institutional policies that prohibited the forgoing or withdrawing of artificial feeding tubes could lead to a lawsuit with monumental implications for the relationship between church and state. Also, what would be the implications, financial and otherwise, for Catholic hospitals that are in cooperative relations with non-Catholic healthcare facilities?

The decision-making process at the end of life is difficult enough as it is. It is a time fraught with tension, pain, suffering, sorrow, guilt, and grieving. The strict implementation of a policy such as that in the pope's allocution seems to us simply to prolong the agony by prohibiting responsible medical and moral evaluation of the patient's condition. Ironically, it would also be at odds with the long Catholic tradition of medical ethics. It also has the potential to cause enormous difficulties for Catholic healthcare facilities and their staffs. While we certainly support every effort to prevent euthanasia, we do not support policies that require medical staff to provide unwanted medical treatment. Such policies might even drive people *toward* euthanasia, by making them feel that they have lost a traditional and sympathetic ally in their final journey.

NOTES

1. The allocution "Care for Patients in a 'Permanent' Vegetative State" can be found on the Vatican Web site at http://www.vatican.va/holy_father/john_paul_ii/ speeches/2004/march/ documents/-hf_jp-ii_spe_20040320_congress-fiamc_en.html or in *Origins* 33 (April 8, 2004): 737 and 739–40.

2. Congregation for the Doctrine of the Faith, *Declaration on Euthanasia*, in *Origins* 10 (August 14, 1980): 154–57.

3. For example, see T. A. Shannon and J. J. Walter, "The PVS Patient and the Forgoing/Withdrawing of Medical Nutrition and Hydration," *Theological Studies* 49 (1988): 623–47; J. Torchia, OP, "Artificial Hydration and Nutrition for the PVS Patient," *National Catholic Bioethics Quarterly* 3 (2003): 719–30; G. D. Coleman, "Take and Eat: Morality and Medically Assisted Feeding," *America* 190 (April 5, 2004): 16–20; T. A. Shannon and J. J. Walter, "Artificial Nutrition, Hydration: Assessing Papal Statement," *National Catholic Reporter*, April 16, 2004, http:// natcath.org/NCR_Online/archives2/2004b/041604/041604i.ph p; R. Hamel and M. Panicola, "Must We Preserve Life?" *America* 190 (April 19, 2004): 6–8; M. Panicola, "Catholic Teaching on Prolonging Life: Setting the Record Straight," *Hastings Center Report* 31, no. 6 (2001): 14–25.

4. G. Kelly, "The Duty of Using Artificial Means of Preserving Life," *Theological Studies* 11 (1950): 203–20.

5. G. Kelly, "Tissue Transplantation," *Human Body: Papal Teachings* (May 14, 1956): 380–83.

6. Pope Plus XII, "Christian Principles and the Medical Profession," *Human Body: Papal Teachings* (November 12, 1944): 56–58.

The Pope on PVS

Does JPII's Statement Make the Grade?
John F. Tuohey

A recent address by (the late) Pope John Paul II regarding the care of patients in a persistent vegetative state (PVS) has left many people—Catholics and others—scratching their heads. If the withdrawal of tube feeding or artificially administered hydration can be the equivalent of "euthanasia by omission," do we all need to rethink the decisions we have made in our advance directives and living wills? What immediate impact will this statement have on Catholic hospitals, for both Catholic and non-Catholic patients? Part of the difficulty in determining the weight and moral authority of the statement is that it comes from John Paul II himself, and it can be hard to separate the message from the messenger. Notwithstanding the authority of the messenger, the message deserves examination on its own terms. How might we read this text if it were, say, a thesis proposal submitted to an interdisciplinary committee for review at a Catholic university? Here is one possibility.

Dear Student:

We have read your proposal with great interest, as it addresses a topic about which there is much public debate. The ongoing case of Terri Schiavo in Florida is just one example.

In brief, you propose to show there is a moral obligation to maintain

From *Commonweal*, June 18, 2004, http://www.commonwealmagazine.org/print_format.php?id_article =854 (accessed November 21, 2005). © 2004 Commonweal Foundation, reprinted with permission. For subscriptions: www.commonwealmagazine.org.

nutrition and hydration, "even artificially administered," for the PVS patient, saying that doing so is "necessarily ordinary and proportionate." You affirm that this is "not a medical act," but a "natural means of preserving life." In short, you say it is required whenever it works to maintain life.

While we are pleased to accept your proposal, we would like to bring up some issues to which you will want to pay particular attention as you continue your work. Our brief comments below will refer only to the 1980 *Declaration on Euthanasia*, the most authoritative statement by the church to date on the topic; the 1995 Pontifical Council's *Charter of Health-Care Workers*; and some older traditional references that represent the long-held moral tradition on this subject. Other sources will, of course, also need to be explored as you continue your work.

First, you summarize the clinical reality of PVS by stating that PVS is not a diagnosis, but "only a conventional prognostic judgment." You will want to be a little more precise here. In fact, PVS refers to a medical condition, defined by specific clinical indications that make it possible to distinguish a person in PVS from someone who is temporarily unconscious or in another form of coma— PVS includes periods of arousal and the return of sleep-and-wake cycles, when the patient seems "awake" but unfortunately is never aware. You state the person "seems unable to interact with others." In fact, what is misleading about PVS is that the opposite is true: although they remain unconscious and unaware, PVS patients may appear to be interacting. You then go on to suggest the possibility that PVS patients may recover from their condition. This possibility is a key part of your argument that we must not forgo nutritional support.

Your proposal, as now written, might be taken to suggest that a person's diagnosis—which is distinct from his or her medical condition and prognosis—is the key in deciding whether to continue or to forgo nutrition/hydration. More specifically, the person would seem to need to have a diagnosis of a terminal disease. Since a person in PVS is not, it would seem, terminally ill, administering nutrition/hydration would be considered "ordinary and proportionate" and forgoing it would constitute "euthanasia by omission." But an emphasis on diagnosis in making these decisions will be difficult for you to argue, for the *Declaration* states that we must consider "the results that can be expected taking into account the state of the sick person." In other words, the patient's prognosis and medical condition. In the 1950s, the moralist Gerald Kelly, SJ, concluded that forgoing nutrition/hydration was permissible when a patient was in a condition described at the time as a terminal coma: a condition from which he or she was unlikely to recover. Clinically speaking, patients in PVS today can be said to be in terminal comas. (Kelly is particularly important in this discussion since he played a significant role in developing the concepts of "ordinary" and "proportionate" care.) Another highly regarded traditional source of that time, Charles McFadden, noted that it would be a great hardship to be sustained indefinitely by artificially administered nutrition/hydration. You will need to frame your argument in light of these traditional understandings of the role of condition and prognosis.

Whatever the role of prognosis in decision making, you are clear that the lack of certainty for prognosis is important to your conclusion. It is true to some extent that science "is unable to predict with certainty who among patients in this condition will recover and who will not." But this need not lead to the conclusion that one may never forgo artificially administered nutrition/hydration. In your final work, you will need to distinguish between "clinical certainty," which may not exist in a particular case, and what Aquinas described as "moral certainty" which up to now most writers on this topic have held does exist in most PVS cases. You seem to suggest that if there is doubt regarding the prognosis, the ethical thing to do is to take the safest approach: care for the person as if he or she may recover. This approach has traditionally been called tutiorism. You will also need to engage fully that part of the ethical tradition that speaks of moral certainty in the face of prognostic uncertainty. That is, if there is legitimate clinical doubt that a person in PVS will recover, or if it is unreasonable to expect that the person will recover, it is ethical to make decisions with "moral certainty" that the person will probably not recover—what the tradition has called probabilism. Although in theory recovery is possible, we know that someone with the medical condition of PVS has a very poor prognosis. Recovery is clinically very rare, particularly after three months for nontraumatic injury, such as drug use, and after one year for traumatic injury, such as a car accident. Your final project will therefore need to include a thorough analysis of the work of Aquinas and Alphonsus Liguori in this regard. Other sources that have lent support to this approach are Pius XII's 1957 affirmation that life, health, and all temporal activities are subordinate to spiritual ends; and the *Declaration*'s own affirmation that a person's "moral resources," his or her ability to cope with illness and its treatment, must be considered as part of the moral analysis. Kelly maintained that the clinical certainty should be "reasonable," not absolute, in determining what constitutes "ordinary care." One also thinks of Pope John Paul II's 1992 discussion of "therapeutic tyranny," which cautioned against condemning a patient "to an artificially prolonged agony."

We now turn our attention to your central argument that nutrition/hydration is not a "medical act," but rather "normal care." You describe it as "a natural means of preserving life" when it is capable of achieving its own proper finality of providing nourishment—when it achieves its purpose. That is, it is "basic care," and hence "ordinary and proportionate," and obligatory, when it maintains life by sustaining adequate nutrition and hydration. We believe that making this argument will be challenging. We suggest, first, that it may be helpful for you to describe in detail the different methods of meeting nutritional needs artificially, such as hyperalimentation, nasal-gastric tube, peg or J-tube, or IV. Each of these entails invasiveness, risks, and limitations on usefulness, as well as such medical expertise as anesthesiology, surgery, radiology, dietary, and general nursing. You may find you want to nuance your argument to include only some forms of artificial administration as "basic care."

Another challenge to this argument will stem from the tradition's usual understanding of ordinary and proportionate care as referring not to the ability of some intervention to achieve its purpose, but to its ability to offer what McFadden called "the sound hope of providing benefit" by doing so. The *Declaration* makes this same point stating, "it is also permitted to interrupt these means where the results fall short of expectations," not simply because they fail to achieve their purpose or are burdensome.

We would also call your attention to the language traditionally employed in such discussions. The *Declaration* speaks of "techniques" and "remedies," not the "medical act/natural means" distinction you propose. Your project will need to show how this new designation better serves a tradition that has not heretofore recognized the need for it.

Finally, we would like to make one comment on your use of sources. In one place you write, quoting the *Declaration*, that "there is an obligation to provide the 'normal care due to the sick in such cases.'" But citing "normal care" as obligatory is curious. Your thesis is not that there is an obligation to provide normal care, which this reference would support, but that "normal care" includes artificially administered nutrition and hydration. The *Declaration* does not address this issue, so your reference to it here may be misleading. More problematic is your reference to the Charter, which you cite as stating, "normal care . . . includes, in fact, the use of nutrition and hydration." The 1995 Pontifical Council's Charter actually reads, "administration of food and liquids, even artificially, is part of the normal treatment always due to the patient when this is not burdensome for him." You will want to use greater care in your final project.

We are hopeful that you will find these comments helpful as you continue your work.

Sincerely,

Your Thesis Committee

On the Death of Terri Schiavo

Edward J. Furton

Terri Schiavo died March 31, 2005, after more than thirteen days without food or water. Before her feeding tube was removed, she was physically healthy, except for her diminished cognitive ability. When one looks at her death certificate, one will not see any illness listed as the cause of death. She did not die of "the persistent vegetative state." She died of a lack of food and water.

What brought about her starvation and dehydration? The case of Terri Schiavo can be reduced to this simple point: her death was caused by the decisions of those who should have been caring for her.

THE ISSUES AT STAKE

Let us be clear about what was at issue in this debate. We were not talking about burdensome means of preserving life. Terri was able to breathe on her own and did not require a ventilator. Her kidneys were in good working order. She did not require dialysis. She did not face the prospect of a complicated surgical operation. She was not in any pain. She showed no signs that tube feeding was distressing to her. Her body was receiving and assimilating food and fluids without medical complications. There was no infection or problem with aspiration (i.e., the entry of food or fluids into her lungs). She was a healthy woman who was mentally disabled.

From *Ethics and Medics* 30, no. 6 (June 2005). Reproduced with permission The National Catholic Bioethics Center.

This case was also not about the right of a patient to refuse burdensome treatment. One does not need to be dying before one can say no to treatments that are excessively painful, burdensome, psychologically distressing, or too expensive. Terri Schiavo faced none of these problems. She did need a small plastic tube that is easy to place, not painful, and inexpensive. The only significant cost factor was her stay at a medical facility, which could have been significantly reduced by taking her home to be cared for by her parents and a visiting nurse. In the United States, medical insurance absorbs most of these costs. We cannot say, therefore, that her feeding tube was removed on the grounds that it was too burdensome.

This case was also not about appropriate palliative care. Many press accounts used the case of Terri Schiavo to raise the specter of excruciatingly painful deaths suffered by patients held under the tyranny of complex and impersonal mechanical equipment. No one should have to die a miserable death connected to machinery that drags life past its natural end. But Terri Schiavo was not only not dying, she was not suffering—at least not until her food and water were removed. She was living comfortably in her hospital bed, visited by friends and family. She did not need palliative care.

The husband of Terri Schiavo had said that she had told him she would not want to live with a feeding tube. There was no written record of that request and many have raised questions about whether her husband's recollections were trustworthy. Given that Mrs. Schiavo's parents were willing to assume responsibility for their daughter, it seems odd that her husband would not allow them to do so. But that too is not what was at issue here. The fact is that under the law, and in Catholic moral teaching, the husband has the authority to act on behalf of his wife in such cases. Even if Terri Schiavo had asked to have her food and water removed, it should not have been done. We should never be a party to the direct and intentional cause of death in an innocent human being.

EXCEPTIONAL CASES

Neither was this case about the effort of some to impose a rigid rule on others that would necessitate tube feeding in all instances. There are many cases in which it is perfectly appropriate to remove food and water from a patient. Obviously, if food and water are not being assimilated by the body, then they are not effective and may be withdrawn. Sometimes the placement of a tube causes repeated infections. Here again are grounds for removal. Certain patients display agitation at the sight of any tube and may pull it out repeatedly. Though strategies might be devised to attach the tube surreptitiously (e.g., after the administration of a sedative), it is sometimes best not to force the issue. In other cases, such as end-stage dementia, there is no appreciable increase in length of survival following the application of tube feeding. Here the medical evidence speaks for itself.[1] Other patients experience serious complications, such as repeated aspiration and subsequent need for suctioning of the throat. Once again, this can be a reason for ending nutrition and hydration.

In short, the provision of food and water may at times give rise to the same types of burdens that are associated with more complex medical procedures. When that happens, nutrition and hydration may be removed. Of course, if the patient is already dying, there is nothing at all to be gained by applying tube feeding. The pope's recent statement "On Life-Sustaining Treatment and the Vegetative State" did not seek to tie the hands of physicians in such cases. The statement specifically said that food and water should be given only "insofar as and until it is seen to have attained its proper finality, which in the present case consists in providing nourishment to the patient and alleviation of his suffering."[2]

What was at issue in the Terri Schiavo case was none of these things, but the manner in which we treat those who are mentally disabled. The claim that food and water can be removed from patients like Terri Schiavo because their mental condition offers so little hope for improvement is in error. Prospects for improvement are irrelevant in a case such as this. We do not take food and water away from people simply because they suffer diminished cognitive ability. All of us need food and water to sustain life. The fact that these are administered via a plastic tube is no more relevant than the fact that you and I use plates, utensils, and cups. These too are "artificial" means of preserving life.

THE PERSISTENT VEGETATIVE STATE

One of the claims made about Terri Schiavo tells us a lot more about what this case was about than anything else. Many defenders of the death of Terri Schiavo said that she did not suffer from a lack of food and water because, when one is dying, the body naturally begins to "shut down." The refusal to take food and water forms a part of the normal dying process. In such cases, death by starvation and dehydration is "peaceful"—but Terri Schiavo was not dying! She began to die only after her food and water had been taken away. The point had no application whatsoever to her case. How telling that it was so often repeated.

Others gave a different argument to the same effect. They said that Mrs. Schiavo could not experience the suffering of dehydration and starvation because patients in the persistent vegetative state are unaware of themselves or their environment. But honestly, how can we prove that someone is unaware? The question requires us to go beyond all empirical modes of inquiry and into the realms of speculative philosophy. No scientific instrument has ever recorded the existence of consciousness. We can only detect the external signs of that inner awareness, and not all of these may be evident to scientific instrumentation. As Catholics, we hold that the human soul is not reducible to matter. It is a spiritual power that exists even after death. The soul must have hidden capacities for self-awareness that are beyond the reach of science.

René Descartes wrote a famous philosophical work in the seventeenth century in which he argued that our world and all that is in it might be nothing more than an illusion.[3] How do I know that everything I see, feel, and hear is not part of some elaborate dream meant to keep me in ignorance of reality? This led Descartes to his famous assertion, "I think; therefore, I am." The process of thinking, he said, is indubitable proof of my own existence. Although this resolved his metaphysical doubts, it also prompted him to conclude that whatever is incapable of thought does not have a soul.

Terri Schiavo was not capable of thought under the Cartesian standard. She could not deduce her own existence via "I think; therefore, I am." In the mind of many, this was sufficient proof that Terri Schiavo did not really exist. She lacked the higher power of thinking that is the sign of our humanity. From this they concluded that she could not experience any pain.

But does this make any sense? Consider the lowly snail. Does it have any upper brain function? Not at all; it barely has a brain. But stick the snail with a pin and watch how it writhes. Shall we say that the snail is unconscious of the pain that it is evidently experiencing? This is the error of the Cartesian view. Descartes did not believe that lower animals could experience pain because they lacked the power of reason, but the snail's reaction to painful stimulus is evidence to the contrary.

What we witnessed in the death of Terri Schiavo was a very public act of euthanasia by omission, encouraged by those who identify the human soul with the higher powers of human cognition. Did her slow process of dehydration, over a period of thirteen days, cause her any pain? A "no" answer is hard to square with the facts.

NOTES

1. Greg Burke, "Tube Feeding and Advanced Dementia," *Ethics and Medics* 26, no. 3 (March 2001): 1–2.
2. John Paul II, "Papal Address on Food and Water," *Ethics and Medics* 29, no. 6 (June 2004): 2.
3. See Descartes's *Meditations on First Philosophy*.

Part 5

The Aftermath

INTRODUCTION

The death of Terri Schiavo did not immediately bring the controversy about how she died to an end. For months afterward her parents and siblings continued to insist that spousal abuse or neglect might have caused the heart attack that eventually caused her to be placed in a nursing home supported by a feeding tube. Still others argued that Terri was being abused or even poisoned somehow in the hospice where she ultimately died.

The governor of Florida, Jeb Bush, launched an investigation into the cause of her health problems fifteen years earlier. That investigation turned up nothing new or suspicious about what happened the night Terri had a cardiac arrest and was quickly ended. The results of the autopsy, reprinted here, that Michael Schiavo had directed to be performed, showed that not only was Terri's brain massively and irreversibly damaged but that she was blind, had died of dehydration, not starvation, and that there were no signs of abuse present in her body.

Still, the bitterness that had built up over the better part of a decade among the family persisted. Michael Schiavo had his wife's body cremated. The remains were buried in Florida in a private ceremony. A marker was erected with the inscription "I kept my promise" that Terri's parents said they found offensive and insulting.

As Ceci Connolly's story reminds us, death did not stop in Florida hospices with the passing of Terri Schiavo. The hospice where she died kept serving patients and families and did so with the same care and dignity that, despite the reckless charges made against the facility, the staff had provided to Terri. Hospice continues to be an innovative, compassionate approach to dying that has the overwhelming support of medicine and nursing, religious leaders, and the American people.

Americans seemed genuinely horrified at what had happened in the Terri Schiavo case. The nightly spectacle of her image on the notorious videotape made by her parents being shown over and over again on the cable news networks left many feeling that however else Terri had been victimized she had been the unwilling and hapless victim of a media insatiable for images and news about her plight and her family's fight.

Distaste about the case was also reflected in the lack of enthusiasm Americans felt about the intrusive role politicians had played in the battle over what medical care she ought to receive. Despite rumblings from conservatives and some in the right-to-life movement that they would quickly pass laws to insure that no one in a permanent vegetative state would ever have a feeding tube removed, no such legislation was enacted by Congress or state legislatures. The American Medical Association at its June 2005 annual meeting passed a resolution condemning any law that, in the absence of a living will, would "presume to prescribe the patient's preferences."

As both Norman Cantor and George Annas point out, the American people strongly believe that families ought to make decisions about the termination of treatment for incapacitated persons including the termination of artificial feeding. If families do not agree, then local authorities and courts should adjudicate their disagreements. Left-wing groups like MoveOn and the chair of the Democratic National Committee, Howard Dean, found the revulsion against federal intervention in the Schiavo case so strong that they began to use the actions taken by right-wing politicians in Congress, such as Tom DeLay of Texas and Bill Frist of Tennessee, as reasons to raise money for their opponents or to oppose their reelection.

As the articles by John Danforth and Tom Shannon reveal, there was a lot of soul-searching undertaken in religious circles about the stance that conservative religious leaders and the Roman Catholic Church including the pope had taken concerning what was appropriate medical care for Terri Schiavo. Some felt that conservatives had hijacked religious opinion, making it appear that all Christians would oppose the removal of a feeding tube from a person in a permanent vegetative state. Others felt that the religious voices that had spoken out against allowing Terri to die should be heeded and that, as disability groups such as Not Dead Yet continue to argue, it is the duty of the powerful to protect the interests of the disabled lest the stigma which still prevails against those with disabilities is allowed to reduced the resources and care they are given in American society.

Some doubt manifests itself about the adequacy of the terms *coma, permanent vegetative state,* and *brain death* to capture all of the nuances that exist when the human brain suffers severe injury. Arguments are being made that a new category, "minimally conscious," ought to be introduced into medical diagnostics to describe those with severe brain damage but still capable of some forms of cognitive activity. As Ron Cranford argues, mainstream medicine and neurology did not believe that the Schiavo case called for any changes in the way that permanent vegetative state is diagnosed, and subsequent to the death of Terri Schiavo, physicians continue to declare persons PVS using the same criteria that were applied in her case.

Many in law and bioethics had presumed that questions about how to manage someone with massive, irreversible brain damage who lacked an advance directive or living will had been settled by state courts and legislatures long before Terri Schiavo's feeding tube was removed. The controversy over her case cast a great deal of doubt over whether America really had reached a consensus that families ought to have the ability to decide what to do in directing decisions about life support, that spouses should have primacy of decision-making authority, that feeding tubes were a form of medical treatment, and that there should be no presumption or bias one way or the other about what someone incapable of communicating their wishes as a result of falling into a permanent vegetative state would want in terms of the continuation of life support, and that there is no known medical treatment for reversing or improving PVS. Despite the passions, anger, and explosion of opinions that surrounded the death of Terri Schiavo, it would appear that the prevailing consensus weathered this storm.

The law and professional medical opinion continue to hold that families, and in particular spouses, should have decision-making authority. That a husband or wife may act to stop life support for their partner if there is sufficient persuasive evidence that such a course is what the incapacitated person would have wanted. And medicine, nursing, and the courts continue to believe that feeding tubes are a form of medical treatment that may be withdrawn or withheld just like any other form of medical intervention.

Terri Schiavo proved to be a difficult case because her family was so bitterly divided both about what Terri would have wanted and among themselves. It was also a difficult case because Terri had not left any written instructions or communications about her wishes or preferences. Some hope that one legacy of the case is that more Americans will put their wishes in writing about who they would want to make medical decisions for them and what sorts of values ought to govern their care. But relatively few people, especially younger people, bother to compose a living will, advance directive, or durable power of attorney. In the face of such uncertainty and with a deeply divided family, the Florida legal system struggled mightily to try and insure that all possible evidence was heard and that a thorough review was conducted of the decision to allow a feeding tube to be withdrawn from a severely disabled person. There would not appear to be any evidence that adding federal courts or congressional review to this process brought or would bring any additional protection or insight into this type of case. The legacy of Terri Schiavo is that the system of medical and legal protections that had evolved beginning with the case of Karen Ann Quinlan and continuing through the case of Nancy Cruzan worked for Terri Schiavo. It is surely possible and likely that Americans will continue to debate whether Terri should have been allowed to die or not. But it is not possible to look at the events of this case and not marvel at how well the established ethical consensus that each individual, even someone who is severely cognitively impaired, has the right to control all forms of their medical care held up. Despite the firestorm of criticism directed against it, the view that every American has the right to control their medical care or have others they love do so for them would appear to be an ethical norm likely to endure for the foreseeable future.

Our Shining Knights to the Rescue

Norman L. Cantor

Which was greater? Their arrogance or their ignorance? I am referring to members of Congress who zealously tried to "rescue" Theresa Schiavo by making a federal case out of the Florida courts' efforts to fulfill her wishes regarding end-of-life medical care.

The case for arrogance is strong. Senate Majority Leader Bill Frist, a surgeon, gave an opinion about Schiavo's mental status based on viewing a montage of old videos. It contradicted the findings—made by expert neurologists grounded on fifteen years of medical history, electronic scans, and firsthand examinations—that Schiavo was in a permanent vegetative state. His view was echoed by an obstetrician and an internist from the House of Representatives.

Congress suggested that more "due process" was needed in the federal courts even though the Florida courts had ably provided Schiavo and her parents more process than any other medical patient in the history of American jurisprudence. (A specially appointed, neutral guardian could find no taint in the state proceedings, despite investing many weeks in combing medical records, scrutinizing judicial records, and observing Schiavo.)

Some members of Congress insisted that Schiavo was being murdered, though the Florida courts had made careful findings that Schiavo, while competent, had expressed her wishes not to be medically maintained in her current condition, and numerous state courts and legislatures have upheld a person's exercise of prospective autonomy in this fashion.

At the same time, the ignorance is pretty glaring. A congressional committee wanted to subpoena Schiavo to testify, when for fifteen years she had been unable to communicate to anyone (her mother's claims to the contrary notwithstanding). Many members of Congress obsessed about withdrawal of food and water when, according to numerous courts, including the U.S. Supreme Court, artificial nutrition and hydration are equivalent to any other form of life-preserving medical intervention—to be handled by the same criteria governing any other end-of-life medical decision. The reference by members of Congress to the cruelty of "starving" Schiavo to death ignored the fact that palliative care could ensure that her death by dehydration would not be painful (even if a permanently vegetative patient could feel pain, which she could not).

SEEING WHAT THEY WANT

Most important, promoters of congressional intervention ignored the judicial findings that Schiavo expressed her preferences about her medical handling. And they ignored empirical data consistently demonstrating that the overwhelming majority of people do not wish to be preserved in a permanently unconscious state. Schiavo's preferences fit that pattern.

A combination of arrogance and ignorance is reflected in the apparent willingness by members of Congress to overturn twenty-nine years of sound jurisprudence relating to end-of-life medical decision making. In 1976, the *Karen Ann Quinlan* case in New Jersey established that the critical objective of surrogate decision making for a permanently unconscious patient should be to replicate what the patient would want for herself. That is what Michael Schiavo and the Florida courts sought to do.

The *Quinlan* and subsequent cases also recognized that trauma or illness would leave some formerly competent people in such a debilitated condition that (even in the absence of explicit prior instructions) a surrogate, in conjunction with medical personnel, could project that the patient would not want life-extending medical care.

A permanent vegetative state is the prime example of such a situation. A strong majority of states have followed New Jersey's approach in resolving the medical fate of people in a permanently vegetative state—leaving the ultimate decision to caring next of kin under the watchful eyes of healthcare providers.

The right-to-life movement—the primary instigator of the current misinformation campaign—believes that nobody should be able to decide that another person's quality of life is so dismal that life-sustaining medical support should be withdrawn. Yet the majority of deaths in the United States are medically managed; caregivers end medical intervention (pursuant to the requests of next of kin) even though the patient's life could be artificially prolonged.

Realistically, there is no other humane way to proceed in an era in which medical science is capable of preserving lives long beyond a point most people would want for themselves. The alternative is to keep pumping fluids and gases into a moribund patient until the last possible breath. Yet unrelenting medical intervention for fatally stricken patients "transforms human beings into unwilling prisoners of medical technology," as noted in *In re L.W.*, 482 N.W.2d 60, 74 (Wis. 1992).

Congress, perhaps out of ignorance, sought to make Schiavo such a prisoner. For Congress unconscionably sought to interfere with her right to reject life-extending medical treatment as exercised in the oral expressions she made while competent. House Majority Leader Tom DeLay, on the other hand, displayed only arrogance in suggesting impeachment for the judges who upheld Schiavo's rights, Florida law, and the federal constitution.

The Legacy of the *Schiavo* Case

Thomas A Shannon

The sad case of Terri Schiavo has given rise to a variety of discussions within families, religious communities, and various levels of government. There are several consequences that may emerge from these conversations.

The fear that patients' medical requests may not be respected and that they will be forced to endure surviving in conditions abhorrent to them might well generate strong and widespread support for physician-assisted suicide legislation in many states. People may no longer be content to draft a living will in the expectation that their relatives will be able to follow their wishes. They may also fear that even if their relatives seek to implement their wishes, they may be interfered with by any number of advocacy groups. The simplest way to prevent such meddling in end-of-life decisions, in the opinion of some, is simply to enact laws to legalize assisted suicide. That way, people will be ensured that their wishes will be carried out because they themselves will see to it.

This fear of meddling in end-of-life decisions is a real one and must be attended to. A variety of right-to-life groups, along with some conservative religious movements and many politicians, are calling for legislation to mandate various forms of life-prolonging or death-delaying medical interventions. Politicians have been threatened with retribution at the election booth if they do not respond to demands for legislation protecting life through mandated interventions.

Thomas A. Shannon, "The Legacy of the Schiavo Case," *America*, vol. 192, June 6–13, 2005, p. 17. Copyright © 2005. All rights reserved. Reproduced by permission of America Press. For subscription information: www.americamagazine.org.

But even if legislation is not enacted, the atmosphere surrounding the making of end-of-life decisions has changed. When Vatican officials refer to the removal of feeding tubes as equivalent to capital punishment and other religious and political leaders characterize it as murder, those involved in making such decisions may think twice before doing so. This may be particularly true of hospitals, which may not want to become the center of a legal and media dispute. The status of living wills may be challenged if they contain provisions either to forgo or remove feeding tubes. And families might fear intervention as they seek to implement the decisions of their relatives.

While most Americans continue to support the right of seriously sick individuals to make their own decisions and of relatives to implement those choices, the fear that this right is under attack and might be gravely compromised or even revoked is a strong motivating factor that can fuel initiatives for physician-assisted suicide. If more and more people become convinced that their end-of-life decisions will not be respected, they may, in order to protect themselves, support measures that they otherwise might not favor. The zeal to absolutize the right to life might, ironically, turn into an exceptionally strong argument for physician-assisted suicide simply as a way for critically ill people to secure some control over their lives.

A second legacy of the *Schiavo* case could be legislative initiatives, already being proposed by some advocates, to make possible interventions in marriages, particularly if the parents of the married couple do not like some decisions that one or the other spouse takes. While jokes about busybody in-laws are a staple of our culture, such legislative initiatives are not funny. When a couple marries, they establish a separate social unit whose integrity is socially supported. They are legitimate decision makers for each other, particularly if one spouse becomes incapacitated.

We know that many marriages have their problems, that there is a 50 percent divorce rate, and that in-laws frequently disagree with a couple's decisions. In-laws are also frequently a source of help and even shelter during difficult times. We expect this, and most would support such traditional forms of assistance. But to turn cultural expectations of assistance and cultural recognition of disagreement into legislation that would give in-laws veto power over a married couple's decisions would be to strike a substantive blow against the integrity of marriage and the right of couples to live their lives according to their values and preferences.

There is a rather settled process for decision making at the end of life. First in order is the patient himself or herself, then the next of kin beginning with the spouse, and then proceeding to a designated decision maker, a parent or a sibling. When the married patient cannot speak on his or her own behalf, the spouse takes over decision-making responsibilities, unless another legally designated decision maker has been specified. This is a key implication of the marriage relation. Permitting a legal override of spousal decisions would simply destroy the integrity of marriage by potentially putting at risk the legal status of any decision the in-laws do not like.

But even if legislation were narrowly drafted to be applicable only to end-of-life decisions, such legislation would not merely challenge and perhaps destroy significant legal precedents and ethically sanctioned behavior; it would also destroy by legislative fiat the legal standing of the spouse. Those individuals and groups in our culture who have been strong advocates of marriage in recent debates about the meaning and significance of this institution might want to think through very carefully the implications of such legislation.

A third implication is the growing tendency to absolutize the right to life. Clearly the right to life is important. But it is one right among others and is not always the most important right. If the right to life were absolute, then we could not send soldiers into battle, we could not have capital punishment, we could not have people sacrificing their lives to save others, and we could not sanction martyrdom, to list a few instances in which other values—such as the right of self-defense, love of neighbor, and integrity of conscience— outweigh the right to life.

Many involved in the *Schiavo* case argued that life must be preserved even in the face of irreversible physiological conditions, that the right to life is the most important value, and that the right to life is inviolable. This zeal to protect life has turned biological life into an idol, a false god that is seen as a value and an end in itself, to be protected under almost any and all circumstances. This position of idolizing biological life is no longer a form of vitalism, as many have argued. It is a position that is turning into a form of materialism, in which the only value to be acknowledged is that of biological life and its preservation as an end in itself. This is probably not where the advocates of the right to life, particularly those speaking from a Christian perspective, would want to wind up, but this seems to be the logical outcome of their arguments.

Biological life is being absolutized in a way that neither the Christian tradition nor even that of philosophical materialists would defend. Both of these perspectives set the value of life and the right to life within a context of other values and goals. How the right to life is implemented and protected is set within a more inclusive context of beliefs, goals, and values. And even though there are and will continue to be disagreements over the adequacy of various decisions about protecting life, there has been general agreement that the right to life and the value of life are not absolute. This is a cultural agreement that needs protection, lest we have imposed on us a new form of idolatry and materialism.

As frequently happens in cases as publicly debated as the *Schiavo* one has been, all manner of interventions are proposed. We need to think through carefully both the short-term and the long-term implications of such proposals, because the consequences are significant. We know that many political threats are being made; we know that family decisions are being politicized; we know that many have used and will continue to use this case to further their own political and social agenda, and that religion is being subordinated to a variety of political and social goals. We need to be exceptionally careful in our debates and legislative initiatives to prevent long-term social harm through the dismantling of important social institutions and practices.

"Culture of Life" Politics at the Bedside

The Case of Terri Schiavo

George J. Annas

For the first time in the history of the United States, Congress met in a special emergency session on Sunday, March 20, [2005] to pass legislation aimed at the medical care of one patient—Terri Schiavo. President George W. Bush encouraged the legislation and flew back to Washington, DC, from his vacation in Crawford, Texas, so that he could be on hand to sign it immediately. In a statement issued three days earlier, he said: "The case of Terri Schiavo raises complex issues. . . . Those who live at the mercy of others deserve our special care and concern. It should be our goal as a nation to build a culture of life, where all Americans are valued, welcomed, and protected—and that culture of life must extend to individuals with disabilities."[1]

The "culture of life" is a not-terribly-subtle reference to the antiabortion movement in the United States, which received significant encouragement in last year's presidential election. The movement may now view itself as strong enough to generate new laws to prevent human embryos from being created for research and to require that incompetent patients be kept alive with artificially delivered fluids and nutrition. How did the U.S. Congress conclude that it was appropriate to attempt to reopen a case that had finally been concluded after more than seven years of litigation involving almost twenty judges? Has the country's culture changed so dramatically as to require a fundamental change in the law? Or do patients who cannot continue to live without artificially delivered fluids and nutrition pose previously unrecognized or novel questions of law and ethics?

From the *New England Journal of Medicine* 352, no. 16 (2005): 1710–15. Copyright © 2005 Massachusetts Medical Society. All rights reserved.

The case of Terri Schiavo, a Florida woman who is in a persistent vegetative state, is being played out as a public spectacle and a tragedy for her and her husband, Michael Schiavo. Mr. Schiavo's private feud with his wife's parents over the continued use of a feeding tube has been taken to the media, the courts, the Florida legislature, Florida governor Jeb Bush, the U.S. Congress, and now President Bush. Since Ms. Schiavo is in a medical and legal situation almost identical to those of two of the most well known patients in medical jurisprudence, Karen Ann Quinlan and Nancy Cruzan, there must be something about cases like theirs that defies simple solutions, whether medical or legal. In this sense, the case of Terri Schiavo provides an opportunity to examine issues that most lawyers, bioethicists, and physicians believed were well settled—if not since the 1976 New Jersey Supreme Court decision in the case of Karen Quinlan, then at least since the 1990 U.S. Supreme Court decision in the case of Nancy Cruzan.

Before reviewing Terri Schiavo's case, it is well worth reviewing the legal background information that has been ignored by Congress and the president. In 1976, the case of Karen Quinlan made international headlines when her parents sought the assistance of a judge to discontinue the use of a ventilator in their daughter, who was in a persistent vegetative state.[2] Ms. Quinlan's physicians had refused her parents' request to remove the ventilator because, they said, they feared that they might be held civilly or even criminally liable for her death. The New Jersey Supreme Court ruled that competent persons have a right to refuse life-sustaining treatment and that this right should not be lost when a person becomes incompetent. Since the court believed that the physicians were unwilling to withdraw the ventilator because of the fear of legal liability, not precepts of medical ethics, it devised a mechanism to grant the physicians prospective legal immunity for taking this action. Specifically, the New Jersey Supreme Court ruled that after a prognosis, confirmed by a hospital ethics committee, that there is "no reasonable possibility of a patient returning to a cognitive, sapient state," life-sustaining treatment can be removed and no one involved, including the physicians, can be held civilly or criminally responsible for the death.[3] The publicity surrounding the *Quinlan* case motivated two independent developments: it encouraged states to enact "living will" legislation that provided legal immunity to physicians who honored patients' written "advance directives" specifying how they would want to be treated if they ever became incompetent; and it encouraged hospitals to establish ethics committees that could attempt to resolve similar treatment disputes without going to court.

Although *Quinlan* was widely followed, the New Jersey Supreme Court could make law only for New Jersey.

When the U.S. Supreme Court decided the case of Nancy Cruzan in 1990, it made constitutional law for the entire country. Nancy Cruzan was a young woman in a persistent vegetative state caused by an accident; she was in physical circumstances essentially identical to those of Karen Quinlan, except that she was not dependent on a ventilator but rather, like Terri Schiavo, required only tube feeding to continue to live.[4] The Missouri Supreme Court had ruled that the tube feeding could be discontinued on the basis of Nancy's right of self-determination, but that only Nancy herself should be able to make this decision. Since she could not do so, tube feeding could be stopped only if those speaking for her, including her parents, could produce "clear and convincing" evidence that she would refuse tube feeding if she could speak for herself.[5] The U.S. Supreme Court, in a five-to-four decision, agreed, saying that the state of Missouri had the authority to adopt this high standard of evidence (although no state was required to do so) because of the finality of a decision to terminate treatment.[6] In the words of the chief justice, Missouri was entitled to "err on the side of life." Six of the nine justices explicitly found that no legal distinction could be made between artificially delivered fluids and nutrition and other medical interventions, such as ventilator support; none of the other three justices found a constitutionally relevant distinction. This issue is not controversial as a matter of constitutional law: Americans have (and have always had) the legal right to refuse any medical intervention, including artificially delivered fluids and nutrition.

Supreme Court Justice Sandra Day O'Connor, in a concurring opinion (her vote decided the case), recognized that young people (such as Karen Quinlan, Nancy Cruzan, and now Terri Schiavo—all of whom were in their twenties at the time of their catastrophic injuries), do not generally put explicit treatment instructions in writing. She suggested that had Cruzan simply said something like "If I'm not able to make medical treatment decisions myself, I want my mother to make them," such a statement should be a constitutionally protected delegation of the authority to decide about her treatment.[7]

O'Connor's opinion was the reason that the *Cruzan* case energized a movement—encouraging people to use the appropriate documents, such as healthcare proxy forms or assignments of durable power of attorney, to designate someone (usually called a healthcare proxy, or simply an agent) to make decisions for them if they are unable to make them themselves. All states authorize this delegation, and most states explicitly grant decision-making authority to a close relative—almost always to the spouse above all others—if the patient has not made a designation. Such laws are all to the good.

Terri Schiavo had a cardiac arrest, perhaps because of a potassium imbalance, in 1990 (the year *Cruzan* was decided), when she was twenty-seven years old. Since 1990, she has lived in a persistent vegetative state in nursing homes, with constant care, being nourished and hydrated through tubes. In 1998, Michael Schiavo petitioned the court to decide whether to discontinue the tube feeding. Unlike *Quinlan* and *Cruzan,* however, the *Schiavo* case involves a family dispute: Ms. Schiavo's parents objected. A judge found that there was clear and convincing evidence that Terri Schiavo was in a permanent or persistent vegetative state and that, if she could make her own decision, she would choose to discontinue life-prolonging procedures. An appeals court affirmed the first judge's decision, and the Florida Supreme Court declined to review it. Schiavo's parents returned to court, claiming that they had newly discovered evidence. After an additional appeal, the parents were permitted to challenge the original court findings on the basis of new evidence related to a new treatment that they believed might restore cognitive function. Five physicians were asked to examine Ms. Schiavo—two chosen by the husband, two by the parents, and one by the court. On the basis of their examinations and conclusions, the trial judge was persuaded by the three experts who agreed that Schiavo was in a persistent vegetative state. The appeals court affirmed the original decision of the trial court judge, quoting his sympathetic conclusion:

> Despite the irrefutable evidence that [Schiavo's] cerebral cortex has sustained irreparable injuries, we understand why a parent who had raised and nurtured a child from conception would hold out hope that some level of cognitive function remained.
>
> If Mrs. Schiavo were our own daughter, we could not hold to such faith. But in the end this case is not about the aspirations that loving parents have for their children. It is about Theresa Schiavo's right to make her own decision, independent of her parents and independent of her husband. . . . It may be unfortunate that when families cannot agree, the best forum we can offer for this private, personal decision is a public courtroom and the best decision-maker we can provide is a judge with no prior knowledge of the ward, but the law currently provides no better solution that adequately protects the interests of promoting the value of life.[8]

The Supreme Court of Florida again refused to hear an appeal. Subsequently, the parents, with the vocal and organized support of conservative religious organizations, went to the state legislature seeking legislation requiring the reinsertion of Ms. Schiavo's feeding tube, which had been removed on the basis of the court decisions.[9] The legislature passed a new law (2003-418), often referred to as "Terri's Law," which gave Governor Jeb Bush the authority to order the feeding tube reinserted, and he did so. The law applied only to a patient who met the following criteria on October 15, 2003—in other words, only to Terri Schiavo: (a) that patient has no written advance directive; (b) the court has found that patient to be in a persistent vegetative state; (c) that patient has had nutrition and hydration withheld; and (d) a member of that patient's family has challenged the withholding of nutrition and hydration. The constitutionality of this law was immediately challenged. In the fall of 2004, the Florida Supreme Court ruled that the law was unconstitutional because it violates the separation of powers—the division of the government into three branches (executive, legislative, and judicial), each with its own powers and responsibilities.[10] The doctrine states simply that no branch may encroach on the powers of another, and no branch may delegate to another branch its constitutionally assigned power. Specifically, the court held that for the legislature to pass a law that permits the executive to "interfere with the final judicial determination in a case" is "without question an invasion of the authority of the judicial branch."[11] In addition, the court found the law unconstitutional for an independent reason, because it "delegates legislative power to the governor" by giving the governor "unbridled discretion" to make a decision about a citizen's constitutional rights. In the court's words:

> If the Legislature with the assent of the Governor can do what was attempted here, the judicial branch would be subordinated to the final directive of the other branches. Also subordinated would be the rights of individuals, including the well established privacy right to self determination. . . . Vested rights could be stripped away based on popular clamor.[12]

In January 2005, the U.S. Supreme Court refused to hear an appeal brought by Governor Bush. Thereafter, the trial court judge ordered that the feeding tube be removed in thirty days (at 1 PM, Friday, March 18) unless a higher court again intervened. The presiding judge, George W. Greer of the Pinellas County Circuit Court, was thereafter picketed and threatened with death; he has had to be accompanied by armed guards at all times. Ms. Schiavo's parents, again with the aid of a variety of religious fundamentalist and "right to life" organizations, sought review in the appeals courts, a new statute in the state legislature, and finally, congressional intervention. Both the trial judge and the appeals courts refused to reopen the case on the basis of claims of new evidence (including the Pope's 2004 statement regarding fluids and nutrition)[13] or the failure to appoint an independent lawyer for her at the original hearing. In Florida, the state legislature considered, and the House passed, new legislation aimed at restoring the feeding tube, but the Florida Senate—recognizing, I think, that this new legislation would be unconstitutional for the same reason as the previous legislation was—ultimately refused to approve the bill.

Thereupon, an event unique in American politics occurred: after more than a week of discussion, and after formally declaring their Easter recess without action, Congress reconvened two days after the feeding tube was removed to consider emergency legislation designed to apply only to Terri Schiavo. Under rules that permitted a few senators to act if no senator objected, the U.S. Senate adopted a bill entitled "For the Relief of the Parents of Theresa Marie Schiavo" on March 20, 2005. The House, a majority of whose members had to be present to vote, debated the same measure from 9 PM to midnight on the same day and passed it by a four-to-one margin shortly after midnight on March 21. The president then signed it into law. In substance, the new law (S. 686) provides that "the U.S. District Court for the Middle District of Florida shall have jurisdiction" to hear a suit "for the alleged violation of any right of Theresa Marie Schiavo under the Constitution or laws of the United States relating to the withholding or withdrawal of food, fluids, or medical treatment necessary to sustain her life." The parents have standing to bring the lawsuit (the federal court had previously refused to hear the case on the basis that the parents had no standing to bring it), and the court is instructed to "determine de novo any claim of a violation of any right of Theresa Marie Schiavo . . . notwithstanding any prior State court determination . . . "—that is, to pretend that no court has made any prior ruling in the case. The act is to provide no "precedent with respect to future legislation." The brief debate on this bill in the House of Representatives (there were no hearings in either chamber and no debate at all in the U.S. Senate) was notable primarily for its uninformed and frenzied rhetoric. It was covered live by C-SPAN. The primary sponsor of the measure, Congressman Thomas DeLay (R-TX), for example, asserted that "She's not a vegetable, just handicapped like many millions of people walking around today. This has nothing to do with politics, and it's disgusting for people to say that it does." Others echoed the sentiments of Senate majority leader and physician Bill Frist (R-TN), who said that immediate action was imperative because "Terri Schiavo is being denied lifesaving fluids and nutrition as we speak." Other physician-members of the House chimed in. Congressman Dave Weldon (R-FL) remarked that, on the basis of his sixteen years of medical practice, he was able to conclude that Terri Schiavo is "not in a persistent vegetative state." Congressman Phil Gingrey (R-GA) agreed, saying "she's very much alive." Another physician, Congressman Joe Schwarz (R-MI), who was a head and neck surgeon for twenty-seven years, opined that "she does have some cognitive ability" and asked, "How many other patients are there with feeding tubes? Should they be removed too?" Another physician-congressman, Tom Price (R-GA), thought the law was reasonable because there was "no living will in place" and the family and experts disagreed. The only physician who was troubled by Congress's public diagnosis and treatment of Terri Schiavo was James McDermott (D-WA), who chided his physician-colleagues for the poor medical practice of making a diagnosis without examining the patient. Although he deferred to the medical expertise of his congressional colleagues with MD degrees, Congressman Barney Frank (D-MA) pointed out that the chamber was not filled with physicians. Frank said of the March 20 proceedings: "We're not doctors, we just play them on C-SPAN."

The mantras of the debate were that in a life-or-death decision, we should err on the "side of life," that action should be taken to "prevent death by starvation" and ensure the "right to life," and that Congress should "protect the rights of disabled people." The following day, U.S. District Court Judge James D. Whittemore issued a careful opinion denying the request of the parents for a temporary restraining order that would require the reinsertion of the feeding tube.[14] The judge concluded that the parents had failed to demonstrate "a substantial likelihood of success on the merits" of the case— a prerequisite for a temporary restraining order. Specifically, Judge Whittemore found that, as to the various due-process claims made, the case had been "exhaustively litigated"; that, throughout, all parties had been "represented by able counsel"; and that it was not clear how having an additional lawyer "appointed by the court [for Ms. Schiavo] would have reduced the risk of erroneous rulings." As to the allegation that the patient's First Amendment rights to practice her religion had been violated at the bedside by the state, the court held that there were no state actions involved at all, "because neither Defendant Schiavo nor Defendant Hospice are state actors." Whittemore's decision is reasonable and consistent with settled law, and it seems likely to be upheld on appeal.

The religious right and congressional Republicans may nonetheless turn this decision to their advantage. Despite the fact that Congress itself sent the case to federal court for determination, these Republicans may cite the ruling as yet another example of "legislating" by the courts. For they liken the action permitted—the withdrawal of a feeding tube—to unfavored activities, such as abortion and same-sex marriage, that courts have allowed to occur. All three activities, they argue, represent attacks on the "culture of life" and necessitate that the president appoint federal court judges who value life over liberty. A vast majority of Americans would not want to be maintained in a persistent vegetative state by means of a feeding tube, like Terri Schiavo and Nancy Cruzan. The intense publicity generated by this case will cause many to discuss this issue with their families and, I hope, to sign an advance directive. Such a directive, in the form of a living will or the designation of a healthcare proxy, would prevent court involvement in virtually all cases—although it might not have solved the problem in the Schiavo case, because the family members disagreed about Terri Schiavo's medical condition and the acceptability of removing the tube in any circumstances.

Despite the impression that may have been created by these three cases, and especially by the grandstanding in Congress, conflicts involving medical decision making for incompetent patients near the end of life are no longer primarily legal in nature, if they ever were. The law has been remarkably stable since *Quinlan* (which itself restated existing law): competent adults have the right to refuse any medical treatment, including life-sustaining treatment (which includes artificially delivered fluids and nutrition). Incompetent adults retain an interest in self-determination. Competent adults can execute an advance directive stating their wishes and designate a person to act on their behalf, and physicians can honor these wishes. Physicians and healthcare agents should make treatment decisions consistent with what they believe the patient would want (the subjective standard). If the patient's desires cannot be ascertained, then treatment decisions should be based on the patient's best interests (what a reasonable person would most likely want in the same circumstances). This has, I believe, always been the law in the United States.[15] Of course, legal forms or formalities cannot solve nonlegal problems. Decision making near the end of life is difficult and can exacerbate unresolved family feuds that then are played out at the patient's bedside and even in the media. Nonetheless, it is reasonable and responsible for all persons to designate healthcare agents to make treatment decisions for them when they are unable to make their own. After this recent congressional intervention, it also makes sense to specifically state one's wishes with respect to artificial fluids and hydration—and that one wants no politicians, even physician politicians, involved in the process.

Most Americans will agree with a resolution that was overwhelmingly adopted by the California Medical Association on the same day that Congress passed the Schiavo law: "Resolved: That the California Medical Association expresses its outrage at Congress's interference with these medical decisions." If there is disagreement between the physician and the family, or among family members, the involvement of outside experts, including consultants, ethics committees, risk managers, lawyers, and even courts, may become inevitable—at least if the patient survives long enough to permit such involvement. It is the long-lasting nature of the persistent vegetative state that results in its persistence in the courtrooms of the United States. There is (and should be) no special law regarding the refusal of treatment that is tailored to specific diseases or prognoses, and the persistent vegetative state is no exception.[16] "Erring on the side of life" in this context often results in violating a person's body and human dignity in a way few would want for themselves. In such situations, erring on the side of liberty—specifically, the patient's right to decide on treatment—is more consistent with American values and our constitutional traditions. As the Massachusetts Supreme Judicial Court said in a 1977 case that raised the same legal question: "The constitutional right to privacy, as we conceive it, is an expression of the sanctity of individual free choice and self-determination as fundamental constituents of life. The value of life as so perceived is lessened not by a decision to refuse treatment, but by the failure to allow a competent human being the right of choice."[17]

NOTES

1. President's statement on Terri Schiavo. March 17, 2005. http://www.white-house.gov/news/ releases/2005/03/20050317-7.html. Accessed March 22, 2005.

2. *In re Quinlan*, 70 N.J.10, 355 A2d 647 (1976).

3. Ibid.

4. *Cruzan v. Director, Missouri Dept. of Health*, 497 U.S. 261 (1990).

5. *Cruzan v. Harmon*, 760 S.W.2d 408 (Mo. 1988).

6. *Cruzan v. Director, Missouri Dept. of Health*, 497 U.S. 261 (1990).

7. Ibid.

8. *In re Guardianship of Schiavo*, 800 So. 2d 640 (Fla. 2d Dist. Ct. App. 2001).

9. Goodnough A. Victory in Florida Feeding Case Emboldens the Religious Right. *New York Times*. October 24, 2003:A1.

Kirkpatrick DD, Stolberg SG. How Family's Cause Reached the Halls of Congress: Networks of Christians Rallied to Case of Florida Woman. *New York Times*. March 22, 2005:A1.

10. *Bush v. Schiavo*, 885 So.2d 321 (Fla. 2004).

11. Ibid.

12. Ibid.

13. Shannon TA, Walter JJ. Implications of the Papal Allocution on Feeding Tubes. *Hastings Cent Rep.* 2004;34(4):18–20.

14. *Schiavo ex rel. Schindler v. Schiavo*, No. 8:05-CV-530-T-27TBM (M.D. Fla. March 22, 2005) (slip opinion).

15. Annas GJ. *The Rights of Hospital Patients*. New York: Discus Books; 1975:81–84.

16. Annas GJ. The Health Care Proxy and the Living Will. *N Engl J Med.* 1991;324:1210–1213.

The Multi-Society Task Force on PVS. Medical Aspects of the Persistent Vegetative State. *N Engl J Med.* 1994;330:1572–1579. [Erratum, *N Engl J Med.* 1995;333:130.]

17. *Superintendent of Belchertown State School v. Saikewicz*, 373 Mass. 728, 742, 370 N.E.2d 417 (Mass. 1977).

After Terri Schiavo

Why the Disability Rights Movement Spoke Out, Why Some of Us Worried, and Where Do We Go from Here?

Mary Johnson

The controversy over Clint Eastwood's Oscar-winner *Million Dollar Baby* in February gave both the National Spinal Cord Injury Association and Not Dead Yet at least fifteen seconds of fame, if not the fifteen minutes Andy Warhol prophesied.

Those fifteen minutes came two weeks later.

Terri Schiavo's feeding tube was removed March 18. We knew it was coming. We'd known it since March 1, when Pinellas County Circuit Judge George Greer, saying he was "no longer comfortable" issuing any more stays in the years-long court battle, announced the date.

But few disability groups were prepared for the right-to-life, right-to-die political circus the nation was forced to watch between that date and Terri Schiavo's death from starvation and dehydration on March 31. One could almost think that the Eastwood protest had been just for practice.

After the first few days—in which the story was reported as the latest round in the sniping war between conservative Christian right-to-life activists calling for government intervention and progressives and liberals horrified at the assault on a family's right to privacy and individual choice in dying—the disability rights perspective began to emerge.

The *Boston Globe* noted it first, with its story "Rights Groups for Disabled Join in Fight," but by and large, most reporters finally came to see that

From *Ragged Edge*, posted April 2, 2005, http://www.raggededgemagazine.com/focus/postschiavo0405 .html (accessed November 21, 2005). Reprinted from Ragged Edge Magazine Online (www.ragged edgemagazine.com).

there was a third ring at this circus. A glaring exception was the *New York Times*, which steadfastly downplayed the disability rights perspective.

Not Dead Yet seemed to be the group taking the lead. And that was appropriate, given that they exist to "oppose public policy that singles out individuals for legalized killing based on their health status." One didn't hear much from any other disability group, although American Association of People with Disabilities (AAPD) head Andy Imparato, interviewed in news stories and on CNN, spoke cogently about the disability rights point of view.

Now that the sawdust is being swept up, there are a number of objects lying around that we want to take a look at before we move on:

What WAS the disability rights point of view? Was there one?

That this question can even be asked with seriousness points to the way people—including disabled people—understand the concept of a "disability rights movement." Not all African Americans (formerly called Blacks, and before that, Negroes) supported the civil rights proposals advanced by groups such as the NAACP or, during its day, the Southern Christian Leadership Conference. However, there was no doubt in anyone's mind—certainly not the media's—that there were groups that spoke for the issues; that collectively were seen to represent the issues of the "civil rights movement." The women's rights movement has its groups as well, as does the gay rights movement.

However, perhaps more than with any other group, people who have disabilities seem unaware of not only any national disability rights groups, but of any central issues that might unite them. Not Dead Yet (NDY) repeatedly noted that over two dozen national disability groups had in one way or another spoken out over the years about Terri Schiavo's situation with alarm; and that over a dozen had joined NDY on friend-of-the-court briefs raising disability rights concerns about the case.

But most people—even most disabled people—don't know these groups well. To add to the problem, the term "disability group" can be equally applied to a group supportive of rights and to one who rights groups have often seen as part of our national disability problem. Rights groups, charity groups (like the MDA Telethon), groups like the March of Dimes (whose solution to the disability problem is to end disabled lives before they're born), and service and "disease groups" like the MS Society, are all mixed together in the public's mind. Many haven't a clue what their own thinking is on any issue like that we faced with Terri Schiavo. Many were secretly horrified that groups protested Eastwood's movie. "The Brain Injury Association of America, the Christopher Reeve Paralysis Foundation, the Parkinson's Action Network, and the ALS Association—were noticeably silent on the Schiavo case," wrote the *Washington Post*'s Ceci Connolly.

"Cowardice in the face of controversy is not a virtue," said Arthur Caplan, the celeb bioethicist NDY loves to hate, in an MSNBC commentary. "Not Dead Yet spoke up," he noted. "But where were the many other groups who also speak for those with Alzheimer's, Parkinson's, ALS, cancer, AIDS, spinal cord injuries, cystic fibrosis, Huntington's disease? . . . Ducking commentary on the Schiavo case should not be an option."

The disability groups who refuse to speak out do so mostly because they seem to still think that disability is, as disability rights scholar Paul Longmore put it, "a private matter between patient and doctor." That belief has done us far more harm than good, yet it is at the heart of why such groups do not speak out on issues that affect the lives of people with disabilities in America.

Another group created the slogan "silence = death." But it might be useful for disability rights groups to now adopt it as their motto, and act accordingly.

Still, a number of national disability rights groups have been trying for years to be seen as purveyors of a national disability rights sensibility. They have a long way to go; but that doesn't mean they should be treated any differently than national rights groups of other rights movements.

Will the events of February and March make the head-in-the-sand groups reconsider their ostrich policy? Maybe. But that reconsideration may take the form of simply trying to find a deeper hole in the sand in which to bury their heads. All the more reason to appreciate groups like Not Dead Yet, AAPD, and the Disability Rights Education and Defense Fund, all of whose spokespeople were quoted about the Schiavo case.

Why do crip spokespeople, and individual crips, keep comparing themselves to Terri Schiavo?

Of all the comments we've received at Ragged Edge in recent weeks, this is the most common.

"That's ridiculous. Disabled people aren't like Terri Schiavo."

"Terri Schiavo isn't 'disabled'—she's brain-dead!" a number of e-mailers practically shouted at us. "Can't you people see the difference?"

"I'm disabled but I'm far from being like Terri Schiavo. If I ever ended up like her, I'd want the plug pulled."

A number of you felt that by "getting in bed with Terri Schiavo," as one put it, we were doing the cause of disability rights grave harm. The *Washington Post*'s Ceci Connolly, in an April 2 story ("Schiavo Raised Profile of Disabled"), quoted a number of disabled people who felt that way. Particularly telling was Karen Hwang's comment. Hwang, described as a thirty-seven-year-old quadriplegic from New Jersey, told Connolly, "We're independent; we're working, living in the community. . . . Just to have somebody say we are vulnerable, that's patronizing and insulting."

People like Hwang continually return to the issue that what we need to be pressing for is better access, an end to job discrimination, access to education, better healthcare access.

We understand why people want to assert a distinction between themselves and Terri Schiavo. Hwang's comment captures its essence well. And on surface—if what you are comparing are the individual disabilities—the distinctions are vast. But those who make the comparison aren't basing their comparison on individual disabilities but on societal bigotry.

It's the "better dead than disabled" mindset these crips are focusing on. And to that mindset, it's disability itself that seems horrific. And as long as that's the case, the kinds of things that functioning crips want will always be considered too much trouble, too expensive, too bothersome to mainstream society.

The only way disability bigotry of the "better dead than disabled" school has any chance of being stamped out—or even dislodged a bit—is if the disability rights movement is willing to speak forcefully and publicly about the tie-in between emerging public policies that in the guise of cost containment and choice in dying both promote futile care policies and define feeding tubes as "medical care," and the look-the-other-way stances of progressives and right to lifers alike as Medicaid is cut, healthcare services are cut, and anti-access judges are appointed to the federal bench.

Disabled people who see their lives as mainstreamed and OK may not want to acknowledge this, may not want to think about the connect, perhaps hoping that it will go away. They too may want to join the groups playing ostrich. The stretch of sand is going to fill up pretty soon with lots of us digging holes to stick our heads into.

Here are the reasons, as we understand them, that "functioning crips" aligned with groups like Not Dead Yet compared themselves to Terri Schiavo:

1. She was not terminally ill. She was simply a person who would never "recover." Both points, they said, apply also to their lives.

Those are the two related but distinct points that keep getting made by Not Dead Yet members. And the reason they keep bringing them up, it seems, is because they believe that the public doesn't make the distinction. And not making the distinction, they believe, is dangerous for all disabled people.

It is accurate that Terri Schiavo was not terminally ill. Left as she was, with a feeding tube, and with care, she could have lived decades longer. But people ignore that distinction between permanent disability and terminal illness—Not Dead Yet has been making that point for years. Ignoring it, the group says, has allowed right-to-die groups to press for legal sanction for things like feeding tube removal, and ventilator removal, which allow healthy but seriously disabled people to have their lives ended prematurely—often to save medical costs.

It is also accurate to say that Terri Schiavo would not have "recovered." A number of times that point was made in news stories, often as the final sentence, used as an explanation as to why Michael Schiavo justified the removal of her feeding tube. The "will not recover" phrase also appeared in stories explaining why the Schindlers pressed so hard to gain guardianship—that they believed she could receive therapy and perhaps "improve."

When such stories were reported, they also usually contained comments by medical professionals insisting that therapy would be of no use because Terri Schiavo "would not recover." And the phrase also appeared in "context stories" about the issue of people "like" Terri Schiavo who "will not recover"—how much their care cost taxpayers, how court rulings in recent years had made it easier to turn off ventilators, and so on.

In all these cases, the phrase "will not recover" was used, it seemed, to Not Dead Yet protesters, as a kind of shorthand to justify the withdrawal of life-sustaining measures.

And this, perhaps more than any other point, was one we heard made from the Not Dead Yet camp: that people who were seriously disabled with "no hope of recovery" were seen as burdens on society in terms of their costs, their medical care, their needs.

People in the disability rights movement, by and large, are people who have serious disabilities. Virtually none of them will "recover." To them, the phrase—its constant and patently unexamined use—signaled an attitude much in evidence throughout society: that people who could not recover would be better off dead. Or that their families, or society, would be better off—economically, certainly—if they were dead.

That is a hard message to hear. And even if your disability is not on the surface anything like Terri Schiavo's, even if you can think and speak and write and work, if your disability is so serious that you require a feeding tube or a breathing tube or even a catheter—and if you're not going to recover—you fear being treated like Terri Schiavo. Maybe sooner, if you're admitted to the hospital for something unrelated like pneumonia or a tubal ligation and told that you should sign a "do not resuscitate" order—something a number of our readers have reported happening to them. Maybe later, if your disability progresses to a point where you need more equipment, more assistance. But looming always.

2. A feeding tube is not medical treatment. A story in yesterday's *Washington Post* ("Feeding Tube Benefit Questioned") noted 1977 research (much reported in recent days) that showed that nursing home residents "who had feeding tubes did not live longer on average than those without them"—the study, done using elderly "nursing home patients with dementia," seems to be one of those factoids that get dropped into stories willy-nilly when it serves to ground a hot topic. However, what the research doesn't bother to point out but which crips know is that what this primarily shows is that feeding tubes are not "medical treatment"—they're just an alternative device for delivering nutrition. You can live for years—decades—with a feeding tube if you're otherwise healthy. As many crips upset about the "feeding tube debate" are. As Terri Schiavo was.

Yes, Terri Schiavo was healthy. Brain damaged for sure. Unable to "recover," for sure. But healthy. She could have lived a long long time with that feeding tube.

Now maybe that horrifies you—it horrifies many people who are coming at the issue with the mindset of "I couldn't stand to live like that"—but that is beside the point. The point is that Terri Schiavo was not unhealthy. She was not "ill." She was most assuredly not "terminally ill." As the pope is. Pope John Paul II is dying. That is what "terminally ill" is supposed to mean. He will likely be dead when you read this. But he is dying from old age. Terri was not.

It is this distinction that Not Dead Yet crips feel got almost completely lost in the feeding tube discussion, and it is why they latched so quickly onto their "Tube Pride" concept.

That's what this is all about: The feeding tube represents—stands for—all sorts of equipment without which severely disabled people would not be alive. And, they say, slowly but surely the presence of that equipment is being used as justification for encouraging a person to end their life. "How, exactly, did a feeding tube get reclassified as 'medical treatment'?" asks Boston Not Dead Yet's John Kelly.

"Twelve years ago I made a decision to have a feeding tube placed in my stomach in order to prolong life," wrote David Jayne recently. Jayne, who has had ALS for seventeen years, created RespiteMatch.com and lobbies for a change in Medicare's "Homebound Rule."

"I had lost the ability to swallow due to the progression of the disease," he explained.

"Seven years ago last week," he wrote, when he "had one foot in death's door, because my diaphragm muscle was becoming increasingly disabled," he made the decision "contrary to society"—and contrary to what 95 percent of people with ALS say they want—to begin using a respirator. It was, he noted, also *contrary what he would have wanted before he contracted the disease.*

> It is extremely easy for a healthy individual to say how they would not live. I am guilty myself. If someone had told me prior to the diagnosis that I would be totally paralyzed, fed by a feeding tube, communicate via computer with a voice synthesizer and tethered to a ventilator, [yet] that I would find more meaning in life and living, I am certain [I would have thought] that person telling me such a tale was insane.

The night before his tracheotomy surgery, he says, "my now ex-wife told me how selfish I was for wanting to live—that my young children had suffered enough and it would cause them only more pain. It was a sickening sense of abandonment. I have absolutely no doubt if I did not have the ability to communicate my desires the surgery would not have taken place."

This is why the feeding tube issue upsets Not Dead Yet crips so much.

They raise these forgoing points again and again. They focus on those points that they say kept getting made over and over in the Terri Schiavo discussion. The attitude with which progressive right-to-die advocates viewed the Terri Schiavo situation is an attitude that they say they feel is often applied to their lives as well.

Another way of putting this: It is not they who see Terri Schiavo as being identical to them; it is the public, which, although it says that Terri Schiavo's situation and condition is very different than that of a severely disabled but conscious person, nonetheless continues to hold beliefs about nonrecovering severely disabled people which to crips seem very similar. Yes, when pressed, now progressives are making distinctions. But very often, the crips say, the same progressives apply the same kind of thinking toward them— and they say they see it all around them.

In other words, Terri Schiavo represents something to the public that they believe they also represent. She is an example of why people think the disabled person is better off dead.

Another lesson learned: then is not now; now is not the future.

Something else we heard, coming through the opinion pieces and letters to the editor from crips, and from e-mails to Ragged Edge, was that people who are not disabled, despite what they think they understand and would want, have no real clue as to what it is like to live as a disabled person. And there is no way . . . that they can know now what they would really want once they became disabled. Once they had time to adjust, that is.

"[W]hen I discovered I was paralysed in almost 90 per cent of my body," wrote Canadian commentator Ed Smith at the height of the *Million Dollar Baby* controversy, "I pleaded with my wife to have me shot or put down in some merciful fashion. At the time, I didn't even care if it was merciful. That was for the first two days. Now, six years later, I'm rather glad she didn't. Actor Christopher Reeve had a similar experience. So did many people I know who have suffered from catastrophic injury."

This point drove many crips' animus against *Million Dollar Baby*. While it might be true that "Maggie" wanted to end her life—many newly paralyzed people do; even Christopher Reeve did—most people get over that suicidal feeling and get on with their lives, said Eastwood's critics. Only paralyzed people are encouraged to act on that suicidal wish—and given society's blessing and help to speed them to the end, they say. That was Frankie's message, they say. And they hated it.

Thus the general solution to this entire sorry saga—get a "durable power of attorney for medical decision making"—which is what every "expert" on TV has preached in the past few days—may be a snare and a delusion.

Wellesley College bioethicist Adrienne Asch, one of the few bioethicists to come out of the disability rights movement, was quoted in Ellen Goodman's syndicated column on Thursday. Asch told Goodman, "The typical advance directive or living will does not ask the right questions. It asks what sort of medical intervention we want or don't want. The question that we ought to be asked is what am I experiencing? What will make me feel that I have something to live for? What is enough?"

Asch, who is blind and very conscious of societal attitudes toward disabilities, says that if she wrote the living will form, it would ask people to imagine themselves in a range of scenarios. When would we want our lives prolonged by medicine? In her own advance directive she has written that "as long as the people who know me believe that I recognize them and can differentiate them from strangers, I want to be alive."

In the morass of news coverage quoting bioethicists and other "medical experts" on the need for advance directives, Asch's analysis stands out as the only one making the clear point that we hear over and over from disability groups: That people don't really know until they are disabled what it is that they might want. A study reported in the recent issue of the *Journal of Experimental Psychology* found that nondisabled people ("healthy people," the term researchers Jason Riis and colleagues used) consistently "underestimate the self-reported well-being of people with disabilities and serious illnesses." In other words, they consistently believe disabled people are far less happy than they actually are, and imagine life to be far more horrid with a disability than people with disabilities themselves believe it to be. This is not the first study to discover this, but these studies don't seem to have made it into the popular media.

Thus, it is the unusual person who, never having faced disability or lived with others with happily disabled lives, would sign a directive asking to be kept alive if the future meant ventilator or feeding tube dependency. However, what this means is that many many people now rushing to sign directives will say just that—and who knows how they might feel had they had a chance to live with disability?

But why should it matter, you say. If I want my life ended before I wake up on a ventilator for the rest of my life, what does it matter to anyone else? If it's my decision?

It matters very much, it seems, to the community of severely disabled people who make up Not Dead Yet. Although Not Dead Yet's Coleman and Drake are insistent that had Schiavo clearly expressed her wishes, so that there was no debate, they would not be involved in the case, and would not have filed several court briefs in the case over the years, they say they know that many people in "guardianship" who can no longer express their views have lives that are seen as expendable.

Because of those people, the slogan "silence = death" has renewed meaning.

In a recent interview, Coleman told a reporter, "[W]hat we are seeing here is the dismantling of the constitutional rights of people in guardianship. No longer will there be the presumption for life.

"The social presumption that [Schiavo] would be better off dead appears to have influenced the decisions in the case," Coleman said. "We feel threatened by this, almost as if there is a cognitive test for personhood under the law."

Both the evangelical right-to-life movement and the progressive right-to-die movement have broader agendas that go beyond Terri Schiavo. In coming months, as the U.S. Supreme Court prepares to rule on the constitutionality of Oregon's assisted-suicide law, both groups will be pushing their agendas with politicians. And there are plenty of politicians who are already loyal to one or the other side.

But if disability rights movement leadership has learned anything from the past few weeks, one of those lessons should be that it needs to now build on its assertion that it is the one group which can most accurately claim to speak for people like Terri Schiavo. Certainly the disability rights movement can produce a focused agenda—and beyond that, one free of the kind of political overreaching we all grew thoroughly sick of in the last few weeks.

It is, because of this, the agenda most able to lift our nation beyond the left-right hand-wringing we seem mired in.

Not Dead Yet has proposed:

- Meaningful federal civil rights review of contested third-party decisions to withhold treatment in the absence of an advance directive or personally appointed surrogate. Senator Tom Harkin (D-IA) is already working on a bill providing for this. Movement leaders want congressional hearings on how to protect people from death based on decisions of guardians or healthcare providers.
- State-by-state review of guardianship and healthcare decisions laws. They want the review conducted by disability rights monitoring groups like the Disability Rights Education and Defense Fund; they want the review to result in reforms to safeguard against what they call "nonvoluntary euthanasia."
- A moratorium on the removal of food and water from people diagnosed in a "persistent vegetative state" or "minimally conscious state" until they have undergone newer diagnostic MRI procedures, which they say must be a requirement. A recent study done by doctors at Columbia Medical Center noted that patients "who are treated as if they are almost completely unaware may in fact hear and register what is going on around them but be unable to respond."
- Enforcement of the 1999 U.S. Supreme Court Olmstead decision,

which ruled that people with disabilities must be allowed to live in the "least restrictive" setting. For well over a decade, the movement has called for changing the Medicaid law to allow people to receive services at home rather than being placed in nursing homes, saving the government millions. It's time for Congress to get serious about passing the Medicaid Community Services and Supports Act.

- Serious and substantive public discussion about "the difference between end- of-life decisions and decisions to end the lives of disabled people who are not otherwise dying." Disability rights movement experts, they say, must be given equal time in media debates with bioethicists; reporters and editors must begin to turn to disability rights spokespeople as experts rather than relying on doctors, ethicists, and spokespersons on the religious right "to pontificate about our lives."

Now if disability rights movement leadership will only press ahead with them.

We can only hope they will.

Terri Schiavo—
A Tragedy Compounded

Timothy E. Quill, MD

The story of Terri Schiavo should be disturbing to all of us. How can it be that medicine, ethics, law, and family can work so poorly together in meeting the needs of this woman who was left in a persistent vegetative state after having a cardiac arrest? Ms. Schiavo has been sustained by artificial hydration and nutrition through a feeding tube for fifteen years, and her husband, Michael Schiavo, has been locked in a very public legal struggle with her parents and siblings about whether such treatment should be continued or stopped. Distortion by interest groups, media hyperbole, and manipulative use of videotape have characterized this case and demonstrate what can happen when a patient becomes more a precedent-setting symbol than a unique human being.

Let us begin with some medical facts. On February 25, 1990, Terri Schiavo had a cardiac arrest, triggered by extreme hypokalemia brought on by an eating disorder. As a result, severe hypoxic–ischemic encephalopathy developed, and during the subsequent months, she exhibited no evidence of higher cortical function. Computed tomographic scans of her brain eventually showed severe atrophy of her cerebral hemispheres, and her electroencephalograms have been flat, indicating no functional activity of the cerebral cortex. Her neurologic examinations have been indicative of a persistent vegetative state, which includes periods of wakefulness alternating with sleep, some reflexive responses to light and noise, and some basic gag and

From the *New England Journal of Medicine* 352, no. 16 (2005): 1630–33. Copyright © 2005 Massachusetts Medical Society. All rights reserved.

swallowing responses, but no signs of emotion, willful activity, or cognition.[1] There is no evidence that Ms. Schiavo is suffering, since the usual definition of this term requires conscious awareness that is impossible in the absence of cortical activity. There have been only a few reported cases in which minimal cognitive and motor functions were restored three months or more after the diagnosis of a persistent vegetative state due to hypoxic–ischemic encephalopathy; in none of these cases was there the sort of objective evidence of severe cortical damage that is present in this case, nor was the period of disability so long.[2] Having viewed some of the highly edited videotaped material of Terri Schiavo and having seen other patients in a persistent vegetative state, I am not surprised that family members and others unfamiliar with this condition would interpret some of her apparent alertness and movement as meaningful.

In 2002, the Florida trial court judge conducted six days of evidentiary hearings on Ms. Schiavo's condition, including evaluations by four neurologists, one radiologist, and her attending physician. The two neurologists selected by Michael Schiavo, a court-appointed "neutral" neurologist, and Ms. Schiavo's attending physician all agreed that her condition met the criteria for a persistent vegetative state. The neurologist and the radiologist chosen by the patient's parents and siblings, the Schindler family, disagreed and suggested that Ms. Schiavo's condition might improve with unproven therapies such as hyperbaric oxygen or vasodilators—but had no objective data to support their assertions. The trial court judge ruled that the diagnosis of a persistent vegetative state met the legal standard of "clear and convincing" evidence, and this decision was reviewed and upheld by the Florida Second District Court of Appeal. Subsequent appeals to the Florida Supreme Court and the U.S. Supreme Court were denied a hearing.

So what is known about Terri Schiavo's wishes and values? Since she unfortunately left no written advance directive, the next step would be to meet with her closest family members and try to understand what she would want under these medical circumstances if she could speak for herself, drawing on the principle of "substituted judgment." Some families unite around this question, especially when there is a shared vision of the patient's views and values. Other families unravel, their crisis aggravated by genuine differences of opinion about the proper course of action or preexisting fault lines arising from long-standing family dynamics. Here Ms. Schiavo's story gets more complex. Michael Schiavo was made her legal guardian under Florida law, which designates the spouse as the decision maker above other family members if a patient becomes irreversibly incapacitated and has not designated a healthcare proxy. After three years of trying traditional and experimental therapies, Mr. Schiavo accepted the neurologists' diagnosis of an irreversible persistent vegetative state. He believed that his wife would not want to be kept alive indefinitely in her condition, recalling prior statements that she had made, such as "I don't want to be kept alive on a machine."

The Schindler family, however, did not accept the diagnosis of a persistent vegetative state, believing instead that Ms. Schiavo's condition could improve with additional rehabilitative treatment. The relationship between Mr. Schiavo and the Schindler family began breaking down in 1993, around the time that a malpractice lawsuit revolving around the events that led to Ms. Schiavo's cardiac arrest was settled. In 1994, Mr. Schiavo attempted to refuse treatment for an infection his wife had, and her parents took legal action to require treatment. Thus began wide-ranging, acrimonious legal and public-opinion battles that now involve multiple special-interest groups who see this case as a *cause célèbre* for their particular issue. Michael Schiavo has been criticized for being motivated by financial greed, and his loyalty to his wife has been questioned because he now lives with another woman, with whom he has two children. The Schindlers have been criticized for not accepting the painful reality of their daughter's condition and for expressing their own wishes and values rather than hers.

The right of competent patients to refuse unwanted medical treatment, including artificial hydration and nutrition, is a settled ethical and legal issue in this country—based on the right to bodily integrity. In the *Nancy Cruzan* case, the Supreme Court affirmed that surrogate decision makers have this right when a patient is incapacitated, but it said that states could set their own standards of evidence about patients' own wishes.[3] Although both the Schiavo and Cruzan cases involve the potential withdrawal of a feeding tube from a patient in a persistent vegetative state, the family was united in believing that Nancy Cruzan would not want to be kept alive in such a state indefinitely. Their challenge, under Missouri law, was to prove to the court in a clear and convincing manner that this would have been Nancy Cruzan's own wish.

The Schiavo case raises much more challenging questions about how to define family and how to proceed if members of the immediate family are not in agreement. The relevant Florida statute requires "clear and convincing evidence that the decision would have been the one the patient would have chosen had the patient been competent or, if there is no indication of what the patient would have chosen, that the decision is in the patient's best interest." Since there is no societal consensus about whether a feeding tube is in the "best interest" of a patient in a persistent vegetative state, the main legal question to be addressed is that of Terri Schiavo's wishes. In 2001, the trial court judge ruled that clear and convincing evidence showed that Ms. Schiavo would choose not to receive life-prolonging treatment under her current circumstances. This ruling was also affirmed by the Florida appeals court and denied a hearing by the Florida Supreme Court. When Terri Schiavo's feeding tube was removed for the second time in 2003, the Florida legislature created "Terri's Law" to override the court decision, and the tube was again reinserted. This law was subsequently ruled an unconstitutional violation of the separation of powers.

On March 18, 2005, Ms. Schiavo's feeding tube was removed for a third time. The U.S. Congress then passed an "emergency measure" that was signed by the president in an effort both to force federal courts to review Ms. Schiavo's case and to create a legal mandate to have her feeding tube reinserted yet again. Although the U.S. District Court in Florida denied the emergency request to reinsert the feeding tube, the final outcome of Congress's extraordinary maneuver is not yet clear. This sad saga reinforces my personal belief that the courts—though their involvement is sometimes necessary—are the last place one wants to be when working through these complex dilemmas.

Although I have not examined her, from the data I have reviewed, I have no doubt that Terri Schiavo is in a persistent vegetative state and that her cognitive and neurologic functions are unfortunately not going to improve. Her life can be further prolonged with artificial hydration and nutrition, and there is some solace in knowing that she is not consciously suffering. I also believe that both her husband and her family, while seeing the situation in radically different ways, are trying to do what is right for her. If and when her feeding tube is permanently removed, her family may be reassured that dying in this way can be a natural, humane process (humans died in this way for thousands of years before the advent of feeding tubes).[4]

In considering this profound decision, the central issue is not what family members would want for themselves or what they want for their incapacitated loved one, but rather what the patient would want for himself or herself. The New Jersey Supreme Court that decided the case of Karen Ann Quinlan got the question of substituted judgment right: If the patient could wake up for fifteen minutes and understand his or her condition fully, and then had to return to it, what would he or she tell you to do? If the data about the patient's wishes are not clear, then in the absence of public policy or family consensus, we should err on the side of continued treatment even in cases of a persistent vegetative state in which there is no hope of recovery. But if the evidence is clear, as the courts have found in the case of Terri Schiavo, then enforcing life-prolonging treatment against what is agreed to be the patient's will is both unethical and illegal. Let us hope that future courts and legislative bodies put aside all the special interests and distractions and listen carefully to the patient's voice as expressed through family members and close friends. This voice is what counts the most, and in the Terri Schiavo case, it has been largely drowned out by a very loud, self-interested public debate.

NOTES

1. Jennett B. *The Vegetative State: Medical Facts, Ethical and Legal Dilemmas*. New York: Cambridge University Press; 2002.

2. The Multi-Society Task Force on PVS. Medical Aspects of the Persistent Vegetative State. *N Engl J Med.* 1994;330:1499–1508, 1572–1579. [Erratum, N Engl J Med. 1995;333:130.]

3. Gostin LO. Life and Death Choices after Cruzan. *Law Med Health Care.* 1991;19:9–12.

4. Ganzini L, Goy ER, Miller LL, Harvath TA, Jackson A, Delorit MA. Nurses' Experiences with Hospice Patients Who Refuse Food and Fluids to Hasten Death. *N Engl J Med.* 2003;349:359–365.

Medical Examiner, District Six
Pasco and Pinellas Counties
John R. Thogmartin, MD,
Chief Medical Examiner

REPORT OF AUTOPSY

Name: SCHIAVO, Theresa
Case No. 5050439
EXTERNAL EXAMINATION:

The body is that of a 62 inch, 112 pound white female who appears the
recorded age of 41 years. The body is clad in a pink and white gown. Three
pillows and a blanket are also received with the body. The scalp is covered
in thick brown hair with flecks of gray. The irides are brown. There is bilateral tache noire. The eyelids are yellow and dry. The eyes have a sunken
appearance. The ears and nose are normally developed. The mouth has partial natural dentition. The left upper first bicuspid through the molars are
absent. The left lower bicuspid is absent. The right upper second molar is
capped. The left lower first molar appears decayed. The teeth are otherwise
in good repair. The lips and buccal mucosa have no trauma. The neck is unremarkable except for a 2.5 cm tracheostomy scar just above the suprasternal
notch. The posterior portion of the neck is unremarkable and free of scars.
An obliquely oriented 6 cm surgical scar is on the anterior left chest with an
underlying, implanted, medical device. The breasts are pendulous and otherwise unremarkable. There is white powder underneath the breasts. A round,
8 mm scar is on the upper central abdomen. A horizontally oriented 2.5 cm
linear scar is on the central upper abdomen. A faint, approximately 1 cm scar
is on the right mid lateral abdomen. There are a few striae on the hips and

From "Report of Autopsy—Theresa Schiavo, Case No. 5050439," June 13, 2005.

lower abdomen. The external genitalia are normally developed and white powder covers the perineum. The labia are dry. The urethral meatus is visible and 3.5 mm in diameter. No objects or substances are in the vagina other than a slight amount of yellow-white discharge. The anus is patent and unremarkable. Faint, pink-white, flat, 1-2 cm scars are just above the superior portion of the gluteal cleft. A 2.5 cm, somewhat square shaped, brown macule is on the left buttock. There are no open and active decubitus ulcers. The upper extremities have flexion contractures with striae on the medial portions of the upper arms. The muscles of the extremities are atrophic. The lower extremities are partially shaved. The left fifth toe is absent. The skin on the back is intact. The spine has accentuated thoracic kyphosis and lumbar lordosis. The skin demonstrates tenting.

RADIOGRAPHS

Postmortem radiographs show radiopaque shadows extending from the periosteum of the femurs, left tibia, and right ischial tuberosity. Diffuse, severe osteoporosis is present. The 11" thoracic vertebral body has an endplate fracture. Degenerative joint changes are noted in the acromioclavicular joints, hips, right knee, left foot, and pelvis. The left fifth toe is amputated along with the distal portion of the left fifth metatarsal. Radiographs of anterior neck structures and iliac wings are not remarkable. Calculi are seen in the urinary tract. Staples are in the gallbladder bed.

INTERNAL EXAMINATION

The muscles of the chest and abdominal wall are normally developed. The subcutaneous tissues are dry. The panniculus is 2.5–3 cm. In the left chest wall is an implanted medical device with a wire extending through subcutaneous tissues of the left neck and into the left scalp. A flat, four-prong electrical device is in the subgaleal area of the left scalp. A wire then further extends into the cranial cavity. The peritoneal cavity is unremarkable and dry. There are no intraperitoneal adhesions except for an adhesion of the anterior portion of the stomach to the anterior abdominal wall in the area of the previously described round abdominal scar. The organs are in the usual anatomic relations. The pleural cavities are dry. The lungs are well aerated.

The pericardial sac is remarkable for a 1 cm focal area of anterior pericardial adhesion to the anterior portion of the right ventricle. There is some lateral adhesion of the right ventricle to the right lateral portion of the pericardial sac. No other adhesions are noted. The pericardial sac is dry. The diaphragm is intact. The sternum is unremarkable. The ribs have no trauma and are normally developed with somewhat prominent costochondral junctions.

CARDIOVASCULAR SYSTEM

The pericardial sac is remarkable as previously described. The epicardial fat of the 255 gram heart is otherwise unremarkable. The root of the aorta has no atherosclerosis. The arch and descending aorta have minimal atherosclerosis (see attached CV pathology report).

RESPIRATORY SYSTEM

The right and left lungs are 260 and 245 grams, respectively. The lungs have a normal number of lobes and have light pink-red outer surfaces. The bronchi are unobstructed. The well-aerated lung parenchyma is pink-red. There are no anthracosis, tumors, cysts, or infarcts. The upper lobe bronchi contain a scant amount of pearlescent fluid. The proximal bronchi contain yellow pearlescent fluid. The lower lobe distal bronchi contain some scattered areas of yellow pearlescent fluid. The alveoli otherwise contain foamy, reddish-white fluid. The pulmonary arteries contain no emboli. The lower lobes have firm areas of partial consolidation with yellow-green pearlescent fluid. The firm area of the left lower lobe is ~4 × 4 × 3 cm. The right lung has scattered firm areas (<1cm).

HEMOLYMPHATIC SYSTEM

The 215 gram spleen is covered in an intact, gray, somewhat wrinkled capsule. There are two hilar accessory spleens (1.4 and 1 cm in diameter). The splenic parenchyma is dark red-maroon and unremarkable. There is no interstitial fibrosis, tumors, cysts, or infarcts. No enlarged lymph nodes are noted. The bone marrow of the lumbar vertebral bodies is red and soft.

GENITOURINARY SYSTEM

The right and left kidneys are 100 and 130 grams, respectively. The right kidney has a central, 2–2.5 cm, obliquely oriented cleft/scar extending from the central renal pelvis to the upper lateral cortex. The brown-tan outer surfaces are otherwise slightly lobular and granular. The pelvis of the right kidney is mildly dilated. A 1 × 0.6 × 0.7 cm, green-brown stone is in the pelvis of the right kidney. The left renal pelvis has an approximately 0.5 × 0.6 × 1 cm, green-brown stone. The corticomedullary ratios are reduced. The pelvic fat is increased. The left ureter contains pearlescent fluid. The urinary bladder contains ~6 cc of brown-yellow fluid. A 3.8 × 1.2 × 1 cm, white-yellow, somewhat crescent shaped stone is within the lumen of the bladder. The uterus is present and has a normal shape. The cervix is normally developed. The cervical os is large (coned) and contains mucoid fluid. There are a few minute nabothian cysts (<2 mm). A 2 cm, spherical leiomyoma is in the posterior portion of the uterine corpus. The endometrial cavity contains 3 to 4 mm thick, tan endometrium. The ovaries are present, firm, and otherwise grossly unremarkable. The fallopian tubes are unremarkable except for a few adhesions of the fimbriated ends.

GASTROINTESTINAL SYSTEM

The stomach contains 60 cc of green-brown fluid without any solid food fragments. The gastric mucosa is flat, congested, and green-gray. The gastric mucosa is congested. No ulcerations are noted. There are a few congested vessels with minute petechiae around the previously healed ostomy site. An 8 mm blood clot is on the gastric mucosa near the healed/healing gastrostomy site. The wall of the stomach is thin (>3mm). No perforations are noted. The esophagus is not remarkable with gray/pink mucosa. The bowel contains progressively formed feces with the rectum containing hard stool. The appendix is present, but is atrophic/small. The bowel has no perforations. An abundant amount of greenish liquid is in the duodenum. No foreign objects are noted.

HEPATOBILIARY SYSTEM

The outer surface of the 965 gram liver is covered in a transparent intact capsule. There are very few inferior hepatic adhesions associated with an absent gallbladder. Surgical staples are imbedded in the area of the cystic duct. The hepatic parenchyma is brown-green with a slight pattern of congestion. The bile ducts and portal veins appear grossly unremarkable. No fibrosis, cysts, or infarcts are noted. A yellow-white, round, 2 mm nodule is in the anterior portion of the right lobe of the liver.

ENDOCRINE SYSTEM

The adrenals and pancreas are present and grossly unremarkable. The thyroid is mildly atrophic without nodules.

MUSCULOSKELETAL SYSTEM

The upper and lower extremities are atrophic as previously described. The trunk musculature is atrophic. A $1 \times 1.5 \times {\sim}1$ cm area of induration/calcification extends from the anterior surface of the right femur. The anterior/lateral cortical surface of the distal right femur metaphysis is rough and irregular. The cortical bone of the lumbar and thoracic vertebral bodies is thin and soft. The iliac wings have no trauma or deformity.

NECK

The strap muscles of the anterior neck have intact musculature with atrophy of the musculature on the right side. The right sternocleidomastoid is moderately atrophic. There are no hemorrhages. The larynx and piriform recesses contain yellow-tan, mucoid fluid. There is yellow-green, mucoid fluid on the base of the tongue and epiglottis. The larynx contains a scant amount of fluid. The thyroid and cricoid cartilages are intact. The hyoid bone is intact. The tongue is atrophic. There is a yellow-green dry crusted material on the surface of the tongue. The posterior pharyngeal musculature appears atrophic. There are no hemorrhages. A healed tracheostomy site is on the anterior trachea. The carotid arteries and jugular veins are not remarkable. The muscles and cervical vertebral bodies of the posterior neck are not remarkable. The spinal cord and column have no trauma. The posterior laminae are soft.

CENTRAL NERVOUS SYSTEM

See attached neuropathology report.

NEUROPATHOLOGY REPORT BY STEPHEN J. NELSON, MD
June 8, 2005

In Re: Theresa Marie ("Terri") SCHIAVO deceased
Your Medical Examiner Case No. 5050439

Dear Dr. Thogmartin:

On Friday, April 1, 2005, I, along with other forensic pathologists from your office, participated with you in the autopsy of the decedent. My role was as your designated consultant neuropathologist. As such, I personally removed the decedent's dura mater, brain, spinal cord, pituitary gland, a portion of the right gastrocnemius skeletal muscle, and examined them immediately after their removal at autopsy. The dura mater, brain, and spinal cord were then fixed in a solution of 10% neutral buffered formalin for a period of eighteen (18) days with the formalin solution changed often during that time. They were again examined by me in your facility on Tuesday, April 19, 2005 and standard routine neurohistologic sections were obtained at that time.

Neuropathology Gross Description

The head was explored via the standard intermastoid incision. The frontal bone, cut in the typical ahorizontal fashion above the level of the zygomatic arches, demonstrated hyperostosis frontalis interna. There were coalescences of multiple bony excrescences, measuring between 1–2 centimeters each, overlying the frontal sinuses on the floor of the anterior cranial fossa. These excrescences were 4–5 millimeters thick anteriorly, and up to 1 cm thick posteriorly. There was no evidence of subgaleal or subscapular blood, discoloration, or staining. The calvarial bones were intact throughout. There was no epidural or subdural blood, discoloration, or staining. The dura mater was intact and the venous sinuses were widely patent. There was no meningeal staining or discoloration.

A 9 centimeter long implanted neurological thalamic stimulator wire extended outward from the right parietal bone and it was surrounded by a 1 centimeter bony nodule on the inner table. This wire was traced and its tip terminated in the right thalamus. The diaphragma sella was grossly concave and depressed. The pituitary gland was dissected free from the sella turcica using sharp dissection taking care to preserve a portion of the pituitary stalk. It appeared grossly unremarkable with appropriate demarcation of the anterior and posterior lobes. It measured 13 millimeters in transverse dimension, 6 millimeters in vertical dimension, and 9 millimeters in anterior-posterior dimension. There was no gross evidence of empty sella syndrome. The pituitary gland was then trisected in the anterior-posterior plane and submitted in toto in one cassette for subsequent histopathologic examination utilizing hematoxylin and eosin stain (H&E).

At autopsy, the brain weighed 615 grams. A total of 645 milliliters of cerebrospinal fluid (weighing 678 grams) were recovered upon opening the skull and exposing the brain. The brain was small, with widened sulci and narrow and thinned gyri. It was smaller in its vertical dimension as a result of the hydrocephalus ex vacuo tissue volume loss. The worst affected areas were the bilateral occipital lobes. The leptomeninges were opaque and golden-brown throughout. There were no leptomeningeal exudates. The cranial nerves are intact, though somewhat discolored golden-brown. The optic nerves were somewhat thinner than expected, but the remaining cranial nerves were otherwise within the expected limits of "normal." There was bilateral dilatation of the frontal-temporal-parietal opercula, covered by thickened leptomeninges.

The arterial circle of Willis at the base of the brain was that of a normal "adult" configuration. There was no significant gross evidence of atherosclerosis, vascular anomaly, or aneurysmal dilatation.

The pineal gland was grossly remarkable only for the thickened surrounding leptomeninges.

The infratentorial structures were relatively unremarkable externally. There was no herniation. The leptomeninges were opaque, but were also less golden-brown than those covering the cerebrum.

Sequential horizontal sections of the brain (cerebrum, brain stem, and cerebellum) were cut parallel to Reid's base line at 5 millimeter intervals. In all, nineteen (19) slices were made from the superior cerebral convexity, down to the level of the upper cervical spinal cord. There was prominent diffuse ventriculomegaly (hydrocephalus ex vacuo). There is no midline shift of any cerebral or cerebellar structures. The lateral ventricles were markedly dilated, but they were without displacement. The foramen of Monro and the aqueduct of Sylvius were also widely dilated. The choroid plexus and ependyma were intact and grossly unremarkable. The cortical gray ribbon, though intact throughout, was diffusely thinned and attenuated and for the most part, golden-brown. The subjacent cerebral white matter was soft, gelatinous and also diffusely discolored gray-tan-brown, including the bilaterally symmetric basal ganglia, thalami, and hippocampal formations. The thalami appear less affected than the basal ganglia. The mammillary bodies were shrunken and small and discolored golden-brown. The septum pellucidum was intact and thickened. There was no cavum at the level of the genu.

Sequential horizontal sections were cut through the midbrain, pons, cerebellum, and medulla oblongata. The pigmentation of both the locus ceruleus and substantia nigra was appropriate for chronological age. The cerebellum displayed no unusual gross developmental features. The deep midline nuclei of the cerebellum were symmetric and the folia demonstrated significant golden-brown discoloration and widespread atrophy. The medulla oblongata, including the pyramids, were smaller than expected, but bilaterally symmetric.

The entire length of the spinal cord was removed, including filum terminale and cauda equina. A few dorsal root ganglia were also included. The spinal cord was serially sectioned at 5 millimeter intervals, perpendicular to its long axis. There was a subjectively tan-gray discoloration in the lumbar region associated with some narrowing of the cord diameter. The leptomeninges were grossly unremarkable and free of exudates.

A portion of right gastrocnemius skeletal muscle, measuring 2.5 × 2.5 × 0.2 centimeters was excised in cross section to the long axis of muscle fibers and submitted in toto in one cassette for subsequent histopathologic examination utilizing hematoxylin and eosin stain (H&E), and Masson's trichrome stain.

Neuropathology Microscopic Description:

A total of sixty-five (65) glass microscopic slides, from multiple representative neuroanatomic sections, were examined microscopically. All glass slides were stained with hematoxylin and eosin (H&E) and examined, and the paraffin blocks for all tissues (except the pituitary gland and gastrocnemius skeletal muscle) were then re-cut and additional glass slides were prepared utilizing the Luxol fast blue (LFB) staining. protocol for myelin. The histologic sections included multiple sections of cerebral cortex and white matter, subcortical gray matter (basal ganglia and thalamus), hippocampal formations, midbrain, pons, cerebellum, medulla oblongata, spinal cord, pituitary gland, pineal gland, and skeletal muscle (right gastrocnemius muscle).

The changes seen were striking in their appearance, and global in their distribution. They predominately involved the border zone ("watershed") areas and were most severe in the occipital lobes, with relative preservation of the frontal and temporal lobes. There was a readily discernible and noteworthy gradient loss when moving from the anterior to posterior regions. In the thalamus, the most medial portions were relatively preserved (from the frontal cortex). In the basal ganglia, the corpus striatum all but vanished, replaced by extensive astrocytosis (caudate nucleus greater than putamen). This volume loss was impressive and was all but completely represented by non-neoplastic astrocytes. An occasional rare neuron was located. The frontal and temporal poles and insular cortex demonstrated relative preservation. The granular neurons of the cerebral cortex were relatively preserved, while the larger pyramidal neurons were globally absent. There was laminar necrosis involving the middle cortical lamina, in most cortical sections examined microscopically, but this finding was patchy. Hyaline sclerosis of many of the smaller microscopic arterioles was noted and many arterioles also contained widely dilated perivascular spaces. There were calcific vasopathic changes and diffuse astrocytosis in the globus pallidus.

The pyramids demonstrated pyramidal tract Wallerian degeneration. Damage to the midbrain, including the red nuclei, appeared related to Wallerian degeneration from fibers passing through these neuroanatomic structures. The lateral geniculate nucleus (visual) demonstrated transneuronal degeneration with gliosis, while the medial geniculate nucleus (auditory) was relatively preserved. The hippocampal formations demonstrated diffuse neuronal loss (CA 1 through CA 4, and endplate) associated with reactive astrocytosis. The fascia dentata was preserved.

Within the cerebellum there were no recognizable Purkinje cells found. The lost Purkinje neurons were replaced by reactive Bergmann astroglia. In the pons the descending fiber pathways were most affected. The inferior olivary nuclei had no remaining discernable neurons, suggesting this was a retrograde degeneration due to the marked cerebellar cortex damage. The deep midline cerebellar nuclei were relatively preserved, but with prominent astrocytosis. The dorsal motor nucleus was relatively preserved, as was the hypoglossal nucleus. The reticular activating system was also relatively preserved. The locus ceruleus and median raphe nucleus were relatively preserved. The cardiorespiratory centers in the medulla oblongata were relatively preserved.

Multiple representative levels of the spinal cord were examined microscopically. The crossed and uncrossed fibers of the corticospinal tract were abnormal. There was degeneration of the posterior columns. In the cervical-thoracic levels this involved only the fasciculus gracilis, leaving the fasciculus cuneatus relatively uninvolved. The lumbar levels contained a border zone ("watershed") infarct that was symmetrical, extending from central to peripheral. There were multiple foci of loss of the anterior horn cell neurons in the lumbar-sacral regions.

The right gastrocnemius skeletal muscle, stained with H&E and with Masson's trichrome stain using colon tissue as a stain control, demonstrated a mixture of myopathic and neurogenic features. No inclusions were identified. No inflammatory cells were present.

The pituitary gland was histologically unremarkable. The pineal gland contained diffuse astroocytic gliosis.

Impression

    Hyperostosis frontalis interna, skull
    Neurological stimulator, implanted, thalamus, right
    Encephalopathy, anoxic-ischemic, multifocal/global,
        laminar necrosis
        border zone ("watershed") territories
        transneuronal degeneration (lateral geniculate nucleus)
        Wallerian degeneration, descending fiber pathways
    Hyaline arteriolosclerosis, diffuse
    Globus pallidus, with calcific vasopathy
    Hydrocephalus, ex vacuo
    Spinal cord, with
        border zone infarct, lumber
        posterior column degeneration
        anterior horn neuron loss, lumber-sacral
    Gastrocnemius skeletal muscle, right, with myopathic and neurogenic features

Pituitary gland, no specific neuropathologic diagnosis
Pineal gland, with diffuse astrocytic gliosis

Comment: Brain weight is an important index of its pathologic state. Brain weight is correlated with height, weight, age, and sex. The decedent's brain was abnormal and weighed only 615 grams (1.35 lbs.). That weight is less than half of the expected tabular weight for a decedent of her adult age of 41 years 3 months 28 days. By way of comparison, the brain of Karen Ann Quinlan weighed 835 grams at the time of her death, after 10 years in a similar persistent vegetative state.[1] There are numerous publications in both the neurologic and neuropathologic literature of the correlates that exist between the clinical examination and clinical diagnosis of a patient in persistent vegetative state and the subsequent neuropathologic findings at autopsy. The persistent vegetative state[2] and minimally conscious state,[3] are clinical diagnoses, not pathologic ones. The neuropathologic findings of the persistent vegetative state[4] have been well described in the medical literature, including long survival after cardiac arrest,[5] yet there are no similarly published neuropathologic descriptions specific to the minimally conscious state.

The anatomical basis for a persistent vegetative state differs somewhat from case to case, for several reasons. The interval between brain injury and death affects the nature and severity of pathologic changes. Patients in a vegetative state who die early of medical complications are unlikely to undergo neuropathologic changes that would be sufficient to cause chronic unconsciousness in long-term survivors. Furthermore, in patients with chronic neurologic conditions, other complicating factors, such as severe atherosclerotic disease, may independently injure the brain. In such patients, it may be difficult to determine at autopsy exactly which neuropathologic changes accompanied the initial failure to recover consciousness.[6]

Allowing for the above limitations, two major patterns have characterized most detailed reports on the neuropathology of a persistent vegetative state due to acute traumatic or non-traumatic brain injury: diffuse laminar cortical necrosis and diffuse axonal injury.[7]

In diffuse laminar cortical necrosis the pattern follows acute, global hypoxia and ischemia. The principal finding is extensive multifocal or diffuse laminar cortical necrosis with almost invariable involvement of the hippocampus. These abnormalities may be accompanied by scattered small areas of infarction or neuronal loss in the deep forebrain nuclei, hypothalamus, or brain stem. Relatively selective thalamic necrosis may also follow acute global ischemia, although the specific anatomical boundaries for this uncommon pattern have not been well described.[8]

In diffuse axonal injury this abnormality is usually due to a shearing injury after acute trauma. An extensive subcortical axonal injury virtually isolates the cortex from other parts of the brain. Sometimes a diffuse axonal injury is accompanied by small primary brain-stem injuries, as well as secondary damage to the brain stem that results from transtentorial herniation soon after the injury. In patients with an axonal injury complicated by acute circulatory or respiratory failure, diffuse laminar necrosis may also be present.[9]

Only a few pathological reports on the persistent vegetative state describe severe abnormalities of the brain stem. Those that do mainly concern patients in whom severe paramedian mesencephalic damage developed secondary to acute downward or upward transtentorial herniation during the early stage of illness. Lesions confined to the brain stem seldom, if ever, cause long-term unconsciousness, although there has been a report of four patients[10] with severe secondary brain-stem damage in whom coma persisted for as long as six weeks before death.[11]

The gross and microscopic neuropathologic findings here are very similar to the changes seen in multicystic encephalopathy,[12] an encephaloclastic defect originating in the third trimester of pregnancy in which the white matter and deeper parts of the cerebral cortex, as well as the basal ganglia, are transformed into an elaborate glial-vascular meshwork by bilaterally symmetric hemispheric cystic necrosis. There are no accompanying cortical malformations. Similar neuropathologic findings have been described in status marmoratus, a form of hypoxic-ischemic perinatal brain injury, involving the basal ganglia,[13] like cerebral palsy. Smith and Rodeck,[14] and Adams et al.,[15] have both reported patients who also had lesions in both brain stem and spinal cord in patterns that were highly suggestive of cardiac arrest encephalopathy.

In this case, the thalamus was less affected grossly than the basal ganglia, but microscopally they were similarly affected. The presence of Bergmann astrocytes in place of Purkinje neurons in the cerebellum is a typical neuropathologic finding associated with anoxic-ischemic encephalopathy. Ex vacuo hydrocephalus is simply the replacement of lost cerebral tissue with cerebrospinal fluid. Because no imbalance in fluid production and absorption exists, this technically is not hydrocephalus. The right gastrocnemius skeletal muscle demonstrated a mixture of myopathic and neurogenic features, consistent with the loss of anterior horn cell neurons in the lumbar and sacral levels of the spinal cord.

Hyperostosis frontalis interna, an overgrowth of bone at the inner table of the frontal bone, is usually bilateral and symmetrical and chiefly in females over 35 years of age. It has no known clinical significance and is of unknown etiology. It may be associated with irregular cortical thickening of the frontal area and it spares those areas occupied by superior sagittal sinus and venous channels. It may be 1 centimeter or thicker, and it occasionally extends to parietal bones and orbital roofs. It is distinguished by hyperostosis calvaria diffusa, a variant of hyperostosis frontalis interna, that shows more diffuse thickening of vault (involving both inner and outer tables of bone). It is not clear that this disorder is actually rare. Some clinicians believe that it may be a common abnormality found in as many as 12 percent of the female population. The disorder may be found associated with a variety of conditions.

Much discussion took place in the media concerning why the decedent had not undergone an MRI scan of her brain, rather than only a brain CT scan while alive. Last month, the director of the Center for Devices and Radiological Health at the U.S. Food and Drug Administration (FDA) issued an advisory to healthcare professionals that serious injury or death can occur when patients with implanted neurological stimulators—such as the decedent's implanted thalamic stimulator—undergo MRI (magnetic resonance imaging) procedures.[16] The FDA received several reports of serious injury, including coma and permanent neurological impairment, in patients with implanted neurological stimulators who underwent magnetic resonance imaging (MRI) procedures. The mechanism for these adverse events was likely to involve heating of the electrodes at the end of the lead wires, resulting in injury to the surrounding tissue. Although these reports involved deep brain stimulators and vagus nerve stimulators, it was believed that similar injuries could be caused by any type of implanted neurological stimulator, such as spinal cord stimulators, peripheral nerve stimulators, and neuromuscular stimulators.

Neuropathologic examination alone of the decedent's brain—or any brain, for that matter—cannot prove or disprove a diagnosis of persistent vegetative state or minimally conscious state.

Sincerely yours,

STEPHEN J. NELSON, MD, PA
Stephen J. Nelson, MA, MD, FCAP
Chief Medical Examiner
10th Judicial Circuit of Florida

MEDICAL EXAMINER
Pasco & Pinellas Counties

June 13, 2005

On March 31st 2005, the District Six Medical Examiner Office began the death investigation of Theresa Marie Schiavo (ME case #5050439). The chain of events leading to this death investigation began 15 years ago in the early morning hours of February 25, 1990. The determination of her cause and manner of death would include an investigation of the events that occurred and review of available records produced subsequent to that date and time and, regarding some circumstances, extent to a review of events prior to that date.

On April 1st at 0840 hours, a complete autopsy was performed which included external and internal examinations including 72 external photographs and 116 internal photographs. A radiologic survey of her entire body was performed using a digital fluoroscopic C-arm X-Ray) with 58 pre-autopsy images captured. During and after the autopsy a second radiologic examination was performed capturing an additional 28 images including multiple views of Mrs. Schiavo's anterior neck structures, torso, and pelvis. Thus, a total of 274 images were recorded during this examination. Detailed dissections were performed on Mrs. Schiavo's anterior and posterior neck, spine, and brain. Multiple microscopic samples were taken and examined. A Board certified Neuropathologist examined her central nervous system, and a Board certified Anatomic/Clinical/Forensic Pathologist with special expertise in cardiovascular pathology examined cardiac tissue. Genetic testing for cardiac ion channel mutations was performed to detect markers for Long QT Syndrome. Complete toxicology testing was also performed. The vitreous humor chemistry was examined. Court, medical, and other records, including public and confidential DCF and law enforcement documents, were reviewed as part of the death investigation.

1.   What was the cause of Theresa Schiavo's collapse in 1990?
     a.   Did she suffer from an eating disorder?

Mrs. Schiavo was heavy as a teenager, but after high school she tried several standard diets and sought medical help. According to her parents, she was able to lose over 100 lbs. after reaching a maximum weight of approximately 250 lbs. Reportedly, she desired to maintain the weight loss. According to those that knew Mrs. Schiavo, her eating and drinking habits included eating lots of salad, eating a large omelet on weekends, and drinking large amounts of ice tea. No one observed Mrs. Schiavo taking diet pills, binging and purging, or consuming laxatives, and she apparently never confessed to her family or friends about having an eating disorder. Recent interviews with family members, physicians, and coworkers revealed no additional information supporting the diagnosis of Bulimia Nervosa. Indeed, many other signs and symptoms of Bulimia Nervosa were not reported to be present.

After Mrs. Schiavo's resuscitation from her initial cardiac arrest, the first blood draw at Humana Hospital-Northside showed a low serum potassium level (2.0 mmol/L). Several other blood components were also at abnormal levels. Her low potassium level appears to be the main piece, if not the only piece, of evidence purported to show that she had an eating disorder.

Mr. Schiavo filed a malpractice suit against Mrs. Schiavo's primary care physician and gynecologist regarding the care she received prior to her collapse. Her primary care physician reached an out of court settlement with Mr. Schiavo. After a trial, a court entered a medical malpractice judgment against her gynecologist. Apparently, the opposing sides at trial generally accepted the theory that Mrs. Schiavo's low potassium level was the cause of her initial collapse and that Bulimia Nervosa or another eating disorder was the likely underlying cause of her problems. Witnesses presented at trial testified that Mrs. Schiavo did not confess to having an eating disorder nor was any testimony given of witnessed purging. Expert witnesses at the trial including outside experts in psychiatry and gynecology theorized that an eating disorder was the most likely cause of her low potassium level and, thus, the underlying cause of her heart problem and resulting brain damage. Several physicians at trial admitted to other explanations for her hypokalemia including artifact and polydipsia.

Her post-resuscitation potassium level and history of remote weight loss appear to be the only evidence that indicate that she may have had some type of eating disorder.

b.   What caused her hypokalemia (low potassium)?

On February 25th 1990, according to available records, a 911 call was made at approximately 0540hrs. Both Mr. Schiavo and Bobby Schindler were present prior to arrival of emergency responders. They both describe her as lying prone and breathing or at least they describe her as "making gurgling noises." According to her medical records, paramedics began treating Mrs. Schiavo at

0552hrs. The Pinellas County EMS report records her as supine in the hallway with no respiration and her initial cardiac rhythm was ventricular fibrillation. She was intubated within the first 5 minutes. During her resuscitation, she received dextrose solution, five 1 mg doses of epinephrine (1 by ET tube, 4 IV), lidocaine, (bolus and drip), Narcan, dopamine, and seven defibrillations. Although a pulse was documented at 0632hrs, a measurable systolic blood pressure was not recorded until 0646hrs almost one hour after resuscitation was begun. Her time of arrival at Humana Hospital-Northside was 0646hrs. At 0701hrs, her blood was drawn and that sample showed hypokalemia (2.0 mmol/L, normal 3.5-5.0) one hour after her initial collapse and after over 30 minutes of CPR. The results were available at 0725hrs and her doctors began potassium supplementation almost immediately resulting in a rapid rise of her potassium to 2.9 mmol/L. by 0928hrs. Her potassium was measured at 2.6 mmol/L at 1212hrs. and, by 2145hrs, her potassium was within the normal range (3.6 mmol/L).

Mrs. Schiavo was in extremis for over 1 hour prior to her initial blood sampling. It appears that she received approximately 1250cc of fluid in the field (and/or at least by the time she was being worked up in the hospital). She had also received epinephrine, and had suffered a period of ventricular fibrillation all of which are known to cause factitious changes in blood electrolytes and other substances. Factitious potassium levels as low as 2.0 mmol/L have been reported and average decreases of 0.8 rnrnol/L have been documented experimentally. Potassium reductions of as much as 2 mmol/L have been reported. The dosage of epinephrine she received was sufficient to cause such factitious lowering of potassium. Even a cursory examination of cases from the District Six Medical Examiner Office revealed patients with measured antemortem, post resuscitation potassium levels as low as 2.6 mmol/L with various causes of death. Her parents report that on the evening prior to her collapse they all consumed a large meal, and the circumstances of the evening activities would have made it difficult for Mrs. Schiavo to covertly purge the meal. Thus, it is reasonable to conclude that Mrs. Schiavo's potassium level of 2.0 mmol/L measured after a period of ventricular fibrillation, epinephrine, and fluid administration was an unreliable measure of her pre-arrest potassium level. Thus, the main piece of evidence supporting a diagnosis of Bulimia Nervosa is suspect or, at least, can be explained by her clinical condition at the time of the blood draw.

In addition to the abnormal potassium, many of Mrs. Schiavo's initial laboratory values were also abnormal. As expected, some of her blood enzymes were elevated due to the period of cardiorespiratory arrest. Other blood values were also mild to markedly abnormal. The most significant were decreases in her hemoglobin, hematocrit, urea nitrogen, albumin, total protein, globulin, and calcium. Dilution of her blood proteins and electrolytes from excessive fluid consumption is possible, and many of her low blood values may reflect the large fluid bolus she received during resuscitation. Such anomalies have been described in patients in similar clinical settings; therefore, these values are unlikely to be clues to the etiology of her initial insult. Although in the malpractice proceedings the low protein values were suggested as indicators of malnutrition, this is unlikely and not generally characteristic of Bulimia Nervosa.

If her initial serum potassium is to be regarded as reliable, then multiple etiologies are possible given her nutritional history. Bulimia Nervosa involving binging and purging would be high on the list of differential diagnoses. In a young woman concerned with weight loss, use of diuretics, laxatives, or other potassium depleting substances are reasonable possibilities, but no evidence of their use exists. According to the original St. Petersburg Police Department report (90-024846) from February 1990, "various" medications were noted at the scene, yet descriptions of the medications were not recorded. Two were prescribed to Mrs. Schiavo. The toxicology screen performed during her initial hospital admission was negative, but the screen would not detect such potassium depleting substances in that she was specifically screened for barbiturates, cocaine metabolites, opiates, benzodiazepines, amphetamines/methamphetamines, tricyclics, salicylate, acetaminophen, and ethanol. The immunoassay technique used specifically tested for the drug classes listed above and no others, and the technique has limitations.

Her tea drinking habits may also have played a role. Reportedly, she was a habitual consumer of large amounts of tea and may have consumed as much as 1 gram of caffeine per day. Caffeine was not tested for in the hospital toxicology. Caffeine has been somewhat associated with cardiac arrhythmias and hypokalemia. However, considering her activities on the night prior to her collapse and the time of her collapse, caffeine toxicity is unlikely unless some sort of pill or supplement containing caffeine was consumed. No family member or friend reports use of any drugs.

c.   Did she have a heart attack?

The common term "heart attack" is generally reserved to describe the medical condition of myocardial infarction. Mrs. Schiavo's heart was anatomically normal without any areas of recent or remote myocardial infarction.

Her heart (including the cardiac valves, conduction system, and myocardium) was essentially unremarkable except for an apparent incidental finding of focal pericardial adhesions (see cardiovascular pathology report).

    d. Was she strangled?

No trauma was noted on any of the numerous physical exams or radiographs performed on Mrs. Schiavo on the day of, in the days after, or in the months after her initial collapse. Indeed, within an hour of her initial hospital admission, radiographic examination of her cervical spine was negative. Specifically, external signs of strangulation including cutaneous or deep neck injury, facial/conjunctival petechiae, and other blunt trauma were not observed or recorded during her initial hospital admission.

Autopsy examination of her neck structures 15 years after her initial collapse did not detect any signs of remote trauma, but, with such a delay, the exam was unlikely to show any residual neck findings. Even bony anomalies would have likely resolved.

    e. Did she collapse due to other trauma?

Mrs. Schiavo had no traumatic injuries observed or recorded by her initial treating physicians despite numerous physical exams and radiographs. Contusions, abrasions, recent fractures, and particularly, healing fractures would have been visualized during her initial months of treatment (via her physical exams and multiple radiographs) and attempted rehabilitation.

    f. What other etiologies are possible?

Subtle trauma related to commotio cordis or nontraumatic asphyxia is also possible, but no evidence of these exists. Drugs/toxins not typically detected by hospital toxicology testing are also possible. Also, she had received a fluid bolus prior to the toxicology screen and this has been shown to give false negative urine toxicology results. Other substances have also been shown to interfere with TDX urine toxicology screening. An underlying, undiagnosed cardiac anomaly is possible but diagnostics at that time along with postmortem examination of the heart were negative. Mutations associated with Long QT Syndrome were not detected.

2.   Why was a bone scan performed in 1991 and what did the results indicate?

In early 1991, Mrs. Schiavo was undergoing intense rehabilitation at Mediplex in Bradenton. The medical records from that facility clearly indicate that in February 1991, she was experiencing redness and swelling in her knees. During her Mediplex admission (February 5, 1991), in response to this new knee swelling and redness, radiographs were taken that showed severe osteopenia and degenerative changes but no fractures. Her physicians ordered a bone scan to rule out heterotopic ossification (H.O.), infection, or trauma. (H.O. is abnormal growth of bone in extraskeletal soft tissues.) The bone scan was performed on March 5, 1991 at Manatee Memorial Hospital. The bone scan request form listed the history of Mrs. Schiavo as "closed head injury." This is clearly incorrect unless it was meant to imply that the hypoxia was the "injury." The phrase "the patient has a history of trauma" appears to have been derived solely from the erroneous history on the request form. The bone scan showed "focal abnormal areas" including "multiple bilateral ribs, the costovertebral aspects of several of the thoracic vertebral bodies, the L1 vertebral body, both sacroiliac joints, the distal right femoral diaphysis, both knees, and both ankles, right greater than left." Bone scans show the degree of metabolic activity in bone and correlative radiographs described in the bone scan report indicate only a likely compression fracture of the first lumbar vertebral body. No other fractures are noted. It appears that with little or no knowledge of the admitting diagnosis or clinical situation of Mrs. Schiavo, Manatee Memorial staff and radiologists completed the report. This assumption was confirmed after review of DCF report (FPSS#2003-091550) and a deposition taken of the radiologist of record on 11/21/2003. The interpretation made by her attending physicians at Mediplex was early H.O. (a very well known complication of paralysis), and Mrs. Schiavo was treated with Didronel (a common treatment for H.O.). Again, other concurrent radiographs showed no trauma.

Postmortem findings including radiographs and histology support the diagnosis of heterotopic ossification. Postmortem radiographic evidence of H.O. is also seen on the proximal left tibia, left femur, and right ischial tuberosity (adductor magnus area). Degenerative changes and/or fusion were seen in her acromioclavicular joints, hips, right knee, left foot, and pelvis. She also had abnormal bone growth (hyperostosis frontalis interna) on the inner surface of her skull.

This 1991 Mediplex incident was not the first time Mrs. Schiavo had joint problems. She had suffered from swelling of her right knee during her initial hospitalization (early May 1990) and this was treated with "medication and local care." Just like the swelling at Mediplex, this episode of knee swelling occurred during an initial period of physical therapy. Radiography of the knee showed no fracture. The knee was rested and shortly thereafter she was discharged from Humana Hospital-Northside.

As far back as 1991, Mrs. Schiavo was noted to have osteoporosis (a common complication in a patient with immobility and/or paralysis). Compression fractures of the spine and other fractures are common and often incidental complications of this condition, and the compression fracture of the spine was the only diagnosed fracture on concurrent radiographs taken to correlate with the bone scan. A compression fracture of the spine is much more typical of osteoporosis and, possibly, routine handling of the patient than of physical abuse. Multiple radiographs taken during her February–May 1990 Humana Hospital-Northside admission reported no fractures of the spine, and this is the most significant evidence that the L1 fracture of her spine diagnosed in the 1991 bone scan was a later complication of osteoporosis and not a complication of traumatic injury related to her initial insult.

Her postmortem radiographs and autopsy findings confirm the diagnosis of severe osteoporosis. Indeed, the cortical bone of the vertebral bodies was palpably soft. Her 11th thoracic vertebral body was noted to have an endplate fracture in postmortem radiographs. Her first lumbar vertebral body (previously described as fractured in 1991) was noted to have severe osteoporosis.

The other 1991 bone scan finding may also reflect the aftermath of remote intense CPR, infection, bone turnover, artifact, or intense physical therapy that was occurring during this period. Indeed, differential diagnoses were offered in the original bone scan report, in the previously described deposition, and in the DCF interview of the involved radiologist.

In summary, any rib fractures, leg fractures, skull fractures, or spine fractures that occurred concurrent with Mrs. Schiavo's original collapse would almost certainly have been diagnosed in February 1990 especially with the number of physical exams, radiographs, and other evaluations she received in the early evolution of her care at Humana Hospital-Northside. During her initial hospitalization, she received twenty-three chest radiographs, three brain CT scans, two abdominal radiographs, two echocardiograms, one abdominal ultrasound, one cervical spine radiograph, and one radiograph of her right knee. No fractures or trauma were reported or recorded. Although in the acute phase, rib fractures may be difficult to visualize, initial rib fractures would have been going through the healing process during the months of hospital-ization, and, with the serial nature of the chest radiographs, callus formation from any healing fractures would likely have been visible. Moreover, hot spots on bone scans of the ribs do not always represent fractures. By far, the most likely explanation for the bone scan findings in Mrs. Schiavo are prolonged immobility induced osteoporosis and complicating H.O. in an environment of intense physical therapy. Without the original bone scan and radiographs from that period, no other conclusions can reasonably be made.

3. Could Mrs. Schiavo eat by mouth?

The neruopathologic findings, oropharyngeal anatomic findings, and med-ical records clearly indicate that Mrs. Schiavo would not have been able to consume sustenance safely and/or in sufficient quantity by mouth. In fact, the records and findings are such that oral feedings in quantities sufficient to sustain life would have certainly resulted in aspiration. Swallowing evalua-tions and speech pathology evaluations repeatedly record that Mrs. Schiavo was a high risk for aspiration and not a candidate for oral nutrition/hydration. Although in her early rehabilitation, she received speech pathology services, she was later repeatedly evaluated and determined not to be a candidate for speech/dysphagia therapy. According to medical records, she had been treated in the past for aspiration pneumonia Thus, Mrs. Schiavo was depen-dent on nutrition and hydration via her feeding tube. Claims from caregivers of past oral feedings are remarkable, and, based on the autopsy findings and medical records, these feedings were potentially harmful or, at least, extremely dangerous to Mrs. Schiavo's health and welfare.

Mrs. Schiavo's postmortem lung examination had findings that could be considered consistent with aspiration of secretions; however, her decline and dehydration over almost 2 weeks could also have played a role in these findings.

4. After her initial collapse, was Mrs. Schiavo given substances to speed her demise or otherwise alter her medical condition?

In 2003, a former employee of Palm Garden of Largo filed an affidavit with the Court regarding a 1996 incident(s) at that facility. The affidavit detailed inci-dents the employee reportedly witnessed regarding the care of Mrs. Schiavo. Reports from the complainant regarding incidents at Palm Garden were taken by the Pinellas County Sheriffs Office in 1996 and 2003 (report #96-164479, 03-1183/1, 03-1183/2). The Court and the Department of Children and Families investigated these claims in 2003 (FPSS#2003-091550). Review of the Palm Garden records and the timeline of the allegations do not support the claims made in 2003. Comparison of the 2003 affidavit with the 2005 press interviews and review of the above listed reports is essential in evaluating these claims.

On March 29th 2004, a Hospice nurse noted apparent injection sites on Mrs. Schiavo's arms, and what appeared to be a plastic needle cap was also found in her room. Reportedly, these were discovered by Hospice shortly after a visit by her parents. In response to this, Michael Schiavo had her examined at a hospital. Law enforcement investigated and found rational, innocent explanations for the findings. A drug screen was negative and the remaining factors of the case are described in a press release from the Clearwater Police Department (05/14/04) and in a DCF report (FPSS#2004-008306).

There is no evidence to support or the evidence does not support that Mrs. Schiavo was given harmful substances related to these incidents.

In late March 2005, it was alleged in the press that Mrs. Schiavo was being given a morphine drip or otherwise being drugged with morphine to expedite or otherwise ease the dying process. Orders were written and Mrs. Schiavo received morphine sulfate (5mg) suppositories during her final days at Hospice. Her medical records indicate that she received a dose on 3/19/05 and a second dose on 3/26/05. No other morphine treatments were recorded. Her postmortem toxicology showed no trace of morphine in her body. Acetaminophen was detected in her postmortem blood samples at what would be considered therapeutic levels. The finding of acetaminophen is consistent with acetaminophen suppositories ordered by her treating physician, and this drug had no role in her demise. No other drugs were recorded in the medical records nor were any other drugs detected in postmortem toxicology testing. Specifically, according to the Hospice records, no intravenous or intramuscular injections of morphine or any other opiate were ordered or infused.

5. Was Mrs. Schiavo in a persistent vegetative state (PVS)? (See attached neuropathology report)

PVS is a clinical diagnosis arrived at through physical examination of living patients. Postmortem correlations to PVS with reported pathologic findings have been reported in the literature, but the findings vary with the etiology of the adverse neurological event.

6.   What diagnoses can be made in regards to the brain of Mrs. Schiavo?
(See attached neuropathology report)

Mrs. Schiavo's brain showed marked global anoxic-ischemic encephalopathy resulting in massive cerebral atrophy. Her brain weight was approximately half of the expected weight. Of particular importance was the hypoxic damage and neuronal loss in her occipital lobes, which indicates cortical blindness. Her remaining brain regions also show severe hypoxic injury and neuronal atrophy/loss. No areas of recent or remote traumatic injury were found.

7.   By what mechanism did Theresa Schiavo die?

Postmortem findings, including the state of the body and laboratory testing, show that she died of marked dehydration (a direct complication of the electrolyte disturbances brought about by the lack of hydration). The state of her fatty tissue and laboratory findings indicate that she did not starve to death.

8.   What was the cause and manner of death?

Mrs. Schiavo suffered a severe anoxic brain injury. The cause of which cannot be determined with reasonable medical certainty. The manner of death will therefore be certified as undetermined.

It is the policy of this office that no case is ever closed and that all determinations are to be reconsidered upon receipt of credible, new information. In addition to fading memories, the 15-year survival of Mrs. Schiavo after her collapse resulted in the creation of a voluminous number of documents many of which were lost or discarded over the years. Receipt of additional information that clarifies outstanding issues may or shall cause an amendment of her cause and manner of death.

Jon R. Thogmorton
Chief Medical Examiner

Date 06/13/05

NOTES

1.   Kinney HC, Korein J, Panigrahy A, et al. Neuropathological Findings in the Brain of Karen Ann Quinlan—The Role of the Thalamus in the Persistent Vegetative State. *New England Journal of Medicine.* 1994;330:1469–1475.

2. Multi-Society Task Force on PVS. Medical Aspects of the Persistent Vegetative State—Parts One and Two. *New England Journal of Medicine.* 1994;330: 1499–1508, 1572–1579.

3. Giancino JT, Ashwal S, Childs N, et al. The Minimally Conscious State: Definition and Diagnostic Criteria. *Neurology.* 2002;58:349–353.

4. Dougherty JH, Rawlinson DG, Levy DE, et al. Hypoxic-ischemic Brain Injury and the Vegetative State: Clinical and Neuropathologic Correlation. *Neurology.* 1981;31:991–997.

Adams JH, Graham DI, Jennett B. The Neuropathology of the Vegetative State after an Acute Brain Insult. *Brain.* 2000;123:1327–1338.

Kinney, HC, Samuels MA. Neuropathology of the Persistent Vegetative State: A Review. *Journal of Neuropathology and Experimental Neurology.* 1994;53: 548–558.

5. Cole G, Cowie,VA. Long Survival after Cardiac Arrest: Case Report and Neuropathological Findings. *Clinical Neuropathology.* 1987;6:104, 109.

6. Multi-Society Task Force on PVS. Medical Aspects of the Persistent Vegetative State—First of Two Parts.

7. Ibid.

8. Ibid.

9. Ibid.

10. McClellan DR, Adams DI, Graham AE, et al. The Structural Basis of the Vegetative State and Prolonged Coma after Non-missile Head Injury. In: Papo I, Cohadon F, Massarotti M., eds. *La Coma Tramatique.* Padova, Italy: Liviana Editrice; 1986:165–185.

11. Multi-Society Task Force on PVS. Medical Aspects of the Persistent Vegetative State—First of Two Parts.

12. Friede RL. *Developmental Neuropathology.* 2nd ed. New York: Springer-Verlag; 1989.

13. Kinney HC, Armstrong DD. Perinatal Neuropathology. In: Graham DI, Lantos PL, eds. *Greenfield's Neuropathology.* 7th ed. New York: Arnold Publishers/ Oxford University Press; 2002.

14. Smith JF, Rodeck C. Multiple Cystic and Focal Encephalomalacia in Infancy and Childhood with Brain Stem Damage. *Journal of the Neurological Sciences.* 1975;25:377–388.

15. Adams RD, Prod'hom LS, Rabinowicz T. Intrauterine Brain Death: Neuraxial Reticular Core Necrosis. *Acta Neuropathologica.* 1977;40:41–49.

16. Schultz DG. *FDA Public Health Notification*: MRI-caused Injuries in Patients with Implanted Neurological Stimulators. Washington, DC. May 10, 2005.

Onward, Moderate Christian Soldiers

John C. Danforth

It would be an oversimplification to say that America's culture wars are now between people of faith and nonbelievers. People of faith are not of one mind, whether on specific issues like stem cell research and government intervention in the case of Terri Schiavo, or the more general issue of how religion relates to politics.

In recent years, conservative Christians have presented themselves as representing the one authentic Christian perspective on politics. With due respect for our conservative friends, equally devout Christians come to very different conclusions.

It is important for those of us who are sometimes called moderates to make the case that we, too, have strongly held Christian convictions, that we speak from the depths of our beliefs, and that our approach to politics is at least as faithful as that of those who are more conservative. Our difference concerns the extent to which government should, or even can, translate religious beliefs into the laws of the state.

People of faith have the right, and perhaps the obligation, to bring their values to bear in politics. Many conservative Christians approach politics with a certainty that they know God's truth, and that they can advance the kingdom of God through governmental action. So they have developed a political agenda to do so.

Moderate Christians are less certain about when and how our beliefs can

From the *New York Times*, June 22, 2005, p. A–27, col. 2. © 2005, The New York Times. Reprinted by permission.

be translated into statutory form, not because of a lack of faith in God but because of a healthy acknowledgment of the limitations of human beings. Like conservative Christians, we attend church, read the Bible, and say our prayers.

But for us, the only absolute standard of behavior is the commandment to love our neighbors as ourselves. Repeatedly in the Gospels, we find that the Love Commandment takes precedence when it conflicts with laws. We, struggle to follow that commandment as we face the realities of everyday living, and we do not agree that our responsibility to live as Christians can be codified by legislators.

When, on television, we see a person in a persistent vegetative state, one who will never recover, we believe that allowing the natural and merciful end to her ordeal is more loving than imposing government power to keep her hooked up to a feeding tube.

When we see an opportunity to save our neighbors' lives through stem cell research, we believe that it is our duty to pursue that research, and to oppose legislation that would impede us from doing so.

We think that efforts to haul references of God into the public square, into schools and courthouses, are far more apt to divide Americans than to advance faith.

Following a Lord who reached out in compassion to all human beings, we oppose amending the Constitution in a way that would humiliate homosexuals.

For us, living the Love Commandment may be at odds with efforts to encapsulate Christianity in a political agenda. We strongly support the separation of church and state, both because that principle is essential to holding together a diverse country, and because the policies of the state always fall short of the demands of faith. Aware that even our most passionate ventures into politics are efforts to carry the treasure of religion in the earthen vessel of government, we proceed in a spirit of humility lacking in our conservative colleagues.

In the decade since I left the Senate, American politics has been characterized by two phenomena: the increased activism of the Christian right, especially in the Republican Party, and the collapse of bipartisan collegiality. I do not think it is a stretch to suggest a relationship between the two.

To assert that I am on God's side and you are not, that only I know God's will, and that I will use the power of government to advance my understanding of God's kingdom is certain to produce hostility. By contrast, moderate Christians see ourselves, literally, as moderators. Far from claiming to possess God's truth, we claim only to be imperfect seekers of the truth.

At Schiavo's Hospice, a Return to Routine

Scars of "The Siege" Linger for Staff at Florida Facility

Ceci Connolly

PINELLAS PARK, Fla.—In the pre-dawn hours, when sleep is futile and death has not yet arrived, Charles Young and Tom Saviano find common ground in a kitchen permeated by the smell of fresh coffee and stale popcorn. Each is waiting to bury a child.

In rooms less than twenty-five feet apart, Young's twenty-seven-year-old son and Saviano's forty-eight-year-old daughter are near the end. Like Terri Schiavo, the woman who died here about two months ago, they will live out their final hours in Hospice House Woodside. And like Schiavo's parents, the two men are struggling to grasp the inconceivable.

"I can't believe this is happening to me," says Saviano, tears welling up, learning firsthand what hospice is when it isn't on the television, when it isn't in the courts. When hospice is your own private agony. "My wife and I are both wondering what we did wrong."

He is wearing the same navy slacks and golf shirt he arrived in nineteen hours ago, back when he was speaking optimistically of bringing his eldest daughter, Debra, home, back when he still thought she had a chance at beating the cancer now overtaking her. After a couple of fitful hours on a pullout couch, Saviano is up again, prowling the near-deserted halls. It's 4:20 AM, and except for the constant whoosh of oxygen machines and the occasional hacking cough, the single-story red-brick building is quiet.

"We always helped other people," Saviano tells Young. "That's what we can't understand. Anybody who was sick—friends, neighbors—we were right there."

From the *Washington Post*, June 18, 2005, p. A–1. © 2005, The Washington Post. Reprinted with permission.

Young nods, pouring coffee into a foam cup. He arrived from Ohio two weeks ago when doctors confirmed they were running out of options for treating his son's tongue cancer. Dressed in blue striped pajamas, a pack of Kools tucked in the breast pocket, he, too, has been up most of the night, shuttling between James's room and the smokers' porch just off the kitchen.

"You wanna do something, but there's just nothing to do," he replies. "All you can do is just wait."

Two months after the Schiavo case exposed an entire nation to one family's bitter battle with death, the hospice has returned to its normal rhythms. In the past sixty days, 129 new patients have arrived, nineteen memorials have been held, and eighty-eight residents have died, each departing the way Schiavo left—on a gurney, face uncovered, showing that at Woodside, death is not hidden.

Unlike this routine day, the staff has a name for the Schiavo period. They call it The Siege. The two-week sideshow of demonstrators, bomb threats, court rulings, and political interventions.

Now—liberated of the television cameras and police checkpoints, the pastor with the bullhorn and the life-size Jesus on a cross, Jesse Jackson and Randall Terry, the juggler and the monks—the people of Woodside are back to the everyday business of dying. For all the chaos and emotion the Schiavo case elicited, it did not alter the fundamental nature of Woodside and the 3,200 hospices across the country. For fifteen years, they have been the place where anyone, regardless of age, wealth, handicap, or history, can find company on the way to death.

Today, the only visible reminder of it all is a three-foot-tall angel watching over the nurse's station on Beach Avenue, the wing where Schiavo lived for five years.

"To our angels at hospice who cared for us," reads the statue's brass plaque. "Thank you, Mike & Terri Schiavo."

A new patient has moved into Schiavo's room but is unaware she is occupying a space of such high drama. The idea is to move forward. Beneath the surface, however, the aftereffects remain.

To spend one full day at Woodside is to witness the inexorable routines of death. All that seemed extraordinary in March—feeding tubes, last rites, and parents unable to let go—is again unremarkable.

THE CYCLE BEGINS

This twenty-four-hour period begins like most others, though it is Young, dragging on his first Kool of the day, who clarifies what Woodside's version of normal is: "Our minutes seem like hours."

Young has entrusted his son to a unique form of modern healthcare. The purpose of hospice is to provide end-of-life care, traditionally defined as the final six months of life. The goal is support and pain relief, or palliative care—not cures.

Shortly before 9 AM, Dr. Theresa Buck begins rounds on Magnolia, where the most severe cases reside. Entering Room 41, she is greeted by Debra's mother, Corrine Saviano.

"She's still not eating," she tells Buck. "But she is a lot calmer."

With her short-cropped, dark hair and involuntary body movement, Debra Saviano resembles the infamous video of Woodside's most famous patient.

"We'll draw some blood today," Buck says, stroking Debra's hair.

From the bed comes a sound that is both guttural moan and ferocious yell. Tom Saviano's body tenses, fists clench. He turns away.

"We lost our youngest three years ago," he says. It was Debra and Corrine who cared for Dorine after her leukemia was diagnosed. "That's why this is so brutal."

Still, Saviano sees Woodside as a way station, not the end of the line. "We brought her here to clean her up," he says. If Buck can treat Debra's infection, she can go back to the Moffit Cancer Center in Tampa for more chemotherapy.

In the hall, without prompting, Buck answers the impolite questions not asked inside Room 41.

"She's screaming, but she's not in pain," Buck says. "She looks retarded, but she is not. It's the chemo, the side effects, the urinary tract infection. I told the family I'm hopeful, but I can't promise."

Trained as a pulmonary specialist who worked for much of her early years in the emergency room, Theresa Buck, 43, is finally doing the missionary work she dreamed of. Each day she ministers to the dying, utterly at ease with the sights, smells, sounds, and unique language of death.

In the heat of The Siege, Buck, who was not Schiavo's primary physician but who cared for her when needed, tried convincing her parents that not everything they saw in the news was true. To them, the video clips of Schiavo rolling her head, emitting gurgling sounds, proved the young woman was not in the persistent vegetative state that Buck and other doctors had diagnosed.

"I gave up. It was a losing battle," she says, not a hint of anger in her voice. "God knows what I do."

It isn't always easy for Buck to let nature take its course. She admits to being angry when a diabetic in kidney failure recently arrived in bad shape. The woman could be healthy today if she had gotten proper treatment. At this point, though, Buck has little choice but to stop the insulin pump and wait.

"My initial instinct—what I wanted to do—was fix it," Buck says. "She's tired. She wanted to go in peace."

Thomas Broderick, on the other hand, is fighting death with what little strength his body can muster.

"My lungs are congested," the fifty-one-year-old tells Buck when she arrives at his apartment on the Woodside grounds. "I was thinking about that pump."

She jots a note to switch Broderick from pain pills to an intravenous line so he can administer the medication himself. "We'll make a good cocktail for you."

"You still sound horrible, Thomas," she says, listening to his chest.

After his inoperable lung cancer was diagnosed six months ago, Broderick, like many, resisted coming to Woodside, fearing the recognition that there is little time left.

"I'm still in shock," he confides, looking out from under a Yankees cap that fails to conceal his bald head. "I have not cried one tear to this day."

Broderick is afraid of death. But he is even more "afraid that it will be a painful death, like suffocation," he whispers. He heard about Terri Schiavo and knows he should make out a living will, but he is overwhelmed by the legal issues.

"I would like them to keep me alive as best they can," he says at first. "But I don't want to be laying there in pain."

He hopes to make it to Christmas and would like to go to SeaWorld "for my last wish—I like sharks, dolphins, whales."

A WEEKLY RITUAL

Shortly after lunch, Woodside's senior staff—all women, some knitting—gather for their weekly meeting. It begins with a ritual—the reading of the names of patients lost the previous week.

As the first is announced, Jean Ledoux, the chaplain, taps a chime and lights a votive candle. Each name comes with a story. The ninety-one-year-old who hung on until his grandchildren arrived, the childless couple who after nearly seventy years of marriage seemed to need only each other.

For the past two months, Ledoux has been stuck in her own sort of netherworld, caught between her midlife calling to provide pastoral support to the dying and the public portrayal of Woodside as an unholy death chamber. Intellectually, she knows the "people out front were extremists," but she cannot reconcile how self-professed Christians—many wearing robes—could have been so "degrading, hurtful . . . misguided."

"This is sacred ground," she says.

Here Ledoux plays the jester, passing out pie, cracking jokes. But privately, she confesses she is seeing a trauma specialist, hoping to find some deeper meaning in The Siege. For some of her colleagues, it hit like a single, violent car crash. But for Ledoux, "It's more like a creeping-up-the-back-of-your-neck kind of feeling."

At Woodside, death does not end the process.

In the chapel, the Boulgier family is holding a memorial. And on Magnolia Avenue the Savianos have gathered outside Debra's room.

"I don't want her to see me crying," Corrine Saviano says. This is night six in Woodside for mother and daughter.

"She ain't gonna make it. Her organs are failing," Tom Saviano says. About an hour ago, the social worker delivered the news. "We don't know how long—a day, two days, a week. We tried to give her every chance we could."

They have discussed their options, know Debra's wishes.

"I don't want her suffering no more," Corrine says. "If she can't live comfortably, I will let her go."

In the kitchen across the hall, Charles Young is fixing a late supper, buttering two slices of toast. Two days ago, the staff advised Young to "make arrangements" for his son. "There's no reason for him to still be here. His will to live is just incredible. If it were me, I'd let go."

BURYING YOUR CHILDREN

"Morning," Charles Young says, emerging from his son's crowded room at 2:15 AM. In addition to James, six family members have crashed on the sofa bed, air mattress, and lounge chair. Charles Young gets up periodically to suck mucus from his son's breathing tube, or just to have a smoke.

"I know it sounds weird, but you want your children to bury you," he says. "You don't want to bury your children."

Two hours later, Annie Santa-Maria, director of inpatient and residence services, enters her pitch-black office.

"Since the Terri thing, I've had trouble sleeping," she says. "So I just come in. I get e-mail done or read."

Like many of the staff, Santa-Maria is only now processing the Schiavo episode. Her nightmares are the what-ifs. What if one of the bomb threats was real? What if someone had broken past the barricades and given Schiavo a sip of water?

"If they had given her a cup of water, she would have choked to death," Santa-Maria says, her frustration bubbling up. "I just wanted to yell at them, 'We have people die with feeding tubes all the time.'"

Some of her devout Catholic siblings disapproved of her role in the Schiavo case. The Catholic police chief peppered her with questions of ethics and morality. Congress subpoenaed her.

Santa-Maria opens her laptop to a PowerPoint presentation. The working title is "Woodside: A Fortress of Caring." Unlike the television images beamed around the world, the photos depict The Siege from the inside. Police in camouflage patrolling the verdant back grounds, people in wheelchairs pressing against orange mesh fencing, and the signs:

"Feed Terri! For God's Sake."

"Stop the Murder."

"Auschwitz Woodside."

"I would watch volunteers feeding and bathing our patients day and night, and they're out there calling us murderers," she says, her voice piercing the 5 AM silence.

As this twenty-four hours draw to a close, Santa-Maria walks the corridors. She pauses in the kitchen on Magnolia long enough to shake hands with Tom Saviano and Charles Young, who have just discovered their painful bond.

"I wish you could have seen her two months ago," Saviano is saying of his daughter. Even loaded up with half a dozen drugs, Debra always kept her wits about her. "What's the prognosis on your son?"

"He's a fighter," Young replies.

Saviano's mind is reeling—to the doctor's appointment he forgot to cancel, to the final hours with Dorine three years ago, to the call he got late last night from his other two daughters.

"They want to come. We told them not to. We don't know how long it will be," he says, the tears returning to his tired eyes. "They want to see their sister while she's alive."

The cycle of death at Woodside, somehow both heart-wrenching and mundane, continues. Young, his family still asleep in the room next door, heads for the smokers' porch.

"Hang in there," Saviano tells him. He turns and crosses the hall to Debra's room. The vigil goes on.

Case Timeline

December 3, 1963

Theresa (Terri) Marie Schindler is born in Pennsylvania.

Karen Ann Quinlan, 21, who has been on a radical diet, collapses at a party from alcohol and Valium, 4/14/1975.

Vatican Congregation for the Doctrine of the Faith (with the approval of Pope John Paul II) issues *Declaration on Euthanasia* opposing mercy killing but allowing refusal of extraordinary means of medical care and aggressive use of pain medications, 1980.

American Medical Association endorses withdrawal of treatment in hopeless terminal cases and cases of permanent coma, 1982.

Nancy Cruzan loses control of her car and is hospitalized in a coma, January 11, 1983.

President's Commission for the Study of Ethical Problems in Medicine and the Biomedical and Behavioral Research issues report "Deciding to forgo life-sustaining treatment" which calls for brain death statutes to be enacted, living wills to be promoted, and accepts withdrawal of treatment in hopeless cases, 1983.

November 10, 1984

Terri Schindler, 20, and Michael Schiavo, 21, are married at Our Lady of Good Counsel Church in Southampton, Pennsylvania.

Richard Lamm, then governor of Colorado, states in a speech that the "elderly have a duty to die and get out of the way," 1984.

Life Prolonging Procedures Act—Florida Law 765—first passed, 1984.

Quinlan dies June 11, 1985.

New Jersey Supreme Court issues opinion in case of Claire Conroy allowing withdrawal of artificial feeding and fluids from a demented person at the request of a surrogate, 1985.

From Kathy Cerminara and Kenneth Goodman, "Key Events in the Case of Theresa Marie Schiavo," http://www.miami.edu/ethics/schiavo/timeline.htm (accessed July 2005). Adapted and used with the permission of Kathy Cerminara (Nova Southeastern University, Shepard Broad Law Center) and Kenneth Goodman (University of Miami Ethics Programs).

325

1986

The couple move to St. Petersburg, where Ms. Schiavo's parents had retired.

Florida Supreme Court rules in *Corbett v. D'Alessandro* that a feeding tube is a medical treatment and may be removed from an incompetent person by an appropriate surrogate. Decision based on right to privacy found in Florida's constitution.

Hastings Center publishes *Guidelines on the Termination of Life-sustaining Treatment and Care of the Dying*, arguing for right to withdraw artificial nutrition and hydration, 1987.

American College of Physicians issues opinion in *Physicians Ethics Manual* permitting withdrawal of nutrition and hydration as medical treatment, 1989.

February 25, 1990

Ms. Schiavo suffers cardiac arrest, apparently caused by a potassium imbalance and leading to brain damage due to lack of oxygen. She was taken to the Humana Northside Hospital and was later given a percutaneous endoscopic gastrostomy (PEG) to provide nutrition and hydration.

March 1990 ads run by Jack Kevorkian in a Detroit newspaper offering help to those seeking assisted suicide.

May 12, 1990

Ms. Schiavo is discharged from the hospital and taken to the College Park skilled-care and rehabilitation facility.

On June 4, 1990, Janet Adkins, a fifty-four-year-old woman with Alzheimer's disease ended her life with the help of Dr. Jack Kevorkian, a retired pathologist in Michigan.

June 18, 1990

Court appoints Michael Schiavo as guardian; Ms. Schiavo's parents do not object.

June 25, 1990

Cruzan case: U.S. Supreme Court Rules in 5-to-4 vote to uphold the judgment of the Missouri Supreme Court that clear and convincing evidence is necessary for the removal of life-prolonging procedures but that feeding tubes are medical treatments.

June 30, 1990

Ms. Schiavo is transferred to Bayfront Hospital for further rehabilitation efforts.

September 1990

Ms. Schiavo's family brings her home, but three weeks later they return her to the College Park facility because the family is "overwhelmed by Terri's care needs."

Florida Supreme Court rules a guardian may remove a feeding tube from a person who is not terminally ill and not in a PVS state in *In re Guardianship of Estelle M. Browning*, September 13, 1990, based on her 1985 advance directive.

November 1990

Michael Schiavo takes Ms. Schiavo to California for experimental "brain stimulator" treatment, an experimental "thalamic stimulator implant" in her brain.

Federal Patient Self-Determination Act enacted, 11/5/90.

Missouri judge convinced family has produced sufficient new evidence concerning Nancy Cruzan's wishes and orders that the request for removal of feeding tube be honored, 12/14/1990.

Nancy Cruzan dies after removal of her feeding tube, 12/26/1990.

January 1991

The Schiavos return to Florida; Ms. Schiavo is moved to the Mediplex Rehabilitation Center in Brandon where she receives twenty-four-hour care.

July 19, 1991

Ms. Schiavo is transferred to Sable Palms skilled-care facility where she receives continuing neurological testing, and regular and aggressive speech/occupational therapy through 1994.

PSDA interim rules issued requiring hospitals and nursing homes to provide information about advance directives, 3/6/1992.

May 1992

Ms. Schiavo's parents, Robert and Mary Schindler, and Michael Schiavo stop living together.

American Nurses Association issues opinion recognizing provision of food and water by artificial means as a medical treatment which may be withdrawn or withheld, 1992.

August 1992

Ms. Schiavo is awarded $250,000 in an out-of-court medical malpractice settlement with one of her physicians.

November 1992

The jury in the medical malpractice trial against another of Ms. Schiavo's physicians awards more than one million dollars. In the end, after attorneys' fees and other expenses, Michael Schiavo received about $300,000 and about $750,000 was put in a trust fund specifically for Ms. Schiavo's medical care.

February 14, 1993

Michael Schiavo and the Schindlers have a falling-out over the course of therapy for Ms. Schiavo; Michael Schiavo claims that the Schindlers demand that he share the malpractice money with them.

Dr. Bloudewijn Chabot is vindicated by a Dutch Court for assisting in the suicide of fifty-year-old Hilly Bosscher who requested his help for reasons of psychiatric suffering not terminal illness.

July 29, 1993

Schindlers attempt to remove Michael Schiavo as Ms. Schiavo's guardian; the court later dismisses the suit.

President Bill Clinton and wife, Hillary, publicly advocate for living wills after the death of Hugh Rodham, Hillary's father.

March 1, 1994

First guardian ad litem, John H. Pecarek, submits his report. He states that Michael Schiavo has acted appropriately and attentively toward Ms. Schiavo.

Oregon voters pass Measure 16 legalizing physician-assisted suicide, November 8, 1994.

Multi-Society Task Force issues two-part report in *New England Journal of Medicine* on diagnosis and treatment/treatment withdrawal for those in a permanent vegetative state, 1994.

U.S. Supreme Court rules in *Washington v. Glucksberg* that state law banning PAS is constitutional and that there is no constitutional right to physician-assisted suicide, 6/26/97.

Oregon voters again pass a referendum allowing physician-assisted suicide, 11/4/97.

May 1998

Michael Schiavo petitions the court to authorize the removal of Ms. Schiavo's PEG tube; the Schindlers oppose, saying that she would want to remain alive. The court appoints Richard Pearse, Esq., to serve as the second guardian ad litem for Ms. Schiavo.

December 20, 1998

The second guardian ad litem, Richard Pearse, Esq., issues his report in which he concludes that Ms. Schiavo is in a persistent vegetative state with no chance of improvement and that Michael Schiavo's decision making may be influenced by the potential to inherit the remainder of Ms. Schiavo's estate.

Jack Kevorkian indicted after he tapes an assisted suicide (possibly euthanasia) which is then broadcast on *60 Minutes*, 11/22/98.

January 24, 2000

The trial begins; Pinellas-Pasco County Circuit Court Judge George Greer presides.

Jack Kevorkian found guilty and sentenced to prison for 10–25 years.

February 11, 2000

Judge Greer rules that Ms. Schiavo would have chosen to have the PEG tube removed, and therefore he orders it removed, which, according to doctors, will cause her death in approximately 7 to 14 days.

March 2, 2000

The Schindlers file a petition with Judge Greer to allow "swallowing" tests to be performed on Ms. Schiavo to determine if she can consume—or learn to consume—nutrients on her own.

March 7, 2000
Judge Greer denies the Schindlers' petition to perform "swallowing" tests on Ms. Schiavo.

March 24, 2000
Judge Greer grants Michael Schiavo's petition to limit visitation to Ms. Schiavo as well as to bar pictures. Judge Greer also stays his order until thirty days beyond the final exhaustion of all appeals by the Schindlers.

January 24, 2001
Florida's Second District Court of Appeal (2nd DCA) upholds Judge Greer's ruling that permits the removal of Ms. Schiavo's PEG tube.
  In re Schiavo, 780 So. 2d 176 (2nd DCA 2001), rehearing denied (February 22, 2001), review denied, 789 So. 2d 348 (Fla. 2001) (Case No.: SC01-559).

February 22, 2001
The Schindler family's motion for an Appellate Court rehearing is denied.

March 12, 2001
Michael Schiavo petitions Judge Greer to lift his stay, issued March 24, 2000, in order to permit the removal of Ms. Schiavo's PEG tube.

March 29, 2001
Judge Greer denies Michael Schiavo's motion to lift stay issued on March 24, 2000; Michael Schiavo can remove Ms. Schiavo's PEG tube at 1 PM on April 20.
  The Netherlands formally legalizes assisted suicide, 4/10/2001.

April 10, 2001
The 2nd DCA denies the Schindlers' motion to extend Judge Greer's stay, which is scheduled to expire April 20, 2001.

April 12, 2001
The Schindlers file a motion requesting that Judge Greer recuse himself.
  The Schindlers petition the Florida Supreme Court to stay the removal of Ms. Schiavo's PEG tube.

April 16, 2001
Judge Greer denies the Schindlers' motion to recuse himself.

April 18, 2001
The Florida Supreme Court chooses not to review the decision of the 2nd DCA.
  In re Schiavo, 789 So. 2d 248 (Fla. 2001). Case No.: SC01-559.

April 20, 2001
Federal District Court Judge Richard Lazzara grants the Schindlers a stay until April 23, 2001, to exhaust all their possible appeals.

April 23, 2001
Justice Anthony M. Kennedy of the U.S. Supreme Court refuses to stay the case for a review by that Court.

April 24, 2001
By order of trial court Judge Greer, and upon issuance of a 2nd DCA mandate, Ms. Schiavo's PEG tube is removed.

April 26, 2001
The Schindlers file an emergency motion with Judge Greer for relief from judgment based upon new evidence, which includes a claim that a former girlfriend of Michael Schiavo will testify that he lied about Ms. Schiavo's wishes; Judge Greer dismisses the motion as untimely. Also on this date, the Schindlers file a new civil suit that claims that Michael Schiavo perjured himself when he testified that Ms. Schiavo had stated an aversion to remaining on life support. Pending this new civil trial, Circuit Court Judge Frank Quesada orders Ms. Schiavo's PEG tube to be reinserted.

April 30, 2001
Michael Schiavo files an emergency motion with the 2nd DCA to allow the removal of Ms. Schiavo's PEG tube.

May 9, 2001
The 2nd DCA announces a date for the hearing of oral arguments regarding Michael Schiavo's motion of April 30, 2001.

June 25, 2001
Arguments in 2nd DCA regarding Michael Schiavo's motion of April 30, 2001.

July 11, 2001
The 2nd DCA remands the case back to Judge Greer. (1) The 2nd DCA informs the Schindlers that they must address both their desire to have new evidence heard and their perjury claim against Michael Schiavo within the original guardianship proceeding; further, the Schindlers are instructed to file a new motion for relief from judgment in the guardianship proceeding. (2) The 2nd DCA instructs Judge Greer to weigh the Schindlers' new evidence in making a new determination of what Ms. Schiavo would have wanted. (3) The 2nd DCA denies Michael Schiavo's request to discontinue the PEG tube.
    In re Schiavo, 792 So. 2d 551 (2nd DCA 2001).

August 7, 2001
After the 2nd DCA remands the case back to Judge Greer, he again finds that Michael Schiavo may remove Ms. Schiavo's PEG tube on August 28.

August 10, 2001
Judge Greer denies the Schindlers' motion (1) to have their own doctors examine Ms. Schiavo, (2) to remove Michael Schiavo as her guardian, and (3) to disqualify himself from the proceedings.

August 17, 2001
Judge Greer delays the removal of Ms. Schiavo's PEG tube until October 9 in order to allow the Schindlers time to appeal.

October 3, 2001
The 2nd DCA delays the removal of the PEG tube indefinitely.

October 17, 2001
The 2nd DCA rules that five doctors should examine Ms. Schiavo to determine if she can improve with new medical treatment. The Schindlers and Michael Schiavo are to choose two doctors each, and the court is to appoint a doctor. The appeals court also affirms Greer's denial of the motion to disqualify himself.
   In re Schiavo, 800 So. 2d 640 (2nd DCA 2001).

November 1, 2001
The 2nd DCA denies Michael Schiavo's motion to rehear the case.

December 14, 2001
Michael Schiavo petitions the Florida Supreme Court to stay the October 17, 2001, ruling of the 2nd DCA. He states that he and the Schindlers will attempt to mediate the dispute in lieu of further litigation.

December 19, 2001
Attorneys meet with a mediator to determine which tests doctors should run on Ms. Schiavo.

January 10, 2002
State Supreme Court stays all legal proceedings pending mediation; it orders attorneys to report on the status of mediation in sixty days.

February 13, 2002
Mediation between the Schindlers and Michael Schiavo fails.

March 14, 2002

The Florida Supreme Court denies Michael Schiavo's petition to review the 2nd DCA's ruling allowing five doctors to examine Ms. Schiavo.

    In re Schiavo, 816 So. 2d 127 (Fla. 2002) (Table, No. SC01-2678).

October 12–22, 2002

The trial court holds a new hearing on new potential medical treatments.

November 15, 2002

The Schindlers contend that Michael Schiavo might have abused Ms. Schiavo and this abuse led to her condition. They ask the court for more time to collect evidence, and to remove Michael Schiavo as guardian.

November 22, 2002

Judge Greer rules that Ms. Schiavo's PEG tube should be removed January 3, 2003.

    In re Schiavo, 2002 WL 31817960 (Fla. Cir. Ct. Nov. 22, 2002) (No. 90-2908-GB-003).

December 13, 2002

Judge Greer stays his November 22 ruling: Ms. Schiavo should not have her PEG tube removed until an appeals court can rule on the case.

December 23, 2002

The 2nd DCA denies a motion Michael Schiavo filed seeking permission to remove the PEG tube.

June 6, 2003

The 2nd DCA, affirming Judge Greer's November 2002 ruling, concludes that Michael Schiavo can remove Ms. Schiavo's PEG tube on October 15.

    In re Schiavo, 851 So. 2d 182 (2nd DCA 2003) (No. 2D02-5394), rehearing denied (July 9, 2003), review denied 855 So. 2d 621 (Fla. 2003).

July 9, 2003

The 2nd DCA refuses to reconsider its decision.

August 22, 2003

The Florida Supreme Court declines to review the decision.

    Schindler v. Schiavo, 855 So. 2d 621 (Fla. 2003) (Table, No. SC03-1242).

August 30, 2003

Ms. Schiavo's parents file a federal lawsuit challenging the removal of Ms. Schiavo's PEG tube. Schiavos' petition (D). *Schindler v. Schiavo*, Civil Action No. 8:03-CV-1860-T-26-T-TGW.

September 17, 2003
Judge Greer orders the removal of the PEG tube to take place on October 15, 2003. He also rejects the Schindlers' request that Ms. Schiavo be given therapy to learn how to eat without the tube.

October 7, 2003
Governor Jeb Bush files a federal court brief in support of the Schindlers' effort to stop the removal of the PEG tube.

October 10, 2003
Federal Court Judge Richard Lazzara rules that he lacks the jurisdiction to hear the federal case.

October 14, 2003
The 2nd DCA refuses to block Judge Greer's order to remove the PEG tube.

October 15, 2003
Ms. Schiavo's PEG tube is once again removed.

October 17, 2003
The Florida Circuit Court in Pinellas County and the First District Court of Appeal refuse to grant a request by "supporters" of the Schindlers to direct Governor Bush to intervene in the case.

October 19, 2003
The Advocacy Center for Persons with Disabilities, Inc. files a federal court lawsuit that claims that the removal of Ms. Schiavo's PEG tube is abuse and neglect.
  Advocacy Center for Persons with Disabilities, Inc. v. Schiavo, No. 8:03-CV-2167-T-23EAJ.

October 20, 2003
The Florida House of Representatives passes a bill, "Terri's Law," that allows the governor to issue a "one-time stay in certain cases."

October 21, 2003
The Florida Senate passes the bill; Governor Bush issues an executive order directing reinsertion of the PEG tube and appointing a guardian ad litem for Ms. Schiavo.
  Michael Schiavo files a state-court lawsuit arguing that "Terri's Law" is unconstitutional and seeking an injunction to stop the reinsertion of the PEG tube; the court requests briefs on the constitutional arguments about "Terri's Law."
  Schiavo v. Bush. No. 03-008212-CI-20 (Cir. Ct. Pinellas County, Florida).
  The federal court denies the motion for a temporary restraining order filed in the lawsuit of the Advocacy Center for Persons with Disabilities, Inc.
  Advocacy Center for Persons with Disabilities, Inc. v. Schiavo, 2003 WL 23305833, 17 Fla. L. Weekly Fed. D 291 (M.D. Fla. Oct. 21, 2003).
  Ms. Schiavo's PEG tube is reinserted.

October 22, 2003
David Demeres, chief judge for the Pinellas County Circuit Court, orders both the Schindlers and Michael Schiavo to agree within five days on an independent guardian ad litem as required under the governor's order. ("Terri's Law" directs: "Upon issuance of the stay, the chief judge of the circuit court shall appoint a guardian ad litem for the patient to make recommendations to the Governor and the court.")

October 28, 2003
President George W. Bush praises the way his brother Governor Jeb Bush has handled the Schiavo matter.

October 29, 2003
Michael Schiavo files court papers in his state-court lawsuit, arguing that "Terri's Law" is unconstitutional. The American Civil Liberties Union has joined Michael Schiavo.

October 31, 2003
Judge Demers appoints Dr. Jay Wolfson as Ms. Schiavo's guardian ad litem. Dr. Wolfson holds both medical and legal degrees; he is also a public health professor at the University of South Florida. He is supposed to represent Ms. Schiavo's best interest in court, but he has no authority to make decisions for her.

November 4, 2003
Governor Jeb Bush asks Circuit Court Judge W. Douglas Baird to dismiss Michael Schiavo's suit (filed October 21, 2003) that challenges "Terri's Law."

November 8, 2003
Judge Baird denies Governor Bush's motion to dismiss the state-court suit.

November 10, 2003
Governor Bush appeals Judge Baird's decision; the filing of the appeal has the effect of staying the removal of Ms. Schiavo's PEG tube.

November 14, 2003
Judge Baird vacates the stay.

November 14, 2003
In response to Judge Baird's lifting the stay, the 2nd DCA issues an indefinite stay.

November 19, 2003
Governor Bush files a petition to remove Judge Baird.

November 21, 2003
Florida senators Stephen Wise and Jim Sebesta introduce legislation (S692) that would require persons in persistent vegetative states to be administered medically supplied nutrition and hydration in the absence of a living will, regardless of family beliefs about what those patients would have wanted. The measure is withdrawn from consideration on April 16, 2004.

December 1, 2003
University of South Florida professor Jay Wolfson, guardian ad litem, concludes in his report that Ms. Schiavo is in a persistent vegetative state with no chance of improvement.

December 10, 2003
The 2nd DCA refuses to remove Judge Baird, who is the presiding judge in the state-court lawsuit filed October 21, 2003.
    Bush v. Schiavo, 861 So. 2d 506 (2nd DCA 2003) (No. 2D03-5244).

January 5, 2004
The Schindler family petitions the Pinellas County Circuit Court to reappoint Jay Wolfson, the guardian ad litem.

January 8, 2004
Judge Demers rejects the request to reappoint the guardian ad litem, citing the pending court decisions over the constitutionality of "Terri's Law" as reason to wait on any action.

February 13, 2004
The 2nd DCA reverses Judge Baird's ruling (in the case filed October 21, 2003) that denied the Schindlers permission to intervene in Michael Schiavo's constitutional challenge to "Terri's Law." The 2nd DCA explains that Judge Baird did not follow proper procedure. The court also gives permission to Governor Bush to question several witnesses who Judge Baird previously had ruled could not offer any relevant testimony.
    Bush v. Schiavo, 866 So. 2d 140 (Fla. 2nd DCA 2004) (on intervention); 866 So. 2d 136 (2nd DCA 2004) (on request to take depositions) (Case No. 2D03-5783).

March 12, 2004
Judge Baird again rejects the Schindlers' request to intervene in Michael Schiavo's suit that questions the constitutionality of "Terri's Law."

March 20, 2004
Pope John Paul II addresses World Federation of Catholic Medical Associations and Pontifical Academy for Life Congress on "Life-Sustaining Treatments and Vegetative State: Scientific Advances and Ethical Dilemmas." His remarks spark widespread interest and controversy.

March 29, 2004
Nursing home workers discover four "fresh puncture wounds" on one arm and a fifth wound on the other arm; the workers state that a hypodermic needle appears to have caused the wounds. Attendants discovered the wounds shortly after the Schindlers visited Ms. Schiavo for forty-five minutes. Toxicology reports indicate that no substance was injected into Ms. Schiavo. Clearwater police later conclude that the marks might have been made by a device used to move Ms. Schiavo and, in any case, that no evidence of abuse or other wrongdoing could be found.

March 29, 2004
Judge Greer denies a motion filed by the Schindlers seeking to have Michael Schiavo defend himself in a hearing; they allege that he is violating a 1996 court order that requires him to share a sufficient amount of Ms. Schiavo's medical information. Michael Schiavo claims that he has shared an adequate amount of information through attorneys.

April 16, 2004
S692 is withdrawn from consideration in the Florida Legislature.

April 23, 2004
The 2nd DCA rules that the Pinellas County trial court has jurisdiction to hear and is the proper venue for the case Michael Schiavo has filed against Governor Bush asserting that "Terri's Law" is unconstitutional.

May 6, 2004
Pinellas Circuit Judge W. Douglas Baird rules that "Terri's Law," sought and signed by Governor Bush and approved by the legislature on October 21, 2003, is unconstitutional. The governor appeals the ruling.

June 1, 2004
The 2nd DCA grants a motion from attorneys for Michael Schiavo to send the case directly to the Florida Supreme Court and bypass a lower-court review. Meanwhile, attorneys for Governor Bush file a motion asking that all appeals be halted until the issue of whether Michael Schiavo has the authority to fight the governor on his wife's behalf is resolved.

June 16, 2004
Florida's Supreme Court, pointing to "a question of great public importance requiring immediate resolution by this Court," accepts jurisdiction and sets oral arguments for August 31, 2004.

June 30, 2004
2nd DCA affirms Judge Baird's March 12 ruling denying the Schindlers the ability to intervene in the lawsuit over the constitutionality of "Terri's Law."

July 19, 2004
The Schindlers file a motion in the Circuit Court for Pinellas County seeking relief from judgment in *Schindler v. Schiavo*. Based in part upon the recent statement by Pope John Paul II, they argue that the orders mandating withdrawal of the PEG tube from Ms. Schiavo and authorizing Michael to challenge the constitutionality of "Terri's Law" violate her "free exercise of her religious beliefs [and] her right to enjoy and defend her own life and, in fact, imperil her immortal soul."

July 27, 2004
National group of bioethicists files amicus brief "in support of Michael Schiavo as guardian of the person."

August 31, 2004
The Florida Supreme Court hears oral arguments in the lawsuit over the constitutionality of "Terri's Law."

August 31, 2004
Circuit Judge George Greer, opposed for reelection by an attorney who was known to oppose Greer's rulings in the Schiavo case, is reelected by a large margin.

September 23, 2004
Florida's Supreme Court, unanimously affirming the trial court order, declares "Terri's Law" unconstitutional.

October 4, 2004
Governor Bush files a motion and then an amended motion for rehearing and clarification of the Florida Supreme Court opinion issued on September 23, 2004.
Hudson v. Texas following a law supported by then governor George W. Bush the Children's Hospital of Texas is allowed to remove life support from a severely disabled infant against the mother's wishes on the grounds that medical care would be futile, October, 2004.

October 21, 2004
Florida Supreme Court denies Governor Bush's amended motion for rehearing and clarification, as well as a motion seeking permission to file a second amended motion for rehearing and clarification. The court issues a mandate to transfer jurisdiction back to Judge Greer.

October 22, 2004
In Pinellas County, at the trial-court level, Judge Greer denies the motion filed by the Schindlers on July 19, 2004. He also stays the removal of her PEG tube until December 6, 2004.

October 25, 2004
Governor Bush files a motion with the Florida Supreme Court asking that it recall the mandate it issued on October 22 because he will be filing a petition for certiorari regarding this case with the U.S. Supreme Court.

October 27, 2004
Florida Supreme Court grants Governor Bush's motion asking that it recall the mandate issued on October 22. Proceedings in the trial and all appellate courts in the case of *Bush v. Schiavo* are stayed until November 29, 2004.

November 22, 2004
In the guardianship proceeding in Pinellas County, the Schindlers appeal from Judge Greer's October 22 order denying their motion for relief from judgment.

December 3, 2004
Governor Bush files a petition for certiorari, seeking review of the Florida Supreme Court's decision regarding "Terri's Law," with the U.S. Supreme Court.

December 29, 2004
2nd DCA, without opinion, denies the Schindlers' November 22 appeal from Judge Greer's order refusing to reopen the guardianship proceeding.

January 10, 2005
The Schindlers again ask Judge Greer to remove Michael Schiavo from his judicial appointed post of Ms. Schiavo's guardian.

January 13, 2005
The Schindlers file two motions—one in the 2nd DCA, asking it to reconsider its decision of December 29, 2004, and a second in the trial-court guardianship proceeding, asking Judge Greer once again to prevent withdrawal of nutrition and hydration until the 2nd DCA does so.

January 24, 2005
The U.S. Supreme Court refuses to grant review of the case in which the Florida Supreme Court struck down "Terri's Law" as unconstitutional.

February 7, 2005
Florida's Department of Agriculture and Consumer Services cites the Terri Schindler-Schiavo Foundation for failing to register with the state to solicit donations.

February 11, 2005
In Pinellas County, Judge Greer denies the Schindlers' motions, filed January 10 and 13, 2005. The order authorizing withdrawal of the PEG tube remains in effect, although implementation is stayed pending the outcome of currently pending appeals.

February 15, 2005
The Schindlers ask the 2nd DCA to stay the mandate issued when it refused to hear their most recent appeal.

February 16, 2005

Randall Terry, founder of the pro-life activist organization Operation Rescue, appears with the Schindlers at a news conference, vowing protest vigils against removal of the PEG tube.

February 18, 2005

The Schindlers again petition Judge Greer in Pinellas County for reconsideration of the order of February 11, 2005, in which the court upheld its judgment, made in the year 2000, that the PEG tube should be removed.

February 18, 2005

Florida Representatives Baxley Brown; Cannon; Davis, D.; Flores; Goldstein; Lopez-Cantera; Murzin; Quinones; Traviesa introduced H 701 in the Florida Legislature. H 701, mirroring S. 692 (introduced in October 2003 and withdrawn in April 2004), would require maintenance of medically supplied nutrition and hydration in incapacitated persons in most instances.

February 21, 2005

The 2nd DCA denies the Schindlers' motion of February 15, 2005, clearing the way for removal of the PEG tube when the current stay expires on February 22, 2005. Judge Greer schedules a hearing on the Schindlers' motion of February 18, 2005, for February 23, 2005.

February 22, 2005

Judge Greer stays removal of the PEG tube until 5 PM on February 23, 2005 (after he hears argument on the motion filed by the Schindlers on February 18, 2005).

February 23, 2005

After a hearing, Judge Greer extends the stay preventing removal of the PEG tube until 5 PM on February 25, 2005, to permit time to issue an order detailing his decisions regarding matters discussed at the hearing. Officials from Florida's Department of Children and Families (DCF) move to intervene in the case, but Judge Greer denies the motion to intervene at the hearing.

February 25, 2005

Judge Greer denies the motion before him and orders that, "absent a stay from the appellate courts, the guardian, Michael Schiavo, shall cause the removal of nutrition and hydration from the ward, Theresa Schiavo, at 1 PM on Friday, March 18, 2005."

February 26, 2005

The *St. Petersburg Times* reports that a Vatican cardinal spoke on Vatican Radio opposing removal of the PEG tube.

February 28, 2005

The Schindlers file a number of motions with Judge Greer, addressing a range of issues. They also indicate that they will appeal the judge's decision of February 25, 2005. Judge Greer denies some of the motions but agreed to set a hearing date to consider others.

March 7, 2005
The Schindlers appeal Judge Greer's February 25, 2005 order to the 2nd DCA.
     Bioethicists from six Florida universities submit an analysis of H701.

March 8, 2005
U.S. Rep. David Weldon (R-FL) introduces in the U.S. House of Representatives H.R. 1151, titled the Incapacitated Persons' Legal Protection Act. The bill would permit a federal court to review the Schiavo matter through a habeas corpus lawsuit.

March 9, 2005
The Florida House Health Care Regulation Committee considers H.701, voting to approve a Council/Committee Substitute 701 instead of the original version.

March 10, 2005
Judge Greer issues order denying Florida's Department of Children and Families the right to intervene in the guardianship case.

March 14, 2005
The Judiciary Committee in the Florida House considers H.701, voting to approve another committee substitute for the original bill. The *Sun-Sentinel* reports that the House and the Senate have agreed that this bill will come to a vote.

March 15, 2005
The Florida House Health & Families Council considers and approves the second committee substitute H.701.
     The Florida Senate Judiciary Committee passes S.804, providing that medically supplied nutrition and hydration cannot be "suspended from" a person in a PVS if: (1) the purpose of the suspension is "solely to end the life of" a person in a PVS; (2) a conflict exists on the issue of suspension of medically supplied nutrition and hydration among the persons who could be proxy decision makers for that person under Florida law; and (3) the person in the PVS had not executed a written advance directive or designated a healthcare surrogate.

March 16, 2005
The 2nd DCA affirms Judge Greer's orders and refuses to stay the scheduled March 18 withdrawal of the PEG tube.
     The U.S. House of Representatives, by voice vote, passes H.R. 1332, the Protection of Incapacitated Persons Act of 2005. This bill would amend federal law to provide for removal of certain cases to federal court from state court, rather than authorizing use of the federal habeas corpus remedy to obtain federal court review, as H.R. 1151 would have.

March 17, 2005
The Florida House of Representatives approves H.701, after some amendments.
     The Florida Senate votes down S.804.

Florida's Department of Children and Families (DCF) petitions the Florida Supreme Court for relief, and the Florida Supreme Court denies the petition.

The U.S. Senate passes a "private bill" applying to the Schiavo case but differing from H.R. 1332. The U.S. Senate Website, at www.senate.gov, explains a "private bill" as follows: "A private bill provides benefits to specified individuals (including corporate bodies). Individuals sometimes request relief through private legislation when administrative or legal remedies are exhausted. Many private bills deal with immigration–granting citizenship or permanent residency. Private bills may also be introduced for individuals who have claims again the government, veterans benefits claims, claims for military decorations, or taxation problems. The title of a private bill usually begins with the phrase, "For the relief of. . . ." If a private bill is passed in identical form by both houses of Congress and is signed by the president, it becomes a private law."

The Schindlers ask the U.S. Supreme Court to hear the case, but the U.S. Supreme Court denies their petition.

Republican senators circulate a memo on the political advantages of supporting legislation to reinsert Ms. Schiavo's nutrition tube. On April 7, the *Washington Post* reported that "The legal counsel to Sen. Mel Martinez (R-FL) admitted [on April 6] that he was the author of a memo citing the political advantage to Republicans of intervening in the case. . . . Brian H. Darling, 39, a former lobbyist for the Alexander Strategy Group on gun rights and other issues, offered his resignation and it was immediately accepted, Martinez said."

March 18, 2005

The U.S. House of Representatives Committee on Government Reform issues five subpoenas: one commanding Michael Schiavo to appear before it and bring with him the "hydration and nutrition equipment" in working order; three commanding physicians and other personnel at the hospice to do the same; and one commanding Ms. Schiavo to appear before it. The subpoenas would require that the PEG tube remain in working order until at least the date of testimony, March 25, 2005. The subpoenas are included as appendices to the U.S. House All Writs Petition (see just below).

The Committee on Government Reform also moves to intervene in the guardianship litigation before Judge Greer and asks Judge Greer to stay his order requiring removal of the PEG tube. Judge Greer denies the motions.

The Committee on Government Reform files an emergency all-writs petition with the Florida Supreme Court, effectively seeking reversal of Judge Greer's denial of its motions. The Florida Supreme Court denies this petition.

The House Committee on Government Reform asks the U.S. Supreme Court to review the Florida Supreme Court's denial of its petition. Justice Kennedy, acting for the Court, denies the application for relief.

The PEG tube is removed in mid-afternoon. This is the third time the tube has been removed in accordance with court orders.

The Schindlers, as "next friends" of their daughter, file a petition for writ of habeas corpus in federal district court in the Middle District of Florida. That court dismisses the case for lack of jurisdiction and refuses to issue a temporary restraining order because "there is not a substantial likelihood that [the Schindlers] will prevail on their federal constitutional claims."

March 19–20, 2005

The U.S. Senate delays its Easter recess and works on Saturday to reach a compromise with the House on a bill, S.686, closely resembling the special bill it passed on March 17. On Palm Sunday (which holiday is frequently noted in debate), it then passes S.686 and the U.S. House of Representatives returns from Easter recess for a special session to debate S.686.

March 20, 2005

House Democrats and Republicans hold news conferences.

March 21, 2005

Shortly past 12:30 AM, the U.S. House of Representatives votes 203–58 to suspend its rules and pass S.686.

President Bush signs S.686 at 1:11 AM.

Federal District Court Judge James D. Whittemore, Middle District of Florida (in Tampa), hears arguments on the Schindlers' motion that he order reinsertion of the PEG tube while the lawsuit they will assert pursuant to S.686 is litigated.

March 22, 2005

Federal District Court Judge Whittemore refuses to order reinsertion of the PEG tube.

The Schindlers appeal Judge Whittemore's decision to the U.S. Court of Appeals for the Eleventh Circuit.

The Schindlers file an amended complaint in the federal district court, adding a number of new claims.

March 23, 2005

The U.S. Eleventh Circuit Court of Appeals, in a 2–1 vote, denies the Schindlers' appeal.

U.S. Eleventh Circuit Court of Appeals, acting en banc (as a whole), refuses to rehear the Schindlers' appeal, leaving intact the court's ruling earlier in the day.

House Democrats and Republicans hold news conferences.

The Florida Senate, by a vote of 21–18, again refuses to pass S.804. This bill was approved by the Senate Judiciary Committee on March 15, 2005.

Florida governor Jeb Bush reports that a neurologist, Dr. William Cheshire, claims that Ms. Schiavo is not in a persistent vegetative state. The governor asks the Florida Department of Children and Families (DCF) to obtain custody of Ms. Schiavo in light of allegations of abuse. Judge Greer holds a hearing on the matter.

The Schindlers file a petition for writ of certiorari with the U.S. Supreme Court.

Judge Greer issues a restraining order prohibiting DCF from removing Ms. Schiavo from the hospice or otherwise reinserting the PEG tube.

The Schindlers ask again for a restraining order in federal court.

Five members of the U.S. House of Representatives ask the U.S. Supreme Court to file a "friend of the court" brief.

March 24, 2005

The U.S. Supreme Court refuses to hear the Schindlers' case.

The Schindlers file a Second Amended Complaint, adding several claims, in the federal court case. Count X, titled "Right to Life," alleges a violation of the Fourteenth Amendment's right to life because removing the PEG tube is "contrary to [Ms. Schiavo's] wish to live."

The trial court (Judge Whittemore) schedules a hearing for 6 PM and orders supplemental briefs on Count X.

Judge Greer denies DCF's motion to intervene. DCF appeals Judge Greer's order. Judge Greer vacates the automatic stay upon appeal. The 2nd District Court of Appeal refuses to reinstate the stay. The Florida Supreme Court dismisses a motion on this matter because it "fails to invoke" the court's jurisdiction.

DCF Motion in Florida Supreme Court (describing events).

March 25, 2005

Judge Whittemore denies the Schindlers' second motion for an order reinserting the PEG tube.

The Schindlers appeal Judge Whittemore's order to the U.S. Court of Appeals for the Eleventh Circuit. The Eleventh Circuit affirms. The Schindlers announce that they will pursue no more federal appeals.

The Schindlers file an emergency motion attempting to convince Judge Greer to reinsert the PEG, at least temporarily until the Eleventh Circuit decides their appeal. The motion contends her family heard her try to verbalize "I want to live," according to news reports. (This motion and accompanying affidavits comprise Appendix 7 of the Schindlers' Petition linked under March 26, just below.)

DCF appeals Judge Greer's March 23 denial of its first motion to intervene to the 2nd DCA.

March 26, 2005

Judge Greer denies the Schindlers' motion of March 25, 2005.

The Schindlers appeal to the Florida Supreme Court to reverse Judge Greer's refusal to reinsert the PEG tube, but the Florida Supreme Court refuses to do so, citing a lack of jurisdiction.

News agencies report the arrest on March 25 of Richard Alan Meywes of Fairview, NC, for offering $250,000 for the killing of Michael Schiavo and another $50,000 for the death of Judge Greer.

The Schindlers advise supporters demonstrating around the hospice to return home to spend the Easter holiday with their families. The protesters remain.

March 27, 2005

In an interview on CNN, Governor Bush says: "I cannot violate a court order. I don't have power from the U.S. Constitution, or the Florida Constitution for that matter, that would allow me to intervene after a decision has been made."

March 29, 2005

The Reverend Jesse Jackson leads a prayer service outside the hospice and speaks out against removal of the PEG tube.

The 2nd DCA upholds Judge Greer's ruling refusing to let the DCF intervene.

Despite earlier indications that they would pursue no further federal appeals, the Schindlers petition the entire Eleventh Circuit Court of Appeals for permission to file a motion for rehearing en banc although the time to do so has expired. A grant of that petition would enable the Schindlers to ask for review of the Eleventh Circuit decision of March 24.

March 30, 2005

The Eleventh Circuit permits the Schindlers' filing and then, acting both through a panel and as a whole, denies the motion for rehearing.

The U.S. Supreme Court refuses to review the Eleventh Circuit ruling.

March 31, 2005

Ms. Schiavo dies at 9:05 AM. Her body is transported to the Pinellas Country Coroners' Office for an autopsy.

Hospice of the Florida Suncoast issues a statement.

Florida governor Jeb Bush issues a statement.

Judge Greer authorizes Michael Schiavo to administer Ms. Schiavo's estate. On this date in 1976, the New Jersey Supreme Court ruled that coma patient Karen Ann Quinlan could be disconnected from her respirator. She remained in a persistent vegetative state and died in 1985.

April 12, 2005

The Wall Street Journal Online/ Harris Interactive Health Care Poll finds that "most people disapprove of how President Bush, Governor Bush, and the Congress handled the issue."

April 15, 2005

In response to a motion from the media, Judge Greer orders DCF to release redacted copies of abuse reports regarding Ms. Schiavo. Newspapers report that DCF found no evidence of abuse after investigating the eighty-nine reports filed before February 18, 2005. Thirty allegations are outstanding and still being investigated, but Judge Greer earlier had ruled that those allegations duplicated those previously filed.

May 17, 2005

More than six weeks after Ms. Schiavo's death, Lisa Wilson is the last of the hundreds of protesters outside Ms. Schiavo's hospice.

June 15, 2005

Dr. Jon Thogmartin, Florida's District Six Medical Examiner, releases the results of Ms. Schiavo's autopsy. He reports that the autopsy showed Ms. Schiavo's condition was "consistent" with a person in a persistent vegetative state. "This damage was irreversible," he said. "No amount of therapy or treatment would have regenerated the massive loss of neurons." No evidence of abuse was found, he said.

June 17, 2005
Florida governor Jeb Bush asks a state prosecutor to investigate the circumstances of Ms. Schiavo's 1990 cardiac arrest, specifically the amount of time that elapsed between the time Ms. Schiavo collapsed and Michael Schiavo called 911.

June 20, 2005
Despite earlier statements that he intended to bury Ms. Schiavo's remains in Pennsylvania, Michael Schiavo buries them in Clearwater, Florida. The grave marker reads:

Schiavo
Theresa Marie

Beloved Wife

Born December 3, 1963
Departed This Earth
February 25, 1990
At Peace March 31, 2005

I Kept My Promise

Florida voters disagree with Governor Bush's request for investigation 2:1 in poll released June 30, 2005.

June 27, 2005
Prosecutors find no evidence of wrongdoing by Michael Schiavo after Ms. Schiavo's collapse in 1990. They write: "If the available facts are analyzed without preconceptions, it is clear that there is no basis for further investigation. While some questions may remain following the autopsy, the likelihood of finding evidence that criminal acts were responsible for her collapse is not one of them. . . . We strongly recommend that the inquiry be closed and no further action be taken."

July 1, 2005
MoveOn PAC, left/liberal advocacy group begins campaign to block conservative Supreme Court appointments by the president using his actions in the Schiavo case to motivate viewers of their ad campaign.

July 7, 2005
Governor Bush agrees to drop any further investigation into why Ms. Schiavo collapsed in 1990.

December 7, 2005
Michael Schiavo announces he has formed a new political action committee. Named TerriPAC after his wife, the PAC will raise and spend funds to educate voters on where their elected officials stood when they had a choice between individual freedom and personal privacy and overreaching government action. (http://www.terripac.org/)

Contributors

Floyd L. Angus, MD, is an attending physician in the Department of Gastroenterology, Sumter Medical Consultants at Tuomey Regional Medical Center, Sumter, South Carolina.

George J. Annas, JD, MPH, is the Edward R. Utley Professor of Health Law, chairman of Health Law Department at the Boston University School of Public Health.

Robert Barry, OP, is on the faculty at the University of Illinois.

Robert Burakoff, MD, MPH, FACG, FACP, is clinical chief of gastroenterology and director, Center for Digestive Health at Brigham and Women's Hospital, Boston, Massachusetts, and associate professor of medicine, Harvard Medical School.

George W. Bush is the forty-third president of the United States and was formerly the forty-sixth governor of Texas.

Jeb Bush was elected Florida's forty-third governor in 1998 and was reelected in 2002.

Norman L. Cantor, JD, is professor of law and Justice Nathan Jacobs Scholar at Rutgers University School of Law.

Arthur L. Caplan, PhD, is the Emmanuel and Robert Hart Professor of Bioethics, chair of the Department of Medical Ethics, and the director of the Center for Bioethics at the University of Pennsylvania.

Kathy L. Cerminara, JD, is associate professor at the Shepard Broad Law Center of Nova Southeastern University, Ft. Lauderdale, Florida, where she teaches several courses including the Law & Medicine Seminar and Law of Managed Health Care. She also created, was the initial director of, and teaches in the online Master's in Health Law program for nonlawyers.

William P. Cheshire Jr., MD, MA, FAAN, is an associate professor of neurology in Mayo Clinic College of Medicine and a consultant in the Department of Neurology at Mayo Clinic in Jacksonville, Florida. He is director of Biotech Ethics at the Center for Bioethics and Human Dignity in Bannockburn, Illinois.

Ceci Connolly has been a national staff writer at the *Washington Post* since 1997. Prior to joining the *Post*, Connolly was a Washington correspondent for the *St. Petersburg (FL) Times*.

Ronald Cranford, MD, a neurologist and medical ethicist, is assistant chief in neurology at the Hennepin County Medical Center (HCMC), Minneapolis, Minnesota; professor of neurology, University of Minnesota Medical School; and faculty associate, Center for Bioethics, University of Minnesota.

Elijah E. Cummings, a Democrat, represents Maryland's Seventh District.

John C. Danforth, a former senator from Missouri, served as President Bush's representative to the United Nations in 2004.

Tom DeLay, representing the Twenty-second District of Texas, serves as majority leader, the second-ranking leader in the U.S. House of Representatives.

Jon Eisenberg, JD, is an attorney in Oakland, California. He is a California State Bar Certified Appellate Specialist and is admitted to practice in California state courts, the U.S. Court of Appeals, the Ninth Circuit Court of Appeals, and the U.S. Supreme Court.

Barney Frank, representing the Fourth District of Massachusetts, has been in Congress since 1981. He is the senior Democrat on the Financial Services Committee.

Bill Frist, MD, is the fifty-fourth U.S. senator from Tennessee and the eighteenth Senate Majority Leader.

Edward J. Furton, MA, PhD, is director of publications and staff ethicist at The National Catholic Bioethics Center in Philadelphia.

Kenneth W. Goodman, PhD, is codirector of the University of Miami's Ethics Programs, including its Program in Business, Government and Professional Ethics, and founder and director of the Bioethics Program and its Pan American Bioethics Initiative. Dr. Goodman is an associate professor in the University of Miami's Department of Medicine, and has appointments in the Department of Philosophy, the School of Nursing, and the Department of Epidemiology and Public Health.

Msgr. **Orville Griese** (deceased) was director of research, Pope John XXIII Medical-Moral Research and Education Center.

Germain Grisez is Flynn Professor of Christian Ethics at Mount Saint Mary's College in Emmitsburg, Maryland.

J. Dennis Hastert is Republican congressman from the Fourteenth District of Illinois and is also Speaker of the House.

Pope **John Paul II** (May 18, 1920–April 2, 2005), born Karol Józef Wojtyła, was pope for almost twenty-seven years, from October 1978 until his death on April 2, 2005.

Rev. **Brian Johnstone**, CSsR, is a member of the Canberra (Australia) Province of Redemptorists. He is an ordinary professor of systematic moral theology at the Alphonsian Academy of Moral Theology of the Pontifical Lateran University in Rome.

Mary Johnson is a writer and editor for *Ragged Edge* magazine, a successor to the periodical *The Disability Rag*.

Bernard Lo, MD, is professor of medicine and director of the Program in Medical Ethics at University of California, San Francisco.

Thomas J. Marzen, JD, is general counsel of the National Legal Center for the Medically Dependent and Disabled.

William E. May is the Michael J. McGivney Professor of Moral Theology at the John Paul II Institute for Studies on Marriage and Family at the Catholic University of America.

James J. McCartney, OSA, PhD, is associate professor in the Department of Philosophy at Villanova University and Associate Fellow, Center for Bioethics at the University of Pennsylvania.

Charles J. McFadden, OSA (1901–1990), studied philosophy under the late Archbishop Fulton J. Sheen at The Catholic University of America. He taught in the Philosophy Department of Villanova University from 1938 until 1979. He published *Medical Ethics for Nurses* in 1946, one of the first studies of medical ethics published in the United States. His final book, *The Dignity of Life: Moral Values in a Changing Society*, published in 1976, was translated into many languages.

Bishop James T. McHugh (deceased) was vicar for Parish and Family Life, Archdiocese of Newark, and bishop of Camden, New Jersey.

Gilbert Meilaender, PhD, is Richard & Phyllis Duesenberg Professor of Christian Ethics at Valparaiso University and member of the President's Council on Bioethics.

Rev. **Patrick F. Norris**, OP, is pastor of Blessed Sacrament Parish in Madison, Wisconsin, and Coordinator of Health Care for the Diocese of Madison. For several years Fr. Norris was the associate director of the Center for Health Care Ethics and assistant professor in the Internal Medicine Department at St. Louis University Health Sciences Center.

Kevin O'Rourke, OP, JCD, STM, is currently a faculty member at the Neiswanger Institute for Bioethics and Health Policy Stritch School of Medicine, Loyola University of Chicago. He received his JCD (Juris Canonici

Doctor) from St. Thomas University in Rome, in 1958. He also has a doctorate in canon law, and STM (Master of Sacred Theology)—a degree given in the Dominican Order after successful teaching and writing of many years.

Richard L. Pearse Jr., PA, is an attorney in Clearwater, Florida.

Fred Plum, MD, is university professor emeritus of neurology at the Weill Medical College of Cornell University.

Timothy E. Quill, MD, is director of the Palliative Care Program at The University of Rochester Medical Center. He is a professor of medicine, psychiatry, and medical humanities at the University of Rochester, School of Medicine and Dentistry. Dr. Quill is author of five books and numerous articles on issues related to palliative care and end-of-life concerns.

William Rehnquist (deceased) was chief justice of the U.S. Supreme Court until 2005. A former law clerk and Assistant Attorney General, he has been a member of the Supreme Court of the United States since 1972.

Rick Santorum, JD, Republican from Pennsylvania, has served in the U.S. Senate since January of 1995.

Debbie Wasserman Schultz is the congresswoman from Florida's Twentieth Congressional District.

Thomas A. Shannon, PhD, is professor emeritus, religion and social ethics in the Department of Humanities & Arts, Worcester Polytechnic Institute in Worcester, Massachusetts.

Mark Siegler, MD, FACP, is Lindy Bergman Distinguished Service Professor of Medicine and director of the MacLean Center for Clinical Medical Ethics at the University of Chicago.

Reverend Monsignor **William B. Smith**, STD, is academic dean of St. Joseph's Seminary in Yonkers, New York.

Dominic A. Sisti, MBe, is a research associate at the University of Pennsylvania Center for Bioethics.

Rev. John F. Tuohey, PhD, holds the endowed chair in applied healthcare ethics at Providence St. Vincent Medical Center in Portland, Oregon.

James J. Walter is the Austin and Ann O'Malley Professor of Bioethics and the chair of The Bioethics Institute at Loyola Marymount University in Los Angeles, California.

Dave Weldon, MD, is the U.S. Representative for Florida's Fifteenth Congressional District.

Robert Wexler is a Democratic member of Congress serving his fifth term in the House of Representatives for Florida's Nineteenth Congressional District.

The Honorable **James D. Whittemore** is United States District Judge in the Middle District of Florida.

Jay Wolfson, DrPH, JD, is Distinguished Professor of Public Health and Medicine and associate vice president for Health Law, Policy and Safety, University of South Florida, Health Sciences Center, Tampa. He was appointed by the courts to serve as the special guardian ad litem for Theresa Maria Schiavo in 2003–2004, reporting to the Florida governor and the courts.